BROKEN LIGHTS

By the same Author

✳

THE HIDDEN FACE
A Study of St. Thérèse of Lisieux

IDA FRIEDERIKE GÖRRES
BROKEN LIGHTS
Diaries and Letters

❈ 1951–1959 ❈

Translated by
BARBARA WALDSTEIN-WARTENBERG

With a Preface by
ALAN PRYCE-JONES

LONDON
BURNS & OATES

This is a translation of Zwischen den Zeiten, aus meinen Tagebüchern, 1951 bis 1959 *(Walter-Verlag, Olten und Freiburg im Breisgau, 1960).*

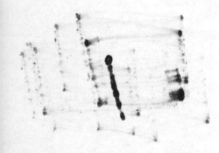

MADE AND PRINTED IN GREAT BRITAIN BY
SPOTTISWOODE, BALLANTYNE & CO. LTD.,
LONDON AND COLCHESTER, FOR
BURNS AND OATES LIMITED
25 ASHLEY PLACE, LONDON, S.W. 1

PREFACE

by ALAN PRYCE-JONES

THE words which Dostoevsky puts into the mouth of the Grand Inquisitor are left unanswered: "We have corrected Thy work and have founded it upon *miracle, mystery* and *authority*. And men rejoiced that they were again led like sheep, and that the terrible gift that had brought them such suffering was, at last, lifted from their hearts. Were we right, teaching them this?"

The "terrible gift" is freedom, and it is the point of Ivan Karamazov's parable that freedom to choose between good and evil is what men cannot bear. Had Our Lord acceded to temptation and cast himself down from the pinnacle of the temple he would have compelled their faith. As it was, he only asked them freely to give it—a gift, so the Grand Inquisitor affirms, which takes no account of the baseness of humanity. Therefore, the Church has had to "correct" the work of Jesus, in the cause of human happiness, until finally the returned Jesus is warned, "If any one has ever deserved our fires, it is Thou. Tomorrow I shall burn Thee. Dixi."

The Grand Inquisitor is not a wicked man. He too has lived in the desert, he too has known the freedom of which he speaks. But he has come to feel that true knowledge is for an élite only. Is it not better for the millions to behave as happy children, lied to by their teachers where necessary, while the teachers alone suffer the knowledge of good and evil?

There may be no direct answer to these questions, but at least it is the part of an awakened civilization to formulate them squarely. There are, as it were, three levels of revelation to be reconciled: the revelation from on high, that of a never-sleeping Church, striving to bring order and clarity into what, of its nature, can never be wholly ordered or clear, and finally the insights of the wise, whether orthodox or no. Each has something to give the others; and if the Church be properly looked on as the pivot upon which all matters of belief must turn, that does not dispense the individual from using the freedom bestowed on

v

him with his birthright in order to formulate from within what the Book of Common Prayer calls "a right judgement in all things ".

Such precisely is the aim of Ida Friederike Görres, whose notebooks are here for the first time published in English. It is not her avowed purpose, but it is certainly her signal success, to take her own part in the permanent debate of mankind with the Grand Inquisitor. The Catholic Church is often reproached by those outside it for a monolithic approach to the truth, for exacting a tribute of intellectual obedience which keeps private judgement always on the curb. Frau Görres brings her own powerful insights to demonstrate, once again, that this is not so. And the demonstration is all the more effective when a little is known of Frau Görres outside the bare facts conveyed in these notes and letters.

She was born into a remarkable Austro-Hungarian family, the daughter of Count Heinrich Coudenhove-Kalergi, and one of the seven children born to the Japanese lady whom he married when a diplomat in Tokyo at the end of the nineteenth century. The Coudenhove family will be remembered for the founding of Paneuropa, a movement which had some success in the optimistic days which followed the First World War, and Count Heinrich himself was not only an outstanding linguist but also an expert in the study of comparative religions. After his early death, his children were brought up in his Bohemian home, Schloss Ronsperg, in accordance with the Anglophile ideas of the time and so, in view of the fact that their mother was an invalid, doubly in the hands of nurses and governesses.

A convent education—the first experience of which Frau Görres in a private letter has wrily likened to that of Antonia White's memorable *Frost in May*—came finally to calm waters at the Mary Ward Institute in St Pölten, near Vienna, which led Countess Ida to enter a novitiate in 1923. Doubting her vocation, however, she took up lay work, and was soon deeply involved in the Youth Movement which made so strong an impression on pre-Nazi Germany. Working under the prelate who later became Archbishop of Freiburg-im-Breisgau, she took part in the active life of the Movement even after marrying Herr Carl Josef Görres in 1935. The war strangled most of these activities, but as soon as it was over, she began once again to write, travel and lecture, until in 1950 a breakdown in health drove her into the seclusion which made these journals possible, not before a score or more of books had appeared, four of which have been published in English.

What will first strike a reader is the breadth of Frau Görres's interests, the scope of her reading and the sureness of intuition—she calls it "Book Providence"—which leads her towards what will be of value to her both subjectively and objectively. Next, the energy of her reaction glows out. She too has been in the desert—in deserts of more than one kind—but they have served to fortify not only her whole-hearted response to her Faith but also a keen critical appraisal of what seem to her surface weaknesses.

Without being in the least "like" Baron von Hügel or Lord Acton, she belongs, as they do, to the race of Europeans for whom there are no effective frontiers other than frontiers of the mind, no final intellectual separations except by consent. She finds, for example, Hassidic teaching and legend full of special perception. She probes with understanding the mystics, such as Boehme and Dame Julian of Norwich. And she brings to her probings a vigorous and, when needed, a picturesque response. She analyses her own reaction to the great occasions of the Church with charming modesty: ". . . something momentous, like the Niagara Falls, is thundering down, right beside me, and there I stand, with a thimble in my hand . . ."; but, in fact, she has a remarkable intellectual grasp of her material. For one thing, she understands people, and particularly young people. "It seems to me," she notes, for instance, "that Baroque art belongs to the pleasure of the second half of life. Youth . . . *must* feel almost repelled by it: first because of the immense gulf between their own meagre mode of life and this triumphant, gorgeous exuberance . . . and then, as spiritual beginners, they must . . . first taste their power to overcome the senses, to withdraw from the world, the process of 'rejecting the images' (C. S. Lewis)." She cares very little for conventional opinion. "Nothing saddens me more," she writes, "at the moment than the pitiable mediocrity and flatness of Catholic Christianity." The phrase "at the moment" is important here. For what she offers is not a considered thesis, but a chain of reactions to a reading or circumstance. So that if she finds it "far easier to talk to a sincere Protestant, or with Jews, even pagans . . . and neo-pagans than with this kind of 120 per cent conservative Catholic" she also displays on every page her loyalty to the best tradition of Catholic Christianity. "I have known no other father but these fathers, the priests of the Church, no brothers but my own dear brothers, the theology students. No mother but the Church. . . . I loved them all and clung to them, not only as a daughter and sister, but as a Japanese daughter and sister, in the intensity of unconditional submission which belongs to Japanese filial piety."

There is nothing insipid about this attitude. Indeed, Frau Görres is a formidable lady enough. She writes that all through childhood and youth she had to stick up for herself, so that now "identifying myself with everything loved, I instinctively, un-consciously assume this to be just as defenceless, just as vul-nerable—as though it really depended on my defence alone".

That is why she cannot bear even a seeming flaw in the crystal of belief. She calls Monica Baldwin's *I Leapt over the Wall* an "awful" book, but for the reason that it indicts an unsatisfactory mode of life. Is not the contemporary cloister ideal, she asks elsewhere, less truly Christian than that of Florence Nightingale? She has no patience with the conventional image of a God "whose every action is calculable, who wouldn't do anything to anyone". She is not dazzled by the saints. "What nonsense it is . . . to think that all saintly persons must be canonized at all costs."

And so on. For these pages are endlessly quotable. It is not Frau Görres's purpose to provide answers to high questions, but rather to ventilate, to suggest, to awaken. She displays her Germanic background not by the dogged wrestling with fact at which German scholars excel, but by a constant seriousness, and a kind of courageous diligence in the tackling of essential problems, however hard of solution. She brings together small points of light and leaves it to others to assemble them into the appropriate *feu de joie*. In doing so, she reminds us of the debt we seldom pay to German Catholicism. The authorities she quotes, the guardians of her own imagination, are likely to be unfamiliar. We do not know names like Bergengruen, Guardini, Baader, well enough. We shall know them better from now on, and join to them that of Ida Friederike Görres.

CONTENTS

DIARIES

❦ 1951–1959 ❧

✻ 1951 ✻

I'VE been thinking for a long time now that marriage today is in a state of transition—passing, as it were, from its Old into its New Testament, i.e. shifting from a purely or predominantly legalistic, social, economic and moral institution into the order of spiritual values. Maybe this is why I cannot view the break-up of so many marriages these days as *entirely* disastrous. Indeed, I'd even go so far as to say that this could be a good thing, in one respect at least, if it would serve to show that there are many people who just can't stand their own rotten ways any longer—that they're sick to death of their sham performances. And as for all this psychological small talk, all this harping on the ominous significance of what is called "the frigidity of modern woman"—this just seems to me a pretty poor comment on the *men*. After all, who can blame women if they find it impossible to respond to advances devoid of all tenderness and courtesy, brutal or bored, maybe, clumsy or simply routine? Besides, I rather doubt whether this much-discussed "phenomenon" is as recent as people like to make out. Did anyone ever ask our grandmothers what they felt about all this?

*

READING the Baal Shem★ again I'm realizing more and more what

★ The Baal Shem Tov, or "Master of the Good Name" (1700–60) founded and inspired Hasidism, the great movement of Jewish religious revival which swept across Eastern Europe in the eighteenth century. The *hasidim*, i.e. devout, or those who keep faith with the Covenant, were communities of simple men who believed that they could best worship God through joy and exaltation of spirit; for them their *zaddikim*, or masters, were the highest embodiment of man's closeness to the divine. While never weakening the hope in a Messiah, the movement kindled both its simple and intellectual followers to joy in the world as it is, showing the way to God who dwells with all men "in the midst of their uncleannesses". It made manifest the reflection of the divine, the sparks of God that glimmer in all beings and all things, and taught its followers how to "lift" and redeem them, and reconnect them with their original root. The doctrine of the Shekhinah, contained in the Talmud and expanded in the Cabbala, of the Shekhinah

3

it means that Jesus was a *Jew*, a very devout Jew. A teacher, roaming the countryside with a bunch of disciples. . . . Perhaps he liked to stay at Bethany to "receive the Sabbath" there as he had been taught by his good parents; perhaps he was happy and grateful that his friends there kept the whole ritual, just as he had known it at home. In the face of such Jewish piety, one can't help feeling very much ashamed if one thinks how Sunday is "kept" by us, even in the most Christian families. Not that the English Puritan "Lord's Day" version is any better.

*

ODD, and unseemly really, that it's not usual with us here to say grace before breakfast. Surely this very first meal of the day, our first gift of "daily bread", ought to be received with special reverence, straight from the hand of God?

*

THAT story of Martin Buber's is terribly revealing—about the rabbi who says his prayers aloud with such fervour that one of his listeners, very much impressed, drags him off to his own special *zaddik*. But, far from sharing his enthusiasm, the holy man rebukes his eager disciple: "What do you mean, my friend, bringing me a man in whose face I can see the tainted image of God?" And then follows the commentary:

> You know that there is a place, lit only by the planet Venus, where good and evil are blended. Sometimes a man begins to serve God and ulterior motives and pride enter into his service. Then, unless he makes a very great effort to change, he comes to live in that dim place and does not even know it. He is even able to display great fervour, for close by is the place of the impure fire. From there he fetches his blaze and kindles his service with it, and does not know from where he has taken the flame.

Maybe this is the clue to characters like Rasputin, Ebel and others, not to mention some priests one can think of! It accounts

as the Divine Presence dwelling in this world, took on a new significance and applicability in the hasidic teaching that every task, no matter how humble, done with fervour and holy intent, brings about the union between God and Shekhinah, eternity and time.

for that curious fascination of the "tainted glow", the "impure" fire which *can* be linked with real and vehement religious feeling and genuine spiritual gifts. What uncanny insight!

*

OCULAR demonstration for early Christian neophytes—and, in all probability, their counterparts in modern China and India: Most of our white Catholic converts these days come out of a spiritual vacuum or from a spiritually under-fed Protestant background. They don't bring in any "spiritual baggage" worth mentioning—they're simply receptive, *tabula rasa*, with few ideas of their own to offer, except questions and objections which they expect to be argued away. But with those early converts—Greeks and Syrians and Egyptians—it was all the other way round; they came to the Church loaded with packs of their own, crammed with metaphysics and mystic experience, with cosmic lore and traditions, and all the rest—nor did they dream of dropping all this on the threshold of the Church and forgetting all about it. On the contrary, they prized these things as heirlooms, as their dowry—to be sifted and smelted, of course, but in the end to be blended with the Gospel. And that was the making of the great theology and mysticism and liturgy of the patristic age.

Maybe it would do us no harm today if a little new blood could be infused into the Mystical Body after centuries (or is it really only decades?) of inbreeding and decadence and empty routine? Not drawn from the watery stuff with no real substance distilled from the "modern" dregs of socialism, existentialism and all the other isms, but from the great common heritage of mankind—Tao and the Ancients (the real ones, not the text-book versions), the Fathers of the Church, and, last but not least, from Jewry. X. told me the other day that he is convinced that we can expect no fresh religious impulse from the East. He views it, in this respect, as no more than "a monstrous disintegration of a festering past", arguing that only the West (the *Abendland*, the True West of C. S. Lewis) still has a promise and a mission and a claim to the Messianic conviction. Well, maybe he's right, but first of all Western Faith itself must be replenished from the very depths of the well. (Of course I don't mean the "deposit of Faith", but rather its interpretations and realizations.) In this connection I'm coming more and more to the conclusion that most things people think—or believe they're thinking—on matters of Faith are really quite irrelevant, more fancywork than anything else. The old lady in Bergengruen's *Tempelchen* put it so well when she told her granddaughter: "You know, if you once start thinking, you can make the most terrible mistakes—as in spelling or the more complicated kinds of sums." Exactly. Which is why it hardly matters.

All of which leads me to conclude how wrong our present method of instructing converts is. We're so fond of telling them that they have to *think* differently and assent to new opinions— and only in the margin, if that, that they're supposed to *live* differently. If we mention this at all, we enlarge upon special "devotional practices", or stress the importance of the liturgy, etc.—as though loving-kindness, pure and simple, were not what *really* counts. . . .

Talking of loving-kindness, I'm deeply ashamed to admit to myself that I've been neglecting charity myself for a very long time, ages, or so it seems now. I simply forgot about its supreme importance—probably just because I stopped trying it. I simply let it fade out of my mind. And yet charity is the twin of true faith—its very Siamese twin—and the cart just can't get along if only one of the horses is in good fettle, and the other is half-starved and lame.

*

I'M reading Buber's *Gog and Magog* alongside of his *Tales of the Hasidim.** The same aching question is forever cropping up. How was it possible that such a deep stream of genuine religious in-spiration—the very Breath of the Holy Ghost—could spring up and flourish *outside the Church*, outside Christianity? What loving searching for the ways of God, what passionate impulse towards

---

* The *zaddikim* kindled the souls of their disciples as much by their actual pre-sence as by their teaching. This inter-relationship between the *hasidim* and their *zaddik* is the very foundation of Hasidism. Thus a great oral tradition of the stories told by the *hasidim* to one another about their masters grew up and endured for a full hundred and fifty years. Martin Buber, formulator of the neo-hasidic philosophy, first collected these "miracle tales" in his *Tales of the Hasidim*, published in English translation by Schocken Books, New York, 1947.

holiness! And yet the answer is not really so hard to find. Even after the rise of Christianity Jewry remained—and still remains —the tree-stump of the Old Testament, lopped and stunted, yet in its faithful no less alive and authentic; the root from which Jesus himself stemmed, and Mary, Joseph, the Baptist, the Apostles. And as for the Jews of latter days born and growing up within this pale and serving the God of their Fathers with all their hearts, expecting the coming of the Messiah as we ought to be waiting ardently for his Second Coming—and aren't. . . . Well, I just can't imagine that the faithful God, the God of Abraham, Isaac and Jacob, that Jesus himself should refuse to accept such souls into his Covenant, on the hidden paths of his Grace.

*

In John 7.38 Jesus says: "He that believeth in me, as the scripture saith, out of his belly shall flow rivers of living water." The Vulgate says "*de ventre eius*" (so does the Authorized Version), but of course we've chastened it to "interior". The next verse is haunting me: "Now he said this of the *Spirit* . . .". I wonder whether one could interpret it along these lines: that even from the lower regions, human nature, the seat of sub-conscious, primitive, animal urges and impulses—unfathomed and uncontrolled by reason and resolve—the living waters of the Spirit will gush forth (a stream, not a trickle)—if only, *if only we believe in him?*

*

READING Buber on the three Sabbath meals, the immersions and other rituals, it is painful to think of the "shorthand" forms in which most of our sacraments are now administered. Who on earth is to make out the seal any more, if the wax it's stamped upon is so thin? The bath of "rebirth" is no more than just a sprinkling or pouring, the bread has become a papery wafer, and in Extreme Unction what they used to call "the sinful zone" of the body is ignored altogether.

*

I WAS reminded yesterday of an excellent passage in one of

7

Von Hügel's *Letters to a Niece*.★ He referred to the raw material, the substance-to-be-worked-upon, *das Bildsame*, which is the indispensable prerequisite for *Bildung*—you just can't shape anything without clay to form with your hands. This is even more applicable to religion. The natural material must be there first—religion can't be planted in an empty hole. Yet our religious education, with its airy contempt for morals, cherishes precisely the delusion that you *can*—which obviously leads to the truism: *"Aus nichts wird nichts"* (Start with nothing, you'll finish with nothing.) It seems to me that our last real contribution here was the stamp of behaviour which used to be called "well-bred" throughout most of Europe. (Compare the "metaphysical luggage" of the Orientals which I noted the other day!) Where even this substratum is wanting, the product of "supernatural training" is most succinctly described, again in the *Tales of the Hasidim*, by Rabbi Bunam's laconic comment: "Anyone who is just pious and nothing more besides is a rogue."

*

A LONG talk with X. in the course of which many of the thoughts which I've been turning over in my mind for ages began to take clearer shape. Matrimony is *the* sign and image of monotheism —i.e. of vital relationship with the Living God. Both are an attempt (so natural and so unnatural to man!) to cleave to One only in perfect Oneness—which doesn't mean just singleness, an isolated bit cut off from all the rest, from the Whole, but rather that Oneness which is one because it is in itself the Whole, because it is ultimate and universal Oneness: "One is One and all alone and evermore must be", and: "Thou shalt love the Lord

★ "I want you, just because you long for religion, to continue to cultivate, to cultivate more carefully and lovingly, also the interests, the activities, that are not directly religious. And this, not simply because, 'Why, of course, we must eat our dinner; of course, we must have our little relaxations'; but, much more, because, without these not directly religious interests and activities, you—however slowly and unperceivedly—*lose the material for Grace to work in and on*—*Hardly any woman works her religion thus;* but then, too, how thin and abstract, or how strained and unattractive, the religion of most women becomes, owing to this their elimination of religion's materials and divinely intended tensions!" I believe this applies to moral and intellectual schooling as well.

thy God with all thy heart, with all thy soul, with all thy mind and with all thy strength". That is why married life is just as hard—or as easy—as our life with God (measured in the proportion of dewdrop to sun, of course, but this is a very true mirror all the same). It is the obvious thing, utterly desirable, the only possible state if and as long as love is alive and growing—it becomes intolerable, a strait-jacket, fetters and shackles constraining all liberty, as soon as love fails or begins to dwindle.

And that's why marriage must be sustained *at all costs*—for better, for worse—that's why it is and must be indissoluble, even if the "image of God" is darkening in one or the other, or in both (just as the face of the transcendent God may grow dark for us in trial and temptation and disaster). That is why married life *must* be carried on, even dragged on, as a shared life (let's concede—as far as possible), just as our religious life must be kept alive in times of aridity, doubt and desolation, even if every vestige of sensible emotion seems extinct. And this, too, is why it *can* go on persisting out of the hidden, the imperceptible yet living core of Love, just as our bond with God can continue to subsist out of naked faith.

And this is also why married love is never so endangered as by the surge of a new affection—"disorderly" love, irregular love —that is, love that has not yet been put in its place, subjugated, ordered; indeed, just for that very reason all things of themselves good and fair and precious are liable to become rivals, to seduce and to sever—*because* of their qualities, not in spite of them. And so, too, every instance of falling away from God is really adultery and fornication, as the Old Testament recognized and stated so uncompromisingly. Maybe this, too, is at the root of the strange "mystical" odium which clings to these sins and cannot be accounted for simply by their social and moral stigma; this is not the outcome of prudery or shrinking from sex or anything of that kind, it attaches to them because they are by their very nature—not because they are carnal—symbols and images of sin itself: lapse from God, treason against his love and faith, surrender to "otherness".

*

I'VE discovered that one can really just as well say the Rosary in the present tense:

> who is sweating blood for us . . .
> who is being scourged for us . . .
> who is carrying the heavy cross for us . . .*

"Christ in agony until the end of the world"—that isn't just a highbrow *aperçu* of Pascal's—he is still suffering bloody torments for us here and now in his martyrs of today.

*

THE doctrine of the Shekhinah† seems to me like a strange image of the Incarnation mirrored against the dark cloud-mass of the late Jewish mind. Of course the original image is changed almost (but still only almost) beyond recognition; but, vague as it is, even this dim reflection, fervently received and responded to, can still work wonders in hearts surrendered to it. For what else, after all, is the Shekhinah—the indwelling of God—but a passionate awareness of *the* indwelling of God in his world, the Word made flesh and dwelling among us? And the desolate, weary figure of the woman pilgrim, seen weeping on a deserted street-corner in the gathering dusk—how like, oh, how very like the image of him who took the form of a servant, who had no place to lay his head, who, being "the radiance of his Father's splendour", yet trod our earth with his glory concealed, "no beauty in him, nor comeliness"!

*

"YOU will suffer from the world, just as I have suffered," said Yehudi, as he bade farewell to Rabbi Mendel. "But try at least not to hate the world—*for, like all of us, it is made up of grace alone.*"

*

READ an article in *Commonweal* yesterday—rather silly really, but telling enough in its way. A discussion in a train between an

---

* In the German form of the Rosary the Mysteries are incorporated into each Ave: ". . . and blessed is the fruit of thy womb Jesus, who sweated blood for us. Holy Mary . . .".

† Shekhinah ("indwelling"): divine hypostasis indwelling in the world and sharing the exile of Israel; Divine Presence among men.

10

American and a mullah about such things as polygamy, the status of women, and so on. If nothing else, it served to strengthen my recognition that the much-discussed "status of woman" is something which belongs to "the region of secret things" and should be approached accordingly and not only through legal and sociological categories. Simone de Beauvoir* is right enough in much of what she says—as far as her *material* goes, that is. But she's got all her accents, illustrations and conclusions wrong. All the same, a good deal of what she says *is* true. For instance that "femininity" (in inverted commas, only this brand!) is in fact largely the product of the male imagination, plus ruthlessness, plus tyranny, plus female complicity. And all these things have combined, wantonly and on a vast scale, to create an overbred species of "differentness" at the cost of human kinship.

It's like that parrot-tulip over there on the table. Lovely as it is, there's something outrageous about it all the same—its petals all slashed and frilled and curled, more like a cactus or an exotic kind of poppy than a tulip. Yet a tulip it is, a tulip which has been deliberately mis-cultivated, almost beyond recognition. Thus a certain type of woman may well be "womanly" too, but what does the "revolt of woman" *really* mean? That women want to be accepted as *real women*—and not merely as females? I think it's important to make a clear distinction here.

*

THE case of the ZZ's is yet another pointer to at least *one* of the reasons why so many women today are unhappy and discontented in their marriages. It would seem that the "cultivated" woman can no longer be two things at the same time, i.e. intellectual and primitive. She only discovered her own intellectual side so recently, only yesterday! She's only just found out that spiritual and intellectual partnership with a man really is possible, that she is taken seriously in a discussion, and that there is such a thing as dialogue on this plane.

The toy is as yet so brand new that she can't bear to let it out of her hand for one minute. The intoxication is so exhilarating, she must just try it out again and again.

* In *The Second Sex*, London and New York, 1953.

11

The ZZ's—bred in the old German Youth Movement*—are a typical example. The poor man is forever being dragged into "discussions", whether he's in the mood or not, forced to take part in family prayers, and so on. If he isn't feeling like it, she thinks that his love, his regard for her as a "mind", in a word all their real partnership is fading out or lost for good—and she feels miserably degraded to a mere Cinderella or even a beast of burden.

Nowadays particularly, with no help available and women physically exhausted by the strain of housekeeping, they do look to their husbands for some compensation, for the mental stimulation of talk to lift them out of their drudgery. But he has spent all day in a men's world, talking shop, and hankers for exactly the opposite when he comes home, dog-tired, in the evening: to hold his tongue and not to be bothered. All he wants is to feel her silent presence about the house. That's that, and it means a lot to him, perhaps more than anything. But to her it means nothing at all, it just makes her feel pitifully unwanted, of no account. Worse still, as in the case of the two couples I'm thinking of, when the husband is of lower class origin and not at all keen on discussing or reading things with his wife—he never did so with his mother who still remains his ideal of womanhood. Of course this doesn't mean that he thinks of his wife as a domestic animal (in between beast of burden and pet), but rather as a domestic *sprite*, a "familiar spirit". But that's all Greek to her, and so the confusion grows—and the soreness of heart.

*

IF one reads Saint-Exupéry's chapter entitled *Thirst*† with due care, one can learn a whole lot about the extraordinary hallucinations which beset people who are tormented by mental and emotional thirst—and the dreams of fulfilment which make up their existence. Odd that these *fata morgana* always seem to take a pleasant form—no mention here of pangs of disillusionment, images of terror, etc.

*

* See Appendix.
† In *Wind, Sand and Stars*, London, 1954.

12

IF we can grasp something of the tremendous significance of the Name of God in Israel, then we can begin to guess what it must have meant to the apostles after the Ascension of our Lord to be able to say: "In the NAME of Jesus of Nazareth"—knowing that it was the same thing.

*

MONICA BALDWIN's autobiography *I Leapt over the Wall* is bothering me. An awful book—why on earth it was so warmly received in the Catholic press I can't think. Probably the reviewers had feared the worst and heaved a sigh of relief that the convent came off so lightly! But what makes it so awful is the fact that anyone could spend twenty-eight years, I repeat: twenty-eight years, in a contemplative convent and come out the sort of person the authoress (wittingly and unwittingly) describes: so vain, callow and stunted. Precisely the accounts of the life of the order (all of them extremely positive and, as such, praised by reviewers) are curiously rigid and impersonal, so much so that I kept wondering whether they hadn't been inspired by somebody else, or even "lifted" wholesale from some religious booklet. At best they could be the work of an enthusiastic theorist who hadn't a clue what life in a convent *really* means—a very young girl perhaps who had done a lot of "religious reading". It all seemed so unreal to me that for two-thirds of the book I had grave doubts as to whether the autobiography could, in fact, be genuine—indeed, I even wondered whether the writer could possibly be a Catholic—so pat, so prefabricated, so reminiscent of High Church fancy-work. . . . But facts are facts, Monica Baldwin *was* a nun, for nearly thirty years at that.

Yet even if only half the book were based on truth, it would still serve as an indictment of the antiquated, mummy-macabre way of life in at least some women's convents. Every page of the book asks the same question, directly or indirectly: how should —and must—the traditions of the ancient orders (I never discovered which one it really was!) be adapted to modern conditions if figures like the writer herself are not to leap over the wall? For it's obvious that this girl who entered with a good will and maybe had a more genuine vocation at the outset than she would have us believe (otherwise her superiors would scarcely have kept her for so long) simply atrophied by slow degrees in her "Saul's armour".*

The habit is a sort of symbol. For girls entering at the turn of the century convent dress was hardly more than a slightly exaggerated version of the sort of clothes they wore anyway: ankle-length dresses, long warm underwear, nightcaps, thick stockings summer and winter alike, large hats. But for modern women and girls, used to wearing next to nothing under summer frocks, with their nylons and no hats. . . . What a radical change! For instance, wearing coif, bonnet and veil indoors and out, no matter how hot it is!—sheer torment, causing perpetual headaches for many a poor nun, using up strength and energy needed for other things. What's the point? And what about the night Office, and early morning meditations timed in the days when bed-time used to be 9 p.m. at the latest? For nuns who, like other modern women with jobs to do, are often on their feet until midnight, this can become a very real form of martyrdom (depriving prisoners of sleep is one of the most refined forms of torture used in political prisons!).

*

In the account of the Last Supper the humility of the disciples is shattering. When Jesus tells them that one of them will betray him, *each* of them asks: "Is it I, Lord?"

*

I've been reading Exodus in my Buber-Rosenzweig Bible, and then the beginning of the Passion in St Matthew. If the Last Supper really was a *seder*, then Jesus would have read this chapter aloud, or told the story: of the lamb to be sacrificed, of the destroying angel, of the sprinkling of the houses with blood and how it ran down the door-posts. No, it's quite impossible to understand the Last Supper solely from the "New Testament angle", even less in the interpretation our theologians put upon it: westernized, European, "spiritualized": without the heavy, reeking cloud which hung over the temple courtyard running

* 1 Kings 17. 38–39.

14

with steaming blood, filling the narrow alleys of the city with its stench; no sound of the bleating and bellowing of the terrified beasts awaiting sacrifice which must certainly have penetrated even to the upper room. (Dorothy Sayers catches this atmosphere very well in her radio play *A Man Born to be King*.) Against *this* background then: "This is my Body, this is my Blood which shall be shed for you." If you think of this connection, and the numerous "lamb" references, from the Baptist to the Apocalypse (especially in St John), as well as that very revealing identification detail, the unbroken bones on the cross: "No bone of his may be broken"—then it's a mystery to me how it can be asserted that only the meal and not the sacrificial character of the Eucharist can be deduced from the Bible. And their further thesis: that the whole notion of sacrifice and the "sacrificial" theory of the Body and Blood as two separate species is simply a late scholastic construction, a sort of philosophical contortion, or a distortion arising from pagan, Jewish, in a word "primitive" concepts somehow assimilated. To which one could well answer (apart from that classical retort: "What's wrong with pagans?") that: (*a*) the theory of the mystery so favoured by the same theologians is pagan too, and (*b*) Jewish, i.e. Old Testament elements are very much a legitimate part of the Christian tradition. Amazing what holes have been torn in Christian consciousness by almost dropping the Old Testament —and how "cleverly" these have been patched.

*

THERE's no redder rag for our modern, progressive Catholics than a certain religious approach to sex and Eros ranging from suspicion to open condemnation and branded accordingly as Manichean, neo-Platonic, Puritan, etc. (why not Jewish and Gnostic as well? I'm thinking specially here of those tales of an androgynous Adam and a Paradise in which there would have been neither procreation nor birth). Quite unacceptable. And yet in these quite obviously heretical speculations there's a barb which, even at first encounter, penetrated to the depths of my mind as the startling confirmation of something "always known", and this ferment keeps on working—all the time. An idea rejected and consciously repressed for many years, but which still kept obstinately cropping up, the idea which one finds in so many apocryphal trends of thought, i.e. that there's definitely "something wrong" with sex in its present form, that is, during this terrestrial aeon—something that is *not* sex in itself, as a whole, but some trait or quality. Something which does not belong to original human nature, but which owes its actual existence to the Fall; in the same sense unnatural as death is unnatural and yet is taken for granted, an inevitable, undeniable factor—in this fallen world. Certainly death can be beautiful, noble, something infinitely precious in the eyes of God—there's even a special sacrament consecrating death. And yet . . . and yet death is still for us not just one but *the* symbol of doom, perdition, which means spiritual or eternal death.

In the primeval mind both these things have always been held to be taboo: death and sex. "Morals" and "culture" have tried their best to tame these two huge and unavoidable phenomena in all kinds of ways, endeavouring to domesticate them —with graves and tombstones, spirit-worship, funeral pomp, the undertaker's art (think of Evelyn Waugh's *The Loved One*!). And then marriage, the wedding ceremonies, all the various rites of initiation, the charms and spells surrounding birth, etc. And in the contemporary "liberal" world we have exactly the same thing attempted through "enlightenment" of all kinds, psychology, depth psychology, hygiene, medicine, law, sociology, and all the rest.

And then that in itself so very strange phenomenon of sexual shame (*pudeur* not *honte*), impossible to explain away by reason —it is and always will be nonsense to attribute this exclusively to false modesty, to warped notions discovered at last by the psychologists, etc., or, for that matter, to "guilt complexes" artificially created and nurtured by taboos. As though it couldn't just as well be the other way round, i.e. that the taboos could, in point of fact, have resulted from the fact that this "shame" has existed since time immemorial? And this is where another significant fact fits in, namely the strange fact that children are most definitely capable of impurity in what they think, say, hear and do *before* they reach puberty. Some people still refuse to believe that this is true, while others chatter away brightly about "childish sexuality" as though this were the most natural thing in the world. In reality this very disconcerting phenomenon would seem to me to demonstrate that "impurity" is primarily a sin of the spirit, applied, as it were, to the body—a sin which can take active form long before the body itself is capable of committing specific acts with the appropriate organs. In this connection it might do no harm to take a look from time to time at the gloomy view Newman took of sins committed by children—it might serve to correct some of the exclusively psychological pronouncements on the subject.

Obviously there's no great point in worrying one's head about what form procreation in Paradise would have taken—any more than we can hope to solve the parallel question as to how mankind would have achieved the transfigured state without the medium of death. All the same it is surely not insignificant that the myth of the virgin birth occurs in so many religions—as though man had never ceased dreaming that birth "in reality" might have been somehow different.

All this seems to me to have a very definite bearing on the Christian, or rather I should say the early Christian, regard for virginity. Indeed, it provides us with the only real answer. For here, too, we're not being strictly honest. The same progressive Catholics pretend that virginity is not meant as a negation of anything, and has no purpose or sense other than that of freeing a man for active service of all kinds, unshackled and completely available (leaving, incidentally, quite a handsome margin for private flirtation—spiritual and otherwise!). Yet the Fathers stated quite clearly that the essential value of that state and these vows lies in continence. Of course not starkly "carnal", as though anatomical integrity were the point—without spiritual foundation; but they did know that continence is just as potent and significant a symbol of one state of mind as bodily love is of another. Yes, the early Christians still had a genuine understanding of the body and all it means—traditional, experimental, age-old—whereas our theological theorists are just bandying words and slogans at each other like ping-pong balls. Oh, those heralds of "frank and uninhibited sex-life", with their arch and artificially naïve prattle, the whole thing like a sort of perpetual sun-bathers' picnic, all fun and frolic, and, please, no ceremonies whatever. . . . Heaven help them, they're even less realistic than the grimmest of old Puritans or the most strait-laced of prudish maiden aunts. "They haven't got no noses, those fallen sons of Eve. . . ."

*

BERGENGRUEN* has sent me a book of his poems. *Die heile Welt*† he calls it—and indeed one can believe him! "Heaven and earth are full of thy glory. Hosanna in the highest!" One long, lovely hymn of joy. The poet's calling as the angels' office on earth.

*

I SENSE so deeply just now that yet again the foundations of my spiritual house, its familiar and tangible basic elements, are gradually disintegrating. It's as though, once more, the whole building were floating upon a cloud, inside a cloud, within which the new framework were shaping, being welded into a form as yet hidden from my sight, perhaps to remain invisible for a long time to come. I've drifted far from the attitude in which I wrote *Die leibhaftige Kirche*, the Church Incarnate, beyond that kind of "denominational" religion which smacks of *Religionspartei*, as they called it in the seventeenth and eighteenth centuries— Churches Political, rival fronts. It seems I'm getting caught up —or is it initiated?—into that great, mazy, marvellous game God is playing with us, his children—a sort of intricate dance in which he is steering and guiding us all into our places, silently intertwining our movements. And he's well able to do it by himself, he doesn't need the fussy help we're always trying to

* Werner Bergengruen, born in Riga in 1892, Baltic convert to Catholicism, outstanding poet and writer. His voluminous and remarkably varied works, ranking almost as contemporary classics, include novels (two have been translated into English: *A Matter of Conscience* (Der Grosstyrann) by Norman Cameron in 1952, and *The Last Captain of Horse* (Der letzte Rittmeister) by Eric Peters in 1953), seven volumes of verse, children's books, travel, ghost stories, criticism, first-rate translations of Tolstoy and Dostoevsky, nonsense (extremely rare among serious German letters) and innumerable tales of the kind Italians call *novelle*. Every book of his reflects his intense and constant preoccupation with the mystery of the universe. He himself has said: "Just as the medieval painters sought to reveal the whole universe in every picture, I too am perpetually trying to show this universe, *visibilia omnia et invisibilia*, in every poem and every story, even if only in the briefest of flashes." (*Trans.*)

†*Die heile Welt*=the whole, sound, good world.

give him, backing him up with nice little salesmen's tricks—pedagogical, diplomatic or rhetorical, however clever these may be. Proclaiming the gospel is something quite different.

*

I DO feel so very intensely the danger for me as an invalid—cornered here in my hole—of growing quite disgustingly narrow-minded and self-centred, irresponsibly irresponsive to God's vast world and his kingdom in it.

It's almost inevitable—that is if I don't manage to snatch the alternative now, at the eleventh hour: and that would mean *real prayer*, excavating an interior space into which I could draw the whole world again—turning my room into a cell, where "matters of God" would be discussed with God, and the concerns of his creatures, too, whom he still leads to me. But, oh Newman!—"Religion, a Weariness to Natural Man"—how he hit the nail on the head, at least for me! I can scarcely ever cope with it, and, when I try, what a languid poor effort it is! And yet I can spend hours day-dreaming about any number of other things. . . . I'd better hurry up and pull myself together, or the Devil will succeed in turning this blessed and unique chance of mine into a wretched fool's paradise of selfishness.

*

I FOUND these wonderful words in one of Emmanuel Mounier's letters: "*Je crois que j'ai été fait pour être . . . de ceux qui sont là pour nouer, en lisière, l'amitié . . . dans le monde des hommes de la foi . . . avec ceux du monde de la nuit.*" I once thought this myself, too. In the range of daylight you can't help being seen—beckoning and gesticulating. But to be noticed at all in the *monde de la nuit*, so as to point a way, to guide—well, you have to *shine*. Like that Princess L. with her Poor Souls.* And this isn't something that can be done at will. On the contrary, the more you think about it, the more you go on *trying* to shine, instead of just *growing* into this state (without once taking a look in the

---

* Germans call the Holy Souls in Purgatory the Poor Souls, insisting on their piteous plight. Towards the beginning of this century a certain Princess L. had visions of such souls, who begged her to help them by prayer and sacrifice. When she asked them why they singled her out, of all people, she received the answer: "We can see you only because you shine."

mirror!)—the less successful you'll be. It's the same old story—
like the recipe for making gold: it only comes off if you *don't*
think of a polar bear while you're doing it.

But how wonderful it is, on the other hand, to think that we
can always begin all over again from the beginning, from the
bottom, as apprentices, as novices, "for in the kingdom of God
there are neither old nor young".

*

THE First Epistle of St John is much more difficult, much darker,
than you'd think. What does he mean, for instance, when he
says that lust of the flesh and lust of the eyes are of the world
and not of the Father? Is not the Creator himself the sole cause
that there is such a thing as "lust" at all, is not he alone the
author of every form of pleasure? How did Creation turn into
"the World"? Is not "the World", in this sense, in fact *man*-
made?—the veil of Maya flung by the fallen spirit of man (C. S.
Lewis's "Dark Eldil"!) across the inexpressible holiness and
dignity of God's creation?

*

READING St John's First Epistle again today I found in Chapter
2. 23: "Whosoever denieth the Son, the same hath not the
Father. He that confesseth the Son hath the Father also." Hard
words for me, thinking of my beloved *hasidim.* . . . But *did* they
really deny the Son? I rather think they, too, acknowledged and
loved him—in the dark mirror of the Shekhinah. And in thinking,
it's only too easy to make mistakes, as we well know. God certainly forgives intellectual errors the most readily of all.

*

TALKING to my masseuse the other day it occurred to me that it
really isn't so strange that good Protestants are often very much
more deeply religious than a certain type of practising Catholic,
even the most fervent kind. After all you can't ignore human
nature in religion either, and for centuries now we've been
practising a kind of negative selection in regard to hereditary
endowment of spiritual gifts. People with more than ordinary
qualities entered religion, men and women alike, whereas those

of the other persuasion married one another and founded exemplary and very large families—and inbreeding was the result.

So many Protestant free-thinkers still have notorious theological traits, not to mention all the renegade theological students or sons of pastors, such as Nietzsche or Hermann Hesse, and certainly countless others too, anonymous.

*

NN. WAS here yesterday evening and disgorged all her troubles. Poor thing. But what strikes me even more forcibly than her side of the case is the realization that celibacy these days would seem to be well-nigh impossible—at least for a vital human being with a gift for Eros—at any rate given our *present* sort of clerical training. The onslaught of female provocation priests are supposed to stand up to—the quantity of "goods for sale", far more than even an ordinary bachelor has to cope with! Priests are expected to behave like salamanders, fireproof, asbestos-coated in the fiery furnace, the blaze re-kindled all the time. And the way so-called good Catholics react when things happen to go wrong! All this wailing and gnashing of teeth as though poor Humpty Dumpty had fallen off his wall for good and all, irredeemably. Surely this attitude is a remnant of Victorian cant, something we really should try to get out of our systems at last? And the very people who fuss so are surprisingly ready to put up with other quite blatant faults in clergy and religious— conceit and pride, bad temper, back-biting, money-grabbing. . . . Perhaps we should look at it the other way round, i.e. that *genuine* continence and virginity are rare and costly achievements—admirable and really extraordinary; the real thing, *nota bene*, not simply a shrivelling of Eros-power by means of life-long taboo injections. The Ancients knew this—they called chastity, honestly, simply and humbly, a *gift*, a *charisma*, to be implored from God with tears and in humiliating experience—not just a simple athletic feat of will-power and self-control. What hypocrites we are! Supposing a normal, healthy, able-bodied man, bound to abstain all his life from eating meat or sweets, were— on top of that—employed in a big hotel kitchen. Would it be fair to be even surprised, let alone aghast, if one day he should happen to snatch a tasty morsel from one of the temptingly garnished dishes he has to handle continually, every day—maybe just out of sheer, irresistible curiosity, to taste just once for himself what he is always recommending and the guests are for ever gloating over? I'm sure one couldn't in all justification *expect* more than that he'd be really sorry—afterwards—and pull himself together, with God's help, and not make a habit of filching.

*

A DECENT fellow, so he seemed,
liked well enough, if not esteemed.
The trouble was—he couldn't wait—
Oh, how he longed to know his fate!
Women and friends, he'd ask them rudely
just what they thought of him, quite crudely.
Those who could lie (and there are such)
declared they loved him very much.
But others, not inclined to spare him,
admitted that they could not bear him.
Small wonder that our friend felt slighted.
(Their judgment he himself invited.)
At last he's come to realize:
to ask too much is most unwise.
Better to face the truth instead:
some things are better left unsaid.

EUGEN ROTH.

It *sounds* funny, but it isn't really a joke. There is far more behind it. The poor man thinks he can elude and exclude doubt and ambiguity and aching insecurity simply by questioning people, by poking and squeezing and extorting answers. But this really only makes matters worse. In other words: he thinks that, possessing certainty, he could gladly forgo faith and trust —and that, of course, is fatal, a profoundly irreligious attitude.

Again: You can ask questions, not only because you want to rip open other people's secrets, but also because, artfully, you want to lay bare your own self, layer after layer (and how often both purposes are identical!)—and both mean the same thing. The idea is that the thing I am disclosing, revealing, is really an offering (whether distress, affection, cleverness, anything), and that, being thus thrust upon the other person, it *must* perforce impress him, convince him, overwhelm him, captivate him. It's

22

not really so very different from the strip-tease technique—which is why a certain kind of "outspokenness" so often seems just indecent and repulsive. Modesty and veils do go together, even where you wouldn't expect it. And this attempt to force admiration, sympathy, love, confidence is exactly the same as the idea of putting merit before grace in religion. And why? Because we actually rather believe in compulsion than in "grace", i.e. in liberty, freely granted favour, election, the element of surprise in love. Rather like trying to substitute magic for prayer. Awful, really.

We can't wait for "the time and the hour" because we don't *believe* in letting things take their course. So we try to put on the clock and think we can arrange everything nicely our own way, convinced we shall be successful if only we can tackle things cleverly enough. How impious, how wrong, how terribly arrogant and yet how fear-stricken this attitude really is! How it reflects the panic of our age in which no one has the courage any more to believe that things come right "of their own accord". Nowadays the maxim preferred is: "What I don't seize myself no one's going to give me". How we've been caught by the spirit of the times and how it has stamped our lives and our actions! And we don't know it, imagining ourselves to be living in a lofty world of our own, in exclusive freedom, well out of its reach. . . .

*

"LYING ill, on the point of death, Rabbi Rafael declared: 'The hour has come to put away every virtue, that there be no difference, no distinction between me and other men.'" If one could realize this before the face of Christ, really grasp it—then one would have broken free to that kind of charity St John's epistles are full of: children of one Father, brothers of one Brother, all of us pied, all of us chequered, none of us really better than our neighbour, only in nuances. Yet we're all thriving on the fond conviction that we *are* "different"—not like X. or Y., and, at least compared with him, something better—not belonging to this particular zoo, but to a superior show. Yet, on the other hand, surely we *must* assert ourselves as individuals against the collective, discerning and acknowledging differences, distinctions of rank and grade among men, despite all this sham equality and levelling? So we are fighting on two fronts even in our innermost heart of hearts. We? Who are we? Why *we* again, and of course: *we*, not the others, we, the spiritual kin, the phalanx of those-who-belong, the minds in harmony, the not-like-that-publican-back-there. . . . Oh, dear!!

Yes, but, hang it all, this *we* does exist—human beings with the same task, the same responsibility and (no hedging!) the same vocation. And yet, apart from the classical and typical German quarrelsomeness, there's surely nothing more divided, spiteful, pigheaded and implacable than our Catholic disunity. Don't talk about the sects, they're much better off, for they're really broken away and set up as independent firms. But we're like a crowd of squabbling relations forced to live in the same house—and each of us sticks exclusively to those who share his opinions, i.e. his spiritual tastes, turning up his nose at all the rest, as best he can.

*

KNOX translates *"Et tentaverunt Deum in cordibus suis ut peterent escas animabus suis"* in Psalm 77 as "challenging God in their thoughts to give them the food they craved for". Here is the difference between trust and presumption: the one honours God, the other challenges him.

Just now this psalm (and others too) force me to think how much more fitting it really is for us not to come begging to God with our own "specialized" wants, but rather to pray along the lines of Bergengruen's lovely verse from the *Die heile Welt*:

> O give us nothing, God, for which we pray,
> Confused, misled by the dim light we see.
> Let us just happen, here to pass or stay,
> As in Creation things are made to be.
> The flight, the fall, the flowering and decay,
> Slow granite growth, the glowing crags' array,
> The salmon's leap, the ivy's steadfast frond,
> The moon, ice-mirrored in the wintry pond.
> Naught give me, God; grant only on my day
> That, like thy stars, the weathered stone, the tree,
> Wise as thy little ones, I also may
> Slip into heaven in their company.

24

Even as I write I can see NN. frowning. The theologian is *not* amused. "But you can't say that!" I know, I know all that. But, just at the moment, anyway, this seems to be my particular bread—the lesson which I have to learn (even if sometimes with brimming eyes): simply to "let myself happen", "to let things happen to me", as opposed to wanting to *do* things, to force things.

*

MAYBE it's quite a good thing—though it does make life more difficult—that we human beings are usually so well packed up, each in his own shaggy covering of thick straw matting, so that one only rarely catches a glimpse of the living human soul within, the soul so akin to God. If one could see God, as he is, then there would no longer be any choice, nor any temptation, so the theologians say—for what could then "compete"? Perhaps, by the same token, if we could see the souls of our fellow men there would be an end of all antipathy. Or would it in this life be replaced by the temptation to idolatry of this *fascinans et tremendum*?

I once heard about an Indian sect in which husband and wife worshipped each other as gods, with offerings of flowers, etc.

*

ONCE again the tide of Carmelite spirituality is drawing me, like a current, and, yet again, I sense its dangerous challenge to my own appointed way. Utter nakedness, utter rejection, utter renunciation—how tempting is this stream of spirituality, with the tremendous nimbus of its glorious and venerable past! But for us who are not monks—for us there are other ways of dying —very real ways.

*

THERE exists a revolting lack of discrimination in love which leads to promiscuity. And there exists, too, the divine indiscrimination of true Christian charity which is never concerned with the value of the object. But I do find it hard to be the *object* of this last sort. To be the *subject* would, of course, be very elevating; but to know oneself to have been picked up on the roadside with all the other rubbish is not pleasant at all—even if one's benefactor were a saint, or even if not a proper saint, let's say, well, the Good Samaritan. For what struck him first was, after all, only the pitiable state of the poor man lying there, and not the "qualities" underneath.

*

I READ again today—for the first time for goodness knows how many years—that passage in the first volume of Spengler which pierced through me like a sword, as a young girl in Stockau, and revealed to me the ultimate sense of my "vocation". "In the Gothic age to enter a convent was to renounce care, activity and will, an act of the highest ethical dignity. It was the greatest possible sacrifice—that of life itself. In the Baroque era even Catholics no longer saw it this way. These seats not of denial but of comfortable living fell a prey to the spirit of the Enlightenment." Only a footnote, on page 430, but how it was to determine my life! And how strange and unquestionable the fact that this vocation has persisted throughout all the stages and forms of my existence, reappearing each time in a different guise.

*

YESTERDAY was Trinity Sunday—the feast on which one can spend the whole day revelling in how *little* we know of God, or will ever know—even in the *visio beatifica*. The Feast of the Incomprehensibility of God, of God Revealed: of the unfathomable abyss of the Divinity, on the edge of which we kneel in adoration, rejoicing in the depth of its silence and the mystery of its Being—*O beata Trinitas!* And—in contrast—all our dogmas and names, all our definitions and explanations are no more than tiny stars, pale against the darkness of the vast night sky. How lovely are the antiphons and the responsories on this day— pure joy in the knowledge of knowing nothing—*O beata Trinitas!*

*

CAN it be that Pietists and Evangelicals (apparently) enjoy so much more in the way of religious experience, enthusiasm, revivals and so on than we do simply because they lack the sacraments? Maybe God makes up for the deficiency in this way?

26

After all they are just as human as we are, body and soul, i.e. designed for visibility of the Invisible, clamouring for it—even if they ignore it or deny it "on principle". And, good will provided, and hunger and thirst for tokens and reassurance, why should God not grant them (like Hagar in the desert) at least the spring of subjective experience, gushing up out of the sand to refresh them?

We have inherited the objective and material forms, and (often enough) we must make do with them, honouring them in simplicity and obedience, performing them—even with hearts parched and blind—"living from faith" in a much stricter sense than Protestants dream of, precisely *because* of the welter and clutter of visible things—and having to live among them solely upon that which is invisible and imperceptible. I've got the impression that converts rather tend to overrate psychological tokens, presages, guidances, etc. They are apt to dislike and to refuse the rational proofs for the existence of God, etc., but they cling all the more to psychological indications, taking these to be the only real signs of the Spirit. That means: spiritual poverty, as above, is what they attain as their very last experience. I suppose this is the special temptation of "spiritual wealth"—it takes a long time for man to understand that even such "property" must be laid down at the foot of the Cross in that stripped and naked faith that seems to deride every evidence and even experience itself.

Devout Protestants, especially of the dissenting kind, actually transpose external and sensory experience from the physical to the mental range, from things visible and tangible to excitements and emotions which are just as "carnal". Which accounts for Newman's dislike, disgust, for this sort of religiosity, which he doesn't even find edifying.

*

I SEE now what a mistake it was these past ten years or so, to make clarity my chief concern in all my writing and lecturing— trying to make things easy, smooth, demonstrable, especially for young minds. And not even out of personal rationalism either, but *ad usum Delphini*—so as not to talk above their heads, to overtax their readiness to believe. Yet this attitude, really, isn't so very different from the "demythologizing" attempts of more renowned contemporaries, i.e. simply deferring to the minds of the multitude—taking the lowest level as a yardstick. I well remember the first time I heard the word "*Entmythologisierung*" from one of our crowd, commendatory at that!—and how shocked I was. Yet in time I, too, lost the courage to proclaim the message fearlessly, recklessly, in season, out of season. I, too, only dared to say what I thought would be inoffensive and palatable, i.e. pedagogic, not political opportunism. And so everything I wrote was wrongly geared, along the surface only, grazing deeper matters now and again, handling them gingerly, but never really breaking new ground.

*

IT seems to me that Baroque art belongs to the pleasures of the second half of life. So typical, really, the way those youngsters "kicked" the other day in that lovely church in Neresheim when we tried to explain. Youth at that stage *must* feel almost repelled by it: first because of the immense gulf between their own meagre mode of life and this triumphant, gorgeous exuberance, utterly alien, incomprehensible to their narrow and drab experience. And then, as spiritual beginners, they must now or never go through their "spiritualistic" phase, first taste their power to overcome the senses, to withdraw from the world, the process of "rejecting the images" (C. S. Lewis!), of glorying in the supremacy of the mind. Only later, after long and painful struggle, will they be capable of that blessed return to things created, to earth's glory redeemed, to the Reign of the Holy Ghost—*after* that long road of self-denial, of stripping and tearing away, of asceticism and even radicalism has been climbed.

Simply to exclude all this, jumping the chasm, steering straightway at the ultimate goal, the unquestioning "acceptance of images"—the very idea seems to me like a pedagogical arch-heresy. Possibly there are exceptions, though surely rare, for people of a specially, almost abnormally harmonious disposition. But in every other case taking the body and the world seriously, in their turbulent and dangerous onslaught, means taking their claim to domination seriously too, their impersonal and compelling power of seduction, answering that challenge with defiance, with a fierce struggle for liberty, with flight or contempt. Only then, when liberty has been attained (somehow), can you return—and revel in reconciliation.

*

LAST Glorious Mystery of the Rosary: ". . . and blessed is the fruit of thy womb Jesus who has raised thee, O Virgin, up to heaven". Amazing what horizons open out from these words— the spiral is sweeping again, backwards, upwards, soaring. I feel I'm glimpsing anew the meaning of *"virgo"* in the austere patristic concept—and really it does only make sense from this aspect.

For here continence isn't just a negation (though useful ascetic training, etc.)—instead it becomes a step along a new way of life, a step beyond, *outside* (as far as man can, by God's grace outstep it) the world-wide collective doom of *fallen* sex. (I must look up Berdyaev!)

Only from here, too, does innocence make sense—no longer just a stilted and emphatic word for ignorance and immaturity, but hinting at a state of exception, exemption, of still standing outside, not as yet immersed. And I can see from here, as well, how the apparent overrating of fornication, as of chastity, really does "rhyme" after all with underlying facts. Virginity means neither old-maidishness, being spurned, left over, unfulfilled, a refusal of life—nor does it mean mere technical independence, mobility for action: it is a genuine presage of "the New Earth". Of course all this is valid only when virginity is coupled with charity, springing from it, rooted in it, expressing it. But how very close such a state must be to Luciferian pride—temptation in a form to which men and women living in the humility and humiliation of the flesh (even in marriage) cannot be subjected. The wonder is not that the Blessed Virgin was "most pure", but that she was most humble.

*

How enthralled I was myself by that ridiculous "progressive" nonsense over the last twenty years—all that bright and breezy, optimistic twaddle, even nowadays *à la mode* among our leading educators. Yet how far they are from reality! How urgent their need to turn back to the hard realism of our forebears—even if we draw quite different inferences from their premisses.

How important it is, for example, to realize that the *rite* of marriage in church isn't just an ornamental fringe and flourish tacked on to the real thing (impossible otherwise to account for the Church's rigid insistence on this ceremony), but a genuine rite of initiation on the threshold of that new "life in the flesh" *as Christians*, which even mere humans can't manage just anyhow. This has quite faded out of the popular mind, thinned out to mere generalizing on matrimonial duties of the moral and practical kind, like providing for the family and fulfilling one's household tasks.

And now, quite unexpectedly, I find staggering confirmation of all my surmises in a stray copy of the Easter Letter issued by the *Berneuchener Kreis*!*—an article on the marriage rite by a Professor Ivan Chetverikov. This corroborates and illustrates exactly what I mean.

In the Byzantine ritual the new couple are compared to Noah in the Ark, to the Three Children in the fiery furnace, to Jonah in the belly of the whale—i.e. to people who ventured into the chthonic depths: the sea, the abyss, the fire, the tellurian powers —and who can exist there only by clinging to Ariadne's thread of grace. What did I tell you?

*

WE'LL just have to unlearn and relearn—and realize the urgent necessity of *telling the truth* about these things. So much seems to depend on this. By and large we still cling to that simple Rousseau equation: "What is natural is good." (When I was young we took the opposite for granted, of course: "What's natural is evil, or at least highly suspect.") But here you bump up against the law that different truths "count" in the early and the later half of life. Of course the Church has always *told* us all these things, but they just don't penetrate into a young mind. Only when you've shared some human experience, despite all warnings, can you "see through nature". Only then! But this lies beyond the threshold.

* A very "High Church" group of German Lutherans.

Again: simply proclaiming esoteric truths at large makes them neither obvious nor credible; they just rebound, are scorned or fall flat. On the other hand they aren't destined simply to be imparted to an Inner Ring (to borrow from C. S. Lewis again) of initiates. We, i.e. our generation in the Youth Movement, tried yet another device: "dosing" the message nicely, offering people only what ought to be digestible, preaching what ought to appeal to them—according to *our* opinions. I'm sure it was a genuinely "pastoral" impulse, but brotherly, not fatherly, democratic, submitting to the majority and deferring to their standards. And where did it get us? To these youth associations of ours, to our own special brand of "enlightened" morals, to a shrivelled theology and a shrivelled form of education. In a word, to the blind leading the blind. What we did, all along, was to exalt our particular, very private, very limited stock of knowledge and experience—the inventory of our twenty, thirty, forty years—as "The Real Thing", "essential Christian thought", etc., and to serve it, thus dubbed, to our public.

Our Lord had the courage to proclaim things to the multitude to which most people were blind and deaf, things they were almost bound to misunderstand. But he well knew that although only those hear who have ears to hear, those who *should* hear really do get their ears opened. Oh, that damned opportunist policy of ours!

*

M.A.'s last good letter: ". . . sink into the great silence, again and again, until it begins to speak to you. . . ." Ah, what a judgment on my own dense, materialistic prayer-habits which have really hardly outgrown the convent classroom! Even now that childish notion that you can barter with God, offering him a price if he would listen . . . as though he himself, the great Lamb of God, had not long since paid every price, in advance and more, for every grace, necessary and superabundant! And for ever trying to "use many phrases, like the heathen," worse still *fine* phrases which impress myself and really ought to impress God, coaxing and persuading him that he really must intervene—and, what's more, offering suggestions how he

31

ought to set about it!! Good Lord, so much of what we call prayer is just plain impertinent meddling, a thing only God has the grace to forgive.

*

X. HAS a very curious effect on me. What he says is not really new, but he somehow sets the very soil moving beneath me. I suddenly wake up to the fact that I'm wildly trying to keep my balance among shifting, sliding stones—and that this has probably been going on for quite a considerable time! *And* that I've gone inarticulate: my very own and innermost thought-language is changing—fixed notions and formulas dissolving like paper in water, dropping away like withered husks, while out of the jostling, racing, ever-changing, cloud-mass of "inscapes" (to borrow from Gerard Manley Hopkins) ever new shafts of light break through, cataracts of terrifying brightness.

*

RE-READING Charles Morgan's *Sparkenbroke*. Very exact, very illuminating, full of insights—delighting *and* disconcerting. That's a book some of our theologians ought to read—it would teach quite a lot of them what virginity really means—integrity in maidenhood and in marriage. That conversation in Lucca. And Charles Morgan isn't even a Christian—but a true Platonist and that, too, is wisdom. Here, once again, I must quote Baader: "Because you once scorned ideas in their divine purity you must tremble now before their diabolic distortions." Precisely.

*

THE X's marriage troubles prove to me yet again how undeniably marriage is *the* symbol of union with God: man facing the (humanly) absolute challenge of love—and even in this he must fail—so it seems—as St Paul says of the Law. He must feel and endure his frailty and his sinfulness, i.e. the insufficiency of all purely natural "virtue", be it in love or in character. Then, but only then, can he be raised by God into a new beginning of pure grace. Is this so in every "serious" marriage? But this, of course, belongs to the most secret *arcana*, which is why one never hears anything about it.

*

In the Office for Corpus Christi a passage right in the middle of the crystalline structure of the great master's text suddenly reveals the heart of Thomas, monk and mystic: the responsories in the Second Nocturn: " *Hoc facite in meam commemorationem.* ℣. *Memoria memor ero*, et tabescet in me anima mea . . ." These antiphons were still poetry. What came later, the Office for the Feast of the Sacred Heart, for instance, is no more than "suitably selected".

*

The close affinity between sexual Eros and deceit is very startling—as in infatuation, infidelity and jealousy: "*Quoniam lumbi mei repleti sunt* illusionibus." For, isolated, it (Eros) is in every sense the most treacherous counterfeit of love, sending a continual flow of self-deception and delusion throughout the world, etc.

*

A long talk with N. about the state of the Church in Latin America—a luscious titbit for Protestant indignation. But after all one must try to see things against their historical background—which was something like this: When first discovered Mexico and Peru still belonged to the Stone Age; under a skin-deep layer of nobility a people still ignorant of wheels and riding beasts; a cult of incredible cruelty—50,000 human sacrifices every year, and with that sparse population! That's what the missionary zeal of the Conquistadores pounced upon—what an extraordinary compound, decked out with Christian trappings, must have resulted! Then, barely 300 years later, the onset of the most rabid anti-clerical propaganda, of Enlightenment, freemasonry and anarchy almost simultaneously. Result: what we see. Over here in Europe we had something to match (but on a far tamer and smaller scale) in the eastern territories of Germany—East Prussia, Pomerania, etc., first "missionized" as late as the thirteenth century by the Teutonic Order, i.e. with sword and violence,* and in the sixteenth century already the beginnings of the Reformation. Result: among other things Ernst Wiechert.†

*

I WISH I could properly discuss the question of the *charismata* and their importance for us with an expert. On the one hand, from the language of Scripture, they would seem to be evidence of the Spirit and "virtue", yet St Paul already declares: "Covet the *better* gifts." On the other hand, it is almost a tradition with us to view anything extraordinary as well as enthusiastic in religion with suspicion and disapproval, always insisting that it is unimportant, unnecessary, misleading and no good at all. This may make sense in dealing with very emotional age-groups, types or even nationalities—maybe that's why Latin spirituality will stress this so forcibly? But when did it start? Anyway it does seem to me that our Catholic training has been overdoing things—breeding that awful unfeelingness, rigidity, all sorts of inhibitions, obtuseness and frustration of heart, a diet on which faith is indeed starving these days—in many a soul.

But what's the origin of this dread and mistrust of all "enthusiasm"? Did the Jesuits start it?—that would mean Spain, that would mean the Baroque age, i.e. a period of such emotional vehemence that the slightest offence called for instant and bloody vengeance, when for nuns the twofold grille in the parlour and the veiled face were essential for sheer self-protection, when the most elaborate etiquette had to be introduced, even between the most courteous and refined, to prevent perpetual brawls and ragings; when histrionics and dramatic gestures were the usual thing (e.g. Madame de Chantal's farewell to her family), etc., etc. Did they really *have* to train people to recognize first of all these volcanic emotional reactions of theirs?—to "weigh" them and to control them? Did the density, the violence of their passions call for an equally ruthless and violent stamping out, curbing, fettering, pruning? Did they

* Recent historical research inclines to a less sinister view of East German colonization. The Teutonic Order did a good deal of genuine missionary work.

† A German novelist at one time widely influential, preaching a strange pagan pantheism with marked anti-Christian undertones.

really *need* it, that training to utmost emotional temperance, so as to make the "voice of reason" audible to all? And all that went on for quite a time.

But aren't we just preserving this attitude—and others as well—like a pattern, with never a question as to whether the psychological situation hasn't definitely changed, and whether people these days aren't ailing—and dying—from emotional consumption, atrophy, paralysis, anaemia and starvation?

*

How on earth can I make a lush and lusty type like that NN. girl understand that, morals apart, there's nothing so likely to wreck that budding friendship as love-making? Just because it's such a simple, handy way of feigning an intimacy, a closeness achieved, whereas in fact things are only sprouting and no one can tell as yet how they will shape out—only that it will take a lot of patience, effort and self-control before they'll mature. But love-making offers certain quick and ready-made patterns, like *clichés* in writing or in art, tokens with a certain current value, accepted as valid expressions of love—and no one bothers much whether the cheque is covered or not. Probably things are not so very different with lots of married couples either—except that here, as in every sacrament, forms really do bring about an increase of what they suggest—the increase of mutual love. But —she'd be sure to retort—they'd do the same for us? Would it be cruel, would it be grudging to reply: The kind of love which is roused and nurtured that way neither exists nor is intended between you—nor may it indeed be. These tokens can only aggravate desire as desire, to fill the emptiness and unreality of your relationship which you yourselves feel and fear. Stop, and see if anything else is left over to fill the curve of your attraction. A very plain comparison: in times of plenty any fool can cook if he or she follows the recipe exactly. The test of a talent for cooking comes when one has to "make something out of nothing", something presentable and really good.

*

In some points men really do have better natures. Supposing, for instance, three men, all friends of a certain woman, were to meet somewhere quite by chance. Other impressions apart, they'd probably consider this mutual relationship a happy augury for their meeting, a gain for each of them. How is it when three females meet and discover that they each know the same man? O Lord! Those searching glances, sword-keen, *almost* imperceptible, the furtive calculation by each of the others' probable degree of intimacy—the cautious veiling of the "true position" (or its wary flaunting in the others' faces). . . . Oh dear, oh dear, oh dear! Too bad that the second part of Eve's sentence is usually as good as ignored—amazing really—the very point applicable to *all* women, not just to mothers. The words about the pangs and throes of childbirth are always remembered, and stressed, but what about woman's desire for man and his rule over her? This applies just as much to girls and to spinsters, and they, too, must somehow cope with it!

*

BERGENGRUEN on writing poetry: "Like talking in a foreign language which one only half-knows. You do not say what you really want and ought to say, but only what you are just capable of expressing. The real things never get said at all and linger on in the poet's consciousness to the end of his life, in an ever-present sense of insufficiency. Happy indeed the man whose sensibilities and thoughts are so limited that he can cover them all with the modest stock of words at his disposal!" Exactly the same thing applies to love. But here it's a very comforting thought, for the perpetual "sense of insufficiency" experienced so often in marriage is really just proof of a *greater* love, not of a failing and *lessening* of affection, as one is only too often prone to fear.

How wonderful it would be if one could apply this to prayer— but, oh dear, here even the most "modest stock of words" still makes up far too big a garment for the poor, thin body it has to clothe.

*

THE Book Providence*: Rasputin, Rosicrucians, still Ritschl, C. S. Lewis's *Allegory of Love*, Dame Julian of Norwich, that

* *Büchervorsehung.*

wild Greek novel, Peukert's Jakob Boehme: the same theme in a hundred variations—mysticism and the Church, "cosmic" religion, the body and sin.

Reading Rasputin, the impression haunts me that the Russian sects aren't sects at all—splinters of the Church, still part of Christendom—but rather relics of quite alien, aboriginal religions, pure heathendom surviving mutely, as it were, in mere practices, the primary beliefs long forgotten and their practice just flimsily cloaked with Christian names and labels. Who could tell, for instance, whether the orgies of the Khlysty, to whom Rasputin belonged, were not really archaic fertility rites and cults? Or whether the crazy incarnation legends linked with these ever meant the Persons of the Trinity at all, and not rather forgotten gods of Nature? Rasputin's women disciples may really have seen him as a deity incarnate, and so have regarded their physical surrender to him as working salvation—exactly the same phenomenon as the temple prostitution of Antiquity. But all those grotesque Christian interpretations, such as "redemption through sin", don't ring true—very belated, far-fetched makeshifts, artificially contrived for the sole purpose of disguising things somehow as Christian. But what shows up with staggering clarity is the mana-power, the numen of pure cosmic force that even in our day dwells in a stark and brazen exhibition of primeval passion, personified thus in an individual: Dionysian power. And this moment of domination, sweeping, possessive, irresistible must have appeared to his victims as evidence of something superhuman, divine and, therefore, good.

*

DAME Julian: God is as worthy of our adoration for what he permits as for what he creates: a breath-taking challenge, so daring it makes you feel quite dizzy! Just try it! To adore God simply for what he *permits!!* Oh, this unbelievably consoling book which, like no other I know, proclaims the absolute sovereignty of God's victory over sin!

Of course in certain dark moments of temptation it *could* be dangerous too, simply because it seems to make so light of sin. Our moral world is reeling—seasick—between the concept of collective guilt, which makes each individual sin as evitable as it is trivial, and that ineradicable Gnostic arrogance which (still!) takes the view that the "elect", the illuminate, the initiated and whatever else they call themselves are incapable of sinning and so can afford to let "nature" have full play. . . .

*

I'VE just finished reading Shakespeare's sonnets, that is, I've read and *understood* them for the first time. One passionate, desolate lament—immeasurable and inconsolable—for the waning, wasting and passing of beauty. At the same time there's something disturbingly un-Christian here—the utterly heathen, desperate keening of the dirges, the grisly dances of death, *danses macabres*, in which death is nothing but the *end*, finality— destruction, not transition. Death as the last word for beauty and life—as though the Incarnation, Easter and the promise of the Resurrection had never been.

*

How mistaken, how far short of the truth it is, that smug bourgeois attitude to friendship for married people! As though there were only two alternatives: either (*a*) a share of the love already bound up, concentrated within the marriage is drawn off, to the benefit of the newcomer, leaving the substance of the marriage drained, diminished, impoverished; or (*b*) a surplus of love yet unclaimed, even unwanted in married life, still "on tap", waiting for the appropriate object to present itself, is then lavished upon this new object, i.e. friendship as an outlet for love left over in wives somehow dissatisfied, childless perhaps, neglected, misunderstood or otherwise unfulfilled.

The third—and real—possibility: here the "new" affection is really new—pure response kindled by the other being, called into existence by its own object, hitherto non-existent. It is as much one with its object as reflection with image, as echo with sound. And yet this sympathy is really a "fruit" of marriage truly lived: quickened by this new stimulus, the wife (or husband) grows and matures, an enriched personality within the marriage, as enduring and virile as ever it was.

*

Hypocrisy is still far preferable to cynicism, so N. said, laying down the law the other day—and he ought to know. But the worst mixture is surely cynicism as hypocrisy. All the same, flippancy and sophistication are not necessarily cynical, any more than every form of camouflage is hypocrisy, except when used to conceal errors or to simulate virtues. The relation between "personal" truth and falsehood is far more complex. It's surely no lie to hide a great love or a religious experience from other people who have nothing to do with it. And anyway how often it is possible to disclose things at all only in a veiled form! And, vice versa, aren't those wild, strip-tease "confessions" to strangers, etc., as often as not only a last desperate resort to camouflage? And what about poetry? Does the poet expose his innermost self, or does he conceal it in words which on the one hand may express all manner of other things within his secret—and, again, can be so "exclusive" while leaving the secret untold, so full of meaning that the reader could well mistake the cup for the contents—indeed this is even sometimes deliberately intended. . . . And then in letters, diaries, and in spiritual direction—probably even more so in music and in painting. . . .

*

C. S. Lewis's (early?) book: *The Allegory of Love. A Study in Courtly Love.** With a quite stupendous wealth of knowledge of late medieval and early Renaissance texts on the subject he sums up the whole in the rather striking formula: the Romance of Adultery—with which he confronts an interpretation of Spenser's *Faerie Queen* as the magnificent rehabilitation and "Romance" of chaste, i.e. marital love.

There is a lot to be said about that—but what I must note are two points on which I differ. First: does this very shrewd, very ingenious interpretation really cover the whole problem and phenomenon of Courtly Love? I don't think so. Of course the historical, sociological, psychological strains he shows up did exist and were blended together in this very multi-form institution. Yet it would seem to me that another factor pervaded too, a true inspiration, irradiating from above: the recognition of the "numinous" element in Woman, apart from all her utilitarian

* Published in 1938.

qualities. Isn't this really the whole point of the "far away Lady", even if another man's wife: that she is (or ought to be) inaccessible, unattainable, of no *use* whatever to her lover, either materially, as wedded wife (in the full weight of that dignity in the clan society of old), or on the level of ordinary gallantry? She is neither *Hausfrau* nor mistress, neither the foundation of his life, nor his companion, neither mother nor home for him. She is no more than a vision—he does not *get* anything from her, or out of her, beyond her mere existence—and in this alone is she the focus of his life.

He may only behold her and sing her—like Dante and Beatrice. This calls for Beatrice, of course, as well as for Dante, and that Beatrices are even rarer these days than Dantes is surely a sorry judgment on both sexes. I don't personally believe the link between devotion to our Lady and this courtly homage was as close as people like to make out here (rather, as Lewis believes, too, the other way round), but it seems clear enough to me that such *Frauendienst* could never have existed without Mary. For it is not merely the apotheosis of mortal woman, but the radiance of Eternal Womanhood—from heaven above, not its culmination "from below".

I suddenly glimpsed something else, too, from this book—rather contrary, I'm afraid, to the author's intention: that marriage in itself is *not* one of the primary, ultimate, supreme mysteries, but only a derivation from them: love belongs to their number, and so does fruitfulness—of the body, as of the mind—and, in as much as marriage *shares* in both of them, it partakes of their character. But, as an institution, it is and will always remain (even in its most ideal realization) only a secondary device, makeshift almost, to preserve and safeguard those "central mysteries" in this wicked world of ours—shielding at the same time a number of other concerns which, though they have no part in these, do belong to marriage itself. Marriage embraces so much, the spheres and planes it crosses are many and various: a hybrid phenomenon, it cannot be proclaimed as an absolute and set among the stars. Our kind of marriage instruction attempts to do both. Such efforts are never quite convincing, even rather ridiculous sometimes—like all forced education.

It's so very important to discriminate between primary and secondary ideals. Some other secondary ideals have very similar implications: the hero, for instance, in war; or work, as such—even monastic life. All these have dignity and grandeur and fascination, a certain translucent quality—a sort of halo—and offer wonderful possibilities. But they all belong to a *fallen* world, and would be inconceivable in Paradise.

But it's awfully difficult to say such things properly—as a Catholic: not confusing people, not hurting, destroying or corroding—keeping kernel and husk in true proportion.

*

St Luke: the storm on the Lake. Could this be taken to mean that our Lord also guides us safely through "Neptune storms",* that he can subdue these as well, at any time, with a single word? "Let us cross to the other side of the lake": does this already imply the promise of our arrival? Here, again, is the same high-mettled, even impetuous Jesus Birgitta once pointed out to me in a talk about St Francis—you can just see him jumping up, angry at being roused from the wonderful deep sleep of exhaustion, and scolding wind and water, as though they were a pair of unruly dogs. And then the devils of Gerasa—surely the possessed man is the living image of a certain kind of lunatic and neurotic: "naked"—stripping himself without restraint in front of everyone; "among the tombs", i.e. living in the past, among the dead, bound hand and foot again and again, yet always bursting his bonds anew (only possible in the fearful spasms and ravings of a fit); driven out into the wilderness, i.e. self-isolation; cutting himself with stones, i.e. tormenting himself, in masochist tortures, or with self-reproach, or in demoniac mortification. None but the Lord can overcome such demons—but he *can*. N.B. He doesn't allow the man to go with him afterwards, sharing his extraordinary vocation, but sends him home, i.e. back to the normal round of daily life, "clothed and in his right mind".

*

That wild Irish novel [*Blackcock's Feather*, Maurice Walsh], a wonderful Elizabethan cloak and dagger story, has started me

---

* Emotional tempests arising out of the unconscious.

spinning again, those same old threads: the link between begetting and killing, i.e. that sex and death must both be phenomena of fallen Creation. Even as a child, reading the sagas, Red Indian books and so on, it struck me that primitive man never really *minded* killing—except in certain circumstances—cowardly, cunning, wanton or cruel killing, yes. In all these stories it is not only the scoundrels who kill—they *murder*—but the heroes as well, the nobles. Just like my Irish-Scotch hero and his generous English foe. They go round protecting the defenceless, granting their enemies pardon wherever they can, they're gentle and good, high-minded and high-hearted, positive paragons of virtue. But they don't turn a hair at killing: in combat— and not only in self-defence either, in attacking too, in avenging a murdered friend—not half-heartedly, against their will, as it were, no, in cold bood, with calm deliberation, they glory in it. If you think of this and countless other pointers, it would seem as though—put cautiously!—at least on a certain level of human consciousness (and this lasted for quite a while), killing, though terrible in itself, was or is nevertheless something sublimely terrible, a *tremendum*, not just something evilly terrible, terrifying. Something granted and permitted to man, within his range, but not for every man, not always and not to be used indiscriminately—a momentous privilege, bound by the severest limits and sanctions—just like procreation. And every arbitrary abuse of either of these functions, outside the order of things, "out of bounds"—man *presuming* on either in unbridled passion—is blasphemy. Why? Because both are really divine prerogatives: to start life and to take life? Something which somehow extends beyond our human compass, power only lent, bestowed throughout the entire epoch of our fallen state only to those who in some way represent the Godhead: king, father, judge—delegated to them to be executed in a sacred act? N.B. Both functions are an exclusively male privilege. From this starting-point it actually seems logical and not merely barbarous that the father should have the right to determine life or death of the new-born, indeed of the whole family.

Maybe this in some way explains the fact that as soon as killing "gets out of hand"—turns into excess, as in war—becomes "promiscuous", the same thing happens with sex: rape and debauchery belong essentially to war. Another odd parallel: the very men who haven't the courage to beget children, to accept fatherhood, are likely to be pacifists on principle, and opponents of the death penalty.

What was it that old Afghan, Mahbud Ali, said to Kim: "When I was fifteen I had shot my man and begot my man!" Obviously very different and utterly ambivalent lines of thought are involved here: the SS, for instance—the same autonomy, promiscuity and anonymity in both these things. And somewhere or other Joseph Wittig comments venomously that it's really no wonder the lower classes don't take priests seriously as *men*, since they are forbidden both to beget and to kill—robbed of his manhood, it is only fitting that the priest is also forbidden to grow a beard! But I would put it the other way round: as representative of God and Christ glorified, consecrated to him, he is absolved from these characteristics of fallen humanity, dispensed, raised above them—neither for ascetic reasons, nor on human grounds, but simply because these are *the* symbols of the "Adamite" order. But an *order* it is, and strict at that, not disorder, and the acts of killing and of procreation are ordained within it, strict, immutable, inviolable—and whoever offends against this discipline is guilty indeed.

*

HIGH time I took the trouble really to plough through "the doctrine of sin"—no easy task, I'm quite sure. Didn't P.B. tell me that St Thomas hasn't devoted a special chapter to sin in the *Summa*? That really makes one think. It's far from easy to know what to think oneself about all this. Dame Julian has taught me to see things from a new angle, but—in contrast to this—remember Newman with those frighteningly sinister views of his. . . . These very definitely cannot simply be brushed aside as remnants of Calvinism, as is the fashion these days. There they are, both of them: apparently utter contradictions, and yet they must both "rhyme" somehow. And here on earth at that.

*

THE night before last I was reading the temptation of our Lord in St Luke—much more suggestive, as so much is left open. Here we have Jesus, "full of the Holy Ghost", not just led into the wilderness, but "led by the Spirit up and down the wilderness",* i.e. driven about, urged on, for forty long days, "tempted by the devil". This sounds far more like a condition of mind than simply an event. It would seem, then, that you can be "full of the Holy Ghost" *and* tempted by the devil at one and the same time—a significant point, especially in considering certain saints and *charismata*, and in interpreting those words: "Swift as the change from good to evil. . . ."

"During these days he ate nothing, and when they were over he was hungry." Again this sounds much less like a deliberate fast than as though he had simply been driven around, forgetting every normal impulse in the storm of his spirit and the storm of the temptation—as though he suddenly woke up to the realization of the situation, the place, his own state—dead, yes, really *dead*-tired, drained to the depths of his very being—like Elias—and there was no way out. For there was simply nothing in that wilderness for him to eat, i.e. to restore his strength and revive him, nothing but the frenzied urge of naked self-preservation, at any price. Was Jesus, then, really famished—like the starving victims of the concentration camps of our own day, even then "a worm and no man"? And at this very moment came the devil: ". . . You've only got to . . ." Was he tempting him to magic, Satan, the Arch-Magician? Surely Christ's very answer shows clearly enough that *this* way is barred to us? "Man cannot live by bread alone." *The* answer in every situation summed up by our desperate: "I can't live without . . ."

And then the second temptation: "The devil led him *up*." Quite clear—people "mounting" are tempted more than those remaining below. A whole new range of temptations, hitherto ignored, opens up here—oh yes, the very fact of being led upwards is already part of the temptation itself. . . .

All the kingdoms of the world—certainly not only in the geographical-political sense, but including all "realms of life", everything which makes up the *world*, everything which can be mastered, used, enjoyed—"the fullness of existence": all the things which really *can* be achieved, amassed by deliberate negation, breaking, ignoring of limits, barriers, ordinances—

---

* New English Bible rendering, roughly corresponding with the German "*in der Wüste umgetrieben*".

even the boundaries traced by God, the Lord, in his world, for mankind, the beings he created.

And finally the temptation of the drop from the pinnacle: does falling, perhaps, feel like soaring?—The lure of danger, of risk? The arrogant hope that *even then* God would still be "obliged" to send his angels?—But what can Jesus have meant by that curious retort of his?

*

I JUST can't help it, I see it more and more clearly: the real explosion-point, the cause of this landslide in our marriage morals and with these what is left of our sex morals too, what has sent it all tumbling down, so that nothing makes sense any more, is simply the refusal to acknowledge that old maxim, so sneered at nowadays: issue is the proper outcome of physical union. Of course this principle was widely distorted in the past— misused, misworded, misunderstood and misinterpreted. They tampered with its very substance, turning it into sheer material- ism, everything impersonal, really awful.

All the same it's still the peg on which everything really hangs, and if we don't succeed in rediscovering its basic truth, winning our way back to it with new insight, new answers, new accents, then there will be no stopping the break-up. Here is a mystery, but it has been buried deep under a mound of platitudes, first affirmative, then negative.

It is indeed curious that people can present solid truth with such idiotic and wretched arguments that others—out of sheer (justified) contradiction, prefer to overturn both arguments and subject rather than accept such rubbish.

*

EMOTION and religion: In last Sunday's collect we not only prayed for love, but also—quite plainly—for its reflection in what we *feel*: *amoris affectum.*

*

PEONIES just flushed with pink, so luminous that it's barely sub- stantial—more like white glowing from within. Wouldn't that be a better colour-symbol for spiritual love than the white arum lily? There's something so lacquered, so papery, unpleasantly scented-soapy about lilies, especially as lifeless rods in the hands of plaster Josephs and Aloysiuses. That's what I must tell Frau Dr X.—that single people living in the world could just as well be peonies instead of fake lilies—which means that they're just as much entitled to friendship with men as other people—friendship meaning *friendship*, not a discreet word for an affair. Friendship is a form of Eros in its own right, and not an outlet for stifled or mutilated sex. Anyway, if it is genuine friendship—which, of course, *is* a form of love!—it develops its own language, and has no need whatever to borrow from flirtation, etc. Obviously this calls for ingenuity, delicacy, subtle sensitiveness, gentleness—but *there can be no compromise.* Friendship may float upon Eros (= the polar tension between male and female!), but it must be kept free, constantly disentangled from sex, which keeps thrusting its way in like a rank weed. Friendship is something quite different from "perfect unity": I wouldn't even say it renounces it, rather it does not aim at it at all. True friendship rather creates its own kind of unity on the mental-spiritual plane, sufficient in itself.

Friendship is *not* "free love" (as **XX.** asserts with her very improbable theory about the Greek *parthenos,* which she sees as a sort of antique *garçonne*), but it has its own particular trend and law: to be the "other" path, to bear witness to the real existence of mind and soul and their relation in a pan-sexual world. *This* sort of friendship could even stand for a sort of modern counterpart to the "courtly love" of chivalry—just as "improbable", just as preposterous in the eyes of the smug—and, for that reason, just as important, if only to keep the air fresh.

Note, too, that physical union is reserved for marriage, neither as the most precious, nor as the basest, element of love—but for an entirely matter of fact reason: because marriage is *essentially* wedded to fruitfulness, not just by accident, procreation being a sacred, momentous, highly responsible charge, which calls for a mode of life fully adapted to it—which is exactly what marriage is intended to be. Perhaps one could say: marriage is the sanctuary of those lovers who may—and must—undertake the great venture together of bearing fruit, each to each. Which brings us back to the old maxim of the Church: children are the "primary good" of marriage.

One often wonders—with all the pseudo-marriages we have nowadays—whether the Church ought not to make far more extensive use of her powers to bind and to loose: whether every couple married in church is truly "married", and whether all those who ask for the wedding ceremony ought to be allowed to have it. To my mind this is far more important than the opposition one so often hears about to indiscriminate infant baptism.

*

THAT critical book of Hilda Graef's on Theresa Neumann* contains a useful lesson for me, even if as "second intention"; the stress laid yet again on the ambiguity and danger inherent in "signs and wonders". Most essential to discriminate between the occult and the pneumatic, the para-psychic and the charismatic!—and who is capable of this?

*

I KEEP bumping up against this theme all the time in Ritschl's absorbing history of Pietism.† It's really exciting to trace back the spiritual genealogy of those intriguing "Gnostic" speculations, particularly their abstruse sex metaphysics, which extend from Boehme and Weigel via Hochmann von Hohenau and Gottfried Arnold down to the Swabian Pietism of Hahn. Androgynous Adam, Sophia myths and so on—all theology very definitely hostile to marriage, viewing all human procreation as "Adamite", earthly and brutish, no longer proper for Christians. Hochmann, for instance, divides marriage into five categories: first the wholly animal kind "which despite the public ceremony is nothing but authorized fornication"; then the kind that is "honourable, but heathen and impure since the persons concerned

---

*_The Case of Theresa Neumann_, Cork, 1951.

† "Pietists" is used throughout this book in a rather sweeping manner, covering a variety of Protestant (more or less) non-conformist movements and groups in Germany during the eighteenth and early nineteenth centuries. Their common feature is reformatory opposition to a petrified school-theology and worldliness among the faithful. They all stressed fervent "testifying" Christian behaviour, enthusiasm in prayer and charity, an actual and emotional experience of conversion and grace, sometimes a strictly puritan way of life. In many points they strongly resemble the English Evangelicals, Methodists and similar groups. In some parts of Germany the influence of Jakob Boehme (see note p. 69) predominated, colouring the "evangelical" strain largely with Gnostic and theosophical speculations and as often as not provoking violent opposition from the ecclesiastical authorities.

are themselves not yet united to God through Christ"; the third is marriage "between sanctified persons"; then come the elect whose fourth kind of union is simply what Catholics call a "Joseph's marriage"; the fifth state is that of voluntary virginity "so that the soul knows only Jesus as husband and the souls which have pledged and sacrificed themselves to Christ may attain the greatest glory in Christ's kingdom".

This last version *sounds* very Catholic, but it's really just the opposite, for here marriage is really *despised*, sex reduced to a shameful fact and virginity exalted merely as its negation. This is real loathing of the body. And it shows up in the results—that awful erotic *Schwarmgeisterei*, deteriorating often enough to wild promiscuity with some very nasty theories. But the really odd thing about it is that such preposterous doctrines found such a ready echo among the lower classes. For these simple people who could have known nothing about ancient heresies, Cabbala and all the rest of it, there can only have been one link: their own factual and unpleasant experience of sex which induced them, indeed forced them, to accept so enthusiastically doctrines which seemed, at long last, to offer an explanation of their own fate.

But something else is revealed here too, just as spontaneously and perhaps even more strikingly: the profound longing for something which would justify, transfigure and sanctify sex by blending it with religious ideas, or at least give it some sort of religious stamp. As I see it, these wild extravagances, often so nauseating—all that fantastic brooding on sinless sex (conceded only to the elect) simply served to fill the gap which occurred when marriage lost its sacramental character, became profane. For either marriage is a really sacred thing, or it surrenders to other powers.

Very curious how both the taboo attached to sex, as well as its transparent and symbolic power are glimpsed here.

*

"To glow is better than to know"—said Bernard of Clairvaux, and then: "Learn from my experience, you will find more in the woods than in books. Trees and rocks will teach you what you will never hear from the masters."

*

48

I'M reading Leisegang: *Die Gnosis.* Amazing really that the young Church managed to survive at all against *such* competition—one thinks of the infant Heracles strangling serpents right and left from his cradle. You can see the reason for all that radical separation from the heretics (St John even declined to set foot in the same baths with them!) and the refusal to share in any form of common life. No question here of broad-minded discussions and irenic attempts to reach an understanding.

How tempting, how intriguing it is, the lure of knowledge instead of belief, to master the mysteries with the mind—i.e. gnosis. After that you can only say the Credo from the depths of your heart: "O REAL, real Father—real Son—conceived by the real Holy Ghost!" And then the blessed refreshment of the Rosary—that sweet and lovely simplicity, the sweet humility of Godhead, the purity of the real, the true, after that huge, pompous peacock's tail whirling of religious fantasy.

*

I WOKE up out of a dream the other morning with the vivid sense of just having discussed "the insignificance of sin" with someone—would it be wrong to fear sin so much as to avoid all occasions, all dangerous situations on principle and consistently, instead of keeping "unspotted *in the world*"? Of course I know quite well that these are two-edged thoughts, and ambivalent, but all the same one must try to follow them to the end. . . . Just now I keep harping on Dame Julian. Surely you can't go pestering God (if I can use such a word!) with endless repetitions of sins long since forgiven—and *so* uninteresting anyway—what's more, right after Holy Communion too, as pious people are so fond of recommending—what lovers, sunk in an embrace, would *dream* of such a thing? Of course contrition is never more vivid, never more scathing than at such a moment, but only the kind of contrition which does not brood first and foremost on one's *own* sins, but remembers *his* love—which is something very different.

*

THE Gospel for Ember Friday: Christ and the sinful woman (Luke 7). The [German] Weizsäcker translation throws a new light for me on Verse 47: "And so I tell thee that many sins *are*

49

forgiven her,"—not shall be!—"for she *has shown* great love. But he who has less forgiven him also loves less."

The Vulgate has *"remittuntur"*, too, not the future; many sins *are* forgiven her, not later on, *now*.

Maybe this means: "You [Simon the Pharisee] see how much love she shows me here and now, washing my feet, tears, kisses, ointment—and so her many sins are already forgiven her, she is reclaimed already, close to God—how could she otherwise love so much?" (N.B. This confirms P.B.'s view that "perfect contrition" is not an act of man which "compels" the grace of forgiveness—as we are so often told!—but rather that genuine contrition out of charity is already an effect of sanctifying grace within us!) "You are not doing what she did, you just don't love enough—much has not been forgiven you, or you would love more!"

*

Persona . . . est ultima solitudo. Not modern either: Duns Scotus.

*

ALL Saints' Day: What blessed beauty in the contrast in the Office between the glory of the Apocalypse and the earthly simplicity of the eight Beatitudes—the humble *back* of the carpet in this our world.

*

MY old, old Inglesant problem, as we used to call it, after the long-forgotten Shorthouse novel, Elsa and I, back in Stockau, discussing it endlessly in the long twilight evenings while waiting for the lamp. Rejection of the world or confident acceptance of the world in faith? This complex and controversial problem really boils down to the simple adage: " You can't have your cake and eat it ", and our attempts to dodge this, somehow or other, to outwit it. You just cannot have the much-vaunted "fullness of life" and purity of life at one and the same time. You need the world to be a full human being, to realize yourself as a person—*and* you must flee from the world to remain "pure". Some have tried, all their lives long, to sacrifice the first to the second. And now, well past middle life, recognition threatens that this decision may have been a mistake. At least the question intrudes: ". . .What if those wolves were not sent from God at all to scare you off your way, but by the Devil ? ? ?" *If* one had attained it, strictly, uncompromisingly, filling one's soul to overflowing with God instead of with the world, that, too, would have been a way to the heights, and to the depths. . . . But all the rest is merely a shoddy, poor and vapid "in-between".

*

NOTHING saddens me more at the moment than the pitiable mediocrity and flatness of Catholic Christendom—I can hardly find one redeeming feature any more. But maybe this is a temptation, and probably the very best antidote would be to get out for a while and knock about in the real world—if I could. I'd soon realize the gratifying difference again!

*

RITSCHL has once more confirmed my "nose" for Church history: Pietism stems largely from the undercurrents of basic Catholic teachings on grace, sanctification, perfection, asceticism, mystical union with God, etc., in a Protestant world which had long since discarded these things. There is, of course, that other line as well, very strange, Gnostic-Cabbalistic, with its outlet in those extravagant cosmogonic and sex-metaphysical speculations (though I cannot prove this, I suspect that the anthroposophists have gleaned much of their philosophy from here)—this is the genuine, patently heretical, even non-Christian layer. And then the third line—far the most attractive for me—which runs from Boehme to Paracelsus, but does not lead from here to Gnosticism and Cabbala, but rather to Scotus Erigena, and then Maximus Confessor and Origen—a chain of tradition *within* the Church, little known, less favoured, but at least tolerated. The bits I know about Scotus E. (from Gilson) are quite intoxicating—so illuminating, full of new impulses. It seems to me he might, perhaps, offer a start for that mystical approach to Creation we need so badly.

*

X. is, of course, quite right in saying that only the orthodox Christian can really profit from Gnosticism. Far from paradoxical—to my mind this goes for every kind of heresy (Dr N. says you can only go in for homeopathy if you have really mastered "orthodox" medicine)—I at least have profited enormously all my life from contact with heresy of all kinds. Not for the apologetic wrangling involved, but simply because even in my most stubbornly correct days the specific fragment of truth at stake shone out for me in its glaring isolation far more clearly than it would have done comfortably embedded in the whole. And so, in a sense, I became the docile pupil of many heresies— and they formed my Catholic mind more decisively than all my "toe the line" training. C. J. has produced another *bon mot* in this connection, by the way. I was quoting Möhler's apt description of the Church as "the unconscious embodiment of all heresies prior to the schism"—wonderful!—and then said that for that very reason a variety of religious opinions, ideas and experience *within* the Church is so much more sound and right than strict conformity to a single pattern. Whereupon C.J. remarked dryly: "Some people would prefer lots of arms and legs to a body—and then they are surprised when the result is just a centipede!"

*

ARMENIAN Gnostic (why, I wonder?) legends about Adam. The idea of the shining body or "garment of light" is so clear that I'm surprised that I ever got along without it. For, of course, Adam and Eve must have been covered somehow—or they wouldn't have dis-covered their nakedness—and since this "something" could not have been material, what then? How illuminating, too, that the first glory of sanctifying Grace, this participation in the Glory of God, was "visible" to the eye, which beheld things spiritual and physical in one and at once.

Strange that motif—and certainly very ancient—of the first sunset, which so terrified A. and E. that Satan wangles their bondage in return for his promise to let the sun rise again. And how lovely that other story is of the angel comforting the exiled pair and reconciling them with the hostile earth by showing them trees, reminder and reflection of Paradise.

And that strange and terrible tale of Adam wrestling for three long hours with the temptation to taste the fruit too—Eve entreats him to eat "so that we shall not be parted", but Adam yields because he sees the beauty of her body and is afraid he will find nothing like her again: "For without this woman I cannot live."

That passage is very significant, too, where Abel was bound to a vine to await his murder, and that wonderfully beautiful idea that, just as Golgotha is above the tomb of Adam, so the Cave of the Nativity is above the grave of Eve.

I can't imagine what's Gnostic about these stories, unless this classification applies to their origin, not to their content. Lovely, too, how the Sun and the Moon stand as two "Ethiopian" men, before the Throne of Glory—"dark against the radiance of the Light of Lights".

No mention here of an androgynous Adam, by the way, but it is said that procreation and birth came *after* the Fall, and then at the angels' bidding, i.e. on divine charge.

*

FINISHED Bischoff's little book *Im Reich der Gnosis*. What I must note besides his main thesis (he traces various lines back to the Babylonian astral myths) is the introduction, though slight, to Philo: his Logos concept, the idea of the demiurge, hypostasis of "Wisdom" (earlier). Significant the comment that the Aramaic post-exilic version of Genesis did not begin: "In the beginning . . ." but rather: "In Wisdom God created heaven and earth."

And all the time my own fundamental question grows clearer, ridiculously childish and simple though it is: What is really *true* in all these doctrines and opinions? How can one judge, for instance, what in these curious Trinitarian cosmogonic concepts is simply "mythology"—or pure myth even—and what is their real core of truth? For in the end the Church did take over quite a lot of first principles, though not without changing them. Of course there's the answer: "In so far as they do not contradict Revealed Truth." *Concedo.* But who knows for sure (and, if so, why?) on what items we have definite pronouncements? In the revelation to Abraham, for example, there is no mention whatever, so far as I know, of cosmogonic things—so he probably hung on quite happily to his "bundle" of Sumerian-Chaldean astral myths (provided these did not involve the worship of idols), handing them down to his sons and his clan. And why not? Maybe he recognized in the God who spoke to him the "First Father", beyond all heavens and all worlds? And Jacob, too, recognizing the angels upon the ladder, must already have been familiar with their image, learnt or inherited from somewhere—and why not from the Sumerian tradition of spirits inhabiting heaven and the planets?

*

VERY significant that Talmudic rule that a rabbi may only discuss secret, i.e. doubtful doctrines "in whispers" with older, mature men, that is, with tried and trusted disciples, and then only pass them on to one or two, for meditation—no question of broadcasting them at random for illiterates.

*

BIBLE reading for today: Luke 6—the "sound tree" which yields sound fruit and vice versa. It sounds so obvious, clear as daylight, as though there were no more to be said. But it's really very tricky. For what is "fruit" actually in a human being, an ordinary human being who produces nothing concrete as his "work", but simply himself? For it's notoriously *we* who have the habit of hanging figs on thistles, and grapes on thorns! A good deal of our "Christian training" means teaching us just this knack. For instance, if a miser schools himself to generosity, or a bad-tempered man to gentleness: is it his *nature* producing its own genuine issue? Certainly not. These are definitely "fruits of grace", i.e. this acquired behaviour—*not* wild growth! —is in itself the "fruit" which proves that the tree has been grafted. And, further, it supposes that the layman, the average spectator, ought to be capable of discerning the difference in taste between such real "fruits", even if grafted, and mere "decorations", just stuck on, hung on (from convention, pious and impious hypocrisy). For we are told to *judge* the tree according to his fruit. This implies things only visible to the eye of

God, but discernible and appraisable by ourselves. But that "palate" which recognizes every fruit in its own quality—would it not be the very "*sapientia*", to which everything tastes as it is? For how else am I to guess what is "fruit" in another person, true product of his innermost self, or merely stuck on, stamped on, counterfeit?

*

"*Vitae repellens taedium*"—I was astonished to find this the other day. How strangely topical. Perhaps this Breviary hymn was the origin of our phrase?

*

I'VE just finished Hugo Rahner's *Maria Ecclesia* book. What amazes me really is that—for the first time in my life—it has really dawned on me that the Church is feminine. And for years I've been talking, writing and reading about the *Mater Ecclesia*, the Bride of Christ, and so on! I simply never *realized* it before. For despite all these traditional names, simply taken for granted, the Church for me was always simply the hidden Lord—Christ living on—for what else is this "Body" supposed to be?

But Rahner's *Ecclesia* is not really this Body—but in some way a super-being which perpetually "gives birth" to this Body—the heavenly archetype of Mary, the Great Woman. This Woman is, however, something very different from the *Magna Mater* of depth psychology—her counterpart, so to speak, her heavenly counter-image, her counter-reality. Here the "Eternal Woman" ceases to be a sentimental, over life-size projection of terrestrial woman-worship. At the same time this heavenly image is no abstract construction, but interprets feature for feature, the living personality of Mary.

The exciting thing, for me, is the extent and intensity with which this early theology already discerned, beheld and stated the essence, the office and the image of our Lady. And yet it never occurred to anyone to cultivate an individual and private devotion to her, invoking her, addressing her, etc. It would, therefore, seem that in this latter sense devotion to the Blessed Virgin really is a late phenomenon, unknown to the early Church

—as all anti-mariologists stoutly contend. But only if this brand of devotion—subjective, individual, egocentric—is supposed to be "the real thing": *this* is certainly a late development, and the result and expression of a completely different mentality. But is this "practical" appeal to our Lady in private cares and troubles really more devout—even better? That other kind of veneration, static, content simply with beholding its great object in awe and wonder, recognizing and acknowledging without any thought of drawing her into individual petty human needs. . . . According to this book *this* has existed from earliest days, and very much more noble, more fitting, it seems to me.

❧ 1951—1952 ❧

FRAGMENTS of Jewish prayers from *The Wall*, John Hersey's book about the Warsaw ghetto and its end:

"I know hundreds of benedictions for all sorts of occasions—for the sniffing of fragrant barks, for hearing thunder, for seeing a rainbow, for listening to a wise man lecturing on the Law, for seeing kings and their courts, for encountering strangely-formed men, giants, dwarfs, and crooked persons—outlandish things. . . ."

On the Day of Atonement: "And Thou shalt cast all their iniquities into the depths of the sea. O mayst Thou cast all the sins of Thy people, of the House of Israel, into a place where they shall no longer be remembered, neither sought after nor regarded any more. Thou shalt keep faith with Jacob and show Thy divine mercy unto Abraham, as Thou hast sworn to our fathers of old."

"Blessed art Thou, O Lord our God, King of the universe, who hast made the creation" = the benediction to be said "at the sight of lightning, or when one has the good fortune to see falling stars, lofty mountains, great deserts, and other wonders".

At the Circumcision of a child: "This is the throne of Elias: may he be remembered for good! On this account, O living God, our Portion and our Rock, give command to deliver from destruction the dearly beloved of our flesh. . . . This little child of Israel, may he become great. Even as he has entered into the covenant, so may he enter into the Law, the nuptial canopy and into good deeds."

Prayer in danger (from the Talmud):

"Thy will in heaven above be done, and grant a joyful spirit to those who live in Thy fear, and whatsoever is good in Thy eyes, mayst Thou accomplish, O Lord!"

Striking how strongly praise and thanksgiving feature in Jewish prayer, and how our own Liturgy has retained this element and this style—just as rooted really in Jewish piety as in the Roman sense for form.

*

TALKING to NN. last night I saw how hard it is to reach a simple crude type of girl like that directly, with words, with reasoning, but how open she is to influence "through the solar plexus", as D. H. Lawrence would have said. If her young man were a Nazi or a Communist, you just couldn't do anything about it! Which showed me, quite clearly, that convictions and ideas are conveyed in three ways: the middle way by argument, verification, recognition, by reason; the two other mediums are like a pair of mirrors, one presenting a positive, the other a negative view. The first is that real, direct participation in the interior life of one's partner in love: union of souls, "fusing of the flames above each head" (Cabbala); the spark leaping from mind to mind, that generation in spirit of which physical generation is really the symbol. The third way is its caricature, following the pattern of animal coupling, far below the human plane: here the passive soul of the weaker partner is "impressed" by sheer brute force, stamped upon; her dull, impersonal, hide-bound emotions are impregnated (consciously or unconsciously) by the sexual urge for possession and domination. Things neither understood nor acknowledged just cling in her mind, are repeated mechanically, and bear fruit in due time. . . . I suspect that this is the way the so-called political opinions—or at least ideas—of many women originate (religious views, too, I'm afraid). The criterion where a conviction belongs is surely whether the thing itself is accepted and consented to freely, or simply swallowed in uncritical subservience to "his" will.

*

"To tread upon serpents and scorpions" and "nothing shall hurt you"—to whom were these words addressed? To the Seventy, not to the apostles. Are they prototypes of priests only, i.e. those chosen for special service, or are the faithful generally meant here? The Seventy were surely just messengers of Jesus, sent out to prepare the way—may we, should we, count ourselves among them?

We ought really to be much bolder, relying on such promises! Of course other things are predicted as well: persecution, imprisonment, death—the disciple is no better than his master: but all the same it shall not *harm* us. And not only on serpents and scorpions shall we tread, but "upon *all the power* of the enemy" —really one shouldn't be so afraid of the Devil, not even in his subtlest temptations from within. . . . All the same the gift "that the devils are made subject unto you" is definitely *less* precious than "that your names are enrolled in heaven". What does the latter really mean? Our names—our real *selves*— safeguarded from human wilfulness and compulsion, fixed in the abiding, the eternal, the immutable, the impregnable—and "enrolled". Is this predestination—rightly interpreted? For certainly HE does not blot out what he has once written. Surely it must take some really terrific counter-exertion on the part of man to obliterate this writing in heaven?

Dare we therefore—like Dame Julian of Norwich—hope that our salvation is well-nigh indestructible? Are our names already enrolled in heaven at our baptism, through our baptism?

*

LOOKING for a corresponding text, I chanced upon the following in Ecclus 2. 9: "Fear him? Ay, and fix your hope in him; his mercy you shall find and have great joy of it." How lovely, how consoling, and what a Scriptural paradox! For, humanly speaking, to *fear* someone is not exactly to expect the best from him. And those who fear the Lord are surely only too aware of their own unworthiness—which "logically" ought rather to make them expect punishment and trials as their due. Instead they are told to fix their hope in him and are promised mercy and joy— because of his love for us. How wonderful!

*

"I WATCHED, while Satan was cast down like a lightning-flash from heaven." Just once?—or is it still going on? That God simply fells the Devil and his powers suddenly, like a thunder-bolt, whenever he will, merely by lifting his hand? The demons in the gospel stories are cast out this way too—not by slow degrees, in a long struggle, the outcome uncertain: this, too, gives one new courage.

*

MM. WAS here today for two solid hours—it nearly killed me! Odd really, she's such a good woman, deeply religious, "a friend of God", no doubt, genuinely living in faith, in prayer and in charity, with a kind disposition and a pleasant manner into the bargain. Yet all the time we were talking two different languages—so much more strenuous than talking to people of other denominations, with most of my Protestant acquaintances. I wondered afterwards, rather sadly, what we really do *feel* in common with such "brethren in faith". For my part I find it far easier to talk to a sincere Protestant, or with Jews, even pagans (Hindus) and neo-pagans than with this kind of 120 per cent conservative Catholic—they strike one as more like a queer sort of sect. Of course we were terribly tactful, taking the utmost care not to tread on one another's toes. Yet all the time I felt as though I were talking not so much at a *stone* wall (which might have yielded an echo!), but rather at a wall of rubber. Everything just glanced off without a sound—oh, that all-indulgent, maddeningly superior, imperturbable, I-know-everything-better smile! No diffidence, no need to verify her own views! Oh no, she was as infallible as the Church herself— in every detail. Extraordinary really: dyed-in-the-wool spiritual pride, and yet in all other respects most unpretentious and, I am sure, even humble.

*

A LONG letter from Fr X. about a certain Sister U. whose cause of beatification he's apparently keen to put forward. She herself declared that for seven years she "possessed the Presence of the most blessed Divinity and Humanity of Jesus in her soul, as though in the Tabernacle, but without the Host". And he thinks this a *charisma* "as yet unknown, even among the greatest mystics in the history of the Church".

I wrote back, a seven-page letter, telling him exactly what I thought! Cocksure it may be, but, as I see it, this probably *is* a genuine testimony of a mystical experience, but disguised in misleading "spiritual" phraseology. Taken literally, it's frankly absurd, inconceivable—both abstract and materialistic: abstract, using the formula "most blessed Humanity" as an excuse for avoiding "Body", i.e. human nature complete; materialistic, since they can apparently only believe in the Real Presence of Christ if the Eucharist is present!—yet this is contradicted again by "without the Host", discarding the very token which implies his sacramental presence. And what's all this "permanent in-dwelling of Christ *bodily* in my *soul*"? How can his "Humanity" dwell in my soul? "We will come to him and make our continual abode with him"—yes, of course, but precisely *not* "as though in the Tabernacle". Anyway, what kind of human being could *endure* a permanent union like that, on the one hand detached from the sacramental, yet still bound to it by daily Communion? All very queer indeed. But the really alarming thing is that a certain spirituality—above all the kind cultivated in convents—is restricting the presence of God in his world exclusively to "the Prisoner in the Tabernacle".

*

THIS touches a personal point. Why don't I mind being excluded for months now from Mass and Holy Communion? Is this an alarming sign—or is it a grace? I don't feel sad about it, or feel it to be a trial or a privation, although religious people feel obliged to condole and console. Could it be simply a kind of anaesthesia typical of this illness of mine?—I don't miss Nature either, at least not as much as I should have thought. But, quite apart from this, just now I'm so intensely aware of myself as a member, as a cell of the Church in her daily Sacrifice and Communion that I simply cannot see what I can be lacking. For to me the Lord's Supper is far more a function of the Church as a body than of individuals—the *Church* herself is fed by the communicants at each Mass. They are her "mouth": but after all the whole body is not mouth only, and even the most distant members are sustained by this food.

A side-light: I can see now that in a period when the sense of individuality was rare and feeble, yet the feeling of Christian community very strong, the faithful could be content to have their priest receiving Communion alone at Mass—as their head and their mouth—they all participating through him.

*

8 DECEMBER: Reading those incredibly bold *Sapientia** texts, always so surprising, I suddenly saw that the Logos = Sophia is

---

* Collective designation in the Roman Missal for the Wisdom (sapiential) books of the Old Testament: Proverbs, Wisdom, Ecclesiasticus. The Epistle for 8 December is Prov. 8. 22–35

the arch-image of Mary, and *therefore* she is the feminine like-ness of Christ on earth—and this because she had to bear Jesus, the Man entirely worthy of the Logos; he could only be moulded according to his *own* character, and, since he lacked a human father, he had to receive this stamp from no other but herself. The misunderstandings start when the Virgin of Nazareth is identified as a matter of course with Sophia, who is as much "prototype" of her Son as she is the creative ideal reflected upon Mary from his Person. When we call Mary "daughter of the heavenly Father", is she not overshadowed here by Sophia, as though by the shining cloud?

*

As Catholics we carry in our pockets the most wonderful treas-ures, like Japanese flowers—those hard, dry, shrivelled little objects you give to children: you put them in water and they suddenly unroll and change into coloured ribbons, loops and blossoms. But no one ever told us to put *our* Japanese flowers into water too, so that they could blossom forth, in their real shape—waters of silence, of contemplation, perhaps even as Bergengruen tells us:

"Just a few drops only—and be they only tears,
And, lo, the rose of Jericho reflowers."

*

CHRISTMAS has come and gone. What struck me most forcibly this year was the double aspect: the Deification of man, as well as the Incarnation of God—"*ut in illius inveniamur forma, in quo tecum est nostra substantia*"—"that we may be found like unto him in whom our substance is united with thee" is what it says in the Missal. But how tame, how cautious this sounds! That we may be found like unto him, him in whom *our matter is present in thee*, immersed in thee.*

*

IF I were to accept literally what the psychoanalysts keep rub-bing in—that one's first seven years determine one's whole

* We must read this in the light of Philippians: "Though he was in the form of God"—*in forma Dei*.

fate—then I could well despair, knowing myself as clearly as I do to be the product of *all* the educational blunders described in their text-books. But there must be other formative elements too. . . .

*

AT long last a good Péguy translation, by Oswald von Nostitz. The astonishing thing about Péguy's *Mystères* is that his meditation stems straight from the Little Catechism, meditated theology, massive, downright, unsophisticated, almost blunt. Some people wouldn't even consider this sort of thing fit for meditation at all.

*

IT seems to me that the span of years between middle age and old age is just as mysterious as the interlude between childhood and that maturity which is supposed to be the core and substance of existence. This phase is beginning for me now. One's fiftieth birthday corresponds with one's twentieth. That day opened the door to a wider life: I reached out to grasp reality. But in fact it was reality which gripped me with its restrictions and constraints and rules which arrogantly claim to be the laws of life, of the universe. To be "grown-up" really meant resignation: one gave in (if ruefully), laughing a little at one's young dreams. But now the walls of reality are folding up again like stage scenery, new horizons appear, and the old dreams return silently, like stars, to their appointed places. They were right, those dreams of ours, only our youthful attempts to realize them were foolish, clumsy or rash, superficial, artificial or otherwise wrong. But what they sought to realize were visions truly beheld—not hallucinations.

*

THAT book of Eugen Rosenstock's, *Breath of the Spirit*, is fascinating, brilliant, but exasperating all the same. Those Jews!! But powerful and authoritative it is, incredibly Jewish in its fervent belief in the flesh, in the word, in the "names"—Buber and Rosenzweig, you can sense their mode of thought throughout, radiant, penetrating. Negatively Jewish, on the other hand, and really irritating, is that intellectual swagger.

*

EPIPHANY: *"Communicantes . . . diem . . . quo Unigenitus tuus, in tua tecum gloria coaeternus*, in veritate carnis nostrae *visibiliter corporalis apparuit."* In the truth of our flesh!

*

SIMONE WEIL—definitely *no.* I'm not impressed. Surely she was a Catharist in essence? It seems the French group (they still exist, and even run a paper!) did, in fact, claim her for their own. I really am trying to be fair to her, but I can't help sensing an extraordinary spiritual self-righteousness. Motives of Jewish solidarity apart, she was convinced that she just didn't *need* baptism—not "desiring" it in any sense at all, considering herself to be Christian enough without it and "dwelling in the centre of love". Père Perrin seems to have shared this view, by the way, maintaining that she had already received baptism by desire. Yet her case does strike me as fundamentally different from Werfel's, for whom it was probably a real and bitter sacrifice to have had to *forgo* baptism for the sake of his Jewish loyalties; S.W. assured her Dominican she would ask to be baptized at once should she feel the divine command—yet for all her belief in Christ and her insistence that she accepted the gospel as his word, she did not feel that it applied to her.

*

IT would seem from the four gospel accounts that John the Baptist was not sure about the identity of that "mightier one" whose way he had been sent to prepare. Was he a superhuman being, the "one yet to come" with the winnowing-fan, who had power to consume the chaff with unquenchable fire? By the "one standing in your midst", was he referring to some unknown person, really present among the throng, or did he mean it in the spiritual sense—just as Elias could have been standing there among them? Even St Matthew implies no more than that John recognized in his cousin a *man* so just and holy that when Jesus asked him to baptize him "he would have restrained him"—rather like two saints or *zaddiks*, each asking the other's blessing first: and then the shattering moment when, in the vision which he shares with the Lord, John suddenly realizes that this kinsman of his (perhaps even, as the legends tell us, his playmate) is in fact the Messiah, the Son of God! Was John the first to know?—after Mary, and even before Peter?—recognizing him as the Lamb, destined as Victim, to perish, not to triumph, despite the Voice from heaven?

And what can baptism have meant to Jesus himself? Did something happen to him? Was he surprised at the heavens opening and the Dove descending, or had he been waiting for this, patiently, fervently? The Arian-Anthroposophist interpretation is really rather persuasive—maybe there's *something* in it after all?

*

I'VE got a hunch that that enigmatic *x* which the mystics *à la* Boehme call the "spirit" of man, what Eckhart calls the "spark", Dame Julian the "substance" of the soul, etc., is, in fact, identical with our own sanctifying grace: the *super*natural likeness to God, the *similitudo* "added" to the *imago Dei*, the garment of light, the luminous body lost in the Fall, perhaps even God's "breath of life" which was breathed into the human clay. This *inspiration* seems to me to indicate, indisputably, that the soul is "born" of God, part of his *Breath*—just what we were taught, in fact, only in such dry language, about sanctifying grace: that which is imparted in regeneration—eternal life, the seed of immortality. The difference is that these heterodox mystics see all this as part of mere human nature.

*

ON intercession: the Hasidim talk about "binding one's soul to the soul of another, so accomplishing the work of ransom". To bind ourselves, to tie ourselves! That's just what one resents about it!—one would be glad enough to help, but from a distance. . . . The difference between nursing the patient yourself at home and arranging for him to go into hospital.

*

THE wedding-feast at Cana. Jesus had the water poured into common or garden water-pots, crude jars used for washing—not even wine-skins proper.

*

SHREWD that remark of Hermann Hesse's in *Narziss und Goldmund*: that Gnostic "loathing of the flesh" is an emotional reaction, not a rational judgment, and that it is to be found almost invariably among the surfeited rather than among the starving.

*

HAHN* again. High time we found the courage to say "divine" again, instead of "supernatural"—the Liturgy has no inhibitions here! Nor had the older devotional writers, who talked quite simply about divine virtues, divine contrition, etc. "Supernatural" sounds so insipid, dead, artificial, remote, empty, its accent purely negative, curbing nature. Pieper's article on Thomas in *Dieu Vivant* explodes like a soundless bomb here: Thomas the mystic of Creation, and of the creature—of the mystery of Being, which is of God, from God, in God and yet not God.

*

REVELATIONS of St Bridget—a formidable volume, at least 700 double-columned pages, printed in 1664! In the judgment scenes we have man standing between his good and his evil angel. Enter the Devil as prosecutor. He's a great moralist, by the way, and knows exactly, down to the finest *nuance*, what is good and what is evil, what man should and could do, and what he mustn't do. He knows our sins and stores them up in his belly, i.e. memory! But he cannot see our *good* thoughts, and so he has no record of these. The good angel keeps a book, too, containing only our good deeds, and reads these aloud "in the love and sight of God". The "ledgers" supplement and explain each other. God himself draws the final balance.

In the great indictment against a good man, by the way, the Devil's *pièce de résistance* is not his misdeeds, but rather the good left undone (what people these days fondly think *they've* discovered—as against "crude" medieval morality!). And, please note, even in a man's virtues and good works the Devil stresses

---

* Johann Michael Hahn, 1758–1819, mystic and visionary, founder of a small dissenting group among the Protestant peasantry of Swabia. As a youth, working on his father's farm, he had a vision of creation and Salvation and spent the rest of his life interpreting and commenting upon what he had seen. Today some twelve thousand adherents to his quaint religious system—very strongly influenced by Jakob Boehme—are said to exist in some four hundred communities in Württemberg.

the lack of supernatural motives, of pure love of God and zeal for his honour. . . . Enter our Lady and all the saints. They in turn stress all the poor man has done to her and their glory. He is finally sentenced to Purgatory, his penance shortened once more through the intercession of his friends in heaven, as well as those still on earth. The exact amount of prayers and alms to be offered by the latter on his behalf is stipulated!

Three degrees of Purgatory: the very lowest, with the real torments of Hell, straight from the furnace of Hell and infernal darkness, and inflicted by the fiends themselves, is the punishment of sins committed, really grave sins. The culprits endure heat and cold, darkness and shame and are terrified by the fear of never getting out again. The second is clearly a state of convalescence (rather like my own just now)—no pain any more, one is languid and drained of vitality, yet still confident that salvation is certain! In the third storey, at long last, the only torment left is the longing for God. Here the people are kept for a long time who on earth were too luke-warm in their desire for the *visio beatifica*. You stay on the second floor until you are rescued by the prayers of friends—or of the Church—a kind of mild detention.

Aren't the souls of the insane really in a very similar plight? "As helpless and defenceless as a child in the hands of a killer", to use St Bridget's own words. Surely we ought to be able to help them too, in the same way?

*

YESTERDAY I came across a comment by one Wilhelm Fraenger (on the back of one of those big colour prints) asserting Hieronymus Bosch to have been a crypto-Adamite and an all-round heretic anyway—which rather shocked me at first. Still, intriguing as it appears at first sight, his idea of the *Garten der Lüste* as depicting the millennium does seem rather flat and far-fetched. True, the label *Garten der Lüste* has a certain taint in German—only in German, though, nothing *louche* about *Jardin des voluptés*, which merely translates the *hortus voluptatis* of Genesis, i.e. Paradise, no more necessarily *louche* than the word *Lustgärtlein*. But the actual *visual* impression is neither paradisaical nor chiliastic. Rather (again, for *me*) that centre panel

is steeped in more wickedness and horror than the panel showing Hell where the damned are depicted merely as "poor devils"
and the demons proper as hefty tormentors, like the overseers in
the concentration camps. But those figures in the Garden itself
are no blessed innocents at play—oh no! Beings bewitched, spell-
struck, drugged by sorcery, with faces like dope addicts—a kind
of infernal paradise. A queer, indefinable whiff of perversity
clings to the whole thing, there's something wrong about it, a
vague, slimy nastiness pervading the glamour—one thinks of
the caves of the Venusberg. If you hold it away from you a little,
so that details are blurred, only outlines and colours predomina-
ting, some of those groups carrying monstrous fruits, grovelling
and worshipping them, or whatever else they're up to, somehow
suggest ulcers, or lumps of offal—"flesh" in all its slippery,
slithery, quivering nastiness.

The figures themselves could well be lunatics performing com-
pulsory antics collectively. Very significant that there are no
children—sheer sterile lust, not fecundity. What is so really
obscene is not the nude figures themselves—some of these are
lovely—but the total lack of privacy. "Visual promiscuity"—
no one couple is really alone, they're all lying around exposed to
the eyes of the others; even those hidden in shells, conchs,
fruits and turrets have their legs protruding, and the "conceal-
ing" globes are of glass! That is why it really is the Garden of
lust, not the *paradisus voluptatis* in the innocent sense.

But this *can't* have been painted by a man who approved or
admired such things—only by someone with a terrible, ruthless
insight into the demoniac depths of lasciviousness.

This picture shows quite clearly that our body is innocent and
"subject to vanity", as St Paul says in Romans 8, only by an
element alien to it—namely, the *spirit* of lewdness. Nature in
travail.

*

GERSHOM SCHOLEM's book *Major Trends in Jewish Mysticism*
really is quite breath-taking. For all its erudition, its critical
paraphernalia and that tedious business of hunting backwards
and forwards between text and notes, it's so fascinating that
instead of growing tired you grow increasingly wide awake.

I discovered here, for instance, proof of what A. once called "the great dialogue between Christendom and Judaism"—perhaps rather between the Church and Israel? Or maybe not after all? For *essentially* it was, of course, quite definitely an unofficial contact. For instance, the latent influence of the Franciscan movement on medieval German Jewry—but as early as the twelfth century, i.e. the movement of apostolical poverty? Quite definitely the influence of the monastic religious tradition on the Hasidic ideal, and (before that also) the influence of Scotus Erigena or Eckhart's concept of an immanent God, God as "ground of the soul", on the Hasidic mystics in Worms and Speyer—and then, five hundred years later, the stream flowing back to water the Protestant mystics—what a cycle!—and now, in our own day, the far-flung seeds of Martin Buber's Hasidic thought in twentieth-century Christendom.

I find it so illuminating (and reassuring!) the way Scholem traces, chronologically and historically (and with what clarity and precision!) the irruptions of Gnosticism into Jewish thought and mysticism—and how the stream meandered from Baghdad via Italy into Provence, and from there into the Rhineland. Why is it I find all this so gratifying? Because it rids me of that secret but most painful suspicion that I ought to be accepting some sort of valid long-lost revelation precisely in the oddest elements of this mysticism.

And then the excitement of discovering in those speculations about the "Glory", the Shekhinah, the mysterious "Great Angel", the "Throne Cherubim", a foreshadowing, as it were, of the Son of God and his Incarnation. Really breath-taking. It's like watching a blind man or a man blindfolded nearly, *nearly* touching something he is groping for. You feel you want to call out "Hot!" or "Cold!". I must look up what Paul has to say about "glory"—Ephesians and the first part of Hebrews. The way everything ties up, and one word leads to another!

Scholem holds the rather startling theory that there's an original spontaneous affinity between Jakob Boehme*and the author of the Zohar. This would, of course, be more convincing

---

* Jakob Boehme (1575–1624) was born and lived in a small and remote country town in Silesia, in a rustic environment, during a period of violence and upheaval. He was one of the most influential German mystics, or rather theosophists. At the

if the Zohar is really the work of *one* man, Moses of Leon (even if a conglomeration of specific trends of thought)—for it's hard to think of the Silesian shoemaker *"harmonizing"* here with a vague mass of primeval traditions. There is such a thing as twin-structures of mind.

*

SOME people, so Dr Mezger told me the other day, can die from a bee-sting—they simply collapse. I think there are people who are spiritually allergic—sensitive to specific spiritual wounds, stings, poisons, etc.

*

BODY and mind: In fact it's the *naturally* *"spiritualistic"* people, for whom really the mind counts, as a matter of course, who now-adays turn out as such passionate champions and apostles of the body, insisting so urgently on its *"value"*, etc.—people for

age of thirty-eight he claimed to have experienced a series of visions of "the inner-most birth of the Godhead", the creation of the universe, the creation of man, the Fall of man and other central mysteries of the Faith. He expounded his illuminations in many writings which raised violent opposition, even persecution, from his Luth-eran Church authorities. He bore this censure meekly, spending some time in exile. He wrote on the three Principles of Divine Nature, on the Threefold Life of Man, on the Incarnation of Christ, on Predestination, etc. His moral teaching cor-responds to the orthodox (Protestant and Catholic) mystics of the age, stressing surrender to God's will, humility, charity, prayer—he wrote a small prayerbook, too. But all this is based upon and interwoven with the quaintest and wildest speculations of definitely Gnostic and Cabbalistic character. This fact is very cur-ious, considering his life as an artisan, among the unlettered class, remote from schools and books. Yet his enormously difficult, well-nigh unintelligible language, which claims to present the message of immediate divine illumination, abounds with Latin words and indubitable alchemistic and Paracelsian vocabulary. In his outstanding book on Jewish mysticism Gershom Scholem says: "Boehme's doc-trine of the origins of evil, which created such a stir, indeed bears all the traits of Cabbalistic thought. . . . In general, if one abstracts from the Christian metaphors (sic!) in which he tried, in part at least, to express his intuitions, Boehme . . . shows the closest affinity to Cabbalism precisely where he is most original. He has, as it were, discovered the world of Sefiroth all over again. It is possible, of course, that he deliberately assimilated elements of Cabbalistic thought after he had made, in the period following his illuminations, their acquaintance through friends who, unlike himself, were scholars." Boehme's thought profoundly influenced most dis-senting mystics of the seventeenth and eighteenth century; in Germany, Holland and England (William Law, Jane Leade). In Germany his influence was most strongly apparent in small sects, now obsolete, who busied themselves specially with his odd sexual mysticism, distorting it crudely and engaging in often revolting prac-tices. But his thought is also evident in philosophers like Schelling and von Baader, and is found in romantic thought and poetry, from Novalis to Bergengruen.

70

whom matter is the far more astonishing marvel. *They*, let's be frank: *We* do this precisely *because*, for us, the body is emphatically "different"—something we must keep on getting used to, so to speak, all the time.

And only genuine "materialists", who take body and matter for granted as "first values", only *they* get excited about things of the mind and about the "invisible reality", and find its very existence strange and improbable—only they could have doubts about it, and turn the possibility of mind into a problem (which we would never do). But when they've once made up their minds in its favour, they become its fanatical prophets, forcing their "discovery" down everyone's throat.

*

SCHMOGER's life of Anne Catherine Emmerich. Not the original, unabridged edition which, unfortunately, seems no longer to exist. Very significant how A.C.E.'s vision of the next world tallies with St Bridget and the Oberlin "map of the world beyond": the various degrees of Purgatory, not only as places of punishment, but also as a kind of pre-Heaven: Abraham's bosom, the Mount of the Prophets, Paradise. And that immense contrast between the poor, whining creature, so tiresomely garrulous and yet so limited, of the official A.C.E. documents, Wesener's (her doctor's) journals and reports to the bishop—and Brentano's sibyl, spiritual, powerful, a natural genius! Which of the two was her true self? Or does Brentano's mirror change too much?

*

I FINISHED Halldor Laxness's *Islandglocke* [Iceland Bell] yesterday, in spite of piles of far more pressing "obligatory reading". It starts off rather badly, a very average, third-rate historical novel—but then it picks up. If the picture is really true, then it's extraordinarily interesting, from the point of view of history and culture. I really must read *Die Jungfrau von Skaholt* again. What struck me was the startling similarity between Iceland and Ireland. Not only the parallel with the Danes and the English, but also in the character of the people, as described here—utterly unlike the sort of "Nordic race" one usually reads about. Even more, that curious paradoxical combination: the most brutal misery on the one hand—drink, decay, filth—with an unquenchable pride of ancestry, poetry, spiritual heritage on the other, with imagination, open-handedness, "memory" in the broad, historical sense. Their scholarly tradition appears—or rather appeared, in the Iceland of those days—to have much in common with the much earlier Druidism in Ireland. It seems that every tramp knew the old poetic sagas and could talk like a skald when he chose. They lived, these people—during what, for us here, was the Baroque era—like a herd of wild swine, plagued and diseased by famine, often half-witted or leprous, lousy, vegetating in caves or under stacks of turf, living on rotting shark-meat. Yet all this indescribable misery could not stamp out the pride or the strange, brilliant spirit of this people. Maybe the similarity between the two peoples passes unnoticed because the Irish remained Catholic, whereas Iceland was "reformed" by the Danes (forcibly, it would seem). But it does strike me that the incredibly strong national consciousness of both peoples has exactly the same quality.

*

By the way: The opposite of assent, as "holding something to be true", is not doubting, but *wanting* this to be untrue: which, fundamentally, is not an intellectual act either, but an act of the will, fed and steered by emotion and only ratified subsequently by rational argument.

*

I've been asked to write about Bergengruen. What a task! Still, it *could* be good. What must I say? That I love Bergengruen so much because he's the poet of the *Universe*, poet of the mystery of Creation. That always and everywhere, in the greatest just as in the smallest things, he sees the world as mystery, the mystery of things created. That *this* is his own particular charism: to recognize the presence of the whole in even the most insignificant symbol. His world is crystal, darkly-clear (like the outer panels of Bosch's "Garden"), floating in the impenetrable ocean of God's mysteries. *This* world must be a mystery, since it is the work of the Creator, this Creator—the very fact that it

72

exists at all is the supreme enigma—and so, even its tiniest splinter is translucent with it. I must say that for us Christians this enigma can never be solved: on the contrary, it becomes richer, growing more and more complex. I'd say something on the point that mystery does not mean darkness or obscurity. There's nothing vague or blurred about a crystal, a columbine, a Red Admiral butterfly—about personality, strong and defined, or a heroic fate. Precisely this "character" constitutes the mystery, not some sort of hazy cloud surrounding it. An unknown script is fascinating and tantalizing, not just a meaningless scribble. Which all goes to show how vitally important awareness, "encounter" with the mystery of the world is for Christians today— for without this experience all sense for religious mystery simply disintegrates and is lost. Indifferent to the mystery of creation, how *can* one respond to the other? Because Bergengruen rouses and nourishes this faculty he "upholds the Christian point of view". The mystery of religion fits into his universe and reveals its deep connection, its kinship with our "real" existence—in his novels, just as in his poetry, in the Rodenstein Book, and in *Feuerzeichen.* Surely this last book couldn't be set in a more prosaic era or in duller, more *bourgeois* surroundings—a small provincial town before the First World War. Yet it's full of demonic flashes, a staggering description of a man possessed, and, in between, that figure of the magistrate's wife, Duschka, sweet living symbol of grace: there just isn't one corner of this world of ours which is not teeming with mystery, not only the creatures of the twilight realm "in between". From anything Bergengruen can strike the spark which ignites any flame, as in his *Lombardic Elegy* in which the meditation on history starts from a tie-pin.

*

BERGENGRUEN's *Die Leidenschaftlichen* [The Passionate]. I well remember when this first version came out (a revised version of *Der tolle Mönch*). How taken aback they were, and how they disapproved, all those readers who had all too readily labelled him "a new Catholic author", i.e. one of those "safe" writers who could be confidently dished up (especially to young people) as "a champion of Christian ideals", describing one particular

3*   73

section of the world, clear, wholesome, useful for the training
of young minds. . . . And now came their regretful verdict (and
not only voiced by fools either!) that Bergengruen was, after
all, a *littérateur*, to whom virtuosity meant more than principles
or points of view. What these critics completely overlooked was
the fact that B's work is a contribution to the theme: "What is
Man?"—no less (and perhaps not really so very differently?)
than that work of Hieronymus Bosch's. Of course his characters
aren't paragons of virtue, but they certainly are "exemplary"
for the species "The Passionate"—for man, that is to say in all
his dark, unfathomable mystery.

*

THE Joyful Mysteries of the Rosary—I was meditating today
on *Maria Ecclesia*: astonishing how you can fit this into all five
mysteries:

1. The Church must continue to receive the Word anew from
   the Holy Ghost.
2. *Maria durch ein' Dornwald ging.**
3. The Church gives birth to the WORD for the world, perpetually, in its tragic "form of a slave"—mute, helpless,
   in hundred-fold humble and humiliating dependence: in
   marked contrast to the maturity, perfection, the imposing
   stature of full-grown man. Even the cave and the beasts
   are there again, each time.
4. In any case.
5. Could it be that the Church even *loses* the Word now and
   again—that she no longer knows where he is any more?
   That he is lost to her eyes, if not to her heart, out of sight,
   out of reach, so to speak—and that she only finds him
   again after a time of fathomless desolation, of anxious
   searching full of self-reproach? That "we as the

---

* Sixteenth-century German carol. Our Lady walks through a tangled wood of
thorn-trees, bearing her unborn Child, and wherever she passes the thorns burst
into blossom:

> Our Lady passed through a thicket of thorn,
> that in seven long years not a leaf had borne,
> but as the Babe through the briars was borne,
> lo, roses ablazing burst forth from the thorn!

Church", so to speak, would find him again in the larger
Father's house, far more spacious than our own snug
little home—*chez nous*—finding him again "in the
midst of the doctors", i.e. among the strangers, the
scholars, the initiates, sitting at their feet, a child in "the
form of a servant"—and they do not know him. But he
asks them questions, compelling them to answer. He
questions them—and he brings their answer back home
with him to the little "mother's house", to be blended
with his familiar speech.

*

In Austin Farrer's *Rebirth of Images* I found a new—really new
—symbol for the Church: the "Angel" through whom the
Lord speaks, who is not the Lord, may not be adored—and yet
the Lord speaks only through him, until his second coming.

I'm gradually collecting a whole series of unwonted images
for the Church: the thornbush, the rock pouring out water
(Numbers 20), Origen's harlot, the Angel of the Apocalypse,
those images of our Lady in the Rosary, that ghastly Goya-
like picture of the mutilated body as seen by Anne Catherine
Emmerich.

*

Just at the moment what preoccupies me—at least in the
"middle storey" of my consciousness—is the "transient"
Church. Meditating on that which is but anticipation in her—
fleeting sign and token, changing, instable, to be superseded, or,
as Origen has it: to be outshone; what is and still must be only
a curtain which must be "rent from top to bottom" (Origen
again) when the time comes. What, in fact, the Church patriot
would like to retain—cost what it may—no matter how rotten or
fossilized—restoring, patching up a hundred times over, fighting tooth and nail against every impulse to discard and build up
anew (yet how magnanimous, how bold the early Church was in
this respect!). In short, the real object of ecclesiastical conservatism—the "letter".

*

QUESTION: To what extent, or when and where does dogma, or rather do dogmas belong to this inventory, and in what sense? Or, one could well ask: Where are they really, those "frontiers" of the Revelation which the Apocalypse closed? And to what extent can that Spirit promised at the Last Supper manifest Itself in "private revelations", that Spirit which, as Jesus said, shall guide us into all truth? How far is this achieved within the office of the Church as *Mater et Magistra*? Feuling's book on dogma doesn't help me much here. It still baffles me how *inaccessible* doctrine is: either reduced to formulae (like chemistry and mathematics), double Dutch to the uninitiated, or watered down for popular consumption—it's hard to fish anything solid out of this brew, something to get your teeth into when you're hungry.

*

BERGENGRUEN and the mystery again. Isn't it human nature to feel vaguely uncomfortable, uneasy, when we master things too easily, get things too cheaply, or see through them too quickly? Doesn't something of this reluctance, this sense of being somehow cheated, cling to our attitude towards a Christianity grown too soft, too petty, too "sweet", to a Faith too plausible, to a world too lucidly explained?

*

BASICALLY, this intense and wearing struggle "between me and myself" (as E. used to say as a child) is the question: Evil and its significance in the world—another Bergengruen theme. Two positions oppose one another here: the one maintains, in the name of God, that evil cannot be allowed to exist at all, that it must be denied, fought against, as far as possible stamped out, absolutely, unconditionally, uncompromisingly; that it is contradiction, nonsense, irreconcilable opposition to God, and, therefore, must be annihilated wherever it is found, without condoning, in the name and at the command of his divine Majesty— consider Newman, for instance, with his terrible teaching that a single venial sin is an evil worse than the destruction of an entire universe; the "rather die than sin" attitude of many of the saints, and mothers praying that their child may die before committing the first mortal sin, etc.

76

And then the other opinion: that evil, though not originally planned, has nevertheless entered into the divine plan later on, as motor, as ferment, as agent, releasing certain vital and even salutary processes which could not have been started without it. And that, therefore, it cannot be negated quite so categorically, but must rather be admitted as a subservient factor, as indeed it is tolerated by God himself: the Devil as God's servant, despite it all. . . . And sin as a solvent, at times indispensable for a new coagulation.

The same old question, insoluble, tormenting, so terribly tempting: How far is it possible, in our present-day world, to live a life without sin, a life based strictly on the moral law? Isn't this only to be achieved within the bounds of a narrow, timorous existence, basically sterile, stunted, impoverished, a life unnatural, unreal, artificial—an existence surely never created by God? A vital question for educators. You cannot guide young people with mental reservations and veiled relativism. What they need is a straightforward "You should!" and "You may not". They need an honest and sound scale of values, not something which is fundamentally ambivalent from the start.

*

HOLY Week is beginning again, and here I am once more, feeling so unadjusted to it, so utterly inadequate. Not that "heart of stone" feeling, simply the sense of being completely out of proportion—something momentous, like the Niagara Falls, is thundering down, right beside me, and there I stand, with a thimble in my hand, and I'm supposed to dip in and collect something, catch it up, assimilate it, reacting properly, goodness knows how. But if you hold a cup under a waterfall, it's not only knocked right out of your hand, but empty to boot; the rushing, tumbling water simply rebounds. The only hope of scooping up anything at all is to hold the cup carefully at the very edge, under a lost thin trickle.

That is how it is with me. I'm standing as near as I can get to the cataract, the thunder and roar of the water is deafening. I can catch next to nothing, and I know very well that one step nearer and I'll be caught up or swept away. But maybe this helpless state of just standing aside, this overpowering sense of not being able to do anything about it is the only sort of adoration I'm allowed just now. One's eyes closed, turned away—this, too, is one way of divining the immensity of this tremendous mystery, of paying reverence, at least, to something surpassing by far either comprehension or emotion. When I was young I used to fancy one could somehow match one's tiny vessel to the onrush from above by dint of emotional wriggling and writhing.

*

THE Blessing of the Palms: meditating on the antiphons, I wondered whether the garments which the *pueri Hebraeorum* spread in the roadway could not well signify "the skin of our hearts", which must be stripped off and thrown before him—to be trodden underfoot—stripped bare, we stand there in all our nakedness. But *they* sang all the time, shouting "Hosanna!"

*

IN the last few days I've come to see how irrelevant it is, how unnecessary that lay-people should have as detailed a knowledge as possible of dogma—up to now I have enormously over-rated the importance of this. Of course it's a fascinating hobby, and for the theologian it's all in the day's work. But it isn't *important* what people think, so long as they've got the *essentials* right. After all, what did the early Christians in the catacombs really *know*? Or the Desert Fathers? Or Brother Francis himself, and the first of his followers? An outline of the doctrine necessary for salvation, filled in not with words and ideas, but with love, fervour, obedience—with a faith which found its expression in "doing what is true in love". It was enough for holiness, for martyrdom. What more do we need? Isn't a lot of our fine talk just wrangling and sounding brass?

*

IF the Cross is a tree, as the Liturgy keeps telling us just now, what is its root? Legend says it stands above Adam's grave and skull. Is it sin?

*

I FRET so about my growing awareness of the "slave's shape" of the Church (Phil. 2. 7). The incredible mediocrity of Catholic

weeklies, etc., of the faithful in general, of their standards
—and, on the other hand, the painful recognition growing within me of the wealth of spiritual gifts and potentialities among
Protestants—things of which we never even heard a whisper.
We were brought up in the idea that holiness, etc., was our own
particular, matchless dowry, our outstanding and intrinsic difference from "the others"—and now, to me, it seems even more
characteristic of them than of us. Has my seclusion removed me so
far from the true life of my beloved Church, indeed so estranged
me from her that I can only see her blemishes and wrinkles and no
longer her "beauty from within"? Of course I cling to the
belief that she is still in possession of these gifts—though
hidden—and know very well that it is a wicked and adulterous
generation that calls for *signs* in order to believe. And yet, and
yet. . . . If the Spirit were really present, surely it must manifest
itself *visibly*? How did Mary Ward put it? "You cannot conceal
Love, any more than you can conceal fire." Or must one have
special glasses to notice it at all? *Must* the Spirit be invisible?
Is it "the flesh" in me which clamours so loudly for the revelation of the children of God? Isn't the very fact that convents exist
dazzling evidence enough of the presence of the Spirit, unsatisfactory and odd as their inmates often are?

*

ANOTHER instance of the tradition hidden within the Church:
Actually lots of those wonderful insights of Dame Julian's,
her loftiest revelations on sin, contrition, etc., were contained in
the First Confession instruction we got from good little Sister
Leontia at the convent orphanage in Ronsperg: "In Confession our Lord washes the stains out of the shining garment of
our soul . . . and afterwards this dress of sanctifying grace is not
only as white and beautiful as ever it was, but even finer than
before—for in place of every spot and every hole he sets a
gleaming pearl."

If you came across such a passage reading one of the old
mystics, you would marvel at its profundity. But it was only old
Sister Leontia, Sister of Charity in a little Bohemian country
town.

*

LAST night I was reading, with growing disgust, that appalling book on Padre Pio by —. Really nauseating—watery gruel, diarrhoea of pious platitudes, hardly one dry, solid statement in the whole book—which, considering the subject, would not have been such an impossible feat. Instead, everything coated with thick, sticky, cloying jelly—brrh! This kind of treatment can turn even the most serious religious phenomena into emetics. Pondering over these things afterwards, frankly, uneasily, I asked myself: Is it just spiritual conceit that I simply can't stand this kind of stuff any more, that it frankly makes me sick? Could it be really good and pleasing to God? Or is it we who are just a lot of conceited "know-alls" in his eyes? God knows I don't mean it that way. As the "others" see it, the 120 per cent R.C.'s, probably my attitude, *our* attitude, is a disgrace to the Church, grievous, offensive, only to be put up with by heroic indulgence. Crazy.

*

GLORY be to God for his kindness! If *only* the enthusiasts of Suffering and Atonement were right, then I ought to despair, thinking God had forgotten me, or dropped me—for I am having such a good time. On the other hand, I do see more and more that there's such a thing as an office of thanksgiving too, of wonder and child-like joy at his good gifts—and that we must make a point of cultivating this attitude as long as we can. Strange really, how good Christians can presume to upset our appeciation of divine benefits, lowering God's most obvious bounties to second-rate and even suspect gifts, suggesting a decrease in grace—whereas pain and suffering are glorified as the real, essential—certainly higher and nobler—tokens of his love. Is there not a time and place for everything? For the moment anyway, my barometer's set at "Fair"—at grateful enjoyment, delight and praise: Blessed be the LORD! Praise the Lord, my soul, and all that is in me bless his holy NAME!"

*

CABBALA, Boehme, Hahn, Julius Kerner's Prevorst papers: On the fringe of the established Christian theology of the Churches —which I had hitherto held to be the only genuine theology— certainly as a consistent whole—there's another vast network of "theosophy" (more a web than a block), cropping up under different names and in various places—but with a marked persistence—within the Christian world: with Pietists, Dissenters, Separatists, Occultists (and, nowadays, Anthroposophists). Surprising, how the basic structure of cabbalistic thought permeates all these varieties—but in Germany they all stem from Jakob Boehme.

*

Is there any Catholic book which really honestly deals with the various and paradoxical "overlappings" in marriage and love? A book which admits how little marriage as an institution is really bound up with love—how very late, really, love became involved in it at all, let alone assessed as its condition *sine qua non*—how dangerous and highly explosive the attempt is to build the most permanent thing on the most incalculable factor in the world!—how marvellous and adventurous and utopian the very *idea* of a "love match", of marriage *based* on love—anything but to be taken for granted! A book as far from pessimistic cynicism as from airy optimism.

Goethe's letters, which I'm reading in between as relaxation, fit in beautifully here. Of course his *liaison* with Christiane was really marriage, even though incomplete until the seal of matrimony could be given in October 1806 by a binding public avowal and pledge. And yet, those seventeen years of living together, and the children they had—that was far more "marriage", less of a fragmentary connection, than the fourteen years of friendship with Charlotte von Stein. That bond, existing on a quite different and undoubtedly higher plane, was yet inferior for all that. Of course it was love, human, personal love in the highest degree—but it lacked the gravity of a union for life, and of fecundity.

*

ASTONISHING how the *Gloria Patri* gains volume in the light of the Cabbala—how the NAME seems to expand . . . and what new dimensions open out when one begins to understand the "divine attributes"—justice, mercy, and so on—as God's "emanations". I remember that a central tradition of Catholic spirituality always held devotion to the Blessed Trinity to be the ultimate peak of interior life—perpetual contemplation of this mystery and obedience to its inspiration.

*

GOETHE, whose letters I've been reading very intensively during the past few weeks, is always stressing *Verträglichkeit*— agreeing to live and let live—as the most important element of friendship: we shouldn't try to *change* people, but simply let them be as they are, making the best of even partial concord, instead of trying to force a fictitious perfect harmony. I think we, i.e. at least my generation, were hampered here from boarding school days by the notion they kept hammering into us that friendship must *à tout prix* have "ennobling", "elevating" effects —oddly enough always on the *other* person, never on oneself! It was taken for granted, with the utmost naïveté, that in whatever one's friend differed from oneself, it was *she* (a he-friend was not even conceivable!) who badly needed improvement, for her own good, of course—to be brought up, gently but firmly, to one's one level. . . . Heavens above! Nobody realized what dynamite and fuses we were laying for later life.

*

HAVE just started on a little book of selections from Origen. Glory, glory, hallelujah! The Book Providence again, answering precisely so many of those questions of mine about "the soul spark", etc. Origen even states what I was groping for in Pietist mysticism, i.e. that "spirit", for them, means sanctifying grace. What a fool it makes me feel now, remembering those first *Volkshochschule* courses* when everything was still in ruins —I simply hadn't the courage in those days even to hint at these realities, *similitudo*, etc., keeping gingerly to the "similarity to God" on the *natural* plane. What a coward I was! I see now that I only ventured to give information, not Truth. But this shows, too, how little I myself had discerned of the image of man, the

* General re-education courses started for young people in Stuttgart jointly by Catholics and Protestants, 1946–47.

nucleus of Christian anthropology. These essentials seemed so marginal, almost a flourish, to be discarded for prudential reasons, without any loss to anybody.

*

ACTUALLY the Jews must have a special affinity to speech, language, etc.—"the word" in general—since the whole point of their being at all is that God spoke to them, and spoke to them directly. They received THE WORD twice over—in the Old Dispensation—as God's "word of mouth", and then, in the New Testament, incarnate in the Son of God. As a people, as a race, they seem to have a special relationship to sex, too—a fact lots of people have noticed and which (see Freud) is usually chalked up against them as a rather unpleasant trait. But they were "invented" solely that the WORD might be made flesh among them, begotten and born of them, the last of that long line. Strange that after that almost timeless lineage the very last genetic link was omitted—with the Virgin Birth as the culmination.

*

PSALM 118, "the psalm of rejoicing in the Torah", as the Hasidim call it. How very comforting it is. I'm sure quite a number of us cradle Catholics, really law-abiding people, are seized, at least now and again, by a secret, stealthy panic that maybe the others could be right after all—those others who taunt us, supercilious or pitying, that we've spent our lives in narrowness and fear—indeed that we've *missed* life altogether for the sake of the Law and its letter. But the psalm well knows that:

> My *delight*, Lord, is in thy bidding,
> Duty's path my *choice*, I keep thy law ever in remembrance.
> Disappoint me, Lord, never, one that holds fast by thy commandments.
> Do but open my heart wide, and *easy* lies the path thou hast decreed.
> Ever let my choice be set on thy will, not on covetous thoughts.
> Eyes have I none for vain phantoms;
> *Let me find life in following thy ways.*
> Each command of thine I embrace lovingly;
> Do thou in thy faithfulness grant me *life*.

Freely shall my feet tread, if thy will is all my quest.
Go not back on the word thou hast pledged to thy servant;
There lies all my hope.
Lest I should sink in my affliction,
Thou hast given thy covenant to be my comfort.
Thy promises have brought me *life*.
Heritage, Lord, I *claim no other* but to obey thy will.
Is not the law thou hast given dearer to me than rich store of
gold and silver?

One really ought to know it by heart—so precisely does it state the same thing over and over again in a hundred variations.

How I'd like to write something comprehensive, really valid on this matter—on the real significance of the Law: not remotely, not in the faintest degree contrary to personal conscience—as voices keep insisting here, ever louder, ever more stridently decrying the Law as constraint, tyranny, distorting the voice of conscience, dead letter, convention, and all the rest of it. No, commandments, orders, decrees, ruling, bidding: the whole psalm is full of such weighty, massive words—and how gladly the soul responds in joyous surrender, ardently, tenderly—a bride, not a captive seized and raped. Yes, yes, and yes again, assent welling up from the innermost depths! But I suppose only someone who knows love can really understand this, who knows what it means to fuse with the will of the beloved, deliberately, of one's own volition, surrendering one's own will to his— someone who has really experienced the union of two wills.

*

THE grain of mustard seed and the leaven once again. The Kingdom of Heaven can take root and sprout up in a human heart from the very tiniest beginnings, virtually without human assistance (the mustard seed was probably never sown on purpose, but dropped by a bird or blown by the wind)—yet it really took root, grew into a "tree", sturdy and enduring, steadfast in all weathers, and the birds of the air (divine inspirations, etc.) can *really* nest in its branches. But it's "in the garden" for all that, in a cultivated demesne, i.e. man must *do* something himself—at least keep the soil raked and hoed, so that a chance seed blown by the wind can settle and be nourished.

The leaven: "We prefer our yeast pure" says C.J., meaning Catholic piety in the form we all know—instead of mixing it with the flour of the world around us, of ordinary everyday life, and letting these three measures of meal be leavened. We're so afraid of spoiling the yeast by taking it out of its nice hygienic little cellophane packet and breaking it up, stirring and mixing, past recognition. And then you must remember to set the dough aside to rise, leaving it to itself for a while, else nothing will happen at all! Both parables stress the insignificance of beginnings. One must have the courage to scatter even the tiniest, most inconspicuous, unheeded suggestions at random, leaving it to God to make what he will of them—if anything.

＊

Who can *not* enter by the narrow gate? What *is* this narrow gate? The back door—for servants, tradesmen, beggars. . . . Who cannot get in this way then? (*a*) Those who only deign to use "portals", who don't care for the sort of people they might encounter around the back; (*b*) Those, too (especially true for the rear entrance!), who can't stoop to low and narrow doors— too fat—puffed up—too much flesh!—who've brought too much luggage with them, etc.

That disquieting dialogue with the master of the house reveals plainly enough that he is talking not to strangers, not to chance passers by or outsiders, but to *familiares*: "We have eaten and drunk in thy presence!"—in our own day: "We have received thy sacraments!" "Thou hast taught in our streets"— openly, and on every corner, i.e. in good Catholic territory. They are "practising Catholics". But he says: "I know nothing of you, nor *whence* you come", i.e. for all that, you were not children of the Church.

＊

God "ignores" the wicked, so Origen says. And the outsiders come from the four winds. *Loathing* at the sorry recognition, ever-growing, of the religious poverty and pettiness within the Church—and the luxuriant wild flowering "outside". . . .

＊

Is all this reading, Pietists, Gnostics, Cabbala and so on a danger to my faith? Some of my good friends would certainly think so, and worry about me, at least privately. My grievances against certain patterns and habits of thought and doctrine inside the Church— and methods of spiritual life too—are, in fact, thriving enormously, much in favour of the Pietists and Hasidim. Of course this is painful and distressing, but I don't think it is *wrong*. Every genuine struggle for renewal must be roused, fostered and guided by profound insight into the complaints which call for reform, and maybe that insight can never be probing and ruthless enough. But probably it ought to be balanced by as vivid and vigorous an insight into the real treasures of the Church. And that's where I am in a scrape just now. I feel as though I'm facing a friend of whom I thoroughly disapprove—at present—and yet I am honestly trying to stick to my good opinion of him—but, for the moment anyway, this is a matter of resolve rather than sympathy. Just now I see the Church (not the "great" Church, of course, the present-day, "little" version) like a fossil in amber, or rather as the amber surrounding the fossil, or as the little box of mummified Japanese flowers . . . as a fellah guarding the pyramids of antiquity and their hidden treasures. Maybe I ought to read more *Herder-Korrespondenz*,* keeping myself informed about what's really going on within the Church? But, oh, isn't the spectacle of the *Orbis Catholicus* far more disheartening and depressing than inspiring and comforting? Or is it simply that I am being cut off from the Eucharist for too long— and maybe my idea about participating with the "Church Communicant" is an intellectual fad after all, not enough to prevent atrophy by starvation. Somehow or other these theosophic speculations sometimes seem more convincing to my mind than the corresponding bits of our own theology . . . they *appeal* to me so much more; on the other hand I am perfectly aware that heresy always seems more intelligible than orthodoxy, for the simple reason that mere human thought is more akin, more attuned to our mind than the "thoughts which are not your thoughts".

Another thing: I well know how vague I am about doctrinal definitions, in general and in particular, and that I ought really

* Leading monthly periodical giving international Catholic news.

86

to do something about this. But whenever I poke my nose into a volume of the *Summa*, for a change, both the approach to the problems and the problems themselves strike me as utterly remote and abstruse: nothing for me, it just doesn't apply; it's all as uninteresting as it is incomprehensible, I feel myself rebelling inwardly, as though I were forcing myself to read a book about income tax. It's a foreign language. The door is open, but I don't want to go in.

The queer thing is that men like Hahn, and even Boehme, for all their abstruse style, still had a gift of expressing subtle and complicated esoteric teachings in plain language too, so that peasants and craftsmen could understand what they meant—whereas our theology has been turned into esoteric lore, carefully preserved and handed on in a most exclusive lingo for adepts, only really intelligible for Latin scholars—with a wretched tasteless stew of the same stuff as sermons.

Luke 13. 31-35. Christ could cast out demons and heal the sick—but he could *not* gather the children of Jerusalem under his wings—because they wouldn't come. The devils obeyed his word, and so did nature, too, in his miracles—only man can resist him—above all the son of the Holy City, the paragon of virtue, the religious expert, i.e. the Pharisee—*he* can resist more stubbornly than all the demons.

*

EVEN read in such broken bits Origen is real food and drink. You can feel it being absorbed, right away, into your very blood. How terse, how compact he is! All this modern stuff is barley-water in comparison.

*

I'VE been lucky enough to get hold of Buber's German translation of the Bible. Reading Josue, Judges, Samuel and Kings one realizes for the first time that the epiphany of God in the Old Dispensation was no whit less humiliating than the *"non horruisti Virginis uterum"*. God appears here really as a wild tribal deity, rampaging for blood, God of "the savage Jews", as Else Laske-Schüler so fittingly calls her biblical forefathers. What savages they were—and their enemies along with them!

—is shown to the full in the tale of their exploits in this archaic version: quite a Red Indian epic, Gedeon slaughtering Madianite chiefs Raven and Wolf at the Raven's Rock and the Wolf's Wine-press, cutting off their heads and sending them around as trophies (just like Hemingway's wild Spaniards—1936!). And even David's great psalm of thanksgiving is not very different. David, that chief of outlaws and woodland bandits in their eyries and caves. . . . Their perception of God is a lurid reflection on dark night clouds, caught in the flare of blood-red torches: and yet it is HE, HE who *really* manifests himself to them, who *really* speaks to them—to *them*, not to Greeks and Hindus, Chinese and Egyptians, full of sublime speculations and dreams about him. Almost as though he had revealed himself to the Sioux Indians or the Zulus in the nineteenth century, by-passing the civilized races, and they had recorded it in their tribal chronicles and on their totem poles, and then—presented it to us as gospel. I can just imagine the reaction of the highbrows of ancient Greece when they encountered this Jewish God! What a tall story it all is.

*

C.J. TOLD me yesterday I had a "defence complex". He may well be right. All through my childhood and youth I had to stick up for myself, never knowing what it was to be protected, to find anyone to defend me—it seemed sheer impossibility; and now, identifying myself with everything loved, I instinctively, unconsciously assume this to be just as defenceless, just as vulnerable—as though it really depended on my defence alone. Even "Truth" and the Faith, and the Church. How hard it is to learn that everything one loves is in God's keeping, that one can really safely leave it in his hands.

*

BERGENGRUEN's short story *Die Krone*: yet another parable of material evil—the fraud worked on the queen, on the whole nation, the nurse's oath to conceal the identity of the murdered as well as the rescued child—and yet what happens is virtually right and good. It seems things can happen this way. I'm so uprooted and confused in my own moral theological notions, at least on the rational plane. I only know one thing for certain: that on countless occasions, emphatically, clearly, unequivocally, our Lord bade us to keep his commandments; that in his farewell discourse he set this on a par with the charge to remain in his love—and that his bitter Passion is the price paid for the breaking of God's commandments. Which is why there can never, under any pretext whatever, be any question of "freedom to sin" or "obligation to sin", whatever the "mystique of sinning" adepts may say. I can still only go on clinging to Psalm 118. "If you *love* me, keep my commandments!" Nothing here of fear, stereotype conformity, etc. There is a passion for the Law which is love of God.

*

EACH of the Easter gospels has the same persistent, mysterious undertone: that during the forty days (which somehow present a pattern for this last aeon of ours between his resurrection and our own) his manifestation, his epiphany, his dwelling among us do not assume one shape, always recognizable: he appears as a stranger, an unfamiliar figure, unknown, easily taken for someone else—as the gardener, the pilgrim to Emmaus, the stranger on the lakeside. Even "his own" did not recognize him straight away. He was different from the Jesus they had known, as they remembered him. They had to learn to see anew—just as, right at the beginning, the women, too, had to learn to look for him—"Why are you seeking one who is alive, here among the dead?"—when they came to the tomb. I see here a disturbing, confusing, consoling parallel to the Church which is also the Body of his epiphany.

*

JUST now my chronic horror of "institutions" is specially acute. All the same I know perfectly well—and unshakeably—that we cannot do without them as long as this world of ours lasts. "Once the walls protected the city—now the city protects its walls" is apt here; and that remark of Goethe's about the general who in defending the entrenchments is protecting more than just mud and stones—I must look up the exact words. This is very important.

*

THE Law is as full of mysteries as the Faith. One can grumble about both from the outside, but they can only really be understood from within, and in practice. For God as truly conceals his will in his law as he hides his light in dogma. Both times it's in a nutshell—and both times it is hard to crack.

*

Soulier de Satin yesterday. A middling production (except Prouhèze), but nothing can really spoil that marvellous poetry. But, here again, that curious Claudel twist: the sudden taste of something bitter in your mouth, and, without warning, the most sublime passages are somehow suspect—pitched too high— an accent is false—a passage rings hollow, treacherous. . . . Alas, the very passages on which you'd like to tread most firmly—as though on the stone arch of a bridge.

*

THE sin of Paradise. I can't help it; when I examine my stock of religious notions and images, simply looking up, checking the inventory, I'm afraid that optimistic concept of original sin just isn't there any more. I simply cannot believe that this sin affected Adam and Eve *alone* (and their progeny, of course), and not the whole universe, and that it was spiritual only, just pride and disobedience. Surely the very act of eating the fruit was physical, not merely spiritual? We're always being told that the Fall had nothing whatever to do with sex. No, I can't believe this any more. The verse about their nakedness which follows seems to me only too clear—even though this also includes the loss of the "garment of light". The unique role of sex in human consciousness is only too significant. C. S. Lewis is perfectly right: a bawdy joke would be inconceivable among animals—even talking and thinking animals. And then, human beings don't make "indecent" jokes about eating—coarse jokes, yes—though there are uncouth and ugly abuses enough in eating and drinking, goodness knows. But *this* sort of shame has a different quality, though people will keep trying to treat these alike. Something must have happened to human procreation since the Fall. Not that procreation, as such, would never have been without the Fall (as some enthusiasts pretend). That's nonsense, to my mind; but somehow or other it would have been *different*. This opinion is rooted in solid and ancient tradition too. If it's true that St Thomas held other and more optimistic views on this subject, this doesn't disconcert me one bit. Maybe an "angel-type", as he was, endowed with the charism of virginity, would be incapable of realizing the depth of the Fall in this domain. What is always attributed to latent Manicheism in St Augustine might well be the realism of experience. But perhaps, in this case, the "angel" could hardly measure the real depth of our redemption either, or the height of our transfiguration.

It seems to me that the pendulum has swung too far in the optimistic reaction to those late medieval Manichean trends— as though in "apology" to the Creator and his Creation. But surely this detracts unduly from the momentum, and, inadmissibly, from the depth of the Fall?

*

BOUYER's article on evil. Good and yet not good. His attack on scholastic metaphysics which whittles evil down to mere negation, i.e. abstraction, and, as he says, illusion—and his attempt to balance this positively by "the Evil One" seems to me simply to shift the question on to another plane. For the *real* question still remains: why, and how, the Evil One is evil, and how he could become evil, since he was created good—and since, as one reads, his *nature* was not changed by his Fall?

What is *evil*, as distinct from what is "bad"? Ugly, terrible, harmful, dangerous, etc.—is still not *evil*. And if only things actually opposing God were evil . . . how little in the world would then be really evil! Would it apply, after all, only to mankind and angels—and everything else would be good?

*

ON the other hand, we shouldn't be scared when we're charged with "spiritualism".

For me the word would seem to embrace all kinds of phenomena. There is a spiritualism as "demonic negation", for instance, which, as A. says, is part of the nihilism of our age. In opposition he is—and lots of us are—insistent in their praise of body, form, matter and senses. But the spiritualism of my youth was something quite different—the Franciscan kind, no Luciferian negation of the visible, rather the consequence, the shadow, the shell of a far more passionate affirmation of the Invisible: of an eschatological impatience, really and truly eschatological, borne on the wings of faith, hope and charity, and *therefore* impatient of everything temporal, dull, dense and heavy, everything trammelling. Unfair, of course, to our fleeting, yet "given" Creation, but still far removed from nihilistic, demonic repudiation.

Both these elements may well be found in Christian ascesis— not in principle, but as an historical phenomenon—according to motives and personal dispositions. The neo-Platonic denial seems to me (like the Hindu) more negative; but even the puritanical brand is, in its upper fringes, no longer purely Manichean, but at least ambiguous.

*

IT is dawning on me: that very disquieting tendency of Boehme- schooled minds (*and* Graham Greene!) to justify evil—the deep places, the slimy darkness, the disreputable and scandalous —it might be, in its ultimate depth, an infinitely pathetic attempt to accept, to embrace, the *entire* universe, i.e. every existence willed (or permitted!) by God, even in its most puzzling and repulsive aspects—thus forcing it to yield the secret, shining core which must, *must* somehow be hidden within it; an attempt to decipher, to detect, to reveal in what seems lost its essential transparence, its kinship with the Above. This might also lie behind the curious Hasidic challenge to penetrate into the Above and the Below, uniting the one with the other—to redeem the "captive sparks".

It's part of Bergengruen's fascination that in his books he has actually achieved this—at least to some extent—and in the most perfect way, in play, as it were, "on the light fantastic toe". Of course it makes one impatient, bitterly disappointed, to see the faint-heartedness of so many Christians, refusing to join in this vital task of retrieving, redeeming these "sparks", for fear of infection, of compromising themselves, of being misunderstood.

But is it possible to express this at all, except in the cipher of the Shekhinah and of the "sparks"? Is there any equivalent purely Christian myth? Yes, fairy-tales: *Beauty and the Beast, Allerleirauh, The Frog Prince,* etc. Christian? Not just Western? It would be important to know just when these stories originated, whether they are pre-Christian foreshadowings, or wonderful, naïve disguises for the story of the redemption. Actually this is also the problem in *Kranz der Engel* (Gertrud von Le Fort)—only here it has been transferred to the rational, moral plane where it is hardest to deal with—for which reason that attempt is a failure.

Badness is not only something to be fought against, refuted, crushed, but also illuminated (you hold dark amber against the light), ransomed, drawn into the transfiguration. . . . *De facto*, badness is not absolute, not evil in itself (having no being of its own, in good Thomist phraseology), but rather good subjected to evil, by curse, by spell, something disfigured, violated, which *can* be restored. . . . Not only man, but *everything* can be included in this process. I must try reading fairy-tales along these lines. I know the depth-psychologists have had lots to say about them, but from the Christian point of view they're still as good as unexplored.

❧ *1953—1954* ❧

1. BOOK PROVIDENCE

I'M reading Inagaki Sugimoto's *Daughter of the Samurai* again and marvelling how near this world really is, for all its distance. Mother's father must have been born in 1834—he died in 1910 at 76. Which means 34 years before the great Japanese revolution which put an end to the shogunate. Not only his childhood and youth, but his early manhood as well were, therefore, spent in feudalism roughly comparable to the Hohenstaufen era in Germany. But what I find so baffling is that amazing affinity, the almost sisterly likeness, between the civilization of Japan and our "Old World" (and there were certainly no "borrowings" or interchanges in this case). It must just be that the "Old World" really does express "human" values in *all* its cultural forms—which is what P. thinks is still keeping Antichrist at bay. What a pity that the new Japan should have turned so definitely towards America rather than to our own West, taking on their stamp as that of the whole white race as such!

*

JUDGING from Karl Rahner's *Kleines Kirchenjahr*, it really does seem as though "aridity", darkness and parched emotions in religious life are the chronic state of all the "better" sort of people in the Church, i.e. all really mature, adult Christians. Only children and people who refuse to grow up are dispensed and are allowed to play about in fragrant pastures. Probably because they're no use for anything else. But the others have taken upon themselves the burden of the world around them—or at least it has been laid upon their shoulders—like Simon of Cyrene. This is the *Christian* way of being "far from God".

*

Liebesbuch für Mädchen (a modern book about love for girls) : infinitely well-meaning, but two basic blunders. First of all, the pooh-poohing and tabooing of any physically distasteful aspect of sex—just as mistaken as the old-fashioned prudery was, and maybe even more injurious. For if girls go believing this sort of thing and then discover for themselves that there are some things they don't like, and that with the best will in the world they can't talk themselves into thinking everything in the garden is lovely—then they'll almost certainly end by thinking that there must be something wrong with them, that they're hopelessly and morbidly decadent, and develop awful inferiority complexes, or—if they force themselves into it—maybe become perverse. Secondly, the flat denial of *spiritual* love (platonic) which, after all, is an experimental fact and cannot just be written off as non-existent. Why must these people always go pouring out the baby with the bath-water?

*

RE-READING D. H. Lawrence, and feeling—as every time anew —as though I'd really understood him for the first time. He is a past master in the art of voicing the voiceless, the incommunicable—almost unbelievable, and how precisely he does it—terse, mordant, graphic, even colourful. Strange, incredible that he was only 45 when he died—how wise, how knowledgeable he was at that age! *Women in Love* was published as early as 1920, so he must have written it before he was 35. He just "knew" more than his own individual mind could contain—his was the consciousness of a whole hitherto unconscious class, emerging from obscurity; it is their dumb experience speaking out of him.

*

RE-READING Galsworthy's *Forsyte Saga*. For all its irony and aggressiveness, for all its sarcasm, it's still (unintentionally) a powerful apologia for wealth and possessions—property as the rock upon which all civilized human life is based. For it makes for leisure and detachment, providing barriers, so that things don't get so jumbled, providing privacy; in short, all the things which life these days threatens to sweep away. The romance itself is really rather stupid. A lot of fuss about nothing. Actually it's

Soames (intended as the villain of the piece) who's the only reasonably likable person in the whole family. Irene, supposed to be the attractive heroine, is too disgustingly selfish and vindictive. In the end, the whole book is really nothing but a direct attack against the "old" form of marriage—and not only against its abuses, against its very structure as well.

*

IN that sound little book of his on *Austerity and Vice* Fichtenau quotes and expounds St Augustine's prescription for curing by *contrasts—contraria contrariis*—and its applications. But wouldn't there be some homoeopathical way of curing souls as well?

*

KNOX's *Enthusiasm* is really fascinating. Very English—neither too "thorough" (in the professorial sense), nor too "profound" in the German—and, I suspect, not always *too* accurate either. But full of flashes of insight, humour, analogies, brilliantly apt wording. If I could write like this about Mary Ward . . . ! I found quite a lot of side-lights here, incidentally, although she herself isn't mentioned. But: *why* was she hounded so long by the suspicion and odium of heresy although they were never able to accuse her of it directly, and, in fact, never did? Surely not just to class her with other contemporary "cases"? As I see it, the reason lay in the *atmosphere* in England at the time—in Rome alone such a suspicion would never have arisen, or in Germany either, for that matter. But in seventeenth-century England, with Ranters and Quakers, etc., making themselves felt everywhere, anyone informed about these things must have perceived at least certain "family traits" common to their own types of sects: Inner Light, the notion of the invisible Church, lay and women preachers, "prophesyings" by women—all in all a highly suspect mixture. And even if she herself (though perhaps not necessarily!) was as good as ignorant of these things (would she otherwise have been *so* incautious??), the Jesuit General knew all there was to know, not only about the various brands of English illuminates, but about Port Royal too, Alumbrados, the Quietists and those notorious Ursuline nuns of Loudun. On no account did he wish to see his Fathers towed in the wake of

enthusiastic women penitents with an uncontrollable sense of
mission and a zest for reforming. What he seems not to have
known—the irony of it!—was how firmly in tow *she* was in
obedience to one of his own sons.

*

I'VE been reading lots of de Lubac during the past few days.
Astringent, invigorating—like a cold bath and exercises afterwards. Strenuous, but it does one good. This curious Gallic combination of glowing intellect and crystal-cool emotion—just the
opposite of what one so often finds with us : ice-cold thought and
white-hot sentiment. I can well understand young Fr X's
enthusiasm about the spiritual climate in France. The book I'm
concerned with just now—a lengthy treatise called *Le Surnaturel*—
deals with a wealth of the most abstruse specialist's material on
medieval and baroque theological wrangles about the most subtle
and intricate subjects, much of which is beyond me—but how
stimulating those undercurrents are, deep, strong, with those
quaint discussions drifting on the surface like strangely-formed
water-lilies! I can sense the profound, intense *engagement* underneath. And all the time, between the lines, lights keep flashing
out—asides perhaps, not directly intended, but none the less
important and exciting, for me. The whole complex : liberty and
grace, and the thesis, as passionately affirmed as furiously rejected, that the *capacity to sin* is *essential* to every created spirit
during its earthly pilgrimage—because it is created for freedom :
labilitas, fragilitas, vertabilitas, defectio. Part of man's *being*, not
just by chance ill-luck, or as damage inflicted from outside.
What surprises me most of all is my own spontaneous reaction—
I use it like a little magnifying glass to examine general statements. I find my innermost self protesting indignantly, offended
even, against the recognition that man is and *must* be fallible by
nature and of necessity; and how utterly convinced I am, pig-
headed in the face of all arguments, at least of the *potential* perfection of human nature, always expecting it, begging for it!—
and my consternation, my shattering disillusionment (the same
every time!) when someone admired or esteemed or loved
shows his—real nature. Ah, not even in wickedness, simply his
defectiveness. Every time it's as though an angel falls—an

incredible, terrible catastrophe, something un-natural, something which should never really happen, even in its minor occurrences a calamity—anything, anything but just "the nature of things".

Tout être raisonnable est libre, et toute liberté créée est peccable. The latter a basic maxim of both the Fathers and St Thomas. Here I scent an analogy with the Cabbalistic doctrine of the "creation of Evil" on the second day of Creation—when as yet only the spheres of light and darkness existed. To think that a tract full of scholastic theology should proffer me the key to something so very remote! But that's the odd way my thoughts work—over my own head, so to speak. Thoughts can differ as much as a raindrop and a root, but, if they meet, then growth ensues. Good and consoling. Another thing I find very exciting is that the idea of the *superadditum* was originally used *in a negative sense*—not for grace, but for the "garment of skins"—antithesis of the "garment of glory".

*

I READ the Wisdom of Solomon right through to the end today (I'm ashamed to say for the first time!). Very strange those passages about the plagues of Egypt, the "swarms of brute beasts" here, the night of death—quite different from Exodus. From what sources does all this spring—or not sources at all, but apocryphal symbol-spun legends which we can no longer decipher?

*

GRAHAM GREENE recognizes and understands supernatural evil, but not supernatural good, which he depicts as mere "virtue".

*

I READ two thrillers last week: Dorothy Sayers' *Whose Body?* and *A Gun for Sale* by Graham Greene. What a difference between the two! Dorothy Sayers: despite the grim case (murder, after all!) amusing in the extreme, a clever game of brains around a preposterous fable, brilliant, frothy dialogue, Lord Peter at his best and not the slightest hint at possible fun passes unnoticed.

But with Graham Greene there's not a trace of humour—not even a smile—stark, naked tragedy—yet miles apart from those stupid American thrillers where horrors, cruelty and hair-raising shocks are simply used as *art pour l'art*, heaped at random on top of a very indifferent plot. Even in this book—which only ranks among his "entertainments" and isn't one of his serious novels —he touches on the most profound and poignant human problems: what is guilt? who is guilty? and whose fault is it? what is a "born criminal"? That boy, Raven—a variant of, or perhaps a sketch for, Pinkie in *Brighton Rock*?—son of a drunkard and a suicide, straight from the orphanage into the gang (was there ever a *real* character like Kite, "teacher" of both Raven and Pinkie?). Then, after Kite is killed, he becomes a venal assassin, hired by industrialists to murder a statesman somewhere in Central Europe (Prague?), to start a war—paid (a very appropriate symbol) in forged notes—which puts the police on his tracks. And the one good girl, the first of that species he ever encountered—the first creature to treat him like a human being, arousing tremendous expectations in him—well, she just hands him over to the police, conscientiously, dutifully, like the good girl she is.

*

A WHOLE series of "signals": that Mexico film, D. H. Lawrence's *Lost Girl*—quite a few in Tolstoy's *War and Peace* (Natasha and Anatole!), and now these nasty Stefan Zweig novels. One theme really, all the way through, differently disguised each time: unfounded love, love for a worthless object— muddy puddle-mirrors of divine love, so tragic, yet so pathetic, for here—for me—God's love seems somehow to shine out more clearly than in descriptions of happier, well-deserved love—where the inexpressible paradox of divine love for sinners doesn't strike one nearly so forcibly. Maybe, after all, it was the *Jew* in Stefan Zweig who wrote this—telling more than he was aware —and not *only* the decadent Viennese *littérateur*, versed in all the tricks of the trade—but even in the turbid swamp of his novelist's fantasy, the supreme mystery of the World Above is mirrored out of unfathomable depths. For God *so* loved the world, yes, so much. Curious, by the way (and certainly unintentional), that in all these stories it's the women who personify Agape, even if they haven't the faintest inkling of this.

Frau X. might well be capable of something of this kind incidentally—I'm afraid one shouldn't keep on lecturing her with appeals to her good sense. It might be that she is destined for something better, something rarer. That's what is puzzling me, what makes me so ashamed: this poor little "lost" woman *never* condemns anyone, even when she knows and sees through it all, even where the weakness, sin and stupidity of other people, of men, have made such a mess of her life. Doesn't that make up for quite a lot of muddled thinking?

*

RONALD KNOX's *Creed in Slow Motion*: not nearly so good as his *Mass in Slow Motion*. But all the same I've come to love this book for the one (patristic?) idea he puts across rather cautiously, almost shamefacedly: the Psalms—indeed the whole Bible— are full of the praise sent up to God by the mountains, stars, etc. —how can this be by Nature "inanimate"? Yet this is not just a manner of speaking, for this echo of love is really the Holy Ghost himself, perpetually flowing back in thanksgiving and longing from God's "second Son"—Creation—to the Father, even as he flowed from him. What a wonderful thought—how bold, and yet how natural!—strange really, that I should only stumble across this truth now. . . .

*

KARL RAHNER's unpublished Assumption book. This extra- ordinary knife-edge precision—is it a special gift, is it *art pour l'art*? Or is it simply a device to ensure soundness in the "embodiment" of religious thought? According to Georg Volk, even a slightly damaged nerve can cause a lasting deform- ity, e.g. instead of a nail, a mis-shapen cuticle will grow, no matter how often you cut it away. Perhaps the same thing applies to things of the mind, i.e. that out of seemingly unimportant, but faulty, premises, wrong inferences keep on growing, like weeds. And just because these insignificant, peripheral, scarcely heeded thoughts can grow in such rank profusion, theologians must be so insistent in their concern for the correctness and precision of all such statements.

*

A ZADDIK of Buber's loved the cheerful sinner in his community best of all—because "the basest form of pleasure still mirrors divine joy, whereas even the noblest sorrow is a consequence of sin".

*

I've started on Franz von Baader. In Schelling's (first) appreciation of him I chanced upon what is surely the most wonderfully apt description of NN.—*cum grano salis*, of course: "I know a man, subterranean by nature, in whom knowledge has become as much substance and concrete existence, as in metals sound and light have become solid matter. He does not *know*, being himself a living, ever-mobile, complete personification of *knowledge*."

Baader's interpretation of that Jewish and Jakob Bochme speculation about Adam's double temptation seems for the first time to make sense of the doctrine to me: for here Eve is not—as Hahn thinks—*punishment* for Adam's spiritual and mental Fall into the animal world, but, on the contrary, his *salvation* from this temptation. One could well enlarge on this still further, and say she was given him as the incarnation of Sophia (= the first spouse of Man), the first, earliest, very faintest foreshadowing of *the* Incarnation—as the visible manifestation of grace. In Eve Adam finds himself facing no alien nature, but his own substance, his own heart in bodily presence—to be chosen, to be loved, and giving herself to him—instead of one of the fawning, extraneous creatures. What depth here!

Marc Oraison's interpretation of the Fall fits in perfectly at this point: *superbia*, yes, but *realized* by the arbitrary seizing of the Creator-power in sex—instead of waiting for the hour appointed by God.

*

Peter Pan, film and book—strange that this should rank as a children's story, a classic even, like *Alice*. In point of fact it's an extremely astute, subtle, melancholy, almost cynical book:

wrapped up in a playfully contrived fairy tale is Barrie's gently mocking analysis of the Eternal Male—in the specific form of the dashing and brilliant youth, who refuses to grow up and settle down—always escaping from home, mother and mothering— "Adventure" the permanent form of his flight from every tie, which is precisely what makes him so attractive to the "womanly" girl, who tries every ruse to lure him into security and domesticity—which attract her as much as they repel him. He's always toying with these things, nibbling at them, only to disentangle himself again, and it's just this game of homesickness, longing and flight which makes the whole thing so piquant for him. No, anything but a book for children! Astonishing, really, that the depth-psychologists haven't pounced on it long ago— that scene, for instance, where Wendy tells the little lost boys on the Robinson island "the story of the mothers"—and Peter Pan's tirade about the betrayal of mothers! Or where he returns to her out of his wild woods after three times seven years, ageless, eternally young—Pan and Cupid in one—and then woos her daughter—who falls for him just as her mother did as a child— generations come and go, he himself remains, always the same. This is more than a made-up fairy story—it's almost a real one.

*

THE German translation of Sven Stolpe's novel *Sacrament* in MS. Strange how very different the spiritual climate of the Church is in different countries! One German publisher has turned it down already, as too unreal, negative in its approach to life, etc. Not much hope for it, I'm afraid, in the German Catholic world of today: reviewers would certainly unanimously condemn it as old-fashioned, cramped and (of course) "Manichean". And the French would probably call it *bourgeois*, individualist, ivory tower, etc., unruffled by contemporary social problems. I find it a provocative testimony to the picture Catholic reality presents to a man emerging from the veritable jungle of our age, unencumbered by any Christian tradition. He sees it from afar, but (for this very reason) he sees it *right*. He looks at it the way an early Christian convert would see it, his eyes neither dulled nor irritated by too close proximity, by habit or by detail.

That couple in his story, standing on the edge of the mountain? They gaze down at Vézelay, lying there below them, in pure, sweeping lines, raised against the sky's infinity, no blemish, no break to mar the eye's clear view. And what does the pilgrim behold in this radiant vision? The other world, the ascetic—and the rational—element. He beholds the sublime affirmation of the Invisible and the sublime negation of the Devil, the Flesh and the World—and a new clarity, light and trust for the mind of man, aware of his communion with the Divine Spirit—all things of which he had hitherto never dreamed. Which is why he's so overwhelmed by things like convents, deliberate choice of virginity, voluntary chastity, liturgy, cult, and the great classical theology. The whole book is really a hymn to just these things. He sees it all in pristine freshness, and he finds it wonderful. For us the pseudo-spiritualism of the nineteenth century, the unreal rejection of the world (out of sheer weakness) has blurred our vision, and when we do catch a glimpse of the original, it hardly seems genuine any more. We're so fed up with insipid repetitions and poor reproductions that the real thing no longer "takes".

Yet, for all that, Stolpe is no spiritualist. He devalues nothing which belongs to the normal good things of life—neither beauty nor tenderness, art, science, nature, the simple pleasures of existence—he only shows that everything, really *everything* can still be outsoared in an elemental, upsurging flame of love.

Which is, perhaps, why genuine "pagans", i.e. people with a vital, naïve, unhampered approach to life (natural or decadent), are rarely shocked or put off by true ascesis when they are converted: on the contrary, they're attracted by this. For the first time in their lives they prepare to take the jump—in wonder and in joy, not in fear—the leap over the visible and tangible, that wonderful, incomparable Icarus flight. As for us, latter-day Christians of Germany (and perhaps of France, too?), the first lesson when we are "converted" is to learn anew "the humility of the flesh", gratitude for our simple existence as human beings here on earth—to conquer that insincere, arrogant pseudo-spirituality of our Catholic ghetto.

*

2. MARRIAGE, EROS, WOMAN

How significant that our Lord should have spoken of marriage as "two in one flesh", and not "one in two bodies". For that would be something quite different. The former ensures the inviolability of the individual as a person, even when fused in the densest tissue of life-flesh: it is still always *two* people who experience this union, each time anew, and it doesn't matter that they are two, as long as their "one flesh" is recognized and not ruptured. Even in such marriage as consumes and exhausts itself merely in a union lasting as long as flesh endures (which, after all, is our allotted span on earth). Maybe for many couples this form of marriage is really sufficient and complete—as task and achievement—and when it is done, they have done with it, are acquitted and discharged. Those who, *beyond this*, have become one in spirit as well, carry this union across into eternity. Yet it seems to me that this is by no means *essential* to marriage, which, as an "earthly" institution, is more modest in its demands. Rather it is a superadded grace, something which, though it might have been lacking at the start, yet grew up and flowered out of the mysterious soil of the sacrament, transforming and fulfilling marriage with love. Our modern Catholic prattle about marriage takes much too much for granted, in assuming love to belong to marriage as a matter of course, a prerequisite even, as though marriage without this element were something inferior, doomed to failure from the start. Just the same as all that hot air they keep talking about "womanly" jobs for girls, appealing to and appeasing their feminine instincts, etc. What disillusionment *must* follow such exaggerations! Expectations—and demands—screwed up to high tension, artificially, and quite unnecessarily too.

*

IN marriage, too, it is God who determines my role, not I myself. Perhaps one is nowhere else so autocratic, or at least would like to be, wanting to lay down the law on just what the other person is to "have" in one, to set one's *persona** for him. And probably it's part of our training in love that this

---

* *Persona* in the sense of C. G. Jung is the ego-figure of my ego as I want other people to see and appreciate me.

never succeeds, and that one has to put up with standing poor and naked before him, anything but the fulfilment of his dreams! Here, again, is that problem of merit and grace, and in the end one comes to see what is just as true of our relation to God (of which marriage is the most impressive mirror) : that love consists in uncomprehending, grateful, wondering acceptance of love ever undeserved, never to be "earned"—love that is grace. For what *is* grace but simply loving for its own sake, without "getting anything out of it"?

The claim to be all in all for another—is this not virtually a claim to divinity—or almost? What human being could be so presumptuous, and who may accept such a challenge? Surely this is just another proof of what X. said that day in Schloss Solitüde: that Eros really embodies "Advent", expectation of God? Yes, but, if so, no one can *demand* that this Light be reflected only in himself, that the beloved behold it in no other mirror, that he smash all the other mirrors in his life. St Francis de Sales defines jealousy as the expression of a violent but impure love. Does he know how it can be purified, I wonder? Or must it die slowly—in its own festering sore, as it were—burning, oozing out, the way a wound cleanses itself before it heals?— or, alas, until the whole body has been poisoned to death?

Jealousy corresponds with desire; where there is no desire, only good-will ungrudging, one no longer nurses jealousy. Where the physical ego is not engaged—or no longer engaged—jealousy manifests a claim, a claim unmet, and it is the third party, the rival, who, entering on the scene, deflects and attracts that yearning to himself. Or is the core of jealousy one's own sense of inadequacy, of not coming up to the mark? And its sting in the fear that the rival would seem to offer exactly what one lacks oneself? Here jealousy would be despair resigned or rebellious.

*

A visit from YY. who was shocked by a lecture she'd heard in which old symbolic images, such as the eye, etc., had been used to interpret "knowledge", in its double meaning. Surely there is, basically, only *one* single vital function, omnipresent, divided into stages or phases: encounter, contact, fusion, exchange, fruitfulness—extending over various planes and through various media: beholding, listening, smelling, tasting, breathing, eating, embrace, knowledge, artistic conception and birth, prayer, rising even to *unio mystica*: are all these not *one* structure, *one* process, *one* scale of variations? Whatever is wrong or offensive about knowing this, or stating it openly?

*

Wort und Wahrheit has published a long review (more of a synopsis really) of the last number of *Etudes Carmélitaines*. Sex —Eros—Mysticism. Very clever, very erudite, but—to my mind—just missing the point. For one thing it seems to me questionable and misleading to translate *continence* as *Keuschheit*. Just like Germans to muddle the difference! And then, the reviewer seems to keep confusing sex with Eros. These "modern" Catholics are unable to get away from prudery as their *starting point* for every discussion (having a guilt complex on that score, feeling open to blame and justifiable reproach), which is about the worst line they could take. You can't shift everything into the proper position just by contradicting contradictions! Furthermore, they stare as though hypnotized at the crudely biological aspect: "Nature" for them, which must be justified at all costs against the "disparagement" of the old days. But both reactions are inept, both hamper fair and square judgment. This discussion doesn't even focus genuine Eros, on which, after all, the whole problem hinges. But, above all, the whole approach is wrong from the outset, trying to explain and to interpret sex from *below* instead of from above. This seems, to me, the fundamental error of the whole debate. In their eyes the biological facts are the basic, original thing, which may—and ought to be—reflected and repeated and sublimated on a rising scale of analogies, each feebler and less real as they are "elevated": instead of beginning with the phenomenon of divine and spiritual love and fecundity, watching it descend into countless manifestations, each slighter and dimmer, hardening and narrowing down to the very specific bodily analogue—yet recognizable in every rung of the ladder. If I could only say this properly!

*

106

I FOUND something wonderful today: a cutting from some book on art or ethnography, showing two Shiva-Shakti groups. The eternal nuptial embrace of the gods. (I well know that there are other representations as well, pretty ghastly ones, but I'm not concerned with these here.) But I've never seen anything like this before, and marvel at the beauty, purity and serenity of these figures, especially of the seated pair: Vajradha (whoever that may be) with Shakti. Nothing in the least offensive, or embarrassing. Nothing even faintly obscene. No hint of lust or anything gross: only a wonderful solemnity and simplicity—everything so clear, unselfconscious, so calm and composed, so full of peace. Two beings, sunk in one another in the deepest contemplation—really "knowledge". Nothing lubricious about it, nothing suggestive. No trace of constraint. As natural, as pure, as children asleep. Compared with *this*—alas!—Bernini's St Teresa is crude and coarse, so loud—so revoltingly outspoken. It is the *tranquillity*, the absolute stillness, which makes this Hindu work so moving: ". . . almost a star, ever-circling, so are we". "Turned to a cloud, the lovers drifted. . . ." Or perhaps, as in the *Sonnets from the Portuguese*:

> When our two souls stand up erect and strong,
> Face to face, silent, drawing nigh and nigher,
> Until the lengthening wings break into fire
> At either curving point. . . .

But these verses mean only the *souls*. This is the same thing in shape, in sculpture, and I feel a touch of sadness to think that among Christians, aware as we are—or ought to be—of marriage as a *sacrament*, and of the tremendous weight of symbolism attaching to nuptial love, such representations would be utterly *inconceivable* (even if they could be achieved, which is equally hard to imagine!)—and probably most of one's friends, even the finest people with a really mature outlook, would find such attempts intolerable. Can one imagine a Christian artist venturing to illustrate the Song of Songs with pictures like this? He couldn't help giving the impression of blasphemy—or at the very least of ludicrously bad taste, exorbitant, just "impossible".

*

ADDENDUM to my manuscript on celibacy. There is yet another relationship between "apostolic" women and priests. Mary Ward is the prime example. The woman for whom the priest is her *animus* figure, in the strongest, most intimate sense, not just in general, as man, or as masculine type, but specially: as the embodiment of her very own dreams, dreams she knows can never be realized, since she herself can never be a priest. And so she sees the "exemplary" priest as her deputy, leading her own life by proxy, as it were, representing the whole purpose of her life. The bond between many of the saints must surely be seen thus, not as "spiritual matrimony", as it is often so inappropriately termed; this would really only apply to St Francis de Sales and Jeanne. For marriage implies being *personally* there for each other, within its own intimate sphere, whereas relationships like these cannot be classified or compared with any other sociological model—they are a *modus per se*.

*

SURPRISING really how much outright contempt for women you often find among priests—sheer "biological" prejudice, they just don't *count*! Yet you'd think that the priest, meeting women all the time in the religious sphere, women, in their relation to God, in all their needs, of faith and of conscience, ought to find it easy to appreciate and accept them as persons, as "souls".

*

Amare amare: quite different from loving the *Du*, the "Thou". Love and art: whom and what does the artist love?—his subject? painting? his picture? Isn't the subject quite often just the thing which starts him off, to be discarded after a while? Can he not (see the moderns) get along quite happily without a subject at all? The same parallel exists in religion: you can be in love with religious life—with its pursuits and experiences, with religious situations and moods—without loving God. Surely there's no more powerful or subtle stimulus to self-enjoyment than "piety"? Religion, plus love: what a mixture for dope!— the very drug for one's ego. Perfectly legitimate on the one hand: two transparencies blending into one, until the screen seems to dissolve so dazzlingly that you feel you are touching it

108

already—it? Beatitude itself! But wrong on the other hand, for, before you know it, this experience becomes itself the hinge on which everything else turns. Here marriage is the second form of "Christian Utopia". Which is why marriage, and religion, must necessarily exist (at least in stretches) in darkness and in drought—to show the difference between the real thing and just "being in love".

*

IT's very suspect and not the stamp of unselfish and devoted love to keep wanting—and forcing—the other person to *need* one, always trying to be useful, in demand. Just one way of veiling the wish to be indispensable. Needing someone means being dependent upon him, in his hands, at his mercy, i.e. the dependence of the one corresponds to the power wielded by the other—a typically feminine form of domination, despite all assurances to the contrary. For it is the one who is "needed" who really has the whip hand, no matter how unassumingly and submissively he (or she) may seem to serve. He or she (this indispensable being) can keep the other person dangling, leave him in the lurch, whenever and for as long as he or, again, she likes, not vice versa, even if it happens to be "only" an indispensable servant or employee! And it turns a relationship between friends into a tie—but a very spurious one, for its bonds have been selfishly knotted—by both parties—out of just what most contradicts real love—calculation.

*

LOVE: the power of union—Dame Julian would say: oneing— and bearing fruit. Sex is the symbol which stands for it, *not* the thing itself.

*

"MASCULINE discretion": woman, as a whole, is essentially "open", made to receive and to transmit, both good and evil. Man, on the other hand, is "closed", in the same degree. Which is why so many couples have difficulties and disagreements about "sharing" (that Ransom novel!). She loves to share everything with her husband, or at least to talk it over—every little happening, no matter how trivial; but *he* wants his privacy. (There are, of course, wives who claim that you can enjoy yourself better at a party *without* your husband—and the very idea of having him around while you're having a baby makes their hair stand on end!) But, even for the woman, it takes wounding—bodily, mental—to dis-close her. . . .

Maybe even the attitude we call "open-mindedness" is different in men and women. You could say: because she is an "open" creature, she needs some kind of enclosure, of boundary round her; whereas he, being naturally shut up in himself, must open out into the world, to the world, filling it with himself, setting his stamp upon it. She must remain exposed, a man can always withdraw into himself, putting up his defences. A woman cannot help betraying that and what she has received and conceived, and even from whom; a man can conceal it, revealing it only indirectly in the objects of his encounter with the world.

*

TALK with Father W.: which special features mark the "likeness" to God in women, as the divine attributes of power, mind, domination, etc., are reflected in men? Perhaps beauty—joy—grace—love in its special shape of "gratuitous" love—as man must represent it in his own form: wooing, conquering, possessive, protective love?

*

WHY don't our convents attract more young people these days? Because the mystique of virginity no longer exists for us, it just isn't there any more—the *real* thing, that is, for the sort of "spouse" idea cherished by many good nuns isn't genuine, but simply an outworn, empty ideology, wrapped up like a mummy, in terminology obsolete for years. Or the unmarried state is "excused" by a lot of high-sounding talk about unhampered freedom for social work, charitable activity, etc., etc. But all these things are, in fact, really effects, not *causes*. We have no true mystique of virginity for the very simple reason that we have no mystique of marriage, i.e. love lived as unity *and* fruitfulness. And the "and" here is the important thing. If we cannot recapture the mystique of fruitfulness in marriage, then the other thing just doesn't make sense. We've already won our way back to a "new" understanding for marriage as the mystery of personal union, but there it seems to be stuck. The very people who've grasped this aspect have fashioned it into a highly emotion-ridden battering-ram against the "old-fashioned" view of marriage: "issue" as the "end" of matrimony. Now both these elements must be integrated. If we could succeed in realizing this, achieving *this* image as a presence in the world, complete, visible, then the true ideal of virginity would stand out plainly against this background: virginity as the mystery of *divine marriage*: love in oneness and fruitfulness *in ordine religionis*. No invention of mine, of course. The sparrows have been chirping this from the roof-tops for ages. The trouble is that what we mostly hear is "motherliness"—which sounds more "spiritual", more refined than plain, down to earth fecundity. And the whole point is lost in sloppy sentimentality (which colours our moral training here, too)—and as though all this only applied to women anyway—with the husband supposed to stand there, gazing from afar in awe and admiration!

*

IN Paradise, continence, St Thomas observes, would not have been praiseworthy, but simply a refusal of fertility for no reason. In the existing order, on the contrary, it is praiseworthy "not because it is infertile, but in consequence of the disorder of sexual lust, for in a state of innocence sexual union would have been fertile *but without lust*". The same teaching, according to C. S. Lewis, of the Doctors of the Church. But does this really mean a cold fecundity, devoid of all feeling? I can hardly believe it. Surely the *libido* itself would have been *ordinata* as well?

It would seem that medieval man found it hard, indeed well-nigh impossible, to believe in "pure" erotic love; yet I think they did not mean this solely in regard to the body, but had observed that, in nine cases out of ten, erotic love is mixed with a whole variety of other weaknesses, faults and sins. The Ancients were less inclined to abstractions than we imagine: they took the thing as a whole. I remember how struck I was by that passage in *Kristin Lavransdatter* where Kristin reflects on "all the sins *inherent* in love: defiance and disobedience, rancour and hardness of heart, obstinacy and pride"—and all these stem

111

from "the white-hot, consuming fire which fetters the whole being because it excludes all reason ", i.e. understanding, *ratio*, the reason which orders, clarifies—as they understood it in those days. In other words, this means simply that love stirs man to the very depths of his being, and this ground is very ambivalent indeed. If there were nothing dark and muddy to stir up here, then surely that rapture, that intoxication would be pure ecstasy—flight and not fall? We must distinguish between flesh become transparent—and flesh set up as an idol. A good many quite well-meaning people seem to confuse the two pretty frequently—and what an unholy mixture results from it!

*

IF marriages are going to remain deliberately sterile, then there is no longer any logical, conclusive argument against homosexuality.

*

BAADER* says: "In love, i.e. marriage, man should aid woman to rid herself of femininity as incompleteness (*Unganzheit*, nonwholeness), woman aiding man in the same way, so that the original archetype of mankind in its entirety may become inwardly manifest in both of them." I think this is very good: "Femininity as incompleteness", as a mere rudiment of human-ness, as stunted humanity—all this was surely a product of the development which ended with the nineteenth century. It was *the* caricature against which the "good" feminists' movement rose in revolt—their aim was to seek "woman as human", and to restore her: woman as human being, not as mere female. But that trend disintegrated quickly enough into the fake slogan: Woman as human *instead* of womanly, and, soon enough, the equation : man = woman : woman *as* man, in order to be human— see Simone de Beauvoir.

*

BAADER again: "In every union devoid of love sex is aped in its brute form." Nothing new, I know, a truism—but it is

---

* Franz von Baader (1765–1841). A highly original and eccentric Catholic thinker, now rather obsolete, who expressed his often startling insights in the most obscure language.

112

significant for me, all the same, inasmuch as it shows me, yet again, that every human union really is a mirror open to two possible reflections: from above or from below. Which is just why it is so degrading when it chooses to be an imitation of the lower kind: not even "exactly the same thing"—for this it *cannot* be—but rather a step lower, a caricature, a fake of brute mating, lacking that very originality which confers value and meaning on animal coupling.

*

IT's always taken for granted that physical motherhood is the whole point, the real thing, and its spiritual and intellectual counterpart just a pale, artificial analogy. . . . But maybe it's really the other way round, i.e. that physical birth is, in itself, but "image and likeness", in the same way as bodily love is symbol and image, and precisely in its symbolism, imagery, transparency lies its "real" value and meaning. Which is why this particular tangible "shape" is fading out of this world of ours, perishing, disappearing, abandoned by its *spirit*. It just cannot exist among humans by itself, merely on the animal plane.

*

SOMETHING or other in that book of Albert Mirgeler's*about Europe set me thinking again about "courtly love", the *Frauendienst* of chivalry—an extraordinary phenomenon, not to be compared with any other form of love: that sudden, brief, flashing epiphany of luminous "Eternal Womanhood" in a densely male world. This was no culmination, flowering, double or sublimation of the "dark" Mother Image, but rather a radiant counter-figure, floating down, as it were, from above. Visible only for men, and, therefore, never to be "achieved" or developed by women—and certainly never to be claimed as her due or her right—for if a woman is seen and beheld as "Grace", then it is because she has received grace herself: *gratia plena, quia respexit Dominus ancillam suam.*

*

* *Geschichte Europas*, Freiburg, 1953 (3rd edn. 1958).

THREE booklets about Maria Goretti (one by an American, one German, and one translated from the Dutch)—one more awful than another. And now I must consider the phenomenon in itself.

Is Maria Goretti really a martyr of *chastity*, of purity? I'd rather say of the *Law*, in the sense of Ps. 118: of obedience and of simple, living faith. Decisive that she should have heard that sermon in Netto just before, in which the priest, speaking of Christ's Passion, said: "Whoever commits a mortal sin crucifies Jesus anew!" That places her obedience in a sphere different from mere conventional morals, or so-called "fear" of the law; or also from an exclusive or even a predominant devotion to *chastity*. For this child would naturally have reacted in exactly the same way had she been asked to keep watch for a burglar or to swear a false oath.

Lewdness assaulted her in the most terrifying, threatening form, crude—*un brutto peccato*—not as "seduction", as far as heaven or hell from any impulse of love or even captivation of the senses, just filthy and sordid—no hint of allurement, without the slightest response from her side: can one really talk of a martyrdom of purity or chastity here?

I wish I knew of some "real" martyrdom for chastity, i.e. that a human being had renounced love of the body, unto death, for Christ's sake? Silly question. Of course this is the typical, focal point of the "unbloody martyrdom" of virginity. Which is why, in contrast to its bloody counterpart, it remains a secret—for no one could possibly guess it except the lovers themselves. (This, too, could be a martyrdom of obedience, "as the law decreed".) For some early martyrs, such as Agnes, Dorothy, etc., it was always a case of resistance against un-chastity—never, as far as I know, resistance against the seduction of love. But probably such instances could be found as well. Difficult to control, to relate events in this sphere, though, for the very sin itself can hardly be assessed—see our Lord's words about looking at a woman "so as to lust after her". Besides, it seems too narrow, to my mind, to limit the meaning of this passage merely to "sins of thought"; I think it applies rather to the sensuality of the soul, which can be just as intense as that of the body—and which, presumably, is just what makes up the particular sinfulness of such bodily lust—otherwise it would be just a rather trivial variant of gluttony. Yet chastity is really something more than *just* fasting. Nor can I quite see how (according to Pieper = Thomas) it can be just a variant of temperance. For in that case it would be motivated, and valued, merely by morals (almost hygienic!)—not linked at all with the great mystery of Eros. Could one put it this way: *temperantia* = chastity is only the substructure, the first step towards "holy" chastity?

*

RECOGNITION of truth seems always to be receptive, acquiring, conceiving: but at the same time it is conquering, piercing, instilling: so the human mind is androgynous too. Facing Truth it is "feminine", receiving, accepting; facing the World: transmitting, representing, materializing Truth—it is virile, fighting.

*

SOMETIMES I think men view their capacity to make money as a sort of potency (which is even a connotation of the German word for fortune, *Vermögen*). Being im-potent in money-making is felt to be a symptom of weakness, a lack of virility. And to experience weakness is always humiliating. Another side-light on the problem of career-wives. . . .

*

So much is written and talked these days about the "revolt against the father-image" (not paternalism only, but against all it stands for). Yet I'm inclined to think sometimes that the revolt against the mother-image is far more wide-spread, and far more ominous, just because it is less noticeable. It's the *daughters* who are rebelling: against the old ideal of the mother, against the ideal of their own mothers, against the lot of their own mothers—conditional and unconditional; the itch, the claim to "have things better", protest against the mother's fate, against motherhood, primary and secondary, bodily and spiritual —and so against qualities, standpoints and methods of training which induce this, building it up.

Rebellion against the mother, against motherhood, is rebellion against what is feminine in the world. Which accounts for the curiously strong antipathy towards devotion to our Lady,

115

since Mary is the archetype of everything feminine in the world, *the* epiphany of woman—irremovable, indissoluble. All pretence that such aversion is rooted in the silly kind of exaggerated, sentimental veneration of our Lady is, in the main, just a rational attempt to justify this deep-rooted, unconscious impulse. And from this cause, as well, stems at least part of the revolt against the *Church* from within herself: in the name of immediate, untrammelled access to God—even in the name of Christ himself.

So the whole human race must be in revolt? It would seem so. Clear enough if you think of the refusal of the double decree: "In the sweat of thy brow"; and the pangs of child-birth, and "He shall be thy lord". Flight from the land and "birth strike", the ever-swelling Utopia of affluence and ease—all symptoms of the same thing. And, since very real sin leads itself *ad absurdum*, the first brings its own punishment in the present-day "total working world", with manager-disease in all colours and sizes, no Sundays and no leisure; and for the second sin we have a sex-ridden world in which woman is more the slave of man than ever she was, so much so that outside of sex she can no longer see any point in life, any justification for existence.

*

How little the mystery of Mary is really understood is evident in the kind of fanatical Marian devotion which claims "equal rights" for our Lady: Mary = co-redemptress with Christ, the Redeemer; Mary = Mediatrix of all graces beside Christ, the Mediator; Mary = the Queen beside Christ, the King.

*

PINSK'S* article in *Michael*: Marian devotion, so he writes, is not a specifically Catholic feature; it is just as appropriate for Protestant Christians. The real differences lie in the doctrines of the Creation and of the Church. But this is surely only true when Mary is seen merely as an historical figure: the mother of Jesus, the maiden from Nazareth?

* Johannes Pinsk: Well known in Germany for his books on the liturgy and a leading figure in the liturgical movement. His *Towards the Centre of Christian Living* has been translated into English and published in 1961.

De Lubac's insight goes deeper (the final chapter of his *Méditations sur l'Eglise*)*: the extraordinary parallels between Marian doctrine and that of the Church, in the course of history, too: how they rise and fall together, both growing clear or fading, the precise interpretation and even the exaggerations. And I'm sure it could as well be proved that the figure of Mary is just as closely linked with the doctrine of the Creation, for these three subjects—Mary, Creation, Church—are simply three transparencies held against one another. Probably Sophia—the "feminine" image of Logos—stands behind each. The Feast of the Immaculate Conception proclaims the "immaculate" origin of Creation before the Fall, just as the Feast of the Assumption represents the mystery of the New Earth after the transfiguration of the Church and, in an orthodox sense, the *Ave Maria* can well be addressed to the Church too.

What a pity that statement of the good old apocryphal tradition—ranging from The Book of James to Anne Catherine Emmerich—that Joseph was a widower with sons should have been so definitely dropped! Probably only since some "spiritualist" (Manichean?) group or other felt they must at all costs hold up St Joseph as a virgin. Yet what simpler, more beautiful, more plausible explanation could there be for the "brethren of Jesus" who seem to exact such an unconvincing display of philological acrobatics? And, from the human angle alone, how much rather one would think of our Lord growing up among a crowd of brothers and sisters, rather than as an only child—difficult to imagine such a thing in that archaic, ancient society!

*

To "bear" is womanlike. Or maybe you could put it the other way round: the female, the feminine is what bears, is destined to bear, to bear with, to carry burdens. So her place *must* be "below", at the bottom = "fundamental", isn't that obvious? Woman must be somehow "lower" than man, more "lowly". Not in value, simply in function. *Humilis* really does mean on the ground, low. But if you are to bear, you must accept a burden, and people run away from burdens these days. There's nothing they hate more than to be burdened or tied. This accounts for

* *The Splendour of the Church*, London and New York, 1957.

117

this perverse cult of youthfulness: youth is in itself the *yet* unburdened state—so we worship youthful looks as the sign and symbol of that craving, almost the promise of its fulfilment. But to attempt to keep it for ever only leads to sterility in every sense: monstrous perversion of youth, destined as blossom of the fruit. . . .

Is that why so many "little" saints are canonized these days, humble ones, *humiles*, almost anonymous, symbols of the bearing of burdens, of loads accepted willingly, voluntarily? According to the principle of the tightrope dancer in Buber's story: "Whenever you feel yourself toppling over to one side, lean to the other!"?

Charles de Foucauld only wanted to lay foundations, nothing more, leaving the building and "establishing" to others. His followers go "underground" and want to stay there, purposely not "rising", even when the chance presents itself and they could be much more "useful". No, like mothers, they are simply "present".

*

Pius X had a definitely motherly function in the Church: "feeding" the faithful. (The motherly function of the priest: to feed, to cleanse and to forgive.)

*

Seasickness—nausea, disgust!—is caused by the "ground" rocking, reeling, turning upside down *and* downside up! (which is actually the very process of vomiting). Here "the people" appear as a parallel to women. They don't want to be "lowly" any more, they refuse to be burdened, downtrodden, anonymous, obscure—but rather the opposite of it all. It seems these are states to be *chosen* nowadays, since they are no longer accepted as decreed and taken for granted. Of course the burden really goes on in the revenge of distorted ideas: in the enslavement (never more relentless) of the working world, even of the so-called "free" professions and easier forms of work, as well as in the lot of the career-wife, doubly burdened with job and family, a phenomenon which, though so widely condemned, seems to have come to stay.

And this is why only through a new, *fundamental imitatio Christi* as God's "servant" (Ph. 2. 7–8) a kind of salvation could come.

Democracy insists on "self-government" of the people by projecting and representing itself, instead of being governed by a "representative of God". And so we have the "little man", the upstart come to power, as the most ruthless despot. There's so much talk these days about man torn out of his environment, uprooted, unsettled, damaged himself, as well as destructive. But who is willing to be "ground" any more, foundation, firm, stable, quiet ground, soil in which others could take root and settle?

Newman, too, had to descend into the "cave", dwelling in obscurity, oblivion, inactivity, so as to "lay the ground" for the century to come, to be himself the foundation, corner-stone, basis of a new future.

*

FIRMAMENT and fundament are related—as "the waters above" and "the waters beneath". In the beginning they were one, the solid Earth and the solid vault God called Sky (like man and woman??). In Mary's assumption into heaven they become one again: the handmaid, lowly, bearing, burdened by her life on earth—and the Queen of the World.

*

THE men who laugh at the emancipation of women would do well to reflect that the most unwomanly women rank high among the all too credulous and faithful disciples and even imitators of the women-scoffers. They've learnt only too well from the men to despise women as inferior, contemptible creatures, etc. On the other hand, some of them have come to their senses—the better sort—refusing to accept their masters' view as gospel any longer and to identify themselves obediently with those objects of male cynicism. That they've jumped from the frying pan into the fire here is another story.

It is a pity that priests should look down so on women, despising them, in a good-natured sort of way, but all the same. . . . For them only the lowest, crudest type of woman is really genuine and natural—in good, and in evil, too—and any woman who is "different" is rated at once as unwomanly, even degenerate. Women, in their eyes, are either kittens, shrews or servants. How *can* they appreciate the archetype of woman in Mary, in the Church? Yet in every raw and lopsided lump of a man, no matter how biased or dense, *we* are expected to see and to honour, willy-nilly, the Man, with all the implications of the First Image. This has led to that other curious form of Marian devotion—a poor, stunted attitude: our Lady simply as paradox, chosen and elevated not *because* but *although* she was a woman; only because God wanted to teach a lesson to the strong, i.e. to man—to humiliate him!

*

CANDLEMAS. The actual "process" of birth really does extend over 40 days, so that it's quite fitting and proper to keep the Crib until then, commemorating Christmas. Is not Simeon the last counterpart of Abraham? the old man carrying the Child, the Son, in his arms—into the Temple? Surely everything offered in the Temple, offered up, "lifted", as Buber says, is sacrifice? What is the origin of the ancient idea (see breviary) that Simeon was a very old man, *had to be old*? And Anna, the prophetess, is a very mysterious figure, too: two old people from Jerusalem, man and woman, the *Nunc dimittis* of the Old Dispensation— which ought to have then receded, to make way for its own rebirth in the Son.

*

FATIMA, the miracle of the sun: surely this is the ancient symbol of the whirling wheel of fire which Ezechiel saw in his day, and Brother Klaus? Thousands have seen it, dozens of people have written about it. Odd that no one, as far as I know, has yet suggested this key. According to Alfons Rosenberg the turning wheel is the symbol of change, of return, rebirth and eternal life.

*

DECEMBER 8. *Nondum erant abyssi, et ego iam concepta eram.* How significant that Mary–Sophia, heavenly archetype of everything womanlike, is earlier, more ancient than the abyss, the earthly feminine counter-image—chaos, sea, the dark tellurian primeval mother.

3. FAITH, THE CHURCH, SPIRITUAL LIFE

THE sins of our educational system (Catholic) : How we ourselves were wronged by it and how we wronged others in its name. What people call "moral training" is really a political activity— representing a particular community and its "vested interests", which is why it is so liable to political sins and blunders.

It took the monstrous caricature of totalitarian education to show us how little religious and how very political our own "Catholic" education was—and probably to a large extent still is. Its aim was direct, tangible *success*—something which could be registered—with results all planned beforehand, mapped out down to the last detail, everything nicely calculated, nothing left to chance—and as little as possible to the oh, so incalculable and often so unplausible intervention of God. Based on distrust instead of confidence, as G. once said so bitterly : "On the *canaille* element in human nature". Pupils are gauged as "material", the main feature is pliancy, they must be easy to handle, easy to manage. This kind of education is mainly precautionary and prophylactic, set on avoiding bother and complications—time-robbing and tiresome hold-ups. Which is why they must resort to scaring and bribing—punishments and prizes on the spot— big threats and paltry rewards. And what they called "the wrong spirit" was the only *real* sin known.

I'm inclined to think that one of the most significant, if banal, roots of the prudery fostered in the convent boarding schools of my own day lies here—in a strange, twisted roundabout way. Taboos are so handy, sparing the teacher the trouble of grappling with the ominous problem itself, as well as of convincing each child individually. The great idea was to prevent the girls from stumbling upon problems by themselves, directly or indirectly. Anything which might have offered a hint or a glimpse was simply eliminated. Illustrations of Greek statues were discreetly touched up and even words which could have "put ideas into our heads" were neatly pasted over in the volumes of our recreation library. They don't do this any more—even Sigrid Undset is allowed, but, so I've been told, not before the book is spoilt for the girls by censorious comments on its more improper items.

And secondly, friendship, like Eros, is the domain of privacy *par excellence*—of two people by themselves, alone—even secrecy. Both break away from the crowd, both endeavour to escape supervision, both seek solitude, i.e. independence. What is more, the bond between them backs up each otherwise isolated individual, increasing the power of resistance. Which is why both these things must be *verboten*. This is the only explanation I can find for the hostile attitude towards friendships in our convent schools. I can't imagine that our good nuns actually feared such a thing as perversion among us.

*

I'M constantly struck by the "demonic" aspect of the institutional even when reading Ronald Knox's extremely interesting book *Enthusiasm*, about the sects, particularly in seventeenth- and eighteenth-century England and France. Loyal and ultra-orthodox as the author is, and for all his concern to exonerate the authorities and their methods—even when they've hardly got a leg to stand on—you can sense what a tussle this purpose often costs him as an objective historian. And, despite it all, you can't help noticing what a sinister role the clergy's struggle for monopoly, or at any rate hegemony, in the direction of conscience played in the Molinos quarrel. That they could hardly be expected to tolerate a spiritual trend which dispensed with frequent confession, examination of conscience, etc., is obvious. All the same the Quietists did seek "direction", though in other ways, cultivating very close ties with their confessors.

Yet more disturbing is the often nebulous borderline between "genuine" and spurious mystics. For Joseph Bernhard, for instance, Madame de Guyon is a true saint. Knox's picture seems to me far more convincing: he shows her as quite as hysterical a type as Frau von Krüdener, whom, curiously enough, he doesn't mention at all.

*

I THINK I'm really and truly fathoming the *seductive* power of images for the first time—what is at the bottom of all iconoclasm.

Of course it is really God's "own fault". The radiance of his glory is so immense, so intense, that a human being (who has been given eyes to see with!) could well drown in even a single

drop caught in the tiny cup of one of his countless mirrors—
someone who could divine the whole from the fragment. What
makes images so seductive is precisely their similarity, their
very "likeness", *similitudo*—and so, though not themselves
Reality, they still possess something of its fascinating power.

It is easy to see from this why all the mystics are so adamant
in their exclusion of "signs and images"; not that they reject
images or the body, as such, or are blind to their value—but
because they know the spell of these things too well—and their
own susceptibility no less.

Image—*eidolon*—idol: for the first time I see the terrible
depth of this implication.

*

THE gods, too, are images of God. And man is the last of the
gods—the last in the double sense of the word: ultimate,
supreme. For he is *the* image and likeness, in his outer form, as
in his being. Man himself is the greatest temptation to idolatry,
for himself, as well as for others, for he is the most tangible
reflection of God: the most intense, mysterious image, revealing such dimensions. . . . So much more "approachable" than
the angels.

*

DOES the sight of some wonderful effect of light, a rainbow, for
instance, a rose-flooded evening sky or a landscape before a
storm make me want to turn away and look for the source of the
light somewhere else, out of another window perhaps? No. I
simply stand there, steeping myself, as it were, in the radiance
before me, just letting everything it so wonderfully transmits in
its glory sink into my being. At that particular moment I
certainly don't think of the source . . . not then. But surely this
is *intended*? The purpose of the Inventor? At the theatre, for
instance, I wouldn't dream either of turning my back on the
bright stage before me to look for the flood-lights, nor would I
stop watching the sea to go in search of the lighthouse.

*

THE "process of belief" which has been going on within myself
over these last years is probably part—a very essential part—
of that other process of "growing poor", stripping, which seems

to belong to every real growth in our relationship with God. That story of Buber's about the riches of the Hasidim is so terribly applicable. . . .

My "property" in matter-of-fact, clear, diamond-sharp, sparkling, apparently indestructible concepts, notions and definitions used to be the very heart of my spiritual fortune, the thing most precious, incomparable, guarded most carefully, jealously, passionately defended: the only thing which seemed to me really stable, unshakeable, inviolable, never to be questioned—absolute.

And now this is beginning to dissolve, disintegrate—in part, at least. *Not the substance*, but the form. And even though I know that both are not identical (as I believed them to be for three-quarters of my life, or more), I know just as well that substance cannot exist without form. Which accounts for this strange dread as yet another bit of form melts and trickles away. For who can tell whether it isn't gone for good? Will I ever get it back again? When, and how? It is transformation, not annihilation. But in the same way as death is *transitus*, transition via dissolution, retrogression, return to a nothingness out of which the new body is crystallized—no, not nothingness really, but chaos. Just as in translation the matter must be "withdrawn", going back beyond the bounds of language, into its liquid original element, and then recast, poured into a new mould, to regain its novel shape. But—can this be done? Isn't there just the same risk that it will remain in this state of dissolution, that I'll never be able to capture it again?

Which is why I'm scared of "letting go". This awful anxious feeling, oppression, element of agony. And even more, perhaps, the fear for the treasure entrusted, the *depositum fidei* and the grace of faith, granted personally to me: the fear of wronging a very sacred thing, of impairing and imperilling its majesty and integrity, of surrendering, yes, forfeiting this, betraying it. For what? For the sake of a spiritual adventure, for the mere chance of deeper penetration?

*

WHO can say that such and such a concept of God is wrong? Could it not be that it simply contains *more dimensions* than my former one? Surely it only contests certain fashions of speech, not the substance of faith? and even then formulae, only on the philosophical plane? As for this feeling of being at sea, floating, vagueness which attaches to this state of mine? Surely no worse than this petty worship of the letter, the craze for formulae of skeleton logic enunciated by certain theologians. Aren't most of the religious books (and so-called mystical literature) advertised in Christmas book lists simply intolerable, just too awful? Small wonder really if the poor publishers' readers who have to spoon up this watery gruel all day long as their job get fits, faith-cramp. . . . Is there *anything* nourishing in a diet like this, any real food to satisfy the hungry? No! I'm not going to ladle out of this pot any longer, simply doling out platefuls of this dreadful soup to all and sundry as though we were in some People's Kitchen. Is this pure arrogance, going on strike?

*

MUSTARD seed and leaven. *Abscondit*: the woman *buried* the leaven in three measures of meal. The ferment has to disappear completely, till you can't tell it's there any more. No little, hard, tell-tale lumps. . . . It only reveals its presence by changing everything else—not *"pure"*. But it must change *everything*. It's no good if the flour still remains flour, the milk separates, and the other ingredients fall apart. Then something has gone wrong. Nothing has happened—the yeast wasn't the real thing, or it was "dead".

And if the mustard seed is to grow into a tree (and we're first of all reminded how tiny it is), this, too, means that it must assimilate a whole mass of strange elements, out of all proportion to its own minute size, yet all the same active, determinative, formative. For it does not dissolve into this heap of raw material, but rather forces this into a new form. And this alien matter, too, must assume a form as different from itself as the original mustard seed must become from its first form. In both parables we have change—the changing of two different elements into a third—neither of these, but their product.

Of course, the inevitable question: When does this process come to an end? Is there really *any* end to it? *Is* the Church a tree, or bread—or would this, too, mean an end, ossification? I think the Fathers said: the Church is neither flour nor yeast, but rather the woman who hid the leaven in the meal. And this isn't a unique dramatic event, but a perfectly normal procedure, to be repeated scores of times, an everyday, workaday occurrence. Nor is the Church the loaf of bread which comes out at the end. . . . And the Kingdom of Heaven embraces all four: the woman, the yeast, the flour and the bread itself.

The tree, too, is a growing, living thing: it must grow taller, expand, i.e. the mustard seed must be constantly at work, changing the mass of new material *and* the elements—earth, light, water. We can never sit back and say: "That's enough. The bush is quite big enough. All we have to do now is to look after it and keep it in trim. It needn't grow any more."

This passion for keeping everything "pure", this inbreeding, this Catholic exclusiveness, for ever repeating old conventional forms is so utterly wrong. Deadly.

*

AN invasion of nieces. Long, rather disturbing discussions with the girls. What *do* these young people think about Truth? Do they think about such things at all? Is their standpoint really so very different from that idle, indolent attitude typical of so-called Society in, say, the "twenties"? I well remember talking to R.: "Of course if one were to consider the dogmas seriously, really think them out, one would automatically turn Protestant —if not lose one's faith altogether. But then, what self-respecting person would? Certainly not our sort of people." . . . Or is it perhaps faith as *fides*, not as assent? Faith as an act of dedication, not as an intellectual position, as "argument"? But dedication to whom, for the sake of what? For God's sake, for Christ's sake, even for the sake of Truth—or just because these young people sense that the Church alone is the core and the star, the anchor and bulwark of the age-old, eternal world ideal which they glimpse from afar with such yearning in the midst of the chaos and havoc of our age? "Even if the Pope were to serve us up a new dogma every morning for breakfast it wouldn't worry us one bit. . . . *That's* not the important thing. . . ." Or: "I know a lady who's been wanting to become a Catholic for ages—there's nothing she wants more—but she just can't bring herself to believe in transubstantiation. . . . I can't see how it can be so important what one understands or doesn't understand about such details. . . ."

Is this sort of attitude just a "positive" version of modern utilitarian, collective thinking? Can it be that the era of *personal* decisions, of the "intellectual conscience", as we used to call it, is really *passé*? Was this just a psychological phase, a brief interlude between two epochs in which personal convictions were unknown and people merely shared the general creed of their own particular community or set? Are we the last of the Mohicans here too?

*

AND yet it's amazing really what clear vision this war and post-war generation often has, how open they seem to be to what is valid, objective. Their scepticism of the Church is roused by the sort of Christians who capitulate and retire to the catacombs, seeking "the interior life", privacy, instead of facing the world out in the open, setting and applying standards—and accepting the consequences. (Where this *does* happen—see Spain—they are indignant or shocked, of course!)

All the same these are facts worth noting and thinking about.

*

THE Advent breviary—oh, the beauty of these antiphons and responsories! Sheer poetry! This last week I was specially struck by: "*Aegypte, noli flere, quia Dominator tuus veniet tibi, ante cuius conspectum movebuntur abyssi, liberare populum suum de manu potentiae. Ecce veniet Dominus exercituum, Deus tuus cum potestate magna, liberare populum suum de manu potentiae.*"

This is a mystery indeed. Egypt, land of death, realm of the flesh, of darkness, of slavery: yet it is Egypt who receives tidings of the conqueror to come—*Dominator, Dominus exercituum* —i.e. as the strong one, the Lord who will triumph over her in power and in battle, liberating his people, sighing and weeping under the yoke of the oppressor, *cum potestate magna*. But *is* this last sentence really implied? For then it should actually read: "*Egypt, weep and tremble!*" Or is it a *promise*—not a threat!— addressed precisely *to the wicked*, to Egypt herself, not merely to her victims . . . not to the poor wretches of sinners, good-natured enough, longing captives, trapped by the powers of darkness, compromising out of sheer weakness, poor and abject, incapable of helping themselves—but to the genuine sinners, ready to make common cause with their masters, no longer willing to make a stand against tyranny. The Lord sees their misery, too, the silent tears and sorrow of heart which is the only sign of their plight, for they no longer call upon him in prayer. He sees them, too, and he is stronger than they. As sovereign Lord and master he will break their bondage as well, bringing them the freedom in which they had ceased to believe, indeed hardly even desired any more.

*

FOURTH Sunday after Pentecost: the miraculous draught of fishes. How significant that our Lord should say: "Let down your nets . . ." *Laxate*. Loosen the nets, let them be. Passive, not active. Not "Cast out your nets!" as we so often hear in so-called "free translations". No parade-ground command here. Let down the nets, let them just float—not striving, contriving, snatching and catching, not sparing and grudging either—but prepared to take a risk—maybe they will break, or be washed away—but they mustn't be weighed down, or tied up, or hooked on to things for fear they could come to some harm. And twice over, though with different words, it says: "Draw back from the land"—and then: "Launch out into the deep!" Into the *deep*. The nets must be let down in the deep, not just close to the shore. Far out in the midst of the "sea", where the fisher himself drifts over the unfathomable depths in his nutshell—what mysterious words!

*

JESUS, the Vine: that tapestry in our church grows more and more beautiful. This morning I spent the whole of Mass contemplating one single detail: the cluster of grapes bleeding out of the wound in the right hand—no: the wound in the right hand bleeding, as these grapes, into the chalice. The *dextera Domini*— the power of God himself, helpless, wounded, yet filling the empty chalice, our chalice, which otherwise *remains* empty—our sacrifice, still only a vessel, which cannot be filled of itself. And this—and his wounded side, which also "responds" to the piercing lance with a bunch of grapes: with fullness, with sweetness, with strength and healing, this whole Body "answering", from all its wounds, with Wine, with fire, with spirit, with fruit. O Church of the East, thou Body bruised and wounded! Shall our dry, empty chalice be filled from thee? *Corpus Christi salva nos.*—And these wounds are inexhaustible, ever-flowing, they will never run dry—for this, his Body, is *the* Vine.

*

ZACHAEUS. Because he was "small of stature" he could not see our Lord on account of "the multitude". *Tout comme chez nous.* Precisely the "little" people, with their shortcomings, lacking in vision and broad outlook—they still cannot catch sight of our Lord because "the multitude around Jesus" blocks the view, especially those close to him, his "professionals". So he has to run on in front and climb up into a sycamore tree, a wild fig tree, i.e. he hangs on to something natural, grown wild, for support—and he really "rises"—advances. From up here, raised aloft from this somewhat precarious and rather ridiculous position, he can hear the Lord's call to him—which maybe might never have been audible down below, on the solid, firm ground of everyday life. And the Lord's first revelation to him is a request—he needs him, if only to be put up for one night in his house. And on the answer he gives him Zachaeus' salvation depends. Just like a fairy-story (or the other way round?). Isn't his "*quadruplum reddo*" typical of the amazing largesse one so often encounters among "little" people, among the "short-legged" stock whose narrowness and pettiness we're so fond of joking about—as though magnanimity were the prerogative of the "long-legged?"*

*

PSALM 118—my solace and my blessing—unfathomably deep. It is my backbone. I turn to it again and again, seeking in those countless repetitions the reassurance that I really am on the right path. And it confirms me, giving me confidence and strength. It tells me that my naïve, dense clinging to the Church, to her laws and her teaching and doctrine, often even to the letter *is* in accordance with the will of God—true service of God, pure and

---

* "Short-legged"=*Niederbeine,* "long-legged"=*Hochbeine*: special terms in Bremen dialect for well-bred and vice versa.

acceptable in his eyes, even if people laugh at it, calling it narrow-minded, simple-minded, fear-ridden and immature. But no, true, willing, faithful and—God grant it—humble submission to the Word is of far more worth, far more precious than all one's own special notions, all those extra special things, all private "Gnosis".

*

CHRISTMAS. Lots to say actually about the theology of the Christmas tree and the gifts it brings: symbol of desires fulfilled, of surprise—"no eye has seen, no ear has heard"—the bread containing all sweetness in itself, all joys in abundance, the twelve-fold fruit of the Tree of Life in the Paradise to come.

*

FEAST of St Thomas. The true Body of our Lord is ever to be recognized by its wounds—only then is it *real*, no projection, no image born of wishful thinking.

*

ACTUALLY we were brought up to ingratitude—on a monstrous scale at that, above all in the discipline of so-called self-sanctification, what was termed "striving for perfection"—a relentless training through which we were taught to find nothing whatever good in ourselves, whether natural or spiritual. Of course we were *told* about thanksgiving for God's good gifts. In practice, however, we learnt to look another way, and when some quality or other did reveal itself even against our will, then we were quick to cancel it on the spot by finding some flaw in it, or by conjuring up some past failure, blunder or lapse. And how diligent we were in our flea-hunt for even the tiniest fault! Conquering pride and conceit, they called it, practising humility, self-praise is no praise—all very well. . . . But surely with the same amount of patience, precision and perseverance such temptations could just as well have melted into gratitude—and the far more genuinely humbling recognition of the *unmerited* "*magnalia Dei*", in me too? Was pride *really* crushed by all this snubbing and humiliation? Was it not rather "repressed" in such a way that it came bursting out elsewhere, from the rear, as it were, in a hundred artifices, skilfully camouflaged, but very much there all the same? Worse still, we learnt this way to cultivate the "devil's mirror" eye of Hans Andersen's *Snow Queen*, over-vigilant, super-critical sight, sharpened to discover the worm in every bud, even the tiniest plant-louse! For if one practises this sort of discipline on oneself, day and night, it is asking too much—at any rate of a young girl—to judge one's neighbour by another yard-stick. All the time one's lynx-eyed consciousness remained on the alert, quick to pounce on everything negative—in you and in myself. And since this sort of thing was deemed a pious practice for oneself, it was hard to see why it should be wrong as applied to other people. Hans Andersen well knew how near this attitude is to blasphemy.

*

Just as we must learn to dissociate the practice of religion from "feeling pious", so we must also learn to help, independently of sympathy. With the best will in the world you cannot "acquire" a warm, compassionate heart, no matter how hard you try, if it never was there to start with, or has dried up with the years—or other processes of absorption. And, oh how feeble and inadequate our hearts are anyway! But to *see* the needs of others, where you yourself could help, you only need use your eyes and ears, and a little common sense. Not that I'd call this charity, by any means, indeed not even mercy—which means really taking the sufferings of another as one's own. But it is at least benevolence, poor as one knows one's heart to be, and even this little is worth a good deal, as useful and necessary in this poor world of ours as all the other things we do out of duty, unprompted by spontaneous feeling. You could almost say here that conscientiousness does duty for quite a lot of what we lack in virtue?

*

Demonstratio ad oculos for Christians *en route*: Driving to Lake Constance with the K. children. Christiane never tired of asking, all the time, at every turning, at every village, at the sight of every roof in the distance: "Are we nearly there? How far is it to grandpa's? Is that the road to grandpa's? Is that grandpa's house over there? Is grandpa's behind that hill? How long till we get to grandpa's?"

*

FLOORS polished too highly are dangerous. Moral: overdo virtue and you make other people slip.

*

CERTAIN minor virtues serve only as weapons and tools in our fallen state: diligence, frugality, self-control, a certain kind of cleverness—all virtues which would never have existed in Paradise. Courage and patience? Certainly—yet it does seem to me that these belong to a different category. Jesus was courageous and patient, but whoever could picture him as thrifty, intent on economizing and making money?

*

FRAU X. gave me a pious pamphlet entitled *The Holy Sacrifice of the Mass, a Hidden Treasure*. She (and probably countless others like her) finds it wonderful. But it sets my teeth on edge like lemon juice. Why? I think it's the method behind it. The canker of this sort of Catholic piety would seem to lie in that boundless introspection and the kind of unreal abstraction which goes with it (there's a sensible kind as well!) which indulges in the fanciful, almost mechanical connection of suggestive words, superlative topping superlative, in logical succession, just like knitting—stitch after stitch, row upon row: one plain, one purl —serenely indifferent to hard truths.

And behind it is the fanatical attempt to express the unutterable, what ought never even be dared: like putting into words —in detail—the intentions and emotions of Christ himself during his Passion, or, today, in the Sacrifice of the Mass—as though this *could* be constantly forced into human awareness, reenacted by will, consciously! No one sees that this just cannot be done explicitly, though an implicit intention in this direction might be admitted. What a lot we must get rid of, get back to, before we can regain the old, simple essentials!

132

And what an awfully misleading form of Marian devotion grows out of all this! Once Scheeben* is quoted: "Mary is the Mystical Heart in the Mystical Body."

This makes sense, the only sensible sentence in the whole booklet!—and it ought to be enough for us. But no, they must go taking her pulse, counting her every heart-beat, rationalizing everything down to precise intentions and resolutions. But thousands of really religious people find this sort of thing helpful and illuminating. They just lap it up—their minds are completely "blocked" by such trash. Their minds—yes, for, spiritually, the genuine love and humility with which they try to re-enact this nonsense is probably a sure and effective "antidote", so that perhaps, instead of doing them any harm, it could in fact even be good for them.

*

To my joy the Vine tapestry is back again in church. What strikes me most forcibly every time I look at it is that *sweetness* drops from the wounds of Christ. From *his* wounds—ours suppurate, oozing bitterness and acid, long after the injury. . . .

*

How readily people admire visible self-immolation—and how seldom those are appreciated who have to keep themselves for the sake of a higher mission!

*

WHAT does "luck" really mean? Is it just another expression for long-term success easily won? I'm less and less inclined to believe that it's a result of qualities like efficiency, dexterity, ingenuity, intelligence, energy, aptness, etc., but rather a quality in itself, like beauty. Although, of course, even cosmetics can do quite a lot these days. . . .

*

THE new edition of Schamoni's *Seven Gifts of the Holy Ghost* now arouses a very dubious echo within me—yet how this book impressed me when it first came out! Isn't it really centred on

* Matthias Joseph Scheeben, great Romantic theologian, contemporary of John Henry Newman.

purely *personal* "perfection"?—everything seen exclusively from the pedagogic, ascetic angle?—evidence of that curiously intoxicating preoccupation of the individual soul, spinning round and round, intensely, exclusively, about the *reflection* of its own conscious relationship to God?—what in our youth we mistook for "the spiritual life", indeed for religion itself?

The fascination of this kind of religiosity strikes me today as most ambivalent: the sacred is only one of its poles: the other, hidden away underneath but often far more subtly powerful, lies in the fact that it's a not only legitimate but positively "canonized" form of self-worship. And so, for some people, it's the delight of all delights. (Makes me think of Frau H's devastatingly innocent remark after that lecture (a Catholic doctor's talk on sex-life in the aftermath of the war): "Lord, what a treat for the girls—to be able to listen to all that indecent talk —and for once with a perfectly good conscience!").

For lots of its adepts (though not all, of course), this kind of "mysticism" means legitimate, perpetual, passionate preoccupation with self—in all good conscience and guaranteed with the highest motives—poring over their every impulse and reaction, however faint, with a magnifying glass. A very similar temptation exists in love—St Augustine knew and wrote about it: *amare amare* and *amare amari*, the love of being in love. If in religious life everything else is cut out except myself and my Creator, the ego—as his sole counter-pole and partner —only too easily attains to an almost God-like position in its own consciousness.

*

A propos the Great Supper: the gospel for the Tuesday after the First Sunday in Lent also states that the blind and the lame came to Jesus *in the temple*, and he healed them (i.e. you find cripples inside the sanctuary as well as outside).

*

Somewhere, deep down, I've the feeling that where Meister Eckhart and his school may perhaps have gone wrong, fundamentally, is in claiming the soul to be God-begotten, akin to him by nature, where the Church teaches that these qualities are only conferred in Baptism, in re-birth to sonship. But couldn't one say: "In the beginning it was not like that", i.e. in the beginning Man received *both* as his nature, in the moment of his creation, unmingled and undivided, and it is we—poor progeny of Adam in this fallen aeon—who have to pick these elements apart so laboriously, since we can only receive them singly and separately? In talking of the soul, these mystics don't mean the subject of our individual experience, but rather the soul of Adam. Adam was both *imago* and *similitudo*, so the masters tell us; for us only the *imago* remained, and *similitudo* is restored by Baptism. And here my head goes bang against the wall of the Tempter's taunt: "And how much, pray, do you *see* of all this in that crowd of your precious regenerates?" Ah, most of us are still only embryos in the womb of the Advent Church—picking her way through the thorn-thicket of time.

*

EVEN the matter of the divine attributes appears in a new light. In reality only the reborn have a claim to the *imitatio Dei*, and then only in fulfilment, at the end, in the third birth into eternity, in the state of resurrection and glory; here on earth we are bound to the *imitatio Christi*. It is not proper for us, as human beings, to achieve a status above the "form of a slave" which Christ took upon himself. The servant is not above his master. That always smacks of usurpation. It might be granted to a privileged few, as an exception, perhaps as a kind of "memento" for us others, to remind us how man was meant to be in the beginning. St Ignatius' Third Grade: not only pedagogic and ascetic good sense, ontologically right, too.

*

HUMILITY is related to "brains" in just the same way as chastity to Eros: not as negation, but as regulative, a purge, more than that: the "setting" within which both these powerful urges can take on and retain their valid form. How the mind calls for redemption! How "carnal" it can be, how corrupt, how susceptible to even the faintest breath of temptation, how it calls for control! "Reason the harlot"—did Luther coin this himself, or did he take it over from some older tradition?

Anyway it couldn't be more apt, betrays quite astonishing insight, real genius. . . . But even reason as harlot is after all just the distorted image of the queenly virgin Sophia.

*

WITH his intransigent anti-rational attitude X. really is an exact pendant to these "anti-carnal" prophets of ours. For he's always railing against precisely the same perils, drawbacks, incongruities, seductions and symptoms of decay they keep abusing in Eros. The third element would be power. Yet these three very elements: power—wisdom—love, are really the three window-panes, the three transparencies in the true sense of the word, through which we here on earth can catch a glimpse of the divine reality. *Sapientia* and *scientia* correspond to Agape and "adoration"—and isn't power, in its divine form, "glory"?

*

How important to rediscover baptismal innocence as "glory". Otherwise it's going to get swept under the table altogether as mere inexperience, infantility even, in that "sinner-and-grace" brand of mysticism *à la mode* nowadays. Those old, child-like images: the white dress, the burning candle. So simple, yet how full of meaning. . . .

*

WE mustn't jumble up "personal" and "individual", as such. The individual, even as a Christian, cannot counterbalance the collective, only the whole can do it, the Church as a *body*. No use being good and pious, not even a blameless and consistent personality will do: they simply lack power and momentum. Read up de Lubac's *Maria Ecclesia*, also Hugo Rahner's book, Karl Rahner's ecclesiological doctrine of the sacraments, etc.

*

NN. RANG me up just now, back from Paris. Everything at sixes and sevens there on account of the worker-priests [3.3.1954]. "They didn't convert us, we converted them!" so the Communist press is triumphing. Easy enough to picture the effect of all this on the "People's Churches" behind the Iron Curtain. . . .

For me the real tragedy here follows exactly the same line as that of the Reformation (I must look up Lortz), i.e. to all appearances, at any rate, the fire, the enthusiasm, the real appeal, the dedication is all on the side of the rebels, the innovators, no matter what mistakes they may have made—and on the side of authority? Nothing (at least in the majority of cases) but sanity, correct behaviour, a sharp eye—and submission—no flame, no risk, no pioneer light or decisive action. Oh, the pity of it! Yet perhaps this is outweighed by the suffering and heroic obedience —the Isaac-sacrifice—of those worker-priests who have submitted?

The whole affair has yet another very personal barb. A chance remark N. made commenting (not at all to my liking!) on the introduction I wrote for Sven Stolpe's book on Joan of Arc is pricking me again: "What and who *is* actually 'the Church'"? For all the new views about laymen in the Church, revised principles, etc., surely it is still largely the clergy alone whom we credit with this holy name—out of tradition grown almost to second nature?

Do we not still too exclusively mean the "ecclesiastics" when we say "Ecclesia", as though they were herself, and not just one of her organs, however vital? Are we not applying Christ's "he who listens to you, listens to me" too one-sidedly, to those in orders? Surely we ought to have the courage to recognize the Holy Ghost in those "prophetic" men and women as well who are very much an organ, and not the least one, of the Church?

And yet, and yet: "What greater follies than those of compassion?" Isn't this true of the worker-priests, too? What strengthens and furthers the militant Antichrist of Bolshevism— *de facto*, of course, not intentionally!—*can* this really be from God?

*

THE absence of God among the faithful seems to me often even harder to bear than the godlessness of the unbelievers.

*

N. TELLS me he finds that Lourdes article of mine in *Hochland* so exasperating because I was trying here to smooth away things which, in fact, cannot be smoothed over, except by smothering and by word-juggling. The heretic is the man who has the courage to face, to assert and to back up the clash—more honest than we are, since he leaves the cross standing where it is, whereas the all-explaining Catholic tries to argue it away.

I've re-read all my three bits on Lourdes, but, quite honestly, there's nothing there I could retract, or even tone down. I can't help it, what I said is true. Never for an instant do I *deny* the cross, or try to "modify" or explain it away. On the contrary. Which is why the article met with such bitter criticism and a flood of angry letters! But what I want is to point out *this* cross of the Church, precisely this one—being not only the form of the servant but also the form of the sinner—I'm trying to denounce it *as well as to accept it*: because we love the Church. Not because these things are right, but because they are definitely *not*. The Church really is androgynous—virile-fatherly on the one hand: law-giving, dividing, passing judgment, rejecting and excluding, too; yet, on the other hand, "motherly": embracing, forgiving, sheltering and protecting, inexhaustibly patient and forbearing.

*

OCTAVE of SS. Peter and Paul. I see today's gospel as a tremendous parable of the Church—yet I can hardly make it out, it's like some old script for which I've forgotten the cipher.

What can it mean: that Peter's little boat had to fight its way across the sea in the night, "hard put to it by the waves, for the wind was against them", and *without* our Lord? And he appears suddenly walking towards them *from outside*, overtaking them, perhaps even coming from the opposite direction? That they saw him as a wraith, i.e. something unreal, sinister, born of darkness and chaos, indeed the very culmination, so to speak, of these hostile powers.

And earlier on it says: he *compelled* the disciples to take ship without him, leaving him behind to go up alone "on the hillside", in solitude, out of reach.

How did his answer come to them? Did he "outshout" the storm and their cries of terror, or did they suddenly hear his voice, quiet, unmistakable, in their hearts?

And it's *Peter* who answers him, stepping down out of the ship, and walking across the watery element of the abyss—

towards the Lord. And the temptation came—"he lost courage and began to sink"—only when he had reached Jesus—because then he no longer looked at *him*, but only had eyes for the wind and the waves. And Jesus stretched out his hand—the *dextera Domini*!—and in his answer you can hear the reassuring laugh: "No need to be so frightened! Why? *I* was calling you!" And then they go on board *together*, and at that moment the wind drops. . . .

*

As heretics attack the Church, so rebels debunk society: protesting, laying bare the hidden rifts and cracks. Both expose the "intolerable" things the respectable people iron out so messily with their sacred smoothing-irons.

*

JULIAN of Norwich has helped me no end to see the subject of priest and prophet, i.e. office and charisma, more clearly: Her "shewings" are flashes, not lamps. The seer *needs* the Church, for she alone provides the background against which his visions really make sense—instead of being simply isolated, crazy arabesques. The priest has to keep the *whole*, whatever is enduring, universal, catholic—to the prophet is committed the *part*, the renovation, what is new—as well as what must be renovated. His is the *special* task. But the second cannot be accomplished without the first. Only against the "common" outline of the whole, within its proportions, can the flash-lit details be understood. No point in enlarging a photograph of an eyelid, for instance, unless people know the face.

*

MATRIMONY and the Church: in both the most intimate things are most public and vice versa. And when both no longer correspond, then something has gone wrong.

*

SECOND Epistle of St Peter. Curious, and very remarkable, how identical the pattern of false teachers remains throughout the whole history of the Church: here in St Peter, no less than in St Paul and St John—even in the apostles' day already full-grown and recognized down to the very last detail and *nuance*! The same combination every time: heresy—carnality—pride—delusion—allurement. The erotic-sexual element as compound in the spiritual seduction of the mind, that peculiar "emanation" in the influence of the heresiarch. . . .

That's another reason why I'm not so readily convinced by the assertion that the extolling of chastity in the early Church was rooted in Gnosticism, born out of a Manichean, spiritualist, depreciation of nature. Rather the other way round: although this tendency (virginity) does not actually appear in the gospels—only later on, in St Paul!—it is surely their genuine issue and natural heritage, and precisely in those early days a vital antidote, immunizing against this sort of seduction. An important trail to follow up. St Jerome cannot be held responsible for everything here. Think of the host of early virgin martyrs, starting with Thecla! Surely they prove an older origin?

*

PETER BAMM: *The Invisible Flag*: "Scientists tend to think their theories are as reliable as the results of their experiments." How true of theologians, too!—not to mention historians, psychologists, philologists. It seems it lies in man, the prepotent urge to balance his own fancies and notions against the weight of things created.

A propos: by and large the faithful are completely uninterested in theological explanations. They're content to accept anything they are offered—even the craziest "explanations" of the Mass, for instance. Yet they still believe substantially in the thing itself, would die for it. Surely, then, reflection—always subsequent—plus all the attendant formulae, isn't really so important?

It's like the modern craze that no course of instruction for marriage is complete without the usual doctor's lecture on chromosomes, ovulation, elementary genetics, etc., etc.—even for country-women and servant girls. People have been having children for millions of years without this sort of knowledge, and a hundred years ago even the leading gynaecologists were ignorant of such *finesses*.

*

I'VE been reading Sara Alelius again. Left me—as so often—nostalgic for the *simplicity* of the Protestant faith, and for the sweet purity, strength and depth which springs from it. Their asset is the clear outline, single-mindedness. Our weighty heritage is profusion, really *embarras de richesse*! Our little mind cannot possibly master it, even begin to grasp it, let alone pick out the salient points. . . . And so people are either trying to reproduce the Church as a whole in their own religious life, to become the Church in miniature, like a pocket dictionary in microscopic type—the idea being that the Church is a mosaic, with each little stone representing the whole design, only on the tiniest scale—or they cling to some specific, isolated aspect, picked out at random.

The whole thing is so vast, so heavy, so rich that it would need an immensely broad supporting structure, with the weight distributed over many zones: liturgy, ways of life, morals, personal religion. When the "objective" supporting elements disintegrate—as today!—then the whole mass falls back solely upon the individual mind—impossible. Things remain theoretical, abstract intentions, just casual, capricious toying with details.

We are no longer living our life with the whole, drawing our life from the whole, sharing more or less unconsciously what is happening within the changing seasons: which is why "they" must go forcing everything into awareness, with arguments for this and explanations for that, every tittle brought home to us, literally, with "How to keep feast days in your family", etc., etc. —all *against* the tide, on purpose, insisting on training, apologetics, propaganda. Handy little devotional formulas all nicely thought out, contrived and constructed, distributed from headquarters in stencilled patterns, mass-production, no roots.

How our *real* stock has dwindled! How many prayers, for instance, does the average Catholic still know by heart? How many saints does he really know, is he devoted to personally? How many religious classics does he "own"—and not on the bookshelf alone, in his heart? Protestants have the immense advantage that their "iron rations" consist of the most authentic and living substance—psalms and hymns. Actually in this they are living within a far more genuine tradition than we are, real, enduring, unfading—whereas *chez nous* one can hardly keep pace

141

with all the "religious practices" and devotions chasing one another at hectic speed: Enthronement of the Sacred Heart, Fatima, consecrations to our Lady, etc.—mostly from periods of the very worst spiritual taste and the most thread-bare, moth-eaten tradition. Stamped and punched, not *grown*—no wonder these fashions are dropped in due course. They can't last, they simply serve to allay, for a time, religious appetites pepped up by artificial stimulants. They no longer touch the archetypes of the soul. There are, of course, some really weather-proof forms— the Rosary, the Stations of the Cross, the Crib. But, alas, they too seem to be disintegrating these days.

*

WE haven't even water in the pots any more, mostly just sand. We must ask for water again before it can be turned into wine at all.

*

JOACHIM of Fiore* made me re-read Newman's texts on the Church in the two-volume Karrer edition. Very important. How much more clearly than Joachim did Newman see the transparency of Christ's incarnation in the Church, through all the veils, far beyond these! The divining eye of love, quite the opposite of projection, of ideology.

These "realists" make me think of that flat, sour state of "being sensible at all costs" which follows disillusionment in love. When you see, to your shame, how far you've overshot the mark, all the things you've projected into the other person, idle, secret dreams; and now you're grimly resolved to stop making a fool of yourself and to see the other person "as he really is". Yet this very attitude proves that the former ideal was never recognition of the real face, but merely wishful thinking, retracted now in angry disillusionment, cancelled for good and all.

---

* Joachim of Fiore (1145?–1202), Cistercian monk and mystic of Calabria. Founded a new monastic order, the Ordo Florensis, in San Giovanni in Fiore, absorbed by the Cistercians in 1502. He divided time into three Dispensations: of the Father, the Son and the Holy Ghost, foretelling a third Kingdom of the Holy Ghost to supervene on the second Kingdom of the Son in 1260. The Spiritual Franciscans claimed that St Francis's apostolic and poor friars fulfilled this prophecy. Though his teaching was not accepted by the Church, he has not been condemned personally.

What these people call "the stark and sober facts about the Church" corresponds in reality to one's partner's naked, empiric ego, no longer or not yet loved, i.e. it is nothing but the unimportant surface layer, the barest outline, the ambiguity of his undeciphered behaviour.

But when Newman talks of the Church he sees her in her true reality, he is speaking of her queenly soul, dwelling and animating her poor body, no matter how disguised. Newman did not need to seek the Holy Ghost in the near or distant future —he saw him clearly enough in the present: he knew him, real and living, as the Spirit of Jesus in the Church.

*

THE Church, too, has her own bold Utopias: powerful, daring enough to make history, to change people: first, breath-taking in its audacity, monasticism: to live like the angels—fiery messengers of love and of truth—hovering above sex, possessions, power, struggle. The other, marriage: for ever indissoluble, an incomprehensible union of sex, Eros, friendship, love, Agape, fertility—all things which the Ancients assigned to diverse and often hostile gods: and in this and beyond it symbol, too, of the mystery of the "oneing" of God and man, God and creation.

*

I WONDER why people dislike holy places? They're not so hundred per cent democratic about other things. I think what makes them feel uneasy is that they imply *selection*. For "choosing" means an active, free and sovereign God, a God who makes decisions, surprising, startling, baffling us, setting us puzzles —very different from the "tame" God often pictured, whose every action is calculable, who wouldn't do anything to anyone.

*

I KEEP finding the Church all the time in the Zohar! She is the Torah, she is the Shekhinah, she *is* the First-born, she is the Body of Him who, as "Glory", is the Son, and as the Son is Glory; she is the dwelling-place, the tabernacle in the desert, and the temple in Jerusalem.

*

WHAT strikes me most forcibly, reading Jungmann's great work on the Mass,* is how incredibly slowly the Church developed, how long the mind took to realize itself. Centuries passed until the Church discerned one or other facet of the Mass, and still longer until this was penetrated, formulated, embodied into the rite, finally adopted and popularized among the faithful. How can you, in all justice, expect every individual to grasp all its implications, sacramental or symbolic, really partaking in these to the full? One shouldn't be alarmed by one-sidedness, so long as it isn't "exclusive", so long as it remains open to amplification and expansion. It's the faith of *all* of us which makes up the faith of the Church. One can't repeat this often enough.

*

PEOPLE tend to treat blessings and consecrations as just another unnecessary trimming to the hem of the Church. Yet actually it is one of her principal functions on earth to be *Heiland*.† Healing and hallowing, protecting and gathering to herself, safe-guarding within the house of God—all this belongs here.

*

WHEN did the Church actually cease to be a revolutionizing power and begin to represent in the main the conservative element? A conundrum. When the rest of the world grew revolutionary *à tout prix*, cutting itself off on principle from every "principle"—as "*princeps*" as well as beginning—(prince, aristocracy, authority, tradition, identity, permanence)! Till that time when all the dangers lay in ultra-conservation, existing conventions, traditions, the *ordre reçu*, the Church = the Spirit, *had* to be a restless, turbulent, irrupting, fermenting element. Afterwards it was, and is, the other way round. Today, in fact, she alone represents the Great Memory of mankind and man's primordial energies. But this alone is no longer sufficient.

*

* Joseph Jungmann, S. J., *Missarum Sollemnia*, Vienna, 1949. (*The Mass of the Roman Rite*, 2 vols., New York, 1951.)
† *Heiland* = the Saviour, i.e. healer.

SLOWLY, slowly, painfully, in anguish and soreness of heart, I'm learning to see that theology, too, is only *one* language for God's Truth, and not the only possible and valid one. Not just "not identical". And that to express the same content otherwise is no greater sacrilege than to say it in German or English, instead of in Latin. Theological thought is just a language, that's all. Not "the living garment of the Godhead".

The tongue of my fathers, of my brothers—how hard to depart from it! For I have known no other father but these fathers, the priests of the Church, no brothers but my own dear brothers, the theology students. No mother but the Church. I am a daughter of the Church. I loved them all and clung to them, not only as a daughter and sister, but as a Japanese daughter and sister, in the intensity of unconditional submission which belongs to Japanese filial piety. What others feel for their kin was transposed for me, completely, to this plane. And so what is happening to me now is really "leaving father and mother" for a new face of the living Christ in the Church—a face strange until now. This is real "conversion". Just as converts must break away or at least travel far from the childhood home of their Church, from their brethren in faith and the faith of their fathers with its sweet, familiar habits and ways of thought, so I, too, am now travelling in a certain sense, from Catholicism to the Church, from Catholics to Catholic Christianity, travelling from the small, accustomed vision towards new horizons, huge, awe-ful, unfamiliar. And so, at fifty, I'm gradually becoming a Catholic at last.

*

ALTHOUGH he doesn't mention this specifically, Karl Rahner's course on the Sacrament of Penance in the Church prompts one to ask, merely from the historical standpoint, whether the reception of a convert into the Church today would not be the nearest thing to the ancient rite of reconciliation. And the further question: whether this ought not to be recognized accordingly, as a genuine form of the Sacrament of Penance in itself, and whether it should not thus either dispense converts (as in the case of adult baptism) from the private general confession which follows on it today, or at any rate include this confession as its focal point, not just tagged on, as it is now, shamefacedly, as an appendix. And in instructing converts, surely far more attention should be paid to this aspect of *reconciliatio cum Ecclesia*, instead of limiting efforts to imparting knowledge and altering opinions or convictions in matters of dogma, etc. . . . . It's exciting to note how this growing insight implies for me a certain shifting of my concept of truth and of faith from individual assent to specific points of doctrine to an explicit assent to the Church as a whole.

*

IT seems there's nothing left but to participate in the mysteries of the Christian life with one's eyes closed, without knowing more than the splinter of a splinter. But isn't this actually always true where *life* is concerned? What do we know, after all, about the "essence" of even the simplest vital functions, such as breathing, sleeping, eating? Which is why even the most "elementary" Catholic life honestly lived is, in this way, religion really experienced—not reasoned—unconsciously embedded in the immeasurable tissue of God's *real* presence on earth.

Curious that some critics of the Church should keep telling us that our religion is merely theoretical, cerebral, no longer religion truly lived and experienced. This surely only applies to a very small section of "highbrow Catholics". How poor, fleeting and trivial in comparison is what Pietists (all brands) insist on calling religious experience—nothing really but the chance reflection, "echoes" of truth in emotions (often enough "enlightened" and fostered by just such intellectual reasoning). We shouldn't be carried away by these eloquent descriptions: they're deceptive. I seem to remember something H. said years ago in this connection: "Faith makes one speechless, unbelief loosens the tongue."

*

THERE is moral evil and mystical evil. The first is merely a negation of good—the second its reversal, its perversion, and has the same fascination as a reflection in a mirror. Then there is good which is just the negation of evil, or simply its avoidance, and good which is the surmounting, outshining, redemption and restoration of a good falsely, distortingly, bound up in evil. It's the second which really matters; the first is only a defence measure, a feeble makeshift. (In the same way as in the Counter-Reformation—and often enough since then, alas—Catholicism was merely "anti-Protestantism"—no longer all-round fulfilment and superabundance of the real and legitimate concerns and claims of the Reformation.)

In moral training it would be so very important not to *start* from evil, which then appears as basic reality, with "good" as merely its corrective, protesting against it—a line adopted by many puritans.

*

A PROBLEM of religious life: Someone who has never obeyed in her life before, and now naturally finds this terribly hard. Difficult for me to imagine. Question: Would this type be in fact the "real" monk, i.e. perhaps he alone is really capable of practising true obedience, of his own free will, in contrast to someone brought up in drill and the *habit* of submission? Or is it vice versa? Perhaps just such a person lacks something profoundly human, having never yet submitted to natural authority, never having accepted any form of human will out of natural humility or love, willing only to bow in submission to God alone, without any natural model?

*

CONFESSION. Curious really, how it persists, that old childish notion that it is the *number* of sins that makes confession worth while! As though one single sin were not enough for contrition and purpose of amendment. On the other hand, it isn't as simple as we try to make out either. Nowadays—for want of bulk!—the emphasis is laid on the sins of omission. Good. There's certainly a good deal in that. All the same, there is a great difference between things I don't do although I could, in fact, very well do them with a little effort, and things I simply cannot do, because I'm not made that way. It would be ridiculous to accuse oneself of being short-sighted or of not being able to sing. And where real faults are concerned, too: We thought it a wonderful idea when they set the fashion that you ought to confess what you *are* and not what you *did*—and it became the thing to make use of confession for elaborate self-analysis. What rot! No

147

wonder the confusion between confession and analysis grew. The confession of *guilt* is something very different from describing one's negative or missing qualities. But when the recognition grows that single peccadillos actually committed are merely the expression of a "wrong" moral attitude or perhaps disposition? I find it more and more hard to confess such things: I just don't see the point of it. Firstly because an increasing realization of the boundless love of God is accompanied by a growing insight that such trifles cannot really "grieve", let alone "offend" him— so long as there was no ill-will involved, just silliness and weakness. Those flaws which make up our wretchedness, are they not part of us as created beings? I cannot keep on for ever asking my husband's forgiveness for having a mole on my neck or for having to wear spectacles!

*

FLORENCE NIGHTINGALE: I've been thinking about her so much just lately, and somehow it aches. The question is: was her life the life of a saint? A life of faith and love, humility and dedication, full of suffering unnoticed, tremendous yet unselfconscious discipline for the sake of the cause, not for the sake of "perfection"—single-minded, unsparing. Is this not more than the lives of hundreds of religious?—even the lives of founders, some modern founders anyway, who so often strike me as tarnished somehow, diminished by their violent self-preoccupation, their "striving for perfection", or crippled by efforts to adapt their ideals to historical conventions within outworn forms, cut down to the point of sterility, by preconceived ascetic principles?

Florence Nightingale, this really great *lady*, boundless in magnanimity, with her flaming, insatiable Eros-nature: is all this not more than if she had turned her back on men in total renunciation, tying up her will in obedience, perhaps under a narrow and incompetent superior, robbing herself through poverty of most of the chances to help and give pleasure? And did she not *still* live up to all three evangelical counsels, and on a heroic scale at that: virginity, forgoing the cravings of her heart again and again for the sake of her vocation; obedience, to its wearing, merciless claims; poverty, in the austere and selfless privations involved in her utter surrender to the "one thing needful".

148

Is her broad, glowing, generous Christianity not more truly human, more *truly* Christian that at least our present-day cloister ideal? Did she not, in fact, do more than found an order—she established a new way of life!—in the spirit of the genuine, historical founders of old? Did she not awaken countless vocations, save countless bodies and lives, alleviate suffering, enabling souls to breathe again?—or is it "worldly" to think like this? But surely it's sheer bigotry to dub her as a mere philanthropist, as some Catholic critics do, dismissing her life with a sigh as "an immense step forward, but unfortunately outside 'the *Way*'"?

She is the glorious embodiment of the best of the nineteenth century—with its enthusiasm for Progress in all its pristine freshness, as yet unencumbered, though, to be sure, as yet untried—quite different from what came later, the prey for cancerous growths, defeatist and palsied. She is a true all-round individualist of the kind only possible then, in the narrow strip of time between the old world of tradition and convention and its decay—and then only in a select upper class, that fertile greenhouse in which a few choice seedlings of the best stock could thrive undisturbed in incredibly favourable conditions, enriched, really "cultivated" by the very best and richest heritage. And then the splendid products of this fortunate constellation could be placed at the disposal of others, prepared for service complete, untrammelled, lavish. What giants they were—and what dwarfs and cripples we are in comparison!

*

Florence Nightingale and Madame Curie, "the saint without God": how far are they apart, or how near? And how far (measured by our current Catholic yard-stick) are they both "beneath", let's say, a type like NN., still nursing, painstakingly childish, her old convent-school piety of yore . . . or any average "nunlet", for that matter, hoarding her "sacrifices" and totting up her sins, making up spiritual posies, with confession every week and Holy Communion every morning, etc.—and never really *growing*. Is it really justifiable to counter this with talk of "invisible grace" which will show its fruit in heaven only? Isn't all this stressing of the supernatural often just a subterfuge—wearing blinkers—so as not to have to face reality, to acknowledge it, to live up to it?

*

INTROVERSION isn't a virtue simply because "worldly" people are so often extroverts.

*

IT is a dangerous temptation to imagine you've got to have money in order to be able to help or to give—in other words that you've got to have money to be able to indulge in charity. This naturally implies that "bounty" consists above all in material gifts, and is therefore necessarily bound up with property.

And yet it's a salutary temptation too, for, so long as you've no serious material worries of your own, it's fatally easy to adopt that lofty Pharisaic, puritan attitude: "Money is the root of all evil, wealth is bad for your character", etc. (It's the same with power and sensuality!)

Yet actually wealth, just like power, fertility, beauty, is also a divine attribute—not merely its symbol—indeed it is also one of the natural likenesses to God: the capacity to be splendid, generous, high-hearted, creating things, founding—a kind of fertility, too—helping, relieving, in a word, magnanimous. Which is why a king, as one of the "natural" images of God, must also be rich. And not to be rich means a certain restriction of personality, and thus a kind of humiliation—precisely on the higher, not simply on the material plane, since poverty means "impotence", i.e. precludes a certain kind of radiance, of divine healing and hallowing effluence. Somewhere or other Saint-Exupéry tells the very strange story of a Moroccan slave, liberated after many years, whom he had watched when his plane landed in civilization: the first thing the man did was to buy cheap toys and sweets to give to the strange children who were hanging around: the very first gesture—expression of the dignity of man regained!

And so it would seem that poverty, at first, is a lack, a fetter, paralysis, like illness. But *then*—second stage, i.e. when it has been sublimated, transferred from the sphere of the body to that of the spirit, through recognition, acknowledgment, agreement, willing acceptance—then it becomes "humiliation beneath the hand of God", an act of adoration, expectation of grace as help, as surprise, as the power of God manifesting itself—even in miracles. In this sense poverty is a virtue of the *creature*, i.e. an intrinsic virtue, specifically, exclusively human, not a reflected divine attribute. Strange, actually, that Christ should have set us an example of precisely these and related virtues: humility, self-denial, patience, obedience—living these qualities far more distinctly than the primary traits of God-likeness— which is why they are, literally, more "Christian". This possibility was unknown to the heathen (in Europe only surely?), that is, they strove after the splendour of the "primary" divine virtues . . . which, perhaps (?), might have been the virtues of Paradise. But *eritis sicut dii*: this danger naturally lies hidden in all such striving, which is why this "noble", high-flying kind of striving can so easily deviate into presumption, pride, man's ruin instead of his elevation.

It was Christ himself who first "canonized" the other, secondary, human virtues. Up until then they had simply been the results of adaptation to circumstance, virtues of the underdog, of slaves, of women and children, i.e. typical embodiments of created existence: dependent, surrendered. The fallen state as the actual state of man, man as pilgrim, was first acknowledged, confirmed, sanctified through the Incarnation—before that he had had to live from the borrowed or simulated glory of old, something only possible for a tiny minority. But being poor also means being a receptacle of kindness. You don't waste gifts on a rich man.

*

IT's easy to tell yourself—or let other people tell you—that your work isn't progressing as it should because you don't pray enough. Perhaps. Yet it seems to me really rather a shame, even irreverent, to fall back on prayer as though it were an irrigation plant for my so-called productivity, a prize fertilizer. . . . In other words turning—or trying to turn—my relations with GOD into a *means*—in his service, of course, not for purely earthly purposes, but all the same. . . . Something fishy here. Actually it ought to be the other way round. Being filled with God should crave expression—one shouldn't have to pad and prop up one's poor, flat, flabby output by prayer. And all official, formal, normal, prayer is so hard for me just now, so infinitely wearying and alien, somehow or other "impossible", in the second sense of the word. Like a dinner off those dolls' plates and dishes with toy foods stuck on which used to delight us in the nursery. Pretty little counterfeits, but how can you offer such things to HIM! At the same time I know perfectly well that the "other" kind of prayer just trickles out, dissipated, if the form is neglected altogether—form of the word, of words, which is, after all, immensely important, a mystery even, transcendent, never quite understood.

*

A MOMENT ago I set a butterfly free. How madly it had fluttered and battered against my window-pane! I simply took it by the wing-tips, as it lay there utterly exhausted, and flung it out—and away it drifted, borne aloft by the wind and sunlight. All it lost in the process was a little wing-dust, and no doubt it will get this back again. I haven't the courage to do the same with my poor soul, for all that it often seems to me like Meyrinck's* man in the bottle.

*

ACTUALLY there is but one weapon, one antidote against sadness: thanksgiving. *Te Deum.* "Blessed art thou, my Lord, for our Brother Death whom no living man can escape"—and for everything which heralds his coming, foreshadows and mirrors him. . . . Curious how the simplest Christian truths, commonplaces really, such as "he must increase and I must decrease" and the like, always strike one as something new, startling, shattering. Really one is as obstinate as a pig.

My exterior life is so extremely sheltered. I'm spared so much, surely one has every occasion to thank God for at least one thorn in my flesh, one pinch of "salt", i.e. penance, to prevent one from getting flabby, from rotting?

But why, *why* does it *have* to be this way? Because of the physical law of connected vessels?—solidarity with suffering

---

* Gustav Meyrinck (1868–1932). He wrote a weird story about a clown enticed to perform in an immense glass bottle and then corked up in it.

humanity, so burdened, so sorrowing, from whose common destiny none of us may exclude himself, even when—no, especially when our own lives are "easy".

Of course these things are really incommensurable, but all the same. Or is that "fear not to have to suffer" just sheer prejudice, conventional thinking a sort of conjuring trick, an attempt to underbid or bribe fate? The fear of having too easy a time? There are pious people who even say: "I think God has forgotten me!" Yet sometimes this sounds positively blasphemous to me: for surely it is the normal thing, entirely in accordance with Creation, God's own will and intention, that his human beings should be happy? And fear and pain, menace, etc., ought to be an exception, a morbid growth, arbitrary restriction and limitation, distortion and violation of existence? But we often talk as though it were exactly the other way round. Surely the few tiny islands whose lives are "whole" ought to strive to keep this way, to safeguard this blessed state, instead of "sacrificing" themselves, hurling themselves as well into the general decomposing mass of evil, to be dissolved in this themselves? BUT "As you would have men treat you. . . ." How this smarts.

*

INCIDENTALLY—in Ecclesiasticus—in the great "Marian" wisdom passage of all places, riches and honour are referred to as *fruit* of the flower of wisdom.

*

NEWS of YY. and that tragic marriage of his. As a young man he married an old woman, or rather he let her marry him, because she paid for him to study. Same theme as in *Islandglocke*,* by the way. Ah, how weak we all are—precisely "intellectuals" are prone to the crassest materialism, just because it can so easily seem as though *everything* were allowed, even to sell oneself, for the sake of "higher values". If Sonia (Dostoevsky) could go on the streets for the sake of her family and end up as a quasi-martyr, what's to prevent the scholar from selling his body and his presence, so as to be able to read and devote himself to research in peace?

* See above, p. 71.

Only in the religious sphere would the deception be even worse—first of all because the object is supreme, and then because the "clear conscience" can find yet a better cloak here: *ad majorem Dei gloriam*. Doesn't this theme continue the thread I started spinning yesterday—poverty and riches, the purpose and privilege of possessions, etc.? Surely only relentless ascetic discipline can save us from this net of subtle, barely conscious, deluding and delusive forms of slavery to the most massive "world"?

*

AND yet pain *is* a good thing. In spite of all my theories and objections to the contrary, pain is good, merely because, fused with HIS own, it is ransom, too—apparently the only kind really valid on earth. Ah, but *why*, I wonder?

*

THE Maid of Orleans* (Sven Stolpe version). Fascinating, the yet unsolved enigmas of her life in which so colourful an exterior destiny so completely conceals what was hidden within.

1. Her undoubted opposition to the visible Church. You cannot defend her smugly by saying that the bribed episcopal court "wasn't really the Church"—*we* know that today, in retrospect, enlightened by umpteen documents and investigations. But Joan herself didn't know it, couldn't even have dreamt it: for her these clerics did represent *the* competent and legitimate ecclesiastical authority.
2. Her betrayal of her Voices in the cemetery at Saint Ouen. Both these things are especially important, since each constitutes an exception to the rule (perhaps not merely from the accepted patterns!) of sainthood.

*

MY radio script on *Gratitude* is worrying me. What should—what *can* you say here? What is killing the zest of life? Why does it die? What's the cause—physically, too? Only very rarely can you answer: pain. Toothache, in which the whole

---

* English translation, London and New York, 1956.

154

world seems to shrink, concentrated in one point of the jaw, isn't really typical. I rather think the answer lies in a feebleness of the senses—dull-wittedness, a growing less and less susceptible to what is beautiful, good and pleasurable in the world, the incapability to appreciate things, to enter into them.

I don't believe people are blasé and apathetic from sheer gargantuan greediness, but rather vice versa, from an ever-dwindling capacity for pleasure, all round (which, incidentally, is what they maintain in all this modern talk about frigidity!). Everything must be overstated to "get across" at all, every form of attraction and stimulus—the loudest music, the shrillest sirens, the crudest colours. All the subtler, finer, muted nuances of pleasure, of delights experienced, are lost. Small wonder that the world seems insipid!

On the other hand, if this blunting were really *genuine*, then you'd think it would make itself felt on the other side, as endurance in suffering. But it doesn't. On the contrary, people are more inclined to whine and complain—negative sensitiveness is on the increase. Some sort of mysterious principle of selection seems to be at work here, which is why people react to some things and don't mind others.

*

Is it selfishness if the suffering of the world doesn't spoil one's own sense of well-being, or at any rate barely touches it at all? Yet how rarely is the sort of person who "suffers from the woes of the world" really convincing!—one so often feels that it is just *panache*—and a magnifying-glass for his own private grievances. If these were to disappear, the plight of humanity would certainly be far less depressing for him!

*

PONDERING on "pedagogic imposture" gives me no peace. For it's everywhere: in morals, in dogmatics, in education and culture—which reveals its "political" nature. Yet it does not only appeal to the *canaille* element in human nature, as I once thought, i.e. operating with terror and bribery, but appeals just as well to the highest urges: dedication, sacrifice, readiness to help, etc.— exactly the line taken by all demagogues. For which reason it is so successful. An appeal to the evil instincts probably wouldn't meet with anything like such a favourable response! Which makes it all the worse. Just as in politics, this propagandist imposture is, basically, a manoeuvre prompted by fear, taking the line of least resistance. It can only be overcome by courage, and by trust in grace. Yet in a way you can hardly blame teachers for not wanting more trouble than they have to put up with anyway—that's surely sound and justifiable good sense. We hear a lot these days about the genius of Don Bosco and how modern his system of education was. But, if I remember rightly, it consisted chiefly of constant supervision, of never leaving the children alone for one moment—anything but liberty and trust. Yet up to a point it may have worked, in immediate results, that is, but how long did these last is the question?

*

OTHER *lumières*: Thanksgiving is the same thing as blessing. "Say grace!"

*

THE introduction to the Stolpe St Joan book finished at last! Some time I really must write something about the three "doubles": Holy obedience—unholy obedience; holy poverty—unholy poverty; holy chastity—unholy abstinence.

*

THE numinous element of the French Revolution (and the other revolutions which followed it). No, these victims were not sacrificed to the profit of man alone, but to gods. But not the ancient gods, which, after all, were really epiphanies of the divine attributes. These "new gods" are somehow related to the facts of the Gospel, under the surface, isolated and secularized: to the SON. And the image of man which appears here as apotheosis is not the original one, but that which was only raised up by the Incarnation—"lowly", labouring, suffering man.

It is Satan's aim to tear apart the image of the Son from the Father and to stake the Son against the Father—that's what every form of spiritualism does—yet rejecting, on the other hand, the Incarnation: the nearest approach surely to breaking up the Trinity, i.e. separating the Spirit from his relation to the world = Creation = Father, as well as from the Incarnation = Church = Son? You cannot play off the Brother against the Father, as our "leftist" Catholics are so fond of doing.

These tendencies are just as much mixed up with our asceticism as with the enthusiasm of all heretics.

*

SAINTS as transparencies. A.R. said the other day that St Sebastian, for instance, was a symbol of primeval man as well, which seems very convincing; the naked man, in the full beauty of youth, bound to the tree—Tree of Paradise and tree of the Cross in one—defenceless against the arrows—*Deus sagittarius est*—unarmed, exposed to the far-flung arrows, the inescapable, which later on concentrated, crystallized, as it were, in the terrible spectacle of pestilence. St Cecilia with the organ, St John Nepomucen, standing high above the waters with the finger of silence raised to his lips—they surely mean something of the same sort, too.

*

STRANGE really, for years I've been saying the Little Office, almost every day—without understanding it in the least. Probably no different from countless "nunlets"—or so I suspect. Yet what momentous things it contains! The hymns alone—alas, untranslatable, into German anyway: our versions are just caricatures, intolerable. The aspects they express are no longer to be found in our present-day Mariology: cosmic on the one hand, and then the profound, massive emphasis upon birth, as bodily, womanly function. Nowadays all this is turned into subjective motherhood, with the emphasis primarily on private psychical or moral features.

"*Quem terra, pontus, sidera*"—"*Intrent ut astra flebiles*"—Incredible how long one can simply "read past" words like these. Now it is dawning on me, for the very first time, that these texts are an abyss full of mysteries, sealed caskets of jewels, only to be opened by meditation.

*

WHAT does it actually mean, to greet someone?

157

I know you—I recognize you—I acknowledge that I know you—I own before other people that you belong in some way to me, to my life. And *saluer*—salute—*salve*—hail—*Heil*: is this not the same as wishing salvation, akin to blessing?

Greeting: joyfully noticing another person, welcoming him, accepting and acknowledging him with words.

*

Legenda Aurea: Genesis lessons in my breviary. What nonsense to try to "verify" them, squeezing them into the letter, these vast, weathered outlines engraved in the profoundest rock-bed of human memory!

*

IN all their concentration on "efficiency" and emulation (maybe forced upon them?), convents these days seem to have lost sight of the fact that they were once asylums too, i.e. sanctuaries for refuge. Nowadays all they want are strong, healthy, normal people, capable of working hard—they've no use any more for those sickly, odd, defenceless individuals, in some way weak and unfit for life, who cannot adapt themselves *in the world*, but who might very well develop special gifts, indeed a real mission, in some sheltered corner, close to God. It is very doubtful whether someone like St Hildegard for instance, would ever have got through a modern novitiate without being sent away as unfit. And lots of people one knows, for that matter, yet the holy "keep" surely ought to be intended and responsible for them too?

*

"RELATIONSHIP to Christ": what do people actually mean when they talk about this? I've noticed so often my own uncomfortable shyness—aversion even—to this stressing of the "historical" figure of Jesus. Isn't it really rather overdone? Surely we *experience* the Transfigured Lord all the time, active, as a Being alive within his Church—why, then, keep looking back on the figure of his earthly span, long since past? True, he can only be *re*-cognized, met, if we already *know* him well from the accounts of his humanity (what disgusting abstractions!—what *is* "humanity" here?), the stories about Jesus of Nazareth, i.e. if we meditate his life in the Gospel and "live with him" there. On the other hand, the "historical Jesus" does seem to me— sometimes—to be simply a starting point, like the kernel from which the Tree has grown—the whole, tremendous reality of Christianity, of the Church. Why, actually, should one go to such trouble to picture this kernel so vividly in one's imagination (moreover you *know* that such pictures *can* only be more or less beside the mark, far short of the real thing), thinking of him as he *was*, instead of on the grown Tree, as he now *is*? What do we *know*, anyway, about the present reality of the Transfigured Lord apart from his manifestation in this his terrestrial *persona*, the Church? About whom and what are we actually talking, when we try to subtract this actual apparition on earth? The SON from the beginning, Wisdom, the Logos, "The Glory of his Father's splendour"—and "Jesus, thy servant".

*

ALL the strange, multicoloured side-lights thrown on the mystery of the Trinity by Gnosticism, the Cabbala, Boehme, etc., only serve to emphasize the burning central importance and indispensability of the doctrine of the Incarnation. (But at the same time increasing my own scepticism of accounts of private revelations to modern mystics, their dialogues with the Trinity. "Dialogues" between the Primeval Abyss and the Abyss answering HIM—the idea of putting *this* into human words! St Paul well knew that it is neither possible nor lawful for man to repeat words heard in heaven!)

*

I CAN never quite get away from the Catharists. Somehow or other I feel them to be extraordinarily congenial. They protested against work, property, marriage, war. Heretical, yes: but actually all these things are not expressions of "life", as such, but very definitely only of our *fallen* life—all those things would never have existed in Paradise—at any rate not "like that".

Whatever else the Manichees may have wanted, surely this was an attempt to construct a life strictly in accordance with the *imago* — or at least to exclude its fallen distortions? It could, of course, be interpreted otherwise, i.e. the spiritualists refuse to accept original sin and the fallen state of nature. They postulated at least one group of elect to whom these things do not apply, who choose to live outside their conditions and precisely by this choice are raised above the *massa damnata*. But the monks?

*

THE Cabbalistic Eros doctrine: "Everything forbidden in the world below is allowed in the world above"—i.e. what some are striving to attain, *behind* distorted images, exists in the world beyond in its pure form. Or, as Bergengruen puts it in the final lines of those lovely verses of his:

> What we touched on earth, we never held—.
> Fragments only, raised against the light.
> But the hidden fruit itself is whole.

*

THE same old theme again. If you belong "wholly" to God, how can, how may you "really" love any other person or thing? —love him so much that you belong to him?

What does it mean at all: to belong? How can you "give" yourself to God, since you are completely his in any case. What does it mean, then, to belong to another creature? Words? Reality? Basically, is it not exactly the same question as: How can anything exist at all "outside" God? Or: where does anything exist which is not in God? Is the "barrier" between him and his creature not altogether a *mysterium stricte dictum*?

The Cabbalistic doctrine of the "contraction" of God to make room for his Creation is really the only convincing answer for me here. There must surely be some sort of analogy on the human plane as well.

How does a woman belong both to her children and her husband? Or someone like NN., for instance, so strongly attached to her father, how can she belong to him *and* to her husband? Or, in the old feudal times, how could a man belong to his lord and his wife at one and the same time? The circle is probably the original figure. But the ellipse is a figure too, encompassing not one, but two focal points. But is the latter a natural shape, I wonder, which has always existed, or has it just been invented, constructed by mathematicians?

I think it's a question of precedence—not "side by side", so to speak, but of above and below. Who ranks before whom in every situation which calls for decision? There is nothing "next to" and "outside" God; but, horizontally, following the hierarchical order, quite a lot of possibilities do exist—even in his Presence. . . . In the lives of the saints even. How did Péguy put it in those lines of his about St Joan in *Eve*?

> *n'était qu'une simple enfant perdue dans deux amours,*
> *l'amour de la patrie parmi l'amour de Dieu. . . .*

❧ 1955 — 1957 ❧

I'VE come to the end of Von Hügel's voluminous work on St Catherine of Genoa. For such outlay in erudition, such an immense scholarly apparatus, it's basically an oddly unrewarding book (for me!), but full of interesting side-lights nevertheless.

Curious, for instance, that Catherine, always universally cited as *the* recognized "authority", the most important and competent witness to the nature of Purgatory, should actually never have had a vision of it—neither as "shewing" nor as "visiting in spirit", as other mystics did, Anne Catherine Emmerich, for instance, St Frances of Rome, etc. Her statements are pure *conclusions*, analogies, based on her own spiritual experiences of suffering and bliss: "So that's what it must be like in Purgatory!"

*

VON HÜGEL supposes strong Platonic and Platonizing influences, especially in regard to Catherine's "doctrine of the soul"—we may call it that. But *could* all this be just "borrowed" from books and conversation? With that youth of hers, and her *mondain*, unintellectual past? Or perhaps hers was a typical case of what scholars so seldom recognize: that the same truth can be revealed to different kinds of people in different eras?

But, even if he's right, is all this traditional lore about the soul really only Greek? And what is "only" anyway? Why should *everything* of this nature in the Bible be "revelation"— didn't quite a lot exist already as "Semitic presuppositions"?

He talks, for instance, about the neo-Platonic concept of the pre-existence of every soul, perfect and immaculate before its incarnation; and how profoundly Catherine's mind and feelings were influenced by the notion of the "lapse" of every human soul into a body at the Fall, and he goes on to say that, despite its echo in the deutero-canonical books of Wisdom and a non-doctrinal passage of St Paul (??), this is not Christian but rather

162

neo-Platonic; yet this idea, with its vehement rejection of the body, could not fail to appeal to mystics. But—must this appeal really be rooted in "aversion" to the body?—are not quite a number of other, and more important, factors involved here?

Catherine herself said (I'm "quoting" from memory): "So long as a human being is still capable of speaking of divine things, can savour them, understanding, remembering and desiring them, then he has not yet reached the harbour." "Should a human being think he truly beholds spiritual things as they really are, let him pluck out the eye of his presumption."

"From time to time I have the feeling that certain instincts [urges? involuntary impulses?] are being annihilated within me, which have hitherto seemed good and perfect: yet as soon as they are destroyed I perceive how evil and imperfect they were." This strikes me as very important, for it shows that the judgment of conscience can change, and precisely in someone whose conscience must already have been particularly highly developed, sensitive and illuminated.

And how significant for a contemporary of Luther's—one ought always to have this passage handy for discussions: "I would not that as much as one single meritorious act be ascribed to my separate self, not even if it should convince me that I would never fall again and that my salvation would be certain as soon as I had accomplished it: for such an imputation would be for me *as though from hell*. I would rather remain in peril of eternal damnation than be saved by such an act of my separate being, and furthermore to be aware of it."

Incidentally, Von Hügel admits with an admirable conscientiousness, which other hagiographers could well emulate, that Catherine herself never wrote down a single word of her mystical doctrine. It was, all of it, spoken in conversations with her friends and *protégés*, straight from her warm and loving heart. The cold, even chilling process of deliberate composition contributed the least part to the final product, and it was not hers.

She held the soul in its essence to be eternal rather than immortal. (This is most significant in comparison with Dame Julian, who lived as a recluse a good hundred years earlier, long before all Renaissance Platonism and quite outside the learned world!)

Catherine did not go to confession for ten years. Von Hügel "justifies" this by quoting a statement by St Thomas on Easter confession: "that since, strictly speaking, that divine institution and obligation only applies to confession of mortal sins, a man not aware of having committed any mortal sin is not obliged to confess his venial sins: that it suffices, for him, to keep this commandment by presenting himself to the priest with a declaration that he feels free from every suspicion of being in a state of mortal sin". No question, then, of simply dispensing oneself from Easter confession in such a case—as many good Christians probably do these days—but rather of submitting to the ruling of the Church all the same, in this special way. This really makes sense—and is behaving fairly.

*

CURIOUS how this book should have left me feeling restless and uncomfortable rather than "edified", for all its wonderful, indeed sublime thoughts, etc. I think it's because Catherine is the very purest type of what I call the "God alone" school of mystics, i.e. those who reject and even despise and loathe Creation with as vehement a passion as they seek and love God. And there simply *is* something wrong with this attitude, extolled as it is by writers on ascesis.

Maybe Von Hügel is right in attributing this to Catherine's very special and personal need for *self-defence*—against her own fiercely possessive even hysterical temper. With her unrestrained, insatiable "claimfulness" she would—had she been allowed—have seized and devoured the whole world in the jaws of her Ego, effortlessly, without turning a hair—leaving nothing over from that gulp. Granted that she simply had no alternative—not God or the world—but: God or Myself—and the whole world merely as a sort of handle. . . . Perhaps, and of course it's very wonderful, grandiose, and quite in keeping with one's idea of a Renaissance figure. . . . But surely all the less exemplary for that, *imitandum*, "normal", in the sense of setting a norm for us? Above all there is not the slightest valid statement about the world, just Catarina Adorni.

But I'm quite bowled over by the discovery how much of her "doctrine" about the soul seems to be just Greek—things I've taken for granted all my life simply as universal human belief, as well as dogmatically Christian. With my lamentable ignorance of Greek philosophy at that! Innate ideas? (One really ought to learn Greek—the mother tongue of the mind.)

*

THE Eastern Church views the three vows first and foremost symbolically, above all obedience, i.e. the monk must learn that it does not matter *what* he does, so long as he fulfils the will of God *in the symbol of the abbot*. But the parish priest isn't living in a vacuum, beyond activity, but in his own sphere of very concrete work, with its practical aims, where it is by no means immaterial what he does or chooses not to do. Which is why it seems to me unpractical, to say the least, if he is allowed no latitude, according to his own discretion, in liturgical and pastoral questions—evening mass, or the use of the vernacular in certain instances—but that everything must be decreed by the episcopal authority, or even by Rome. Perhaps it could be put this way: It is not for the parish priest to "practise obedience" as an art for art's sake, as it were—rather he stands in obedience to the Cause which he is serving together with his superiors, not just to the individual bearer; he must obey his office, more especially where the "authority" is no longer either a "person" or even an office, but simply an apparatus. It is not for superiors to put priests to moral tests and the like, but rather to interpret what the Cause demands.

*

THAT note of Beil's in the *Christlicher Sonntag* is very important: Monophysitism applied to the Church, as though she were wholly divine and not human at all any more. The reverse, of course, is just as true: people seeing the Church *merely* as a natural, historic, social structure. Curious how the former process first seized upon the person of Jesus, extending then to the Church herself, and today includes our Lady. For that's how it is, more or less. And some people would even like to go a step further—with Little Thérèse. . . . Whoever, for instance, could picture our Lady as cross, or even mildly put out, let's say by toothache (did they have such a thing?), or perhaps the rigours of the Flight into Egypt? that she could ever have answered dear St Joseph sharply—that the infant Jesus might ever have got on her nerves?—or that she could have asked gossipy questions in the village? Trifles, tiniest ones, all of them. Yet most pious people would think them sacrilege.

The same applies to the violent opposition in certain quarters to my book on St Thérèse.* We're always being told that the saints were "human beings, flesh and blood like you and me", but woe betide anyone who takes this seriously and demonstrates on a living object!

*

THERE is a special kind of clerical narrow-mindedness surely rooted in the fact that the clergy in itself is a genuine caste—its lineage transmitted by brains instead of by blood, but no less "stamping" and restricting. It needs tremendous personality to step outside these patterns—just as it takes a lot for an aristocrat to be something else besides "U", as Nancy Mitford would put it.

*

A PROPOS the parable of the Great Supper: Those who made excuses were all people who didn't "need" to come; who didn't have to accept an invitation in order to get a decent meal for once; nor were they asked for this reason but to do them honour and as friends. The poor and the cripples, on the other hand, came *merely* because they were hungry, honour and friendship meaning nothing to them—maybe they learnt afterwards that they had sat down together with the king, and this knowledge then kindled a new sense of gratitude and dignity. But this wasn't there at first: they only came for what they could get. Perhaps they're the majority in the Church. Those from the highways and the hedgerows are the most "mixed" lot. But how awful are those words that none of those who were first invited shall taste the supper! For they themselves spurned the love of the Lord who chose them—spurned his very choice.

*

* *The Hidden Face*, London and New York, 1959.

THE thermal springs here flow day and night, winter and summer, whether they're needed or not—really an image of the grace of God.

*

My commentary on St Alphonsus Liguori has set the cat among the pigeons: The "holy neurotics" among whom I think I must place him have a mystical vocation—"to pay off the debt which the afflictions of Christ still leave to be paid, for the sake of his body, the Church"—i.e. to endure to the bitter end the ailments and infirmities which he, the Divine Man, was not *allowed* to take upon himself, yet which are so essential a factor of human suffering. In them, his members, he is, even here, "like unto us in all things except in sin". And if, like St Alphonsus (he lived to be ninety—how awful!) they endured such a long life in his strength, they really did achieve the "greater things yet" which he himself foretold for his disciples in his farewell discourse. I even think this "existential" message of St Alphonsus far greater and more important than that of his writings, very period after all—perhaps it may even outlive these. . . .

*

DIONYSIUS the Areopagite: Believe it or not, he was the favourite saint of Thomas Aquinas who is said to have quoted him 1,700 times! Our modern St Thomas opponents wouldn't even dream of it—nothing more contrary to their idea of him as their pet rationalist.

*

CONCERNING "naughting" ascesis: "Someone who is lacking himself can only be healed by being prescribed a dose or diet of himself." That's Novalis.

*

A PROPOS the social background of the clergy: It would seem that the training of boys from the illiterate lower classes for the priesthood calls for *petits séminaires* designed to compensate, as it were, for the "cultured atmosphere" lacking in the boys' own homes. For otherwise what are the universities and seminaries to work on later? On the other hand, it stands to reason that this secondary, artificial ersatz-home training must be a very empty, one-sided affair, since the womanly element is utterly lacking, above all the mother.

Not that our girls are trained "atmospherically" for marriage and a family either. And then they try to make up for this by arranging "pressure cooker" courses for brides, lectures on marriage, etc., etc. As though what ought to have been growing and maturing imperceptibly for twenty years or so could be picked up by sheer brain-effort in a single retreat—or maybe just a few evening courses. What optimism!

*

READING St Luke the other day I came across that odd combination of three verses in Chapter 16. 16–18, beginning with the Law and its letter and then jumping, all of a sudden, to divorce. We're told the evangelists—or their copyists—sometimes strung together unconnected sayings of our Lord just "by chance". But it suddenly struck me that the sequence might be interpreted this way:

"The law and the prophets lasted until John's time; since that time, it is the kingdom of heaven that has its preachers, *and all who will, press their way into it.* And yet it is *easier* for heaven and earth to disappear than for one line of the law to perish. Every man who puts away his wife and marries another is an adulterer, and he too is an adulterer, that marries a woman who has been put away." Could this mean that the man who "presses his way" into the kingdom of heaven, not to seek the will of God more simply, more humbly, more obediently than before, but merely to escape from his old "yoke", is committing adultery against his previous sacred allegiance—he's a fugitive from marriage, and cannot be incorporated into the New Law: adultery against the Torah, as it were, to which the chosen people were betrothed?

A point for converts too, incidentally—as Newman, for instance, stated very clearly.

*

Larion's Law by Peter Freuchen.* An Indian saga written by a Dane who lived for thirty years among the woodland tribes of

* London, 1954.

168

Alaska and even had an Eskimo wife. He ought to know. Very intriguing and exciting. I'd never realized so fully before that when they first encountered the white man (Russians) a century ago, these Alaskan Indians were still living in the genuine Stone Age—which meant that within the span of a single generation they had to jump a couple of thousand years—not like the Japanese, for instance, from the Middle Ages to modern times, a "mere" four to six hundred years! Small wonder really that only a few survived.

Really one is ashamed to belong to a white race. We get so worked up about the concentration camps, the Gestapo and its present-day equivalents, etc., yet what "we" did to Indians, Negroes, Australian aborigines (not even out of political fanaticism either, but as a matter of course, *en passant*)—surely that surpasses even the twentieth-century crimes against humanity?

*

For my special benefit: Novalis: "Fragments would seem to be the most satisfactory form of presenting what is still incomplete, and this means of communication is, therefore, recommended to all those who have not yet achieved integration, but still have some worthwhile opinions to offer."

*

Fragment: Courage to grasp *one* truth which is not yet polished and filed and fitted, but still jagged, with sharp edges and "points" on which you can cut your skin. . . . Incidentally, no fragment stands alone, just by itself—something scholars fail to understand.

*

I'm astonished to realize from those last Bromfield novels just how "period" the era of our parents—our own childhood!—already is, as distinct in itself as Renaissance or our Biedermeier,* and just as interesting as a self-contained cultural epoch. An independent "unit of time", no longer immediately comprehensible to the next generation.

*

* Biedermeier—corresponding to Regency and Early Victorian.

THE Our Father. Did it really only dawn on me today that first and foremost, before all the moral aspects such as awe, trust, gratitude, etc., "Father" means "origin", the being determining the *nature* of the children, their "kind" and thereby their rank? In our case then divine. From the very dawn of man's creation, restored only, not "invented", by Baptism? The Fathers took it for granted. But who really ventures to take this seriously these days? Really to live by this knowledge?

*

ASCETICISM, in the sense of bodily mortification. First stage : The so-called "primitive" human being is still identical with his body, i.e. what touches his body touches his "self", his being. Blows do not only hurt, they also break the will, break pride, they really humiliate him, i.e. they kindle humility, contrition. Convent penances, for instance, such as kissing the ground, kissing the feet of the others, eating off the floor, etc.

Second stage : Man withdraws now from his body—he raises himself above it : now he is "above" his sensations, able to ignore them—like the Indian at the stake, the fakir, the Stoic— or, as a Christian, an ascetic, a martyr even. Nothing inflicted upon him from "outside" can afflict him any longer. Being beaten increases his pride, he depises those who feel really humiliated, even abased by such practices. But such domination of the mind and the independence which ensues *also* mean a split within human nature. They enable not only heroic endurance of bodily pain, but also an unfeeling, callous divorce of Eros from human emotions, rendering people incapable of really meaning, not simply "performing" certain gestures of reverence, courtesy, worship, adoration (kissing hands, genuflection, prostration). Since most people these days seem to have reached this stage, it becomes a problem whether the old penitential practices still the rule in many orders make sense any more, indeed aren't directly harmful. (The discipline, for instance, still used as far as I know in the English Oratory, and by German Redemptorist Fathers, as well as in some nunneries.) Perhaps such things are just "museum pieces" nowadays, left-over relics, negative, serving no purpose, if not actually bad for people?

The third stage would be re-integration. I believe this is *one* reason why Christ's sufferings were absolute: because his nature was "oned" again—like Adam's.

"Carnal sins"—also in the wider sense, such as anger, jealousy, pride of blood, sloth—ought to be punished or treated with penances of the flesh. Surely this would be much more effective!

*

INFANT Baptism as early as possible. This really does seem to be rooted directly in the rite of Circumcision. I'm surprised this isn't mentioned more often. Reception into the Covenant— eight days after the birth—no question of "belonging" before! Makes very good sense when you come to think of it, at any rate as long as there was still some living sense of clanship, of family: they just couldn't bear the thought of the youngest member remaining a stranger, an outsider among them. Mater Anna Neuner (one of twelve children!) used to tell us that they were never allowed to kiss the new baby before it was christened —it was not yet really one of them, "inside" the ring. Austrian mountain peasants used to say: "You can't leave him to stew so long in heathendom." Very obvious!

*

THE Our Father again: Deeper and deeper the insight is growing upon me that father is identical with source, origin, starting point. The most obvious of truisms, I know, but it's so much the fashion here to play down "biological" fatherhood against moral and spiritual paternity, reducing the former to a mere trifle. Ernst Michel, for example, asserts that paternity in itself creates no bond whatever between father and child—indeed that a man only becomes a father by a genuine act of adoption, a "spiritual" act of accepting the child as his own, whereas the mother becomes a mother by giving birth. Typically modern: reality must first be created by emotional experience, as well as deliberate reflection! And yet it is really the other way round: "moral" fatherhood is far more the functional thing, since it is roused—and limited—by the needs of the child (and may cease with these): the father's duty to protect, maintain and

171

educate. These things a father can refuse to undertake, for instance should he choose to remain anonymous. Only one thing —his being "author" of that life, its "pro-creator"—remains independent of his will and resolve, unalterable despite all denials, even perjury. Not for one second can this anonymous father cease to be the physical origin of this particular offspring, even if the child should die. (From this angle the blasphemy of artificial insemination seems more abysmal than ever.)

On the other hand, it is not the best-behaved, most willing, obedient son or daughter, who is the "best" child, the most intensely "child"—or even the child who thinks and talks most about his father and to him—but rather the child who most closely resembles him, shows most of his kin and "kind", who testifies to his father by his very being, his likeness, re-presenting his father, as author of his life.

*

ANOTHER insight into this same web of thought: That for the "great" poor—Francis, Elizabeth, Charles de Foucauld—not poverty as status, but the stooping, the descent into poverty constituted the *imitatio* of the Incarnation. One mustn't forget this. Which is why you could say that only the rich can become poor—and the poor can remain so—none of us being really "poor" by nature—at the most a pauper, needy, wretched, but that's quite a different thing. Those born poor are to be honoured rather as *images* of the Incarnate than as his imitators. Kings, lords, artists, makers of things are "mirrors" of the Father or of the Godhead, i.e. the people formerly "deified". Heroes, on the other hand, already reflect the Son—the Saviour, the Liberator. And who are mirrors of the Holy Ghost? Women—on both planes: mothers and ladies reflect the Lord and Giver of life; the beloved as inspiration, making the world more lovely, reflects the Spirit who "adorns" the universe. The virgin, concerned with sacrifice, renunciation, expiation, belongs to the realm of the Son Descendent.

Is then our *origin* in heaven and not on the earth? Surely this must mean more than that we are just "thoughts of God"? For animals and plants are such, too. Yet we could scarcely say that their *Father* is in heaven—their Creator, yes, but not their Father. Does this only mean dignity of the mind, and not of the entire human nature?

*

Die Frauen von Magliano—a ghastly novel about a female lunatic asylum. Probably a lot of it is true. Our Father which art in heaven—Father of these creatures, too, of these stinking, slavering human beasts of prey, tearing at everything, wallowing in their own filth. Surely they must be possessed? For I simply cannot bring myself to believe that this is "original" human nature — that what comes out here is our real constitution, the "raw material", once abandoned by its keepers, reason and consciousness: that their behaviour reveals the true inclinations and urges of man, let loose at last, untrammelled and unconstrained. I'd rather say that when these keepers are bound, the *enemies* of man take possession of the house left open and unguarded, destroying everything within it—just as the soldiers behaved in derelict houses in war-time: smashing, wrecking, befouling—exactly the same thing. Now they can force the defenceless creatures into a *pantomime* of all seven deadly sins, which would never have been possible voluntarily, in full consciousness. I wonder what would happen if a genuine charismatic exorcist were to enter such an asylum?

*

I'M hot on the trail of the Psyche myth in the figures of virgin saints, especially the virgin martyrs. What traces shall I find, I wonder? Shall I be successful at all? Is the Church the "soul" of the world, and is the fate of the "virgin" therefore the destiny of the *Church* in the world? Beauty and bride, bride of the King, yet persecuted, bound and fettered, thrown into dungeons, condemned to death—miraculously saved again and again, but only as it were to face the next torture—and only through the very last, the inevitable agony of death to enter heaven for the wedding with the King's Son? (Historically a most uncomfortable prospect, alas!)

The likeness: that it is a *charge*—not just an offer—and yet cannot be realized, accomplished, in any other way but in

173

resembling Jesus the Crucified—and his end!—this is gnawing within me, as a silent and painful awareness.

*

PERHAPS it was Benedict Joseph Labre's special task to "redeem" the core of truth in Jansenism? Literally to embody this nucleus, this intention, in absolute purity, in obedience and humility—so that this splinter of truth too might find shape within the Church: and at the same time to atone for the measure of actual heretical pride, self-will and revolt within the general phenomenon of Jansenism in history. For his own concept of God was actually the Jansenist image: the God of wrath, the strict and terrible Judge, all-demanding, to be approached only in fear and trembling—no, only to be adored from afar, never to be neared at all. I was staggered to read that he, who spent all his time on his knees, rapt in ecstatic prayer, actually avoided Holy Communion, even at Easter, and—or so it is said—declined even to receive it as viaticum. A rum crowd, our saints, but the really preposterous thing is that the Church actually canonized them! I'm sure there must be similar vocations today.

*

THAT correlation Virgin–Psyche is even more exact than I'd thought. Of earthly origin, the girl is intended for an earthly man, the god entices her but remains invisible. When she seeks him he vanishes: and then comes the hard quest of purification and finally the union. A certain affinity with the Lohengrin legend, too.

*

THAT book on love for girls again. It's *so* well-meaning, but the *roots* are just wrong all the same. Like its source. Strange how these self-appointed *ex professo* advocates of the body are really the most incorrigible spiritualists! They fancy that the most resistant, obscure, most inscrutable enigmas of "bodiliness" can be perfectly penetrated and pierced by the neon-rays of reason. And if you don't feel like it, shrinking back in awe and wonder, they put you down as having been spoilt by a frustrating education, etc. and try to reform you. They place all their faith in talk, discussion, outspokenness.

For instance, all physical facts must not only be "good", but "nice" too, and "beautiful". Of course, for a doctor even a tumour may be "a splendid specimen" and leeches positively fascinating—taken merely as structures, tissue patterns, etc. But this means complete abstraction, intellectual comprehension as divorced from sensual impression—perhaps rather like the way brain surgery sometimes dissociates imagination and emotional reaction. Doctors and nurses *must* train themselves to such abstraction or they could never endure their profession. But with the best will in the world no one could pretend that excrement, for instance, is *not* unpleasant and stinking, one's repugnance "unjustified" and unnatural, that one ought to react differently to smells, etc., etc. Sheer blather. They simply refuse to admit that there is *anything* offensive, distressing, forbidding *at all*, as though such an admission bordered on sacrilege. What is "morally pure" must at all costs be presented as clean, sweet and inviting on the aesthetical plane as well. They're always insisting that the Fall of man had solely spiritual effects and none whatever in "bodiliness"—our body remaining completely "paradisaical". But upholding this notion would mean closing all five senses to reality. I should think it would be more honest, more human, more Christian to acknowledge and accept one's own and other people's frailty, our injured and abased nature, instead of forcibly denying and idealizing things. Even apart from the fact that such natural aversions might be a most important regulative, like shyness—part of the "fences of the law" in our fallen state. Body and soul having quarrelled, as it is, controlling and curbing the bodily urges would be even more difficult if no physical "brakes" were attached to their allurement. These restraints must be overcome by the soul, in tenderness and love. This makes them a kind of selective principle for sympathy, i.e. selection somehow begins with them—physical resistance only dissolving if a certain mutual harmony exists. Even mouth and breath, for instance, belong already to the sphere within which any proximity of strangers or indifferent acquaintances is felt as offensive, impertinent, to be avoided. Yet it is precisely in the joyous acceptance of even the unlovely elements in the beloved, tokens of his fall and his mortality, that bodily love becomes the symbol of spiritual love. We are human beings,

175

and neither on the spiritual nor on the physical plane can we hope for a wholly ideal partner.

*

I've been reading Sholem Asch, *Der Trost des Volkes* [Comforter of the people], the life of the Polish *zaddik* Yechiel of Pzhysha, "the Sack-bearer", a successor of Yehudi and of Rabbi Bunam. Roughly speaking during the Napoleonic era. Incredibly Catholic, startlingly Catholic, positively and negatively: asceticism, good works, merit; the strictest observance of chastity; "buying heaven"; the very definitely monastic vocations of the young men who left their wives and children to follow the *zaddik*—were the disciples of Jesus any different? Saints, miracles, castigations—sackcloth and ashes, fasting. The unmarried *hasid* is wedded to the Shekhinah = Sophia!! Marriage is the image of the union of God with the *world*. We say: with the soul. But would not the soul = man be an image and symbol of the world? See the Romances of St John of the Cross. How close, how understandable Jesus is in this mirror! He is, after all, a typically Jewish figure, not the least bit "supra-national", cosmopolitan, etc. as people like to make out. "Jesus the *zaddik*", the holy Jew, yes, *the* holy Jew. Which is why I find the figure of the Sack-bearer so deeply moving—a shadow of our Lord. The disciples' vocation, their relationship to Jesus, even the "anecdotes" which actually make up the gospels—how very Hasidic it all is!

*

THE wedding is *the* eschatological symbol. Which is why all fairy-tales end with the wedding—after which eternity begins: "And they lived happily ever after."

*

A CLANDESTINE marriage is actually a *contradictio in adjecto*, for the whole point of marriage is that what was a "private" love affair—secret, concerning none but the lovers themselves—is promulgated in the eyes of the world, acknowledged and ratified by the community.

*

176

ALL these cases of "slipped discs": what a telling symbol of the lack of "backbone" these days, of "carrying" substance! Man is destined to bear things, to bear with things—but he won't do it any more, he just can't bear it.

*

I'M burrowing into that curious anthology entitled *Adam, der Mythos vom Urmenschen* [Adam, the Myth of Primal Man] with growing amazement. But I seem to gather something *quite* different from these "myths"—far from what the author intends to impress on the reader. Crazy scrawls, from which, as you gaze at them, quite another, hidden outline seems to emerge. The whole book is a distorting mirror, rows of them even—and yet they do reflect glimpses of reality, too.

Underneath and in between those "grimacing minds" of the sects (goodness, what a crew of lunatics, some of them!) you catch sight again and again of the secret script, the message of treasure-hunters for lost scraps of revelation.

That *consent* about the primal state, for instance: That man cannot be accounted for from below, but must be explained from above. Not an animal ascending, but a creature fallen from glory. Of course their stuff is, partly, crude mythology (*not* myth!)— but even so their fancy works upon a genuine core. Sophia, for instance, Adam's first spouse—even in the most preposterous disguise she is yet a mythological, even fairy "impersonation" of sanctifying grace.

Incidentally: what about the Irish story of the Abbot St Columba whom God betrothed to the Spirit of Prophecy in the shape of a beautiful queen? [Acta SS. Boll. Jan. 11.]

And the Lady Poverty chosen by St Francis for his bride— isn't it very much the same thing?

*

MOST Christians take sex merely as an animal phenomenon which has to be regulated by ethics and morals, but because they think it is in itself only animal, they cannot get over the "weight" attached to it. Which is why they must keep playing it down by "plain speaking", enlightened talk, etc., attempting to reduce it to insignificance, a mere bagatelle. . . .

Yet the only satisfactory explanation is really the mystical one. Only from this aspect does sex make sense at all and its "apotheosis", positive or negative—for its deification and damnation are no less than this—rightly proportioned. Without this mystical key it *becomes* a merely biological set of facts—as in the animal world—and it's absurd to try to pump it up with a lot of metaphysical reflections and rules, simply for the sake of keeping things tidy.

*

JESUS washes the feet of his disciples. "He laid his garments aside, took a towel, and put it about him." Could this *also* mean: At the Fall Adam laid aside the "garment of light" and put on the apron of fig leaves—proof of his frailty and nakedness!—and those so mysterious "garments of skins"—the animality which now, for thousands of years to come, determined his appearance, his behaviour, his form of existence? And our Lord "re-enacted" this, as it were, divinely, by laying aside the garment of his glory and taking upon himself the shape of a slave—the apron of the slave in service. Washing their feet, cleansing them of the dust and dirt of the earth gathered every day, automatically, simply by "walking the earth".

*

THE paschal lamb: male, first-born, without blemish, as ransom for the Hebrew first-born on the death of the first-born of Egypt, man and beast: signifying HIM, the First-born of God, slain in sacrifice as the "first-born of Israel" = "my first-born Israel", whose blood was shed to redeem all.

One lamb for each household—every supper company must be large enough to consume the lamb entirely—in this they are all united again, one table, one house, one lamb which is consumed by them completely. "Nothing may remain till next day": eschatological. "Next day" the symbol will exist no longer and the meal will be over.

*

Ecce Homo: crowned with the thorns and thistles of Adam's cursed acre, his sceptre a bulrush, grown in the marshes, the swamp—domain of serpents and of dragons.

*

178

FROM that unbelievably lovely book *Strömendes Lob* (St Mechtild of Hackeborn). The Lord told her: "Think of the love which so humbled me unto the bridal kiss with which Judas came to embrace me. Beneath this kiss my heart sensed such love that, had he only repented, I would have won his soul as bride on the strength of this kiss. For at that moment I betrothed unto myself those predestined by me as my brides from the beginning of time." No one could have invented such things—this seems to me to bear the seal of a divine "shewing".

*

MICHELANGELO (in that book of Walter Nigg's about the old masters): "He who would bring forth good works let him withdraw from all trouble and vexation, for art calls for meditation and solitude, and a quiet mind, it will not that the spirit wanders." What a condemnation of our own society which grants pregnant women none of this seclusion which motherhood would call for just as much as art. Such "retirement" ought to be the privilege of all expectant and nursing mothers, as well as those with small babies—as much their due as the right of artists and hermits—while, vice versa, nuns should be led into the world of action by their "motherliness".

*

JEREMIAS GOTTHELF: "Worldly and properly spiritual things are much more closely related than people imagine." This reminds me of the very similar words of Blumhardt the elder: "Man must go through two conversions: from natural to spiritual man and back again to the natural." Both belong to my theme: "Devotion to the World."

*

WHY have we dropped the anointing of the sick, except as Extreme Unction, when death is imminent? Merely in the enlightened fear that it could be taken as quackery, even as magic? And why is baptismal anointing not administered to converts at their reception into the Church? In the Liturgy this does not appear just as a decorative fringe tacked on, to be discarded at will with no loss to anyone, but rather as a genuine function within the process of Baptism, something to be taken seriously. But then that's just it: nowadays the reception of a convert into the Church is no longer a rite of initiation, a "pneumatic" event, but merely a legal act, and for the convert himself no more than a purely private change of opinions.

*

WHAT psychologists call "projection" is, at the best, the search for a "positive scapegoat" on which people can hang all their personal day-dreams and ideals, instead of realizing them for themselves.

*

"SPIRITUAL drought": isn't it a pretty exact analogy to frigidity?—and, as such, a fitting enough modern "penance" for the spiritual *gourmandise* and *voluptas* of those who are perpetually hunting for excitement, pleasure and sensation in religion?

*

MARY WARD: Until the Jesuits arrived on the scene the religious orders were "androgynous": both a masculine and feminine system, the "first" and the "second" order constituted the order as a whole—for the Benedictines, Cistercians, Carmelites, the Franciscans, Dominicans and probably a host of others, long forgotten. The Jesuits formed the first purely male society—bachelors. And with Mary Ward came the spinsters as an independent kind of religious order. But no, not *with* her, *after* her. She always intended herself and her followers as the feminine counterpart and complement to the S.J.—much against *their* will!—planning and pursuing this end with all the energy and vehemence of which she was capable. But this was so directly contrary to the character and will of the S.J. that she had to give in, and so the way was paved for her own community— without a masculine "half". And so the "beehives" began, with the Mother General as queen-bee. For hitherto even the small communities of women religious, such as the Ursulines, with no masculine counterpart still had a male "head" in the bishop, the male guiding counter-pole, i.e. these convents were still enlarged reproductions of the single consecrated virgin who depended on her bishop as the Church on Christ. But now this

180

element was dropped and religious ant-hills began to take form —sterile to the last degree, merely "useful". I wonder whether in her "providential" opposition to Mary Ward (as distinct from pure policy) the Church *also* sensed this break with the past—the break-away of women from the bi-polar world into a somehow un-natural, one-level existence, and endeavoured to postpone this as long as possible? That she was actually prepared to sacrifice the enormous and undeniable *usefulness* of the new institute to the traditional idea of religious? Did the ancient *Zeitgeist* oppose the rising one not *only* out of stubbornness, but also because it sensed instinctively the inevitable consequences? For once this door was opened it could never again be closed. Sooner or later the lone "professional bee"—the "single" female, no longer virgin-bride but simply virgin-spinster— would have to follow in the wake of the corporation, the conventual bee-hive. Single, i.e. "rid" of man—neither bound to him nor really free of him, building up a purely "women's world", in which the female element hypertrophied—and atrophied—ending up at last as a hybrid substitute for the man it believed to be no longer necessary. How significant and how salutary—and what a mercy it is—that with her iron barrier against female priesthood the Church has bolted at least this door against feminine autarchy! Here at least even the religiously emancipated woman still remains tied to man by her spiritual dependence. So that, strangely enough, even in this sphere the Church is once again maintaining the order of nature.

*

I KEEP fiddling about with the Little Flower. Anything but easy to get a grip on what I really mean. . . . It would certainly be unfair to call her "limited", narrow. She was *very* alert and intelligent, and could certainly have gone to university today, passing all examinations with flying colours. But her *horizon* was limited—she was quite definitely a "vertical" person, could only grow skywards and into the depths—no breadth.

How would she have grown old, I wonder? Or has such a type no "disposition" towards ageing, and must reach her fulfilment young because certain dimensions are simply lacking?

*

THAT heavy Pentecost sadness which touches me every year at this season: not to share any more—not to belong where young people experience Pentecost. But do they still really *experience* it, I wonder? I read announcements of religious congresses for young people, and then the reports—and they only serve to increase my sadness by doubt. How dull, how thin, how stale, worn and stereotyped, how unnecessary most of it seems: subjects and problems and approaches—futile, milk-and-watery, conventional. What is supposed to come out of all this? Deep, deep down is the agonizing suspicion that the Spirit abandoned the Church long ago, and we're simply juggling on with empty, hackneyed words—husks. . . . But what else *can* we do? We—who are baptized, confirmed, fed by the Eucharist, living in the sacrament of matrimony or in orders!—The Spirit perhaps, but not grace.

Here and there you meet people in whom you can still believe that the Spirit is really present, silent, secretly, yet living, forming, working. But X., for example, she's a judgment on me—and a scathing one: I'm exasperated with her, she being one of those *impossible dévotes,* whose every religious utterance is infuriating: yet who could deny that, *by faith*—even her silly, childishly frilled faith!—and *only* through her faith, she *is* in fact living miles above her poor futile fossilized beetle's existence. Yes, she does live like a pussy-cat, but right in the midst of that piteous failure still in vivid contact with the world above . . . and truly sustained by her willing participation in its power and its glory.

And it's just as mean and as vulgar to be ashamed of her in front of the "minds" of this world and the "superior people" as it would be to disavow a poor or ill-bred relation, just for fear of being thought dowdy or provincial by the intelligentsia, or classed among the "family narcissists" *à la famille Martin.* Humanly speaking the Church as a whole will never cut a good figure, and her exceptions seem almost like another species.

*

ALL the same: the "Legion of little Souls" *does exist,* and they did become manifest in the Little Flower. True, they get on our nerves more than they edify us—precisely that awful Martin family with their pompous self-preoccupation, their insufferable family worship, a perpetual mutual admiration society—but, say what you will, such people really do *have* religion, in the strictest sense of the word—living contact, authentic "conversation" with God. They do live out of their trust in him, are honestly concerned with seeking and doing his will, they take pains about being kind to their neighbours, for his sake. Is this really not enough? To hell with all esoterics!—Christianity is *not* esoteric, nor is it "democratic" and levelling. On the contrary: not because everybody can claim a right to it, but just because nobody can lawfully claim it, does God send rain and sunshine for good and bad alike, for the geniuses, the idiots and the smug—*non horruisti virginis uterum.*

*

SOLACE of Pentecost: the recognition (truism, as usual!) that God sees the countless tiny glow-worms in multitudes of us, in spite of everything being as it is, far more than one thinks: the countless hidden soul-sparks in good and in wicked people, in the pious and the others, in the smug and the "awakened"— insufferable as we all are, good and bad, deep down below it all flickers the tiny flame, ever-turning to HIM, tiny, helpless, but none the less true. And this minute glow-worm dance in the midst of the darkness of the world may well mark out before the angels the outline of the heavenly Jerusalem.

*

BEEN reading Hardy's *Return of the Native*. Astonishing how moral standards have shifted over the past hundred years: "shifted" isn't the word—a landslide. You feel this, too, in *Anna Karenina* and *Kreutzer Sonata*: probably it was the same thing from Russia to England. One wonders whether the unbelievers of that period once unhappily married *really* stopped short at "sins of thought"? And if they did stop there, was it conscience or taboo? And if taboo, wasn't this, too, really a form of faith, even if no longer recognized and acknowledged as such? Faith as the awareness of a law, dark and anonymous, but valid and absolute for all that, the law which governs marriage, and which can only be broken by the heaviest, the unforgiveable sacrilege which can still never shake this law? How powerful *objective* order was in those days, and, confronted with it, what a puny figure the individual must have felt! Which explains the extent of the triumph he must have experienced when he first challenged this absolute, daring to set himself up against it, first as its equal and then as its master!

In those days a sin which today seems merely banal must have attained, in experience, titanic proportions. Nowadays it's as though people casually ignore or set aside a chance and trivial rule of the game. Today the problems of these nineteenth-century novels strike us as exaggerated, as bathos, even comical—much ado about nothing. But for these people it really *was* a struggle with the gods, very real, menacing, dangerous gods.

*

I JUST can't pray to get well again, I realize this again and again. I really admire the ingenuousness of people who can do this, who are really, honestly, naïvely convinced that

(*a*) they know what is good for them,

(*b*) their well-being is so important that with a good conscience they can "harness" the powers of heaven to this end!!

To me both seem impossible. I'm far too stamped (maimed? crippled? who knows?) by the teaching that everything which can be classified as "pain and suffering" is *precious*—at least for the Christian: and simultaneously by the conviction that, in spite of everything, I'm still so much better off in every respect than thousands of others that it would be sheer impertinence—a downright swindle—to adorn my particular burden with this high-sounding name. Surely one ought to clutch gladly and gratefully at every straw of affliction sent, as though paying a tax overdue—so as not to feel too over-privileged compared with the host of really suffering humanity? Surely every form of hardship—at least so long as it is no worse than mine—is so obviously and directly both a blessing and a gift that it would be ungrateful and simply discourteous to wish to "beg it away"?

Contra: my husband is involved, too, and I therefore ought to try to "pray it away", just as naturally and as honestly as other things distressing or afflicting him.

But, good heavens, no one can have everything, and aren't we both still living a great deal more peacefully and comfortably than thousands of others? When you think of the negative possibilities of suffering and misfortune, how countless, complicated, refined and exquisite these are—then our version really does seem the very mildest and most acceptable.

And to want to change this really would seem like the discontented fisherman's wife in the fairy tale.

All the time each one of us is hovering above an unfathomable abyss of potential calamities of every kind—sensed in that everthrobbing pulse deep down in one's heart: as long as this chasm does not open up to devour one, the "floating island" in any guise whatever must surely be welcome. Wrong notion of God? Asiatic pessimism?

Maybe—but it has its positive aspects, too. For this deepseated fear, this dread of the lurking horrors of unpredictable life breeds at least an enduring and sincere thankfulness—as long as these hauntings only appear in homoeopathic dilution.

*

I WONDER what the Ascension means for us today. I wonder whether for every Christian, at some time or other, Christ must cease to be visible, comprehensible, familiar, disappearing for each one of us completely "into the cloud", so that the Comforter can come? I've always felt vaguely but deeply uneasy about those reconstructions of the "historic" figure of Jesus, both in Catholic and Protestant devotion: novels about him, tales, meditations, all so perfectly informed about him, what he was like—they strike me—without exception—as artificial, contrived fancy-work, never really convincing—no matter how "lovely" they may be. What are these, after all, but retrospective pictures, arrested, glued to something long since past?— whereas he is *living*, here among us, though invisible. Seated at the right hand of his Father *and* to be encountered in the Church and her mysteries. Everything else . . . ?

Or is this just my particular pettifogging excuse, because I don't have any "Christ image" of my own, and never had. Even Bible studies, as far as they are purely retrospective, historic, have always somehow gone against the grain as soon as they

185

attempt more than "scholarship". There's something after all in that mocking remark of Clemens Brentano's about cookery books when the larder is empty. . . . With all due respect and sincere "envy" for the Protestant familiarity with the Bible, isn't it sometimes just a little bit *faute de mieux*, makeshift?

*

"In time of bodily suffering the best mortification is that which God assigns to us, providing we accept this willingly and joyfully," wrote St Alphonsus Liguori to Sister Brianna Carafa on 20 August 1781. There you are! And one is supposed to want to rid oneself of it by prayer?

*

Curious how naked the human being shows up in love, whether he likes it or not—just as in religion. Passion tears away every moral pose, every ethical mask, persona, super-ego, etc. And just as all seven deadly sins exist on the spiritual plane (see St John of the Cross, who makes no bones about this: spiritual pride, greed, envy, sensuality, etc., etc.) smashing all our illusions, you get exactly the same thing in love. There's a special kind of erotic pride, vanity, showing off, envy and greed (called jealousy here), immoderation, lasciviousness, anger and *acedia*. Or are these just typical conditions which could run wild in every sphere of life, simply classical forms of "behaviour" of the ego? We might find the whole scale again in the domain of "property"—and in the field of reason, too: intellectual conceit, envy and ambition in scholarship, lack of integrity (venality of the mind, "Reason the harlot"), *gourmandise*, fanaticism—*acedia*?

*

Women's very worst vice in love is surely their awful possessiveness, their urge for domination. To my mind this "pollutes" love much more than sensuality. For if the latter misuses the so-called "beloved" simply as a means to an end, for personal satisfaction, surely erotic vanity and an erotic urge for domination does exactly the same thing? Moreover in women there's the extra reduplication of falsehood, for precisely the so-called

186

womanly virtues of unselfishness, kindness, readiness to help, etc., provide the weapons and the camouflage for the most rapacious instincts for power and possession. The very tokens of a pure and higher love: comforting, nursing, serving—are abused as decoys for stark selfishness. Decidedly unpleasant.

And *amare amare*—to be in love with love—how many women ever get beyond the stage in which love is but an end in itself, like a game with a casual partner, interchangeable as a chess-man—the object being to keep up the excitement, the thrills, the little triumphs and heart-flutterings of the game. . . . Which is why the fulfilment in every sense is so dangerous a moment—victory, satisfaction. Because now at last is revealed what was the real "end" pursued: the union achieved, or simply the instinct of the chase evaporating with possession of the quarry. To put it bluntly, spiritual self-abuse (as presumably the other kind) destroys the power of love. For here every encounter is simply a fresh stimulus, a new tool serving the same end, i.e. the intensification of ego and the intoxication of its power. Nothing beyond. Actually *amare amare* is the worst perversion of love. And yet, curiously enough, even this becomes translucent somehow: the archetypal image still strangely glimpsed in its perversion, though not in its negation. For "loving", as such, is, in a certain sense, still the highest, most intense terrestrial form of participation in divine nature. God loves for the sake of loving, and "loves himself in everything".

*

Strange, too, how on the psychological plane the fundamental characteristics of man and woman would seem to be reversed in love. For here, often enough, it's the woman who does the woo-ing, aggressive, possessive—demanding, intruding, insatiable in her urge to im-press, to influence the man by sharing her innermost self with him, saturating yet never really satisfying him—to her perpetual rage and grief! As for him, he shies away from such violence—cool, coy, reserved, he evades all her efforts to "open him up", withdrawing behind a "veil" of silence, un-responsive, enigmatic, impenetrable—and so only drives her more mad. But unless she respects that at least intermittent "virginity" in him, she will ruin her marriage, love, friendship, "discipleship"—everything.

*

THAT Somerset Maugham anthology *Cakes and Ale*. How destructive he is, venomous, pulling everything down in biting, corrosive cynicism. Nothing is sacred. Yet somewhere deep down under all the conceit, sarcasm and snobbery is real quivering pain, helpless bewilderment at the inexplicable fact that human nature is "chequered". And what perplexes him is less the common, mean element in "decent" people than the goodness and kindness of wicked, vicious ones. If his *Of Human Bondage* is really his autobiography (he is always stressing the essential privilege of the writer—Goethe), then the core of his own personal destiny must have been a consuming passion for a "lost" woman.

But it is truly a strange riddle, the power emanating from such a woman, overwhelming a young and innocent man—a deeply mysterious phenomenon, you find it everywhere, on all levels (up to Myshkin and Natasha!). Probably its only significance is as a symbol, a very realistic symbol, for the love of God for mankind, as expressed so revealingly in the sixteenth chapter of Ezechiel.

*

"*Dieu ne méprise rien*", says Bernanos.

*

STRANGE what a chain of reactions the liturgy for the consecration of Holy Oils has roused within me. Stranger still that I knew nothing about this before! Yet another important item of our heritage of faith which has been quietly dropped under the table—like the chalice at Communion, or the way the liturgy for the Vigil of Easter (until now) just faded out of the consciousness of the Church. Personally, at any rate, I never realized before that, at least according to the letter of the texts, the Holy Oils are actually just as "sacramental", i.e. indispensable for the effecting of certain spiritual realities, as water in Baptism or bread and wine in the Eucharist. No one ever told me about this before, and I cannot remember having read it anywhere.

Now, for the first time, I really understand the importance attached by Dionysius the Areopagite to "the sacrament of the consecration of Holy Oils"—unknown to us. These days commentators add the note: "He was referring here to Confirmation". He wasn't.

In referring to Confirmation, the new Catechism* simply says: "The anointing with Chrism means . . .", instead of stressing its effective *power*. And in the paragraph: "The Church blesses and consecrates" (p. 148), the consecration of Holy Oils is not even mentioned. Only: "The church building, the altar, the chalice and paten used in Mass, the cloths for the altar and pictures, medals and rosaries, organs and bells, and the graves of the faithful".

And in the relevant questions and the commentaries we have: "What does the Church bless and consecrate, (*a*) on Ash Wednesday, (*b*) on Palm Sunday, (*c*) on the Vigil night of Easter, (*d*) on Candlemas?" Maundy Thursday is not included.

On the other hand, Pinsk is absolutely clear and emphatic (I've just looked up his *Sakramentale Welt* [The Sacramental World], far too little known and considered, incidentally!). In that very remarkable chapter on "The sacramental form of the world of matter" he writes: "In the blessing of baptismal water and all other consecrations which form part of the *Pontificale Romanum* or the *Rituale Romanum*, no actual change of substance takes place, but the wording of the consecration conveys in the most powerful way the *fusing* of the divine life with these elements." Not only, as the Catechism puts it, that "the Church begs of God the well-being of soul and body and protection against evil spirits"—for that would be simply something asked for, not something *happening*! So much for the blessing of the water for Baptism. In the consecration of Chrism, too, we have the words: "That thou wouldst be pleased to sanctify with thy blessing this rich creature of oil and *to infuse into it* the virtue of the Holy Spirit", and "That he may bless with the fullness of the blessing of the Holy Trinity . . . and that he may sanctify them by his blessing." "One can scarcely believe," continues Pinsk, "that in these consecrations—which are preceded by exorcisms annihilating the demonic powers in

* *A Catholic Catechism*—English translation of the official German Catechism, London, 1957.

the elements—nothing *actually* [Pinsk's italics] happens, that the baptismal water after consecration is nothing more than it was beforehand, the combination of hydrogen and oxygen; that after consecration the oil is the same natural product as ever it was. In that case we should be *giving the lie* to the explicit prayer of the Church that the water should be 'made fruitful' by 'This infusion of the Chrism of our Lord Jesus Christ and of the Holy Ghost'; the veneration of the Holy Oils by the clergy, with genuflection and the salutation '*Ave Sanctum Chrisma*' and '*Ave Sanctum Oleum*' would be a *farce* if, after the consecration, all we had were the juice of the olive, as before; or we needs must charge the Church of Jesus Christ with so exaggerating in her rites of consecration that they cannot be taken seriously. But if the Church cannot be taken seriously in her prayer and her consecration, i.e. the very sphere in which her real mission lies, if the Church speaks of an awakening to new life where no new life exists, and of a new glory, where the creature still remains in its old defective state—then when *are* we to take the words of the Church of Jesus Christ seriously?"

But how many of our theologians have the courage to think this way—and to preach this way, despite the rationalistic, materialistic spirit of our age? They're so concerned about conforming to pattern, of avoiding all friction, so afraid of offending the "scientific" sensibilities of their colleagues.

*

No, I'm really none too happy about the new Catechism. They've improved the *method*, it's true, but the fundamental attitude is just as rationalistic as its predecessor.

Right at the beginning, for instance: "The Church is the *guardian* and *teacher* of our faith . . . she puts into our hands the books which help us to learn more about our faith . . ." (illustration: the hands of God holding out the Catechism—with title!—to the human hands reaching up for it . . .). As though book-learning were the first, indeed the only thing the Church had to communicate! So much for p. 4. Only on p. 145 do we find: "The Church gives us the seven holy sacraments in order that we may have *life*" (my italics!). But have we been given our faith and its doctrines simply as "religious culture"?

190

How much more genuine, vivid and convincing is the age-old, traditional figure of the Church as *mother*, not as teacher—why not governess? As mother of our faith the Church does just what every mother does for her children: she feeds them, cleanses them, nurses, cures, protects and warms them, corrects and punishes and comforts them, she tells them about the Father and feasts with them. She doesn't just give them lessons like a governess: at least not as the first and most important thing.

*

M.B. SENT me three numbers of the big Negro colour magazine *Ebony*—which led to a long discussion yesterday about the Negroes in America. A curious situation: an old "archaic" race with no memory of its own past, for its culture entirely at the mercy of a "new" race with virtually no past either—the Americans. Yet surely it's not so different from the fate of the Negroes in Africa, stumbling from the year zero into 19— with no transition by slow degrees over an organic culture of the others' in which they could have "found themselves" and gradually developed?

What would, could, ought to happen were the Negro *really* to find his way into the heart of the Church? Through a real liturgy, for instance, a true initiation to the sacraments deciphering his own concept of the world, really "embodying" it? Will this ever be possible?

*

A. MAINTAINS that "brotherliness" is the watchword and the mark of our future society. I'm not so sure. To me this word, even today, is no more than a slogan, an abstract "wishword", since on the natural plane of experience examples, models and symbols for it are ceasing to exist. Ever since the clan died out. For most people today brotherliness simply means equality, equal rights, service without subordination—i.e. social and ethical relationships. Yet in reality brotherliness is essentially a *vital* phenomenon, earlier than reflection and postulation, not to be re-established by resolve and principle. For brotherhood is rooted first and foremost in the same *blood*, the same lineage: the immense emphasis upon it only makes sense, indeed is only

191

to be found at all, where a living pride in this same stem, this common ancestry, still exists. But it's easier to attain this today through "the people" or the nation than through "the family" which is rarely so vital that all the children truly appreciate their membership as the central thing to be proud of, *respecting this pride in each other*, even if individually they dislike each other or even quarrel.

*

THE lesson for SS. Peter and Paul—Peter's release from prison—could quite well be applied to the psychological sphere where it no doubt occurs too, from time to time: Peter lying in his dark dungeon, shut away from the others—cut off, no contact; the angel "roused" him—none too gently, with a dig in the ribs ("striking him on the side"!)—and the "iron gate" to the city, to the community, swings back. . . .

*

MARGARET TROUNCER's book on Margaret Mary Alacoque is enough to spoil one's taste for all *biographies romancées* (my own included!) for years to come. There are one or two impressive bits all the same, when she quotes the saint's own words instead of trying to interpret her: "He [our Lord] assured me that we should worship the heart of *God* in the shape of his heart made flesh, and desired that a picture *of this* should be set up. . . ." N.B. *not* just a picture of Christ with his heart laid bare, as decreed later by all too scrupulous superiors afraid of possible misinterpretations.

Then that vision of the souls in Purgatory: the nun with the worm-eaten tongue as punishment for uncharitable talk on earth . . . and the other poor soul, Sister de Sirot, who tells the saint: "*I fought against love*—which is why the prayers said for me here are of no avail, and the heart of Jesus himself refuses to be touched by my suffering because I had no pity for those I saw were sad."

*

DIONYSIUS calls the angels "messengers of divine silence".

*

Our heirloom of revelation often seems to me like a huge loaf of bread; there we all are, standing around it like a lot of toothless children who haven't yet learnt to use a knife. . . .

*

Reward and punishment: three different reactions: first, heaven and hell as objects of natural belief (pagans!), and of psychological reactions, i.e. dread or joyful anticipation; secondly, heaven and hell as objects of supernatural belief—in revelation, in the words of our Lord—with a "supernatural" response: the virtue of hope, the fear of God; thirdly—the mystic soars above both in the pure love which makes him indifferent to his own fate without detracting in the least from his faith. But the average Christian these days is *under* (*a*), yet *thinks* he belongs to (*c*). Can he jump the steps like this?

*

I was especially struck by yesterday's epistle: "We are debtors, *not* to the flesh . . .", and "whosoever are led by the spirit of God, they are the sons of God". Here is the weak spot of psychology, or rather our safe-conduct through its tyranny which depicts "the flesh", our disposition and the "damages" inflicted upon it as omnipotent, as our inexorable lord and creditor, ready to destroy us if we dare to oppose his will. On the contrary; "If by the spirit you *mortify* the deeds of the flesh, you shall live . . ."—i.e. we *can* be the stronger party, overcoming it, breaking the ban of mere reflexes, reactions, mechanism. But "by the spirit", not by training alone which, after all, is only "flesh" too, and by no means always its better part.

*

Hans Fallada's childhood memoirs mean much to me, for they reveal—to my surprise—that lots of things I'd always thought were crazy "peculiarities" (in both senses!) of our own school-room were actually typical symptoms of that period, and just as common in isolated country districts and towns which could never have been influenced by one another. That nineteenth century! When you read such things and muse upon them, it's not difficult to see that the explosion was *bound* to come one day

7   193

—an atomic explosion, bursting all this narrowness, this fear and pettiness, all this suppression and control. How far the pendulum has swung. . . . And how much in present-day life is still the unconscious reaction to the tyranny of such "morals" and "virtues", a spectre long since laid.

*

MARVELLOUS, those chronicles of Moses and Josue! Jericho, crossing the Jordan—the vine branch from Nehelescol, the terror of the giants. Surely Israel is the archetype of humanity, of man "the wayfarer"?—pig-headed, lazy and cowardly, ungrateful, full of moods—cock-sure when everything is rosy, moaning and groaning, whining and begging when things go wrong, always on the *qui vive* to rebel and complain: such are we, such am I.

*

AND how strange, Moses talking to the Lord almost as though he were humouring a child, just as an old familiar servant might reason with his young, hot-blooded master: a pity to give the Egyptians this chance to crow over him with this angry decision of his—overturning the chess-board again in the heat of the moment. . . .

Could the Promised Land with its terrors and its treasures be an image of the future, I wonder?—of every future? and the Israelites' refusal to enter it, and the punishment: You shall *not* enter it, but your children, for whose sake you rebelled, *they* shall enter the land and eat of its fruits.

The story of the conspiracy of Korah is surely the revolt of the "general" priesthood against the "official", of the self-appointed "representatives of the people" against those chosen and appointed from above. Do Bible-reading Protestants ever stop to consider this—thinking as highly as they do of the Old Testament?

*

BOOK Providence again, intense, direct, with Régamey* to startle my conscience. For almost everything he says is just as true for a writer as for a painter. For us it is just as urgent to

* Pie-Raymond Régamey, O.P., *Art Sacré au vingtième siècle*, Paris, 1952.

proclaim the old truths anew, in a new way, "stripped", in language swept clean of clichés and façades of all kinds. To speak out, about the Church, about the Faith—on sex, on marriage—saying *really* what one sees, what one thinks, what one perceives—saying what I *myself* see, hold, believe—not "one", not anybody.

*

I'M reading George Borrow's *Lavengro*, strangely familiar from a serial story in *Little Folks* in which two children read this book and then proceeded to try out their "Romany lore" on real gypsies. That was back in 1912. And now, 40 years later, I've chanced upon the original—and, of course, it fits perfectly into the pattern of my current reading!—Fallada and Arnold Bennett's *Old Wives' Tales*, i.e. my constant musings on the nineteenth century. I was amazed to learn from Bennett's book that in Papa's childhood you could watch an execution, which was a public entertainment, a real show, with high prices paid for windows with a good view, and the local hotels doing a roaring trade.

And Borrow: 1803–81, very nearly J. H. Newman's twin! I'm fascinated—and flabbergasted—to think that this autobiography (invent as he may) actually describes *Newman's* England—the reverse of the carpet, as it were. It's quite extraordinary. Reading Newman's sermons, lectures, letters, etc. you don't feel the time-distance, or at least not often. They seem so up to date, the problems, attitudes and situations are so modern, so topical. Yet this England Borrow describes is positively medieval!—or Restoration—our Thirty Years' War—at the latest, with archaic customs and practices of all kinds: snake charmers and horse charms, crazy itinerant preachers, rogues and vagrants, Methodists' meetings, daft specimens of gentry, men of letters, rakes and blackguards—anything but the hum-drum, sober, respectable *bourgeoisie* one would imagine. And if the people are almost Shakespearean, the upper classes are pure eighteenth century—with breeches and buckled shoes, wigs, snuff, and a quaint and freakish kind of scholarship all their own, cranks and eccentrics with three-cornered hats, etc. Hogarth pictures. This, then, was the background, the soil of Newman's childhood and youth—even if he himself noticed little enough of it as a townsman, member of the middle-class, a scholar and a don. But his undergraduates—or at any rate a good many of them—must have come from this strange, still wild world, and those years in Ireland must have been spent in an even more archaic environment.

But, after all, those Swabian peasants addicted to witchcraft, infested with demonic possession, among whom Blumhardt* lived in the mid-nineteenth century were not so very different. And there must surely be people who could describe just such a shady side of society in the first half of our own century—even apart from the war—without exaggerating either, simply from personal experience, if he happened to know those strange, sinister realms which certainly existed, even then. What does "the past" mean at all, what is "progress"? All this was only yesterday and is still part of our own roots. It might well spring up again, slightly changed, that's all.

*

Christlicher Sonntag: Fr Americo with his eight Boys Towns is Portugal's Don Bosco. Fr Flanagan was the Canadian (or Californian?) version. Turin or Genoa have similar figures; I really ought to collect the cuttings, I forget the names too quickly. Danilo Dolci in Sicily; Mother Teresa in Calcutta; the bishop in Rio de Janeiro who brought the "shadow army" of pariahs back to life; the Prado of Bishop Ancelet in Lyons; that consumptive Japanese girl, Reiko Kitahara, the "soul" of the Christian community in the "termite town", one of the slums of Tokio [died in 1958]—actually there are scores of such "charismatics" everywhere, all bearing the same mark, all akin to Charles de Foucauld, even if they've never heard of him. Only with us here in Germany, I'm afraid, most of it is drowned in *talk*, discussion and representation. Or are our saints better at dodging publicity?

*

READING lots of Dickens. *Barnaby Rudge*: the last Catholic pogrom—"No Popery", the Gordon Riots in London—1780, twenty years before Newman was born. He must have known

---

* Johann Christoph Blumhardt, 1805–80. Pastor in Möttlingen in Württemberg. Leader of a revivalist movement.

people who had set fire to the houses, or taken in victims and refugees. Lord George Gordon who led the mob (obviously a religious maniac) died as late as 1793. *Old Curiosity Shop*, *Nicholas Nickleby*—this, too, is part of Newman's background, this gallery of living gargoyles, ghouls and monsters. Might account, perhaps, even for some of Newman's pessimism about the world and human nature, which some attribute merely to his own melancholy disposition?

That nineteenth century!! Asmussen is quite right in what he says about the submerged but nonetheless active grudges and grievances between both denominations on the core of mutual injustice. Yet surely this applies even more socially—between the classes, and, above all, between the two great fronts: authority and the suppressed? Grudge against authority—as such— which featured for so long and to its universal discredit as *tyranny* at home, in the schools, socially, politically? The sins of the patriarchal order—will they ever be redeemed, atoned for? Will the scars they inflicted ever really heal?

*

NN. is weighing heavily on my mind. For she seems to demonstrate so patently: 1. That suffering and unhappiness are two different things—and how very much the latter rests with *us*. 2. How difficult it is for someone like her—hard-working, honest and reliable, unselfish and undemanding, a model of self-control, a paragon of virtue, with nothing to reproach herself for—how hard it is for such a person to see for herself that, in the depths of her soul, she, too, is twisted and warped and desperately in need of "re-turn", of conversion.

*

IT's odd the way pious people tend to view economy as a manifestation of evangelical poverty. Actually it is quite the reverse —that is, when it's rooted in anxious worry for "a rainy day", in reluctance to part with the "nice little bit put away", the craving for security. In this case surely the spendthrift who scat- ters his money regardless whether he has anything or not, improvident, ready to take the risk and face the consequences

197

unruffled, if he thinks it's worth the while, far more nearly approaches the true ideal which, after all, consists in *freedom* from possessions.

*

READING O'Rahilly's life of Father William Doyle I see how right my hunch was. He, too, is a link in the chain of the "little saints" about the turn of the century—the Little Flower was only one of many, by no means the only one, the unique pioneer. Born in Ireland, in the same year as Thérèse, Fr Doyle lived to be fourty-four—he was killed at Ypres in 1917. He, too, was a pious child, full of practical love for the poor and servants. I find it much more remarkable for a boy (only eleven, too, later on he was sent to boarding school) than for a little girl, that he used to get up early to do the housework—like a pixie!—before the maid came down; that he should spontaneously carry the new maid's belongings in those days of rigorous class-distinction, especially in a then British country; that he scrubbed and cleaned the homes of the poor neglected country people himself when he came to visit the sick. Thérèse never undertook such work as long as she was at home . . . in contrast to poor Léonie who did! Thérèse and Céline contented themselves with being nice to poor children, and of course they were considerate to servants, like other devout young girls.

Fr Doyle had the same early longing to be a saint and in his prayers implored the grace of martyrdom. He later became a prefect at Clongowes, conducted missions, and ended as military chaplain. He must have radiated uncommon spiritual attraction. He was just as insensitive to *Kitsch* as Thérèse and found it as edifying as she did. The pamphlet he wrote on vocations for the priesthood had a frontispiece showing a little boy knocking at the tabernacle door and saying, "Jesus, I want to be a holy priest!" And his commentary: "It is not mine but Jesus' work alone, for every word seemed to come from the Tabernacle before which I wrote it, the greater part on the altar itself." (What wouldn't they have made of such words in Lisieux!)

And just the same funny naïve business-mind about spiritual values, rewards: "Golden coins, banking account, step-counting angel, the penny saved for a better and happier world"—

though not, of course, for oneself. And the terrifying, terrific mortifications performed in secret (like the Desert Fathers, or Blessed Henry Suso, or possibly in his case influenced by early Irish monasticism?)—yet he never divulged a word about these ascetic practices and never recommended them to others. Only from the notebooks found after his death—he had a curious almost compelling passion for writing everything down, totting up sacrifices, penances, aspirations, etc.—did his superiors discover these startling records of such a very normal, inconspicuous man. Opinions may well differ whether they really had the right to read these papers—against his express wish—and then to publish them. I'm surprised this book hasn't left a deeper mark, for it contains—often in parallel terms—the whole teaching of the Little Way which created such a stir in the case of Thérèse. But it seems people prefer to accept such things from a lovely young girl complete with smile, roses and veil. One can't help wondering whether Thérèse would have met with the same enormous response had she been hopelessly ugly—a hunchback with a squint, or old. . . .

Fr Doyle: "No, no, God does not lead us all by that same stern path of awful heroism. . . . Sweetly and gently would He lead us along the way of holiness by our constant unswerving faithfulness to our duty, duty accepted, duty done for His dear sake. How many, alas, who might be saints are now leading lives of indifferent virtue, because they have deluded themselves with the thought that they have no strength to bear the 'holy follies' of the saints. . . ." "I will endeavour to perform every task as perfectly as possible: it seems to me that precisely this is what God is asking of me, and that in this way I shall find my main road to holiness."

And all the time, in secret, he was scourging himself with old razor blades, standing up to his neck at night in icy water, and the like—later on he had no need to think up such niceties, the trenches of Flanders were enough. And not the faintest trace of pride —apparently not even the temptation which made Thérèse decide that severe bodily penance was not intended for her own person:

"I do not think I could possibly find food for vainglory in anything I have done, no more than an organ-grinder prides himself on the beautiful music he produces by turning a handle.

. . . I feel ashamed when people praise me for my work, the sort of shame a piano might feel if someone complimented it on the beautiful melody that came from its keys."

And his resolutions:

"Never speak about your worries, troubles, amount of work. Never give yourself relief in small sufferings. Never say you have a headache, etc. Don't complain of others or of anything else. Always be most punctual."

Then, *exactly* like Thérèse, really extraordinary! The peculiar Eucharistic mysticism of that age—diary for 10 July 1912: "I awoke in the middle of the night with the feeling that Jesus wanted me. . . . My prayer was: 'Jesus, come and dwell within my heart as in a tabernacle.' I felt Him urging me to this close union and He seemed to promise me that He would remain with me 'from Communion to Communion' if only I were recollected." Again 1 April 1914: "I write this before my Jesus in the Tabernacle and I have asked Him to make me note down what He wants from me: 'I have promised to dwell *physically* [original italics] in you as in a Tabernacle, from Communion to Communion, if you do what I have asked you—guard your eyes . . .'."

This, too, is always represented as a special *grâce unique* to Thérèse. Stranger still that this "pattern" should recur today. A few years ago I had a curious correspondence with the late Fr Paschalis Schmidt who was keen to introduce the cause of a certain nun, on the strength of very similar words.* He claimed that precisely this was the proof of a grace never as yet granted to any known mystic. The question is: what is actually *meant* by these curious statements by saints or other holy people—anything but clear to me.

His advice to penitents is typically "Little Way": "Go on quietly, loving God and seeking to please Him, without trying to find out in what exact state of perfection your soul is."

"Nothing is too small to offer up to God. . . . What could be less spectacular than the commonplace daily round of the religious life? . . . In the faithful performance of these little day to day tasks lies the secret of true holiness."

He tells them to take little personal faults in their stride: "Love, contrition, and don't look back!"

* See pp. 60–61.

And again, a "verbal twin" of the saint of Lisieux:
"Did I ever tell you that even as a child I was convinced that one day God would give me the grace of martyrdom? When quite small I read and re-read every martyr's life in the twelve volumes of Butler's *Lives of the Saints*, and longed and prayed to be a martyr, and have done so ever since. As years went on, the desire grew in intensity. . . . But nothing came of it and I was left wondering why God should have put that intense longing into my heart when He did not mean to gratify it. . . . Then slowly light came. He did ask martyrdom, but not in the way I thought, a martyrdom far longer and a thousand times more painful . . . a living martyrdom and a ceaseless crucifixion. . . ."

As contemporaries of countless martyrs in Russia, China, Mexico, Spain, etc.—as well as the direct and indirect martyrs of the concentration camps—this use of the word "martyr" may strike us as somewhat peculiar today; but there is no doubt about his seriousness. Was his secret bloody penance also inspired by this sense of vocation?

He, too, made a vow of consecration to the Sacred Heart and also signed it with his blood—complete dedication, and "am I not the victim of Your love?"

And finally, from the trenches: "Just now Jesus is giving me great joy in tribulation, though conditions of living are about as uncomfortable as even St Teresa could wish—perpetual rain, oceans of mud, damp, cold and a plague of rats. . . ." But : "I no longer feel the pain which has passed, nor need I bear that which is to come, so I have only to endure the sufferings of the moment and that soon passes and never returns. . . . I wonder if there's a happier man in France than I am?"

*

HIDDEN holiness within the Church. . . . Probably there are dozens of cases like this, tucked away in convents, and no one thinks twice about them, not even their confessors. And probably every year heaps of exercise books filled with posthumous "notes" and resolutions from retreats, etc. are cheerfully burnt, unread, since no one thinks them interesting—records of obscure individuals which, if published, would be found to be of the same import as *L'Histoire d'une Ame*. This stresses the curious providential guidance in the case of Thérèse: that precisely *her* notebooks should have been preserved—actually entirely due to her sisters with that irrepressible intense family infatuation of theirs. No getting away from it: God prefers to make use of the frailties of his children—to accomplish great things on earth.

*

I MUST ask S. sometime about the Westphalian beggar-pilgrim known as *Betkaspar* who died in Werl in 1911. Kaspar Schwarze was his name—he seems to have been a sort of cross between Benedict Joseph Labre and the Russian pilgrims—probably too "mute" a figure, almost anonymous, to have left any traces. . . . The fact that there *are* such people—that's the point. I remember, back in my Vienna days, that whenever I went into St Anna's—often at the strangest hours—I nearly always saw a man kneeling there, unbelievably dirty and unshaven, half-starved and ragged, sunk in ecstatic prayer before the Blessed Sacrament. Perhaps he, too, was one of this kind.

*

BY comparison: That new book on Thérèse by X. strikes me almost as monomania—the way it endeavours to turn its heroine into a monolith, a very Titan among pygmies. Afterwards my mental stomach felt as if a pint of luke-warm liqueur (the scented kind) had been forced upon me. Their idea is, not only that a glass containing wine must be made of diamond, but also that the wine has oozed out of the glass, by itself!

After this the naïve testimony of Margarete Ebner★ about her own convent youth is sweet and memorable: "What my life was like at that time I cannot say, for I paid but little heed to myself. All I know is that God kept me always in his fatherly love and protection."

Or:

"When I hear about the friends of God and the great things he doeth with them, I have no wish that anyone should know the workings of God within me."

*

★ Dominican nun mystic of the fourteenth century.

*Kirchweih!** The *Schutzmantelmadonna*† is the symbol of the Church. And the priest's hands raised at the elevation remind me always of the "tent" erected temporarily in the desert, with the Host and the Chalice—the Shekhinah—throning on high.

*

WORKING through that draft of NN's comments on St Thomas's tract on matrimony, and very exciting it is, the Aquinas text first, I mean; the commentary warrants a few notes later on.

What is so startling, for me, in St Thomas is the colossal gulf between the highest and lowest interpretations of the phenomenon of marriage.

It is the symbol of the union of divine and human nature in Christ, *therefore* perpetuating the Incarnation. Matrimony is a sacrament = symbol. As a sign it will *cease*, as all signs = sacraments will cease. But the reality represented in the symbol is enduring, finding its fulfilment in the world to come.

And since its archetype is the love of God, it is itself a sign for the future "oneing" of man with God. This also sets a limit upon it. *Like the Eucharist*, the sacrament of matrimony is a pledge of the glory to come.

More breath-taking, if anything, is that quotation from Cornelius a Lapide's commentary on Genesis: "In creating Adam and Eve, God desired to imitate his eternal generation and inspiration. Inasmuch as, from eternity, he begets the Son and the Holy Ghost out of the Son, so, in time, he created Adam in his own likeness, begetting him like unto his son, and out of him he created Eve, *so that she might be Adam's love*, as the Holy Ghost is the love of God." (Marginal note: Ernst Benz, an expert on comparative religion, in his preface to *Urmensch*: "E. L. Dietrich has rightly pointed out that both the Jewish and the Christian religions sought to *eliminate* or suppress *precisely this religious interpretation of sex*. . . . In the same way, in Christianity, this androgynous speculation, indeed all speculations connected *in any way* with the domain of sex, were also *completely*

---

* In Germany the commemoration of their Dedication is observed generally in all parish churches on 15 October.

† The image of Our Lady as *Mater Misericordiae*, gathering the faithful under her cloak.

suppressed. Such suppression could, however, only be enforced in the official theology of the Church."!!)

Further: Berthold of Regensburg: "Of the seven holy sacraments, matrimony is one of the highest which God has on earth. Therefore no falsehood may abide in it." "Effective and participating image of the most sacred unions."

Further: St Thomas's profoundly realistic criticism of sex within the fallen world—neither naïve apotheosis nor minimizing.

Sex is *corruptum et infectum*: the medium transmitting and propagating original sin. Which is why it is in a special way in need of redemption. (Must ponder on this: an argument no longer obvious to our minds.) The urge for food is *infectum*, too, but not *corruptum*: the sex urge was changed fundamentally by the Fall. Like death and suffering, its *present manifestation* first appeared in the world through sin. There you are! So even Thomas ranks in this line of tradition after all—and I always thought he was much more "modern" on this point, i.e. rationalistic, optimistic, but this seems to be just wishful thinking on the part of certain theologians.

*

ALL Saints: Nothing in today's liturgy of "veneration of the saints" in the private, personal, "utilitarian" sense. Entirely eschatological: the World Above—including angels, Ancients and the four living creatures—not only saintly men and women. The Golden City, manifest in its full hierarchy, as Body of the Head which graciously deigns to be visible to our eyes in the Host at the Elevation.

*

IF A.R. is right in what he predicts for the coming World-Age, the Church will be shifting more and more from the aspect "Rock of Peter" towards the "Ship of Peter". Why not? Both images are authentic and original. The "sea" parables will come into their own, become really topical.

*

GETTING back to the Aquinas matrimony treatise—and its commentary. Countless quotations from works on marriage by "eminent" modern theologians, almost an anthology! To my growing discomfort I see the very dubious attitude to the whole

204

sphere of marriage—a curious mixture of crude realism and sloppy sentimentality. Intellectualism has utterly destroyed the taboo character attaching to the *natural* mysteries, the slogan now being: "Let's discuss everything". *Naturalia non sunt turpia*—but not *reverenda* either. Men, students and priests can treat details of (female) impotence, defloration, menstruation, etc. without reserve. Such discussions used to be strictly private, dealt with in Latin in special tracts for confessors—which is perfectly sensible. But these days all this is flung out at large for any public in plain language. Awful really, since it no longer "awes" anyone. For them, so it seems, the "proper" antithesis to prudery is mere lack of modesty, calling a spade a spade, publicity instead of reticence; a hard-boiled "taking things naturally". But doesn't anyone stop to consider the *destructive* effect all this is bound to have, this craze *à la mode* for some years past in our ecclesiastical domain, among priests and parish workers, girl catechists, etc. of discussing everything with every-one? And if things *do* go wrong—a scandal, tragedy of tragedies —then everyone gapes, wondering how such a thing could pos-sibly happen among such people, ready with far-fetched theories of split personalities, Jekyll and Hyde, hereditary taints, etc. Heavens above, does it occur to no one that this persistently "realistic and unemotional" talk could well induce just as unemotional, merely experimental action? Which in fact would be no more than consistent. In the early days of Bolshevism one used to read a lot about their "functionalizing" of sex, the notorious "glass of water" theory—well, they seem to have been just logical. We, too, strip sex of its *real* glamour, take the bloom off, reduce it to clinical processes—and then we're surprised when people trained in this school aren't all paragons of rever-ence, sensibility and natural modesty. . . .

Of course they sometimes do their best to make up for this strictly rationalistic and analytical approach by swathing the profaned and desecrated matter with an ersatz dressing of "emotion". But since such feeling no longer springs from the living depths of the phenomenon itself, from the experience of the numinous, sacred element in human generation and its inherent powers, the emotional factor, the "tension" must be pumped in from outside and from above, either by abstract "supernatural" reflections, or by tawdry romantic notions and moral enthusiasm, which is rather sickening. Schelsky said some very sound things about it: on the persistent confusing of matrimony with "love", either mawkish or truly intimate—or with "union of souls".

Back in my childhood days in Stockau Requiem Masses were still announced: "For the repose of the soul of NN. and for the whole NN. friendship . . .", i.e. kinship. This certainly didn't mean heartfelt intimacy among the various members of the clan. Rather, they took the "bond of blood" literally, as a weighty matter of fact, in no way dependent upon individual sympathies or dislikes, or on agreeing or disagreeing in opinions. The complicated laws governing wedlock between relations by marriage—really an extension of the incest barrier —also go to show how seriously they understood the fusion "into one body" as a fact.

It all hinges—if you like—on the "magic" power inherent in the physical union of marriage, creating new and permanent realities by the "incorporation" of one human being into another and greater body, hitherto alien. *From here*, not from the usual moral considerations, the ineradicable difference between legitimate and illegitimate issue springs, quite obviously. Marriage is the vehicle through which the clan, the *primary* social reality, increases, expanding by alliances between families of equal birth, not between individuals. And the tribe (= the people, the clans "headed" by chieftains who really are "heads" to the clan-bodies) is focused in its "property", here landed estate, called "good" in German, land being *the* token of what is good.

The dominant reality is the blood—the *gens*, the clan; "generation"* in this wide comprehensive sense—pertaining not to Eros but, if you like, to *pietas*. The main concern of the *gens* is duration, fertility. Which accounts for the absolute banning of every form of sex not of its nature fruitful, e.g. homosexuality: and, of course, for the just as well as imperative demand for the dissolution of childless marriages. To me it remains one of the most remarkable victories of the Church, perhaps the most inexplicable, that she could maintain the

* In German this is a play on words: *Geschlecht* meaning sex, generation and lineage.

indissolubility of marriage, even in such instances: for this meant extricating the bond of human personalities from the unqualified submission and surrender to the will and purpose of the clan.

But our modern commentators seem to ignore such archaic realities. If they attempt to champion such alien modes of thought (in proper submission to *divus Thomas*), while deferring to contemporary taste, they resort to limp sentimentality. For example: à propos the child-marriages of his day, not justifiable really, but inevitable nevertheless, especially in dynastic families, Thomas says: "For this act even immature reason is sufficient"—how one senses his contempt for the physical side, as though he were saying: "Animal instinct will do here!" But our commentator declares: "Thomas places his faith in the voice of the heart which here, even in the very young, is reliable and trustworthy", and more in the same vein. What nonsense! As though these child-marriages were ever contracted on the initiative of the children themselves, "prompted by their hearts' desire", and not coldly and brazenly calculated in the interests of their elders!

But something else, something much deeper, strikes one too, precisely in these paragraphs on child-marriage. A curious ambivalence, the irreconcilable paradox of medieval thought: On the one hand the supreme valuation of matrimony *as a symbol*, in accordance with its spiritual character; and on the other the brutal underestimation of its "nature", viewed merely as an outlet for the sheer bodily urge. Thomas reckons "begetting" among the animal functions of man, like "eating, drinking, sleeping, digestion"—not even ranking it on the human plane along with "singing or speaking". What is missing is precisely the mental link of human emotion connecting both extremes. In other words: there is a complete lack of every form of "natural *mystique*" in the sphere of sex and Eros. The begetting of children, so Thomas declares quite bluntly, *is* no mystery, for it happens out of wedlock as well as in it; the sacred character is *first* imparted to the natural event by the bond, its permanence, etc. Strange. It seems that in the Middle Ages people really *lived* in the "mystery of blood" but so deeply immersed in it that they never stopped to reflect on it, indeed were so involved that they could hardly have been aware of it themselves. (Just as our reflections on the Church appear much later than actual life in her.) And once they start theorizing, we get a very poor affair, artificially contrived, borrowed from Antiquity, anything but convincing. But probably this didn't matter much—just as it doesn't really matter how much or how little you know about calories and vitamins as long as you eat enough. But if there's nothing to eat any more, or you can no longer digest your food, and turn to drawing up calorie tables on paper instead? Which is what some of our courses on marriage, etc. seem to be doing—at least partly.

*

To my mind that Thomistic concept runs quite contrary to A.R.'s theory of the medieval interpretation of the whole complex, Eros, marriage, family, children. He maintains that in what he calls the age of Pisces, i.e. roughly speaking the entire Christian era up to now—this sector of life has been determined on one hand by strict, even narrow, acquiescence, even conformity to "natural law", on the other hand by insistence on emotional, even sentimental values. But this, I believe, is true only of the very last stages of post-Renaissance civilization—after matrimony had discarded its impersonal character. Now, of course, something more than the purely animal urge is needed to "justify" sex, and emotions must be pumped in to make the participants feel "nobler" about it.

Although it's all the fashion these days to insist upon it, I just don't see how anyone can call the Christian concept of marriage "natural". Surely strict monogamy isn't natural, any more than absolute indissolubility or total abstinence until marriage? On the contrary: the demands of Christian morality at first ride roughshod over nature, and only a nature long and rigorously disciplined by the spirit can gradually adapt itself, finally even accepting these norms as fit and proper.

The reasons given by Thomas for this "cultural" character of marriage—the three points above—are all strictly on the supernatural plane, rooted in symbol and sacrament.

*

FACED with a provoking "help", one can experience all the temptations of "wicked superiors": that very special kind of spitefulness, snubbing, fault-finding, humiliating, disheartening, biting criticism, abusing the privilege of having the "last word"—even the sin which St Bridget tells us is punished in Purgatory with a hellish penalty: "relishing the other person's pain at correction". You can learn quite a lot of pretty things about yourself in such a situation.

*

HEALING and conversion: I see so clearly how the two fit together—as the gospels so often show. Yet conversion is so often made out to be a purely moral process, an act of will. Whereas the really decisive thing is not what you do, but what *happens* to you. Of course in sickness the patient has also to cooperate. Question: can you be "made whole" against your will—not just patched up?

*

IN the thermal baths yesterday I noticed that as long as the bath is running out, or rather when it is quite empty, the eight-fold jet comes bubbling up out of the pipe-opening in the floor, splashing and flashing, a joy to behold and to hear. As long as the water is rising you can see it moving, powerful at first, then growing fainter; once the water has reached a certain level above the inflow from the source (some 10 inches), everything calms down, you no longer notice the jet surging in from beneath. The water seems to be standing still. Yet actually all this water comes from the single overflowing jet. . . . Moral to point: the charismatic element in the Church.

*

THE main problem of the Index seems to me less the well-known and much-discussed treatment of lay-people than the fact that time and again it's a cleric, an extra super-zealous and orthodox one, of course, who denounces the "offending" book directly in Rome, behind his bishop's back. (I'm referring here to cases in which an *imprimatur* had already been granted.) In point of fact this means that he is *denouncing his own bishop*, and, what's more, for failure in one of the most important aspects of his episcopal office, i.e. as guardian of the faith. An unbelievable affront, actually, and I'm surprised that such high-handed proceedings can be "got away with" in Rome without the bishop having the chance to cite his complainant and deal fittingly with him for this act of flagrant insubordination and disloyalty.

*

A STACK of documents from Regensburg about the beatification of a Flemish priest, "Priester Poppe", a holy little pastor, loved and venerated by the faithful in his district—rather like Fr T., I'd imagine.

But what nonsense it is—sheer hypertrophy and very hard to stomach—to think that all saintly persons must be canonized at all costs—that is, if their friends and devotees have their way! This massive, truly luxurious pomp of pageantry—surely its monstrous machinery *must* have run down by now? How much nicer it would be if we could have little local cults of our own saints—if the bishops would once more be granted the right to beatify—Fr Jeningen in Ellwangen, or Heinrich Suso (if his tomb were ever rediscovered!) in Ulm, Fr Rupert Mayr in Munich, and dear good Dom Wolfgang Czernin, whose monastery grave in Uberaba is quietly developing into a place of silent pilgrimage. If everything is simply geared to publicity for the Universal Church at large, the wheels of this enormous apparatus begin to turn (seven great tomes with a total of 10,000 pages have already been sent off to Rome in the cause of Priester Poppe!), and the simplest of figures is exposed to the limelight, under gigantic magnifying glasses, distorted, out of all proportion. Not everyone can stand this sort of thing. Rilke was quite right that you cannot set up Tanagra figurines in a marketplace. The world stage isn't the place for every saint. How much more effective and comprehensible are saints still embedded in their own soil, at home, roots from the Kingdom of God sunk deep in our own dear earth—accessible and akin to the people of that countryside. So much more convincing than international stars with interchangeable faces and personal particulars. And anyway: international and Catholic! I wonder. I think it's more regrettable than desirable that the new Catechism should have been translated. Its entire approach, its special brand of childtalk seems so very German, so utterly un-English. Such things should be home-grown, not imported.

*

A CHANCE passage in *Dichtung und Wahrheit*, useful for that everlasting squabble about Catholics greedily and mercenarily collecting "merits", i.e. wages for heaven: it shows the change in the meaning of the word itself, a point almost always overlooked, but which certainly has much to do with this problem: *". . . one tends to think rather of the reward one hopes to receive than of the merit one would wish to gain. . . ." "A young man of merit. . . ."* Here the word expresses dignity, "to be worthy of", not calculation or claiming "my due".

*

I'VE been reading Wittig again these past few weeks—Wittig-Rosenstock, *Alter der Kirche* [The Age of the Church]. Odd how *passé* all this already is today—faded, irrelevant, boring, like last week's newspapers. Nothing more ephemeral, of less weight than the "topical". One really ought to shed every ambition of being "up to date".

*

LOURDES was the most powerful "manifestation" = epiphany of our Lord in the nineteenth century. As Saviour, Healer—as Living Water, the spring gushing forth, the pool of Siloe—but above all as *Heiland,** as explicitly as in Rembrandt's etching. "Born of the Virgin Mary", water here called forth by "the Lady" (whose curious independence and isolation—which struck Werfel—used to trouble me too). Extraordinary, in that very era, deaf, dumb and blind to all symbolism, *such* a massive image!!

Our Lady of Lourdes appeared in bridal dress and veil. It's full of significance, pointedly allusive: "adorned like a bride for her husband". Standing on the threshold of the wedding. Watchman, how far is the night? She is the visible Ark of the Covenant (hymn at Lauds of the feast)—a nuptial symbol, too.

* The Healer, favourite name given to our Lord from ancient to modern times in German spirituality.

Is her spring the "counter-flood" of that "flood of water" proceeding from the dragon's mouth, Apocalypse 12?

This fountain is a tangible, materialized "Come unto me all you that labour and are burdened; and I will refresh you." The spring with the power to heal the evils of the earth, the "common" sufferings of the body, of poverty—almost simultaneously with the Communist Manifesto, the revolution from below because "religion" paid too little attention to the sufferings of "the populace".

*

ONCE again I'm reading Freytag's *Ahnen* [Ancestors]—fascinating, badly written though the book itself is. But this isn't the point. What I find so exciting this time is the bone I'm gnawing just now: the power and significance of the family, the clan—though this was probably the last thing Freytag had in mind.

The clan actually was *the* person and the persona. The individual only existed at all inasmuch as he belonged to the tribal family and shared its life. Which was why excommunication, banishment, being outlawed, really was the death penalty, sentence of living death.

*

CHRISTIANITY split the clan asunder like a root cleaving a rock. Obviously there *could* only be clan-baptism at first—absurd to take exception to this. But the axe was already laid to the root when blood feuds, tribal vengeance were forbidden—and whoever accepted this stepped outside the tribe, or rather was cast out, since he could no longer identify his conscience with that of his clan, thus severing himself in this point, a very vital one—the sense of honour—from the tie of common responsibility. For honour is the vital spiritual principle of the clan, just as property, land, is the principle of its material life.

I'm afraid this has been one of the weakest spots in our foreign missionary work over the past hundred years or so, what really has held it up. As modern Europeans our missionaries addressed the individual, detaching him from his tribe, in countries where the tribe and clan were still sovereign and intact, and the individual had neither vitality nor future without it. They missed the mark.

Another point: obviously, in the Middle Ages, on the spiritual plane, the clan could only be replaced by the monastic *order*, the religious houses, they alone offering just as important, extensive and organic a counterpart—the *spiritual* family with its head and members, father and brothers, elders and younger ones, and "posterity". Not by some private form of "lay asceticism", probably also existent, but insignificant. Of course the clan as such could never be entirely christianized, any more than "the nation" or "the State", always only some of its members. It was a *natural* power—and, far-reaching, weighty question: can such natural powers and their incarnations ever be truly redeemed, baptized—not just tamed, domesticated, "dovetailed" into another order of things?

*

At long last I've got down to Tauler's *Medulla animae*, put aside for such ages.

A lot of it is really very dull—an early compendium of all the ascetic catchwords to be found in the *Imitation of Christ*, Scupoli, *Philothea*, etc. Yet it has a certain charm of its own. One thing did dawn on me: that "nature" always referred to by ascetics with a certain negative bias (even in 1924 in the retreat before my clothing) as the ego to be mortified, annihilated, quenched—doesn't mean human nature in general at all, not even our physical nature, but usually quite simply what psychologists these days call "the psyche", i.e. what reacts within us, all the time, to stimuli from outside, automatically, following its own laws—"mechanisms". Nowadays this element of the human being is observed, analysed, hugged, cultivated and cosseted, an immensely interesting and fascinating phenomenon, the object of countless novels consisting solely of its minute description. People seem to hope it can be explained by this method, as though it could be X-rayed, grasped, mastered. The Ancients preferred to ignore it, gagging it, "mortifying" it. For them this was "the life after the flesh" (Knox actually translates: "the ways of nature"!), claiming independence. But neither would they drop it, abandon it—they sought rather to make room in it for God, integrating it into God, not merely into a "self".

The first process, ignoring and stifling, has been supported by moralism. Result: the notorious repressions, complexes, traumas, etc. Nowadays (I'm thinking of Christians!) people believe they can skip this painful procedure, indeed that they *must* skip it to avoid such fatal consequences. Result: nature gets "fresh".

*

ACTUALLY "Devotion to the World" calls for *more* asceticism, not less. But of another kind, you might call it "recoiled". The ancient ascetics (not only, but also) projected into the world what was really in man. *They said "world" and meant "soul"*, a soul huge and marvellously powerful—enough to fill a whole universe! For thousands of years, unconsciously, as a matter of course, it had been nourished through "the five doors" from this world's substance, fed with the fullness of all the forces of Creation and its elements. It had grown so rich that it could reflect its overflowing vitality back into nature in a thousand images of gods, nymphs, etc., and it grew no poorer in the process, for it encountered them again all the time. It had become like the ocean. It had magical powers at its disposal. This was the soul which came face to face with Christianity, or rather with the gospel of Christ. This soul was confronted with God, lifted out of the world, discovering itself as a realm to be conquered for God, a kingdom to be filled by him. And to make room for God it had to be emptied by asceticism, emptied of itself, of the whole world which had accumulated within it in all its imagery. This involved a tremendous conflict, a process so overwhelming that the whole of Creation withdrew before it, vanishing into the background. Only "God and the soul" remained.

But a very dangerous process, immeasurable in its consequences, had set in, too: segregation, divorce from nature, from the rest of Creation, withdrawal, detachment, separation. "Separate" man was born, the umbilical cord was cut. To heal his severance from God, man divorced himself from nature. And out of this separation our culture and civilization have grown, everything we have come to know as the development of Christendom. Yet not without the ominous beginnings of a new desire for nature—desire presupposing separation and tension. In place of the natural ordered whole, a new "unity" had to be constructed with desire as its motive force, greedy for control—with a vengeance, quite literally.

And all the time the soul is growing more and more impoverished, enfeebled, empty—as well we know—but intellect and will-power hypertrophied.

Until at last man is left with too little soul for faith. He is no longer *human* enough. See C. S. Lewis, *Abolition of Man*.

Which is why every form of asceticism which still further weakens, stifles and reduces our "soul-substance" is fundamentally wrong for him. On the contrary, what he needs is cosseting, spoon-feeding—to regain his strength. And how can he except through his senses? *His* asceticism must be applied to what is *really* growing wild and rank: to the new "cold" greed; to reason degraded and unbridled; to obstinate, hidebound will-power; to the monstrous, self-important arrogance of individualism.

*

BUT what about the old "ideal of perfection"? This makes less and less sense to me. For, theoretically, it's linked with "being above" all purely vital impulses and reactions, both sensual and spiritual, indeed it virtually consists of this. Is it really only sour grapes when I say that I don't *want* insensibility, *apatheia*? That I wouldn't have it even as a gift. Not because it costs too much (though probably this has something to do with it!), but simply because to me it's inhuman—because it may be right and proper for the angels, but not for us. Surely it is more fitting, more lovable, more obedient even to God's will for us, that man should be like an Aeolian harp, a responsive—but this means a reacting—creature, intertwined, interwoven, intermingled with the rest of the world, moved to tears and to laughter, alive to joy and to sorrow—in love with Creation? Precisely what the ascetic doesn't want, what he is striving to rid himself of at all costs!

The question is simply: is this sort of "interwoven" existence compatible with the maximum love of God? How intense, how strong would our ascesis have to be to make it possible at all—balanced, fit, anchored in the bedrock, deep down among the rocks, before one could *afford* such swinging and swaying in the psyche-area—before one might venture upon it without giddiness, without self-delusion?

Man in Paradise would certainly never have lived in *apatheia*: he would have been caught up on wings, vibrating with the whole of Creation, with God!

Apatheia can, *must* only be a means, a state of transition—not the goal. But surely, as man is made, this transition, this rigorous cure would absorb his whole life, and, if it's successful, he'd by that time be so done for that there would be precious little left over to be a "harp of the Holy Ghost"? Operation successful, patient dead. By that time all spontaneity, responsiveness, suppleness have been driven out or drastically curbed!

The problem is simply how to survive this cure. What was it old Mother Maruzzi used to say about novices who entered already "conditioned" or not in need of such "conditioning"? "What they need is a little more original sin." But, heavens above, is raw nature really worth while? Is it so marvellous that it would be a pity to chip off a few bits?

*

FURTHERMORE: in this matter, as in everything else, by no means all people actually alive are "contemporaries", i.e. there are certain basic types which are always to be found and other varieties which are only "period". An important discrimination, to my mind, would be between the "conscious" and the "unconscious" types. For almost all these problems actually begin only on "waking". The sleepwalkers—and there seem to be quite a lot of these—must first of all be roused to awareness— that's what I mean by "awakening". But—*must* they really? I'm afraid so, for our present-day world no longer sweeps even slumberers along in the desired direction. You can only steer "straight" *against* the tide, and to do this you need your wits about you. And no matter how modern a man may be, in the sense of heritage, the influence of environment, bearing all the signs of acquired civilization, etc.—as long as he just drags all this around with him in his sleep, he's no more than a chunk of his world, his milieu, an animal . . . a talking animal, no matter how nice. But once awake, come to his senses, there begins for him, too (but speeded up like a film), the long, indispensable process, inevitable, too, in its implications, that same process of detachment, encounter, sublimation, even if these days on a much smaller scale.

But what's the use of wriggling—I can't deny that just "living life" itself, stirring and testing all the energies of body, mind and the senses makes more of a man, shaping and moulding him, developing him all round—than that insistent, intentional, ruthless thwarting and pruning system. He wouldn't even really run wild, the constant clash with facts and realities would chasten and sober him down, I suppose, even more thoroughly than our "exercises". And people do thrive better in this fashion—than we do. Of course this is a very personal issue. I'm so very much the sorry result, the victim of an "ascetic" upbringing, that I can't help my revulsion from such methods. All the same, looking at some of the counter-models one sees around, it's difficult not to exclaim, awful though it sounds: "Lord, I thank thee that I'm not like them!"

On the other hand, take X. and Y. and Z. Surely there are methods enough, exterior as well as interior discipline—including morals—by which a human being could be trained without such mutilation? For it isn't a simple alternative—either ascetic, i.e. crippled, or rank reckless growth, a perfectly ill-bred little pig like NN. Must you become involved in classic asceticism *à tout prix*, just to arouse somebody, to shape him? (humph—I seem to feel Newman and his gentleman hovering somewhere in the background). Yes, quite simply: "Rocks with razors, men-of-war with silken strands." No, he *is* right, after all: even the *honnête homme* with nothing more to him is a poor wretch, with his charming "persona" and the yawning gaps behind it. Like XX.

*

Ah, but the beauty, the sheer beauty of man alive, exuberant, exulting, daredevil, flowering riotously—I've always succombed to that spell—hopelessly, incurably. (Hölderlin: "Those who think deepest love the most living things"?) For me only such a being seems to resemble man in Paradise—never the obedient poodle jumping through hoops of principles and good sense! Is there really no successful combination of (*a*) with holiness—as this, alas, undeniably does exist in (*b*)?

But the *great* saints—in contrast to the little *dévotes*—were they ever faultlessly trained poodles? People like Francis, Elizabeth, Teresa, Philip Neri? Never! On the contrary, here precisely the most rigorous asceticism released and moulded their "natural" glory which without this drastic cure would have grown rank and wild, or rusted, or simply remained crippled—in the case of Francis, for instance, by snobbery, ostentation and extravagance—of Teresa by hysteria and coquetry.

Chinese proverb: "If our lives are mingled with the world, and yet in harmony with the Light, then we shall be living among our fellows, openly, yet in secret, different, yet akin, and no one can tell how. For then no one will notice this secret way of ours." Isn't this an answer too?

❧ 1957—1959 ❧

THAT *Weltbild* annual wants a contribution for young people: an article on virginity, or rather celibacy and virginity. Why is it so hard to start on it? Because here in this country the word, indeed the very concept, is almost taboo. Virginity: people don't care to mention it—or to hear about it. Because, even believing Catholics think it "unnatural", a demand all too exacting—and the sacrifice too great, too devitalizing—for a very uncertain gain. I must show that Christians of old thought it a positive value, not mere negation: a value far outweighing the price paid for it—all costly things cost, that's surely obvious. And this reward is here and now, on our earth. The special union with God must be stressed first, and *then* renunciation, as its condition and accompaniment.

*

THE fear of "standing up for things" in public isn't only due to cowardice or minding what other people think. It's rooted in humility, too, the necessary humility which is shy of showing off, of being forward. How well I understand Kierkegaard's qualms because he was not "authorized" to speak out and to write, and yet he had to! But if you must, then you *must* honour God with a "tongue flowing readily as the pen of the swift writer". After all you can't suppress letters simply because you dislike being hailed as the postman.

*

THE facsimile volumes of Little Thérèse's journals, etc. have arrived. Heavens, what trouble they've taken!! Reproduced to perfection in every detail, not just photostat copies—the notebooks have been got up exactly like the originals, the same cover, paper and ink, complete with blots, erasures and crossings out—you'd think you were handling Thérèse's own notebooks. Every loose slip included separately—everything perfectly arranged. It's exactly like a Bible concordance: glossaries of every word used, its frequency, etc., endless chronological tables, graphological analyses (only formal ones, no mention of character, wisely enough!), notes and commentaries galore for every sentence. Was such tribute ever paid to any poet, philosopher—or any other saint? I can't help it, it just makes me grin. Strange indeed the flowers produced by spiritual vanity, group vanity.

How significant that this work which registers in these tables all the passages deleted or altered by Pauline so precisely, down to the very last punctuation mark, should contain no special list of the numerous *interpolations*, which are every bit as important. You could write a brochure on the mentality of the editors! But I'll leave that to younger brains and simply incorporate what I must in my new edition.

*

THÉRÈSE again. Two problems concerning her inner life are beginning to emerge: vanity—at least self-complacency—and piety.

Thérèse's naïve delight in her own self simply makes one gasp. She is utterly convinced that no other person in the world has received so much grace; that she surpasses the wisdom of sages in her spiritual progress and insight. Dr I. once told me about a Hungarian lady on a steamer trip down the Danube. As they passed Gran with its twin steeples she called out ecstatically: "You can only find this in Hungary!" Explains something of Thérèse's mentality. And then, of course, that atmosphere of family narcissism, gushing out in ceaseless mutual admiration. I suppose God permitted this, since otherwise we would never have discovered these microscopic slides of "ordinary" Christian virtue, so very important today, and increasingly in the future. Who else would ever have *dared* even to *mention* such trivialities at all (headaches, tiny sacrifices, mortifications, etc.), let alone write them down? These things impress many readers as wonderful, "unique"—actually what is "unique" is only that it is put on record. And then her "religious diction". Does this reveal Thérèse's strength or her weakness? Two sides to this. Typically youthful on the one hand. (Those

black notebooks we kept as novices! What very similar out-
pourings!!) In the young wishful thinking far exceeds substance. But the pious reader naturally takes the *Histoire* at its
face value, especially if unaccustomed to this sort of writing.
And then there's her very French delight in flowery phrases,
décor. *And* the convent jargon. Of course Thérèse "ratified" all
this on her death bed : it is all of it *true*. Yes, but this very same
truth could as well be lived without "make up", unreflected,
not in front of the mirror—and it *is* happening all the time, a
hundred times over, mutely, inconspicuously.

Dear old Dom Placidus once told me : "That's temperament,
you know, not religion." This ostentation, this gush, this word-
froth—I suppose it's constitutional, not piety. But the same
piety exists, too—in substance—outside this "setting". And it
must be extracted, revealed.

*

A TALK with NN. Stimulating but most unsatisfactory—time
was short and neither of us would let the other finish what he
wanted to say! He was full of reproaches for the Church for
failing to acknowledge the family as a special state of spirituality, grumbling at the lack of "a proper theology of marriage",
and that issue should still be considered as the fundamental purpose of marriage, etc. Still harping away on the same old strings
—but we must leave it at that, as long as we've got no better
answers to offer.

But do these critics never stop to think that it was impossible
to consider marriage at all except within the family, that this
would have been an impossible abstraction?—outside the reality
which was the clan. And that "the family" always meant the
whole clan, never just the couple. The clan was anything but a
centre of spiritual life!

Nowadays the accent is reversed. These days the consuming,
dominating "ideal" is no longer even the State (except the
totalitarian versions), or society, but a mass-suggestion of the
primacy of "sexual fulfilment". The Christian must find a new
way of breaking free from this collective spell of sex.

*

THE crisis experienced in convents almost everywhere seems to point in the same direction. For their natural model no longer exists; postulants are no longer bred and trained to attitudes corresponding to this pattern—the family structure of the convent is no more than a deliberate make-believe. The old family principle in all its manifestations is irrevocably doomed, hopelessly ebbing away. And in China, where its natural roots seemed most strong and enduring, it has simply been exterminated by force.

*

"DEVOTION to the World." Early Christianity turned its back on nature, the body, etc. This corresponds to the struggle for emancipation from the mother as long as she was all-powerful. But now that we've found her again "in our Father's hand"— just as in old paintings—and have "put her in her place" (in both senses), surely we may, we can, we *must* love her again?

*

CARREL: "The body is at once a phenomenon of permanence and flux, of unceasing self-renewal." Surely this should be equally applicable to the Body of the Church? But we are always trying to preserve everything, even dead cells and cuticles are sacrosanct, to be scattered back over the living Body and stuck on again —while all the time we placidly allow whole organs to disintegrate through neglect and disease, believing this to be progress and "development". That's the awful thing. But thank God most of the bodily processes are not determined by rational thinking or will-power.

*

I'M reading Maxence van der Meersch's gripping novel about doctors, *Bodies and Souls*. Ghastly. But very illuminating, too, for his curious interpretation of Little Thérèse and her message. Roughly speaking he sees them as the consolation offered by one incorrigible sinner to other incorrigibles—the message that even *without conversion* they may still love, and so be redeemed. Behind this, it would seem to me, is an infinite, poignant compassion for the poor creatures who, as the result of ignorance, hereditary disease, etc. are virtually "beyond" good and evil, i.e. beneath moral judgment, with barely a chance of downright, willed conversion—yet perhaps not beyond turning to God in their hearts *in the midst of their disintegration.*

These are the people whom he wants to ransom, for whom he intends this message (which Thérèse herself certainly never meant). But perhaps it should really be the other way round: *first* the blind, deaf and dumb groping towards God's mercy and *then* purposeful conversion?—not skipping conversion, as it were, content with the mere impulse and leaving it at that.

*

GETTING back to that conversation about the family. If there's anything in A.R's astrological-historical theory, then one could say that throughout the whole Pisces era*, right into this last period, the family is an Aries† phenomenon: vehicle of blood, power, authority, fame, possessions, expansion. So closely identified with all these things that it certainly offered no room for spirituality! Which accounts for the demonstrative stand of almost all the typical saints of this era against this idol, starting with Felicitas and Perpetua—indeed all the martyrs, particularly the virgins, for whom severing from the *gens* meant a decisive act—then Radegunde, Francis, Elizabeth, down to Nicholas of Flüe and Jane Frances de Chantal. This struggle, this revolt was lurid, melodramatic, spectacular, and despite all efforts can never be convincingly interpreted as edifying. Which is why monasticism appeared at first less as "sacrifice" than as achievement and victory—liberty from the power of blood, a strange, new, disconcerting freedom! Yet the clan still remained so exemplary, even for its "deserters", that the religious orders have been based upon its model: the religious family, brothers under a father, sisters under a mother—not members of an organization, soldiers under a general—Ignatius was the first to establish this new type of religion without a family.

Only much later, hard on the transition period, did the Church begin to uphold and protect "the family": for this impoverished relic of a once great power now suddenly emerged as the last bulwark against the new leviathan which replaced the Aries deities

---

* Pisces era: roughly the Christian era, up to 1950.
† Aries era: roughly from the Bronze Age era to the threshold of Christianity —the Homeric and saga age, age of gods, demigods and heroes.

by a new idol: the State. All the same, what the Church now defends and protects is *nowhere* the family in the old clan sense. This recent "small" family is in a way just as much an "inner" phenomenon, hinging on interior things, as the clan was extrovert, turning outwards for fulfilment. The "Pisces family" is only now beginning to crystallize, it had barely existed before, at any rate there was no general awareness of it—in reality it may have been there for some time.

The romantic love of the nineteenth and our own half of the twentieth century was the protest against the out-worn clan concept of marriage: the cry for individualism *à deux*. But, rootless and unsheltered, this, too, is overtaxed and dying of disillusionment. It cannot be maintained by itself, as the divorce figures in their millions go to prove. These "love matches" stand more than ever in need of the shelter and security to be found only in something beyond themselves, they must be linked anew to something greater, supported by the whole.

*

St John of the Cross is quoted in the long commentary on Thérèse:

"If love for another creature consists of a purely spiritual affection, based solely on God, then our love of God will grow commensurate with this love in our soul; the more the heart dwells on the other being, the more it dwells in God and desires Him, since both these loves grow together, entwined in one another."

Yes, that's what they all say, I know. But how do they know so certainly when and whether her love was really so "purely spiritual", founded on God alone? In the context the quotation almost certainly refers to the love of the Martin sisters for one another—yet precisely here "nature", the blood-bond, the powerful family tie is so very palpable.

*

Thomas Aquinas. I seem to see and understand him so clearly. If I could only show other people this figure: rock and yet crystal, rooted darkly-deep, his head high in the bright light of reason, like a mountain between night and morning. . . .

*

THÉRÈSE again. Hagiographers are so fond of "blowing up" little frills and fluffs of devotion as characteristics of a saint's particular vocation, whereas in fact they merely betray his "constitution". And so, in the case of Thérèse, everything is built up around tenderness and sweetness and the wish to please —Papa and her sisters—Jesus and God. And she thinks God reacts in exactly the same way. "If one expects only justice from Him, one will receive justice—one gets exactly what one expects from God." That just isn't true—an entirely subjective statement, what's more, revealing a radically false notion of God! Just like that illustration she uses in a letter to Léonie : a mother would *rather* forgive the little pet who cuddles up to her, coaxing forgiveness with kisses, than the poor child who creeps into the corner, rigid and speechless, trembling at the prospect of punishment. . . . As though God—like any good father!— wouldn't turn in his mercy to just this trembling mulish little creature, breaking open its poor cramped heart in his mercy, mercy unreasoned, shattering, startling, overwhelming—manifested in grace : "non *secundum peccata nostra fecisti nobis* . . .". And such statements, well-meaning, but so very limited in their applicability, are then quoted like the gospel. . . . The adulteress in John 8 certainly only expected justice—and what did she find!

*

FR Girolamo Moretti's study of the handwriting of the saints is most interesting. He too admits, if reluctantly, Thérèse's intense self-preoccupation, her passionate craving to be regarded, admired, loved—and to be seen. I see I shall have to re-write my chapter on "the veil"—this was pure *agere contra*, not natural reserve. Fr Moretti claims that Thérèse possessed the highest intelligence, "equal to any male brain"? I really don't want to depreciate her—it's just that I'm immune to her special 120 per cent feminine fascination—which incidentally was exercised only after her death. There's a certain delight in one's own self which is catching, suggestive, casting a spell, literally "enchanting". Moretti actually talks about her "magic"!— which, after all, is expressed by the very word "charm". . . .

*

Legenda Aurea. To think that there's no Catholic edition of this most Catholic book! I remember my brothers sending me a copy of the beautiful volume edited by Richard Benz, illustrated with wood-cuts, back in "claustral" days. But in the full May-time blossom of my brand-new Catholic rationalism I was torn between indignation and shame, declared it an offensive relic of the darkest ages, suspected some teasing prank on the part of my brothers behind this present—and hastily gave it away. I wonder now that my conscience allowed me to get rid of it this way—in those days I ought actually to have considered whether it couldn't harm the Church, since its recipient could have got a bad impression by reading it! Well, I seem to have solved this dilemma somehow, but the fact remains that precisely the religious-minded youngsters of our generation didn't take to this book at all, on the contrary! Benz sees it as epic and myth of the Middle Ages, exact parallel to the Gothic cathedrals. Sunk into oblivion with the epoch, rediscovered through the history of art, in the countless painters inspired by the Legend. Wonderful, costly and beautiful—but belonging utterly to the past, monument, museum: venerable, interesting, imposing— *tout à fait passé.*

But what about us? Lovely fairy-tales from the childhood of our faith, to be read with the same wistful, tender amusement we feel when we come across toys belonging to our parents and grandparents buried in a trunk in the attic—glad all the same that things are different these days? What are we to make of stories like that of St Paul the First Hermit who met a centaur and a faun on his way to Abbot Anthony; Martha, who led the dragon of Tarascon through the town, tame, by her girdle; St Patrick who exposed the sheep thief in the community by making the lamb bleat in his belly; St Christopher, full twelve ells tall, and the eleven thousand virgins? Yet the Archbishop of Genoa wasn't just a dreamy poet—he was a renowned scholar, a critical historian, verifying, expressing his doubts as to sources, traditions, etc. sprinkling his stuff liberally with spiritual and secular quotations. For his time he certainly ranked as a peak of scholarship in general history and Church history, theology and what in those days passed for philology. Perhaps the scholarly works of our own age will rate as amusing fairy-tales in a few hundred years' time? Possibly: still, what is the enduring element in the *Golden Legend*?

We'll never be able to unearth what the medieval reader— and listener—really thought of it all. Certainly they didn't consider it as a report of actual happenings, but rather as a spiritual picture book: a gigantic rose window full of hundreds of colourful figures, all lit by the same radiance, all facing the same focal hub—and comprehensible, translucent in this light alone. What a wealth of ancient traditions is contained in this book— informal lore, not to be found in works on dogma or in the catechism, only scattered here and there in countless works of art, but long since indecipherable for us. Here it is all arranged within the mullions of a single rose window. The spokes are the feasts of the Church year, and perhaps the loveliest chapter is that "on the differing seasons".

It's astonishing what new illumination these side-lights throw even on central subjects. For instance, those words in the Creed: "descended into hell"—what do we really imagine by this today? At the most we argue whether this means Hell proper, or just Limbo, and whether our Lord really shared the torments of the damned. In the Middle Ages they saw this article of faith differently, starkly powerful, graphic: glorious paintings —all of them inspired by the Legend—the gaping jaws of the monster Death, with Christ straddling the cleft like Samson braced for the fight—forcing open a heavy door, revealing Adam and Eve, hoary pilgrims, their hands outstretched in supplication. Or the Lord piercing the monstrous fiend with the staff of the pascal banner and leading out our forefathers, their wrists still fettered. What a powerful Easter message: Christ triumphant, wresting the prey from the jaws of death and Hell, retrieving his own from the beginning of the world? Actually this is anticipating Doomsday—a "dress rehearsal" for our own universal resurrection: what happened then for the just, in their day, will happen for us at the end of all things: the "oneness" of man, of history, of time: a picture message of a future already begun, the "latter days" dawning, eternity already absorbing the past. That Christ is not risen as a lone individual, but, as the Liturgy knows, as the Victor with a host of prisoners in his train. All this drawn out of a tiny chapter—and it concerns each one of us. Such knowledge was once as common as daily bread, handy for everyone, not just caviare for historians, folklorists and psychological experts.

*

THAT league of a thousand years between the hierarchy and actual sovereignty (the tiara! bishops of the realm, royal, imperial!) was another victory of the Ram over the Fishes: the clan triumphant, setting up chieftain and priest in one, so that the High Priest must be the High Chief as well, or the other way round: such an attitude could not fail to produce an "imperialistic" Pope as well as a system of "liege" priests, even serf-priests, until the Emperor wanted to keep the Pope as his own obedient vassal and chaplain.

*

A SACRAMENT consecrating friendship such as A.R. postulates, or rather predicts, for the dawning world-era did exist long ago in the rite of blood-brotherhood. In those days, of course, the friend was raised from a lower to a higher grade of fellowship, to the highest known rank, that of blood relationship, exalted, consecrated—irrevocably, indissolubly.

*

I WAS reading *Swing Door* the other night in bed—a rather silly English novel dating from the 'twenties. The heroine stands, roughly, for Elsa's generation. Accustomed as we are to jobs for women as a matter of course, with career women bemoaning the strain of their lives (and often ready enough to exchange their burdens for a more natural and sheltered domestic existence!), it's very instructive to think back to the beginnings of this incredibly rapid development, so near in time yet already quite forgotten: to recall the struggle of daughters in those days against the truly gruesome and merciless tyranny of the family Moloch which devoured human beings just as ruthlessly and recklessly as careers do today: on the emptiness and pointlessness of such a live puppet's existence, and the salvation of breaking away at last to take up some really useful, fruitful and congenial activity.

*

THAT graphological book on the handwriting of the saints is comforting, but disturbing. Comforting, since maybe there's still a chance for "the likes of us", but very disconcerting, for it shows what lamentable *natural* dispositions some of these great ones really had. Aloysius, for instance, with fits of rabid temper, was mean, vindictive, sensual—this accounts for his ferocious penances. Later on, in the language of hagiography, we then read this sort of thing: "All his life he was protected by special grace from every temptation (? ?) against holy chastity . . . ! " Joseph of Cupertino: born with a streak of "moral insanity", not entirely responsible, with a bent towards passive homosexuality—had the makings of a decoy or a criminal's accomplice! John of the Cross was, in fact, a born heretic, subversive, destructive, could well have become a *"fabbricatore di errori"*: very significant this for the vehemence with which he rejects and demolishes—I would suggest—all things created in his mysticism. . . .

Striking proofs of the victory of grace over nature! But it's disillusioning and frightening all the same, for in our heart of hearts we long to find in these saints of ours the qualities of unfallen man, or at any rate *noble* human nature. But, it seems, Jesus knew exactly why, in that parable, he had the rogues, beggars and cripples invited to his wedding feast—and they came.

*

HANS JOACHIM SCHOEPS, *Die letzten 30 Jahre* [The Last Thirty Years]. "The fact remains that every Jew today, as in the past, cannot but continue to reject Jesus as the Messiah of Israel . . . for the simple reason that we Jews could on no account admit that the Messiah had already come, that we are living in the post-Messianic era. . . . Jewish repudiation of the claim that the Messiah has already come must be as emphatic today—if you like—as naïve as it was 1,900 years ago. *A world redeemed would be very different from the world we know.* We can never admit that the promises of the prophets for the final era have been fulfilled—either literally or figuratively, if we are to accept what Scripture really meant. For we are too painfully aware of the unredeemed state of this world."

Among Christians we hear the same protest: from Joachites,* Rosicrucians: Everything is wrong, intolerably wrong, but tomorrow, tomorrow . . . the long-awaited is already standing in the doorway. They turn to the Church and ask: "Is it thy coming that was foretold, or are we yet waiting for some other?" —and in fact they are still expecting that other.

*

IF I were a pagan, a non-European pagan, I'd have one big objection, one special complaint which would certainly bar my way to the Faith: the fact that the baptized, the white race, have come to be the pest, the curse, the disintegrating ferment for the rest of the world, generally speaking. We, as a body, what is called "Christendom", quite apart from the individuals. That we've branded the whole world with the awful stigma of ugliness, robbing it of its soul, spoiling, violating. By their fruits you shall know them. Can we ever really make up for all this by the gifts of civilization?

*

BUT how infinitely consoling here (like a voice from heaven, hidden so often for me in my Book Providence) is a sentence of St Ignatius's in his marvellous autobiography—what a pity it is only a fragment: "How our Lord dealt with this soul which *was still quite blind* in spite of his *great longing* to serve him in every way to the best of his understanding. . . ." "He had as yet no eye for interior values, nor did he understand what humility, what love and patience really are. Nor did he yet know that sense of the will of God which serves to direct these virtues, imposing the right proportion."—Couldn't this apply at any rate to *young* Christendom, the white race in its youth, as long as it had still some right to call itself Christian?

*

INCIDENTALLY, that strange "illumination" Ignatius experienced by the river—which he himself describes almost *en passant*—

---

* Followers of the twelfth-century Abbot Joachim of Fiore, who proclaimed a third and more perfect dispensation of the Spirit, cf. above, p. 142.

was probably that phenomenon of the "central vision" the Protestant mystics make such a fuss about.

*

LIFE of St Paul of the Cross, founder of the Passionists. Astonishing really that he should be so little known, should have left so little impression, if he really was the figure described here—of much more imposing stature than many far more popular saints. Religious founder and a great missionary like Alphonsus Mary Liguori and Clement Mary Hofbauer, a stern ascetic, too, and endowed with many spectacular charisms, which usually contribute so substantially to fame: clairvoyance, bilocation, mind-reading, power over evil spirits, sickness, animals and the elements (storm, water, air). But he's quite forgotten.

Strangely thrilling that St Paul—end of the eighteenth century! —should have prayed all his life for the conversion of England, pledging his sons to do likewise. Once, during Mass, he had a vision of "my sons in England". But only in 1841, almost seventy years after his death, did they actually set foot on English soil—through Fr Dominic Barberi. It was he who received Newman into the Church—which, incidentally, neither the author nor the translator of my book seems to have known. How strangely they flow, the delta streams of grace.

*

ST Paul of the Cross: *Presenza di Dio:*
"Our devotion rouses the longing in all of us to visit the holy places and the glorious temples of Christendom. Yet our faith teaches us that our inner being is a shrine, for it is the living temple of God, the throne of the Most Holy Trinity. Let us, therefore, resort often to this temple, adoring the holy Trinity in spirit and in truth. Oh, this is truth and a noble devotion indeed!" Sometimes he says jokingly: "Stay at home!" Or: "Go home to your house"—or: "How are things doing there? Your house is your mind and your soul, which is the temple of the Living God, where He dwells through faith."

*

IN one of the April numbers of *The Tablet* I read a very interesting review of a book by the German Cistercian Abbot Wiesinger.* He maintains that all para-psychic faculties are relics of Paradise gifts, gifts once belonging to the "spiritual" body of unfallen man. Makes very good sense to me and tallies with similar views held by Anne Catherine Emmerich. She, of course, makes a very clear distinction between the effect of these powers as used by saints and by "unredeemed man".

*

REAL insight into another human being—such as is granted to one now and again—brings its own sharp suffering. How incomprehensible it then seems, the love of God for his creatures! And then the awful, agonizing fear that all our fine theories about the human being as a "gem", etc. might really be nothing but narcotics, artfully concocted, without which we could never endure such glimpses.

*

STRANGE really, how persistent it is—in some people's minds—the notion that Creation (at least in its primeval depths, the abyss) must be evil and demonic, and that when these depths are "tapped" (see atomic fission) then this reality, veiled with such artistry, is revealed.

Contrary: (*a*) Creation is good—testimony of Scripture, (*b*) furthermore it is even "actively" related to God: praising, proclaiming him. Even dragons and abysses "bless" God, night, cold and lightning—all the terrors of nature, all its menaces and sinister powers. And surely it is precisely this "plumbing of the depths" that discloses new, as-yet-undreamed-of marvels of God's order, revealed, even exactly weighed and measured in microcosm, in macrocosm? Perhaps today, as never before, we can discern, not just sense, what the Ancients felt when they saw the administration of the angels in what was later called the laws of Nature.

When do these forces, fundamentally good, turn "evil"—but not *bad*!—i.e. pernicious, destructive to man? When they grow beyond his control—flood, avalanche, epidemics. When

* *Occult Phenomena in the Light of Theology*, London, 1957.

he must meet them unarmed. A snow crystal is a miracle of delicate beauty, but in a blizzard? Sun and light can be deadly, just like our obedient slave the electric current.

No, man is not the sovereign "lord of Nature" by any means, only bit by bit, laboriously, precariously. True, his domination is increasing, all the time he's venturing on further objects ever greater but not more malignant. To primitive man cold, fire, wild beasts must seem just as "demonic"—Satanic, if he's a Christian—i.e. as mercilessly destructive as the atomic bomb to us. What terrible things a child could do, meddling with the control panel of a power station! Is it not rather a matter of proportion, not quality, whether and when nature seems evil? Pharmacologists, doctors, chemists control, for instance, poisons at whose mercy the ignorant, the unsuspecting would find themselves. The forces "tapped" seem sinister, weird, Satanic (or Divine!) when man has not yet learnt to control them: as long as they're still just brute force. All "untamed" natural power invites mastery. When man fails, we have the situation of the sorcerer's apprentice—which really is almost a myth. But this lies rather in his presumption in meddling with things beyond his control than in an essential evil of theirs. *That* is the sacrilege, and the penalty, i.e. the response of the creature is not evil but just.

On the other hand: the Church exorcizes everything she consecrates, i.e. designates for divine or often merely human service. Does this imply that she "retrieves" the creature, bit by bit, as it were, from Satan, the "god of this world"—in other words that she does *not* regard nature as wholly redeemed—*en bloc?* That she holds special acts of consecration and blessings to be necessary, i.e. is not content simply with the knowledge that all things proceed from the hand of God? Or should one say: precisely in its depths, in its substance, Creation is good: but overlying it like a spell, like a crust, is the power of Satan—the same idea as C. S. Lewis's Crooked Eldil, the dark tellurian spirit Lucifer. And exorcisms and blessings pierce this "glaze" each time, liberating the basic goodness of the creature? Romans 8?

*

THE symbolism of the Sacred Heart is far from fully exhausted—being as yet purely optical, so to speak, never really considered

functionally. For actually the function of the heart in the body is
not to shed blood, to pour it *out*—which is the principal subject of our meditations—but rather to send blood pulsing through
the body, nourishing, warming. Little Thérèse was quite right
here in wanting to be "the heart of the Church".

The devotion, as we know it, is associated primarily with the
idea of a wound—a wound of birth—the Church born out of the
wounded side of Christ—yet all this applied to the Heart of our
Lord is incidental, not "physiological".

*

THERE's an exact counterpart to aphasia, a disease called mental
blindness: eye-sight is still perfect, but memory is blacked out
completely, so that visual impressions remain jumbled, dis-
connected, no longer making sense. Surely there is a similar
disease of the soul? And isn't contemporary atheism somehow
related to it? The function of "religious memory" = tradition in
humanity and in the Church. The enemies of tradition have no
idea what they're doing. . . . They think they're debunking, getting rid of lumber—what they're actually doing is inaugurating a
process of spiritual blindness.

*

HEART and blood: Blood nourishes and protects—purifies. No
one really knows the starting-point of the heart's tremendous
power. Blood flows even into the tiniest capillaries in the skin:
these again being influenced (*a*) by external factors (tempera-
ture, pressure), (*b*) a mesh of the finest nerves, centrally controlled. This outermost network of blood-vessels could well be
called "the peripheral heart". In some way all this must be
equally applicable to the Corpus Mysticum, and expressed
accordingly.

*

FEAST of the Sacred Heart. The same old aching wonder that
I've never somehow been able to achieve what other people
call "a personal relationship to Christ". Despite the fact that
since 1916 the LORD, veiled, has been the star, the core of my
entire existence. But it was *God* on whom my mind focused in
this awakening, not Christ. And ever since 1927: the Church.

Has the Church hidden Christ for me? That, too, can happen. Yet was the Church—for me—ever anything but the shape of Christ manifest—not of God, as such!—just like the Sacrament: *qui sub* his figuris *vere latitas*? Veiling, not hiding. And after all it's He Himself who designed and wove this Veil—and hung it before my eyes.

*

I've agreed to write a radio script about St Elizabeth. It must be made clear that she was a flame leaping upwards—swift, swift—like all who reach perfection early—rushing towards the peak, consuming herself and everything she touched. But the spark came from the apostolic "movement of poverty", as yet darkly smouldering—or, more correctly, from its Franciscan climax. That such a thing should exist: a poverty *movement*! an ideal of poverty, catching thousands in its sway. And not just from "below" either, as self-assertion of the populace, but rather flaming down from above in Francis, Clare, Elizabeth and their like—for they certainly weren't the only ones. What was this in fact? This sudden awakening, long overdue, of a "property conscience", at a time when the urge for possessions, the whole attitude towards wealth was still wild, carefree, unconscious, taken for granted, as natural as in beasts of prey—as natural as the urge for fighting or sex.

Ludwig's death was the decisive test as to whether her yearning for poverty was "idealism", i.e. a passing whim, or serious—so serious that it could even replace the foundation which had been torn out of her life. She passed the test. From then on—no longer borne by her husband—she "foundered", but indeed, in this wreck, reached a new foundation for her life. She was exactly the same age as Little Thérèse when she died. What a difference! Elizabeth's lightning directness, impulsive, unselfconscious, beside the perpetual reflection of Thérèse, for ever bent over her interior life, straining to catch every breath, every changing shade of her ego.

Would Elizabeth as much as dared even to *think* of herself as "the heart of the Church", let alone put this into words? Yet in her "the Heart of Jesus overflowed into the Church", as Peterson puts it. But Elizabeth was far from being a product of the poverty movement! She wasn't even primarily roused and inspired by it—with her it is all much less conscious, earlier, almost instinctive, like a homing bird. It began already in the little girl in the Wartburg, a little wild creature, half-imprisoned, taking the WORD seriously all the same, not the word of book learning (certainly she must have lived in the Wartburg as though in a dream-cave), but rather the image, the crucifix, and the daily picture of the beggars at the castle gate in whom she, gifted with insight, recognized the Lord. It matured with the heart of the girl in love, the bride, the young wife—all without conscious thought, the way her love grew—blossoming into awareness in her encounter with the Franciscans: "This is what I always meant."

*

TALKING to G.S. As an authority on St Thomas and a passionate philosopher and thinker (by no means always the same thing!), he ought to know when he says: Thomas, too, held "Being" as "emanated" from God—and "Creation" means "only" that essence was "draped" round this "*esse*", something other than itself, so that it could be made manifest. Could this also be true of "the spark of the mind"? Was the "soul" "draped" around it in order to exist at all? Is this the point on which Dame Julian of Norwich and, as far as I know, Meister Eckhart were both right?

*

SACRIFICE: what is this really, the A and O of our religious up-bringing? Annihilation or transformation? Annihilation as the way to transformation? Annihilation through transformation? The Ancients certainly didn't hold any theory about annihilation, nor did they want to attain it by sacrifice: this idea must be recent. Fire was surely always the element of transformation, the up-surging flame. . . . But we poor moderns will try to escape the slow fire-death of transformation, to buy ourselves free by a quick jump into nothingness, as we understand it, or by hastily destroying the good things to which we are attached. We thought this sacrifice was "greater". Actually it was cheaper.

*

WEALTH is a virtue which has to be practised, really learnt, if it is to be of any real use to its "owner", turned to good account, giving him confidence, freedom, power and independence—not enervating him, making him dependent, stingy, soft and vain.

And "wholeness", of which health is only the image and likeness—how can this be achieved?

*

COULD it be the special task of the old to bear living witness against the fear of death, whether great or slight? Reconciled to life, reconciled to the earth, they might face, detached and smiling, those still struggling in the upsurge of youth, in the heat and haste of the day—pointing the way to solemn expectation. . . . Old age less as "harvest of life" than as the commission to draw back the curtain, slowly, from the threshold of the new life?

*

THINGS of the world, people of the world are called to work out a clear and clean vocabulary for the heavenly message. For this makes use of picture-words almost throughout: Father, Son, Breath; light, fire, water; birth, wedding, etc. How can anyone read these tidings if the "alphabet" he knows is blurred, smirched, broken and crooked? "On earth as it is in heaven": if this is correct, our earthly script can never be clear and legible enough—otherwise no one will be able to "translate".

*

FEAST of the Transfiguration. "His face shining like the sun and his garments becoming white as snow." Like a winter morning, a snow-clad mountain—these, then, are the images of our Transfigured Lord. In this hour of prayer he must have been sunk in the history of Israel, embracing it with such intensity in his heart that he actually "evoked" Moses and Elias out of Hades—Elias in his body and the soul of Moses? But they talked to him, the "youngest" of their kin, about his end. . . .

*

WHAT does really happen when the factor of "love" withdraws from a human relationship? Is it a loss or a gain? Is the real landscape revealed at last, hitherto "transfigured", but delusive, too, by the driving mist of fantasy? Is it a perverted vision which finds a glowing cloud more beautiful than the solid truth of a plot of earth? And vice versa, what really happens when the radiance, the glamour, begins to take shape, concentrating on a landscape or on a face? It is all concerned with the soul, but what is this soul actually? It is the soul dwelling in the blood. Does one's blood kindle magnetically from that of the other person, and does this set the soul aglow? Or is it the other way round? Probably both ways exist, and both directions. The soul can also begin to glow at a distance, as in pen-friendships—and a meeting can be like an icy shower because the blood recoils. When instead of the other person's thoughts and reflections one is suddenly confronted with his look, smile, smell, his voice and gestures—all external things, yes, but how truly is the inner being expressed by just these, even more reliably than in letters? I've often been disconcerted by people who've turned out to be really repellent—and their letters had been so attractive! Letters, I suppose, often merely reflect the writer's dream-image of himself. But what is the truth, what a person is—or what he wants to be? I cannot answer this question.

*

THAT tragedy with NN. The disappearance of taboos in the erotic and sexual sphere places such an excessive and intolerable burden and strain on the individual that he's bound to come to grief. For it's asking too much of someone who no longer recognizes the traditional barriers, suddenly, of his own initiative, to restore all the safety devices built up by generations over the centuries. Crazy! If only one could make people see that, apart from conformity and rebellion, there's a third attitude: "Earn it if you want to possess it"—Goethe really did put the matter in a nutshell.

*

GOETHE once more. Zelter's diary telling of his meeting with the septuagenarian the winter after the Ulrike episode. "What shall I find? What have I found? A man who looks as though he were love-sick, love-ridden with all the agonies of youth." Goethe grew so ill that his doctors—in November—gave him up for lost. But he got over it and lived another ten years. Fits into my theme: old age. Perhaps only body and mind grow old, not the "soul"? The mind maturing, the body wasting—and the soul remaining unaltered?

*

ELIZABETH: Just like Francis, it's the "descent" which is the point, not the giving of alms: humility even more than charity, even though this was the purpose and lowliness merely the way to it, almost taken for granted. But precisely in this is the descent of the Son of God reflected. Not just a temporary descent, "on a visit", as it were, returning then to the security of one's "proper station", so often the case in charitable and social work; but staying there, for good: like the worker-priests, the Petits Frères et Sœurs de Jésus, like Foucauld, like Danilo Dolci in Sicily: the "modern" charism, i.e. the latest form of holiness.

*

Weg nach Mekka [The Road to Mecca] by Muhammad Asad: An account of his conversion to Islam by a Viennese Jew (Polish), a journalist who must be very much my own age. It is a romance, a falling in love, such as I've encountered in no other conversion story: not Claudel or Chesterton, Péguy or Verkade, Jörgensen, Merton, Edith Stein, Karl Stern. Is this merely the incomparable background, desert, Orient?—or really the flame bursting from this book?

Strange how much Old Testament there is in Islam: tradition holds that Mecca is the place where Agar with Ismael found the well: and the black stone of the Caaba is said to be the last relic of Abraham's sanctuary. What a lovely custom, the wearing of the *ihram*, the white pilgrim's robe which anticipates the shroud, worn by every pilgrim alike and making them all equal. How hideous, in comparison, those tasteless showy churches "we" have built all over the Holy Land. . . .

Why, oh WHY can't *our* faith grip us like this, setting its stamp upon us, as Islam really does seem to grip its faithful?? And when it does—utterly, exclusively, as intransigent as Islam —what's the result? The ghastly phenomenon of the Catholic ghetto, the special brand of Catholicism in the raw. Alas, it was this which finally decided Muhammad Asad—before he took this name—in his brief hesitation between Christianity and Islam: the "type" of the faithful, i.e. Viennese Catholicism—oh, Lord!

But probably it's wrong to take it so to heart, to get so vexed about it. Islam corresponds so exactly to the whole Arab way of life, which in turn is stamped like wax with its seal. It remains to be seen how it will work out once civilization breaks through. What's so disturbing with us here is the false proportion between exaggerating and blurring things.

And another thing: Islam seems to offer the fascinating elements of both Testaments without their burdens: the Old without the Law, and some features of the New: without hierarchy or dogma.

*

I'm reading Günther Anders' *Die Antiquiertheit des Menschen* [The Antiquity of Man]. He's extraordinarily clever, shrewd, has an enviable way of putting things, but is curiously flat and one-sided in his interpretation. That bit about "Promethean shame" impressed me, not so much what he says about this specifically as the more general observations about "the shame of being oneself", the reluctance at stepping out of line, of being "forward", of being looked at. This is entirely true to life. I well remember as far back as my sixth birthday the panic which seized me at being looked at. Yet it's just as natural to man to want to be seen (first step to "recognition"), to want to be outstanding, to be regarded, as to want to hide—and both these instincts—for that's what they are—clash, often with equal force, and you get those strangely paradoxical conflicts, paralysing situations, etc. How clearly I see the Little Flower in this light: from earliest days the focal point for her whole family, yet on the other hand sincerely desiring to be hidden, "taking the veil"— and so wonderfully unveiled to posterity, revealed to the world, set up as an image, i.e. to be looked at!

All this ties up with a further sensitive point: fear of responsibility. A responsible man is naturally "visible", in the forefront, it's part of his job to be "on view". Even in the smallest circle he's a "public" figure and is sized up, weighed and judged accordingly. Woe betide him if he's unable to meet the scrutiny of those he's "responding" to! One must have the courage to make mistakes, to face failure, even to make an ass of oneself— all this belongs to the courage which the venture in itself demands. Which is why the even relatively public character of the marriage ceremony, professions and ordinations is impor- tant—it makes it very difficult to retreat, as very few people dare to challenge public blame.

*

PRESUMABLY this is at least one of the attractions of "spiritual- ism": mental faux pas are not so glaring. Often enough no one notices but yourself. You can get away with this sort of thing far more easily than with burnt stew or broken crockery. The sphere of the body is so very exposed. Which is why people who are afraid of slipping up prefer the domain of the mind for their lapses. We had quite a lot of these types in our Youth Movement. For all our penchant for eccentric clothes, manners, etc., it was fatally easy to make real "test situations" unreal, "escape from self", into the curious anonymity of the typical; socio- logically, of course, this wasn't a jot different from the anonymity of the "society" from which we had fled in such disdain. Yet isn't every kind of conformity really a sort of masquerade, the mask at once conspicuous and disguising?

The great temptation of illness is very similar: it's the perfect alibi for so much—above all for oneself! You can almost always take refuge in the thought: "If I were well . . . then I'd do so and so!" As though in the past you'd been able to do all the wonderful things you would now achieve if . . .—like the social "retro-projections" of so many refugees.

*

A LECTURE for Schramberg on marriage, love, etc. That falling in love which isn't only desire: what really happens here? Per- haps it's a perceiving and touching of the "soul body" which sur- rounds the physical body? You don't notice this at all in most people, or only as a negative aura. In Eros the edge of this cloud begins, as it were, to glow—or the halo shines in one person, kindling the other in response. Sometimes it is sensed and perceived by both, but sometimes only by one, he himself remaining dull and "ordinary" for the other. . . . But when I see another being suddenly "all ringed with light", what is the cause and what is the effect? Must my eyes first be opened so that I really discern the other person?—maybe lots of people "shine", but not every eye is attuned to the spectrum's colour? Or is it a question of the intensity of the ray, its power, the overwhelming fascination which takes even the initially indifferent eye by surprise? Is this the secret behind those fascinating people who simply captivate? Were such vision due to the perception of an actual objective halo, you could neither help nor stop seeing it. Yet experience shows that this aureole, this "magical" radiance, wanders from head to head, descending like Bergengruen's blue flame, now here, now there, and no one knows for how long.

Of course this can simply be called projection and transmission. But there is a third way of describing it: what A.R. calls "clothing with the angel"; maybe this is what the Cabbalists meant when they talked about a partial transmigration of souls, i.e. that a human being can really be "clothed with radiance", just for a time, that a power then rests upon him which is not his being, that as long as this mysterious state lasts he no longer appears to us as himself—but as though he were buried like a fence under a blossoming hawthorn bush, a window-pane covered with frost-flowers. As long as this lasts he is just a mirror, and in him we see something other than himself—a spark of God's glory. But this radiance really does wander at will—no, as He wills.

All the same, some disposition, a readiness, must exist in the lover too. Sometimes it's simply that a certain erotic void, an insatiable craving, induces this "mescalin perception"—as though the customary veil were drawn away from a person's face, sucked away, exposing the hidden radiance beneath. Or is it the starving eye from which the veil is sucked? I've often noticed that the men with the most powerful Don Juan appeal, attracting lots of women, are scarcely ever satisfied themselves—as though there were a magnetic void within them which can never be filled in spite of all the victims engulfed. Contented people rarely emanate this universal appeal.

Whatever way it is, the point does seem to be that this radiance is something taboo: transcendent, not to be touched and certainly not to be enjoyed—just to be revered. With one's hands behind one's back.

Pity you can't say things like this in a lecture.

*

YET again—visible and invisible. The panic of loneliness—not physical, far more moral—arises from the fact that every lonely person is wearing a magic hood,★ against his will: which is tantamount to saying: "If people don't bother about me, it's because nobody is seeing me—seeing *me*. I'm just a piece of furniture in their eyes." If you're well and strong you can don this hood whenever you like and enjoy yourself no end. I remember a rather silly English Utopia novel in which there was one amusing feature: any citizen of this crazy planet had only to mark his forehead with a certain sign and the strictest social convention decreed that he should not be seen—it went so far that people had to stumble over him in the street, out of politeness, to demonstrate his invisibility. A marvellous idea. Enforced, however, such invisibility is rather like civil death, and it's terrible to think how many people must live in this exile—and how often we ourselves impose this feeling of being immured upon others by sheer indifference. Newcomers in a strange world suffer this fate especially, what's more in a doubly unpleasant way: first because no one takes any notice of them since they don't belong, i.e. they're "nobodies", yet at the same time they're conspicuous, in the way, a nuisance, desperately conscious of being just awkward lumps of furniture.

*

WHAT I heard recently about the connection between hypnosis = word = sound confirms the conjecture: that the reputed "supernatural" and mystical *rapport* between ecstatic women and their confessors has, in fact, also a perfectly natural foundation. It is by no means certain, for instance, that it was a special charisma of "hierognosis" that Anne Catherine Emmerich or

★ The *Tarnkappe* of German fairy-tales, a magic cap which makes the wearer invisible.

Therese Neumann even in the deepest sleep or trance, inaccessible to all other sounds, could still hear every command of a priest, and only a priest. One would, of course, want to know whether they reacted in this way to every priest or only to their spiritual director: and then if they could also be reached by thoughts, i.e. where there was no communication by the sound of words.

*

My real problems, the central "existential" issues, are not really on the intellectual plane at all, as people will insist, acquaintances, strangers, even friends. Morality is my vital concern, and has been ever since I can remember—and not theoretically, as a matter of principle, but of *living*. Intellect is just an auxiliary, called in to guide me through the inextricable jungle of life-to-be-lived, and principles serve to hack a path through the undergrowth. The WAY, this is and has always been the essence of my quest.

*

LUTHER said: "God does not uproot evil from man, rather man from evil"? But why "rather"? Surely both operations correspond and the process works both ways?

*

BOOK Providence again with Mircea Eliade's *Images et Symboles*— in the German translation called *Das Heilige und das Profane*.* Very interesting and stimulating, although one never really knows quite how far one can trust these experts in comparative religion. To my mind they are too ready to present as primitive things which still exist today, which will always exist. Similarly, much is treated as religious that is in fact sociological. Take this passage, right at the beginning, part of his thesis on "the sacred area":

"One of the characteristics of traditional societies [what did I tell you, sociological!] is the accepted contrast between the world in which they live and the unknown and indeterminate

* The German translation appears to differ in some respects from the French original and from the English translation *Images and Symbols* by Philip Mairet, but since the author's reflections are based on reading this German version, a translation of this has been used.

region which surrounds them. Their own domain is 'the world', the cosmos; all the rest is no longer the cosmos, but a kind of 'other-world', a strange, chaotic area, abode of ghosts, demons and foreigners—these last placed on the same footing with demons and the souls of the dead."

If that isn't the most apt description of the attitude which we learnt as children and later on at our convent boarding-schools! —learnt, yes, but not through words, simply by osmosis—as the atmosphere we breathed. The "real world", the world which counted, the authentic world to be taken seriously, was only "ours"—everything else wavered between chaos and non-existence. The girls in Pressbaum had a strange kind of geography of their own, a map marked only with country houses and estates, with a sprinkle of small towns in between, which also "belonged", never existing in their own right, merely serving as stop-gaps for providing commodities which could not otherwise be obtained on the estate: needs ranging from the dentist to a passport. The only road system they were aware of was devised for "visiting" purposes. During term the convents were the focal points around which the whole of reality crystallized, and from which it radiated: everything else was The World, in a more or less negative sense, partly as remote as the moon, partly a rather frightening territory through which one would have to hack one's way later on, as though on a bush expedition, constantly beset by perils and ambushes. . . .

And, by and large, doesn't the "good Catholic" look upon the non-Catholic world in exactly the same way, even today? Doesn't he tend to sink all other religions (adage: "Protestants, Jews, pagans!") into the same vague welter of unreality and irrelevance. People regard this as intolerance, spiritual pride, uncharitableness, etc.—actually it's something much more naïve, far more innocent, just this "archaic" area-mindedness, a feeling no one can really help.

"A region as yet unknown, strange, unoccupied [i.e. not yet occupied by us!] still shares something of the liquid, wraithlike state of chaos." Exactly. But that's sociology, not religion.

The chapter on initiation supports the advocates of a somewhat later age for the sacrament of confirmation, and confirms the value of church marriage ceremonies as right and important, a necessity rooted in primitive religion, despite our rationalists and educators who insist on belittling these things as inessential, irrelevant, imported from outside. Truly a lamentable and destructive tendency among us to stamp such things at all costs as "purely Christian", purely "supernatural", detached, i.e. abstracted from every link with primeval man and humanity. As though this would make anything better, "higher", more precious or more credible!

*

AN incredibly stupid letter from a Herr NN. against the Index: interesting merely as evidence of what unadulterated modernist complexes still persist among us (he must be well over eighty); and secondarily of the atmosphere at the turn of the century. In those days it must really still have been considered as 100 per cent heretical to contemplate any change at all, however slight, in any of the existing habits or institutions within the Church. The title "Reform Catholics" had a very unpleasant sound, implying spiritual pride, subversion, self-will—almost treachery.

I remember, incidentally, that even in our novitiate—after the First World War—a saying attributed to St Teresa of Avila was very popular (strikes me today as most certainly spurious!): "She would have joyfully given her life for every paragraph of Canon Law." And this laudable sentiment was to be our model for "Sentire cum Ecclesia". No wonder reaction often turned out so very sour, bitter, corrosive.

*

ON the Lourdes miracles. Nowadays we regard "materialistic" as a term of abuse. Yet actually the "normal" human being, the archaic primeval man, was always very materialistic, though of course not in the earth-bound, wingless manner of latter-day moderns. For him the heavenly world was by no means a separate, invisible domain—"the other-world"—but indissolubly interlocked, interwoven, intertwined with his own earthly world. Indeed he'd have found religion very unconvincing had it been something divorced from the soil of his earth, distilled on a higher plane, occupying only one special sphere. For these unsophisticated medieval Christians signs and wonders were perfectly normal phenomena: speaking crucifixes, bleeding Hosts, weeping images, avenging flashes of lightning, the odour of sanctity and light surrounding the beds of the dying, etc. They would have found it far more scandalous even disquieting had the supernatural *not* been manifesting itself all the time, shining into our world, breaking forth from its depths. Of course it's possible to slip into real and dangerous materialism here, as many pious people in fact do—with their medals and scapulars, setting store by large Hosts, etc. But even the great St Teresa, *the* mystic *par excellence*, felt it an extremely painful and decisive trial, even a *humiliation*, when St John of the Cross offered her a smaller Host than her neighbour at the Communion grille!

It is the "spiritualist" who is really the "non-conformist", the exception: particularly prone to all Gnostic, dualistic, Manichean doctrines, simply because to him matter always seems just a little unreal—nothing but a border, a fringe, a veil hiding something else, full of rents and holes, not strong, solid, certainly not a substance in its own right. Which is why he despises the laws of nature, at least in his heart of hearts, as well as money, technology, finance, economics, society. He, too, hankers after signs and wonders, but his approach is exactly the opposite of our "devout materialists": for he refuses to take the autonomy of matter and its power of resistance seriously, because to him it seems quite natural that it should be swayed, penetrated, controlled by mental power; his "sense of the limits of probability being very undeveloped" (as dear Mother Mossler, bless her, once said resignedly about me!!). Of the "wingless" kind, he will turn into an ideologist, using and exploiting matter, institutions, above all people, recklessly and ruthlessly, violating everything to serve his dreams and ends; and not even from sheer wickedness, simply because they aren't half as real to him as his theories and principles. At best he retires into an ivory tower or devotes himself to spiritual "healing", in its diverse forms.

But between the two, over and beyond them both, often strangely intersecting, runs the "genuine" mystical urge (at least the medieval one) towards "pure", i.e. unhampered encounter with God. There's a great deal to be said about this, of course. For instance:

Even apart from Gnosis or the supposition of an independent evil Nature, Nature—"not divine"—is insufficient in itself for the mystic: the here and now, limited by time and space, the "expanded body" of man, fallen alike with him, maimed, finite, and existing only "on the fringe of God". Which is why the soul, the mind—created, too, yet akin to him in another, immediate way—revolts in the holy urge to break through everything, away from *everything* transitory, relative, "not yet", to spring beyond, to soar above all these things—to touch the Absolute. To such a temper the mirror is not enough either, nor the transparency, the signs and imagery found in created things. Here is the burning desire to penetrate beyond mirrors and fragments, the insatiable hunger for eternal reality. This revolt is far more than "titanic", it is the greatest drama of humanity: the rapturous leap out of Creation into the abyss of God.

For such a man a "miracle" is something else again: the rent in the curtain, the hand reaching from the other side, the moment beyond time.

Yet, for common experience, the craving for miracles is something completely different again—at any rate in these days I should say. It is one thing to believe, generally speaking, that God's omnipotence can supersede his own ordained system of Nature whenever he chooses, measured by our standards!— another question whether, in fact, he must do this in order to produce certain manifestations we cannot understand. But it's quite another thing to regard *my* personal wishes, my private needs as a legitimate occasion for something so momentous. It's this attitude about which I'm so sceptical. How can one think oneself so important?

*

A MOST disturbing book: *Out of the Night* by Jan Valtin (pseudonym for Ludwig Krebs?), U.S.A., 1941. Memoirs of an ex-Communist, and intensely depressing. I never realized so starkly before how powerful it is—this vast, intricate network of thousands of men and women, highly organized, constantly "in action", dynamic, working "in the field" with a heroism, daring, cunning and energy unparalleled. Compared with it, our "Youth Movement" of those days seems wretchedly slack, silly, puerile—ludicrous! Question: What is it that really inspires these people with this sense of mission? What drives them to such extreme and—surely the word is apt here, if ever it is—*religious* dedication? What is it that carries them through danger, through torments, through disillusionment, defeat and privations, through never-ending martyrdom? *What* is it? Love of humanity? Brotherhood? Faith in a better future for all? Hatred alone could never be so powerful a motive force, for all the author's explicit glorification of the power of hate. For what is hated here is, in fact, only the obstacles in the way to the goal so fanatically loved, i.e. what hinders and interferes. Love first and foremost, then, with hate merely as a by-product? Is this "hunger and thirst after righteousness"? In any case it's something *we* haven't got, we Christians, we believers: some priests, some religious, some lay-people, certainly. But no one could say it was usual, the average, normal standard, taken for granted: that people could recognize us by this mark. The Nazis had it. The Communists have it. No wonder some of the worker-priests lost their heads and were carried away when they had been drawn into this whirlpool.

*

BODY and soul. In her long account of Theresienstadt and Auschwitz, Grete Salus comments on the well-known fact that prisoners in these camps did not fall ill, even in the most execrable conditions in which "normal" beings would have succumbed at once: "The body became independent . . . began the struggle for its survival without asking our permission." But is this strictly true? Isn't it, in fact, precisely the other way round, i.e. that self-preservation is an instinct of the soul? Life fights for survival, and in human beings (and animals?) isn't "life" the same thing as "soul"? The "body soul", I'd say, not the *mind*, but you can't tear them apart—it is the soul. Even if the body is its key-board and the soul therefore dependent upon its instrument. If you consider certain well-known mental "menstrual symptoms", ranging from kleptomania and melancholia to religious doubts and emotional crises: it is indeed the body which is at work here, but the soul is "driven" by its power. Surely in the case of starvation it's the soul which fights, ruthlessly, unscrupulously, for its bearer, the body? And is the same thing not true of sex? What is it then, the "bodily" urge? Isn't its independence always just a semblance, already secondary?

*

THE "born" spiritualists and materialists would seem to divide as well among nations as among individuals. I'd rate the Greeks, the Germans, the Slavs and the Indians among the former, and the Mediterranean peoples to the second group, perhaps the Chinese (the Egyptians?)—certainly the Jews.

*

MAN being at once animal and angel, it stands to reason really that types must differ according to which component predominates, just as some children take after their father, others after their mother.

Of late our kinship to the animals is being forced upon my notice from several angles. Primitive man must have felt this so strongly, so naturally, that to him beasts seemed more like "other people" than another species. The bear people, the antelope people of the North American Indians! And the most ancient tales in the *Mabinogion*, that marvellous quaint collection of Celtic legends, tell of downright *wars*, not just fighting against wild animals, individuals bearing names like any other warrior chieftain: Boar Silver Hair, Stag XX—just as against other hostile tribes and their heroes. And then, on the other hand, those fictitious totem animal ancestors, animal names for clans and individuals—incredible really that people still name their children Wolf and Leo. I feel sure that once upon a time we must have had different and much more direct means of communicating and "conversing" with animals. Later on, in the Christian era, man withdrew in an entirely new fashion, passionately, intensely aware now of his own intellectual soul. The gulf widened to the notoriously inhuman treatment of animals in Latin countries. I remember E. telling me about simple Italians who merely shrugged at her protest: "A donkey is not a

Christian!"—in other words: "He doesn't feel it!"—as a popular interpretation of: "Animals have no souls."

*

I KEEP wondering whether that baffling reference to the "garments of skins" in the Genesis account of the banishment from Paradise can, in fact, mean anything else but the descent of man to that proximity to an animal existence which we know was the condition of primitive man.

And what about those rays which Anne Catherine Emmerich saw around the head, mouth and genitals of man in Paradise (the male!) and which "died", turning to hair, after the Fall? Was man in Paradise more or less animal than today? The fact that Adam could in fact seek a mate amongst the animals—both *could* and did *seek!*—points to the former; but that was "in the earlier aeon", i.e. before the garments of skins?

But Christian man is Icarus for all that, even if he has so dashed his wings that today he must creep about in the dirt, maimed and crippled. And mysticism—and even its off-shoot, simple idealism—has surely been his angel's flight, tried out in advance, as it were.

*

A WONDERFUL, terrific book! the life of Brother Albert (Adam Chmielowski), the Polish Foucauld—1845–1916!—in the night shelters for the poor in Cracow, Warsaw and Lvov: "We must be good like bread. Our Lord became bread, we too must become bread for the others." Our neighbours as "sacrament". To be bread, to allow ourselves to be eaten by others, devoured, to be wholesome, nourishing, strength-giving, satisfying, furthering growth.

*

IT's another idea of X's that the soul can be "opened" by certain bodily techniques: fasting = weakening, vigils = deprivation of sleep, scourging = loss of blood—all these reduce the brain's capacity: then, through this ebb, in between these cracks a stream of images can find its way into the body-soul which is linked with the universe. Compare Huxley's mescalin book.* It

---

* Aldous Huxley, *The Doors of Perception*, London and New York, 1954.

would, therefore, seem that bodily castigation would in effect create an artificial state of "malady"—while "we" are still trying to uphold the equation *corpus sanum = mens sana*, especially for ascetics and mystics? Something within me baulks at all this. For wouldn't it mean that the "normal", healthy, sound human being is after all really the "limited", hide-bound man?—and the wounded, the chastised the superior, higher being? And can anyone venture on such excursions "across the border" at all, by means of drugs or through such drastic cures, without paying the penalty, that is, by seriously damaging himself? If this were so, then they'd really be right—the people who exhort us to despise, scorn and reject normal Nature, i.e. this world as it has been given to us. In that case the Platonist would be right, and it would in fact be no more than a frontier, a wall, a dungeon to be burst open, to be overcome—by force, if necessary—to reach freedom outside, to attain the heights and the depths.

Inveterate old spiritualist that I am, of course my heart thrills to the flash of such questions. And then I still turn back to the world—trying to excuse it, to stand up for it—our poor narrow earth, God's beloved world!—and I find them so ungrateful, these people who want to treat it merely as a spring-board to be kicked away, as they soar out far above it.

*

WERFEL's Jeremias novel [Hearken unto the Voice] strikes to the marrow: Jesus is mirrored here, unmistakably, with a frightening intensity. Yet again I realize that only in the Jewish mirror can I recognize our Lord as Man at all—Sholem Asch, the Hasidim—every "white" depiction seems so cheap, the real image painted over, disguised almost beyond recognition. Jeremias is the Word of God, breaking forth, spurned, hounded to earth, to death. Werfel must have known and meant this. In that scene where the prophet is standing in the mire of the cistern, the Word sent from heaven, descended into hell, abased in the dirty abject figure of the punished slave—here the transparency is breath-taking, and you know: that's how it really was.

*

THE conflict in which particularly "conscious", i.e. aware people, often find themselves with "unconscious" has the same ruthless, helpless character as that between adults and children—seen from the child's angle. But in this case it's actually the "grown-up" who is helpless, for it is not only most cruel but also very unfair to go raging at these unaware people, scolding and reproaching them for things they cannot possibly understand, impervious in the innocence of their incredible unwitting "otherness". But can they really be allowed to do just what they like, simply because they're blind and ignorant? When they're playing with fire and uncorking bottles of poison—for themselves and other people?—dropping precious things on the floor without noticing? Must I really stand by and watch idly while a blind man goes stumbling over my loveliest flower-bed, or let an unsuspecting child tear up my manuscripts to make paper boats? No. But I mustn't shout at him either, or box his ears, or offend his dignity. I must take the blind man gently by the arm and lead him out again, courteously, without making a scene.

How right Dominikus Ringseis was: Looking after sick people is so good for us because we *must* always treat them the way we *ought* to behave towards everyone. But instead one is apt to get into a panic, genuine panic, terrified of the dumb, sucking force, the pull of precisely these unconscious trends, blind, inexorable—ready and able to turn the human being who unwittingly succumbs to them into a puppet against his will.

*

BERGENGRUEN's sparkling little book about the poet's privileges is most illuminating—slightly distressing, too, but a reliable guide for the mere "writer". Writer and poet are related, I believe, rather like priest and prophet (and at times I feel like a busy little cleric who suddenly feels the prophet rumbling in his inside like the colic).

*

THERE's an uncommonly violent storm raging outside, whistling, howling, rolling like an organ—snow, gossamer-soft at first, now a wild blizzard. We've grown so unused to this sort of

thing these days that it strikes one as positively "unnatural"—
rather like a stage storm.

*

THE "psyche" is surely just as much a natural structure as the
body, determinate, subject to strict laws—something rather
than somebody. Only in union with the mind does it become
something different.

*

IN the "nether world" the mother is the link between the father
and the son—the Church. And Mary? Only "in God" is no
mother needed. Which is why the Christian needs the Church if
he is to be a son of his Father—as St Augustine, I think, first
put it. But precisely on this point the "masculine protest" is
roused in so many—they would like to be immediately connected with God. The mother's task is essentially to bear witness
to the father, to talk of the father, to lead her children to their
father. After all, she herself is only a mother because there is a
father. The combination mother and child alone doesn't really
exist, it's just make-believe.

*

MY lecture on marriage again: Man must be changed, transformed, and the most potent means and instrument is love—or
solitude: the one positive, the other negative. Each of these
states challenges the best in us—or the worst. Each asks too
much of us, thereby teaching us to recognize our limits, each can
only be endured, can only itself endure by grace—by which we
can step beyond our limitations.

*

BACK to my "mescalin" ponderings. I'm inclined to think that
we're less receptive to finer, more subtle impressions nowadays
not so much because we're insensitive, i.e. thick-skinned, but
rather because our consciousness is cluttered, as so often in
prayer, with inessentials—"jammed" with other things. You
just can't cram anything more into a lumber room which is full,
or at any rate not as much as into an empty one. Probably our
"capacity" for natural and supernatural things isn't really so very
limited, it's just blocked.

I know quite well myself, for instance, that my personal awareness and perception of "Nature" has diminished and been obscured since my marriage. For the simple reason that one's consciousness is never really quite empty any more, never again quite free to take things in with the clear and naked eye, with undivided concentration: one is constantly aware of the other person, or at least half-aware, in a diffuse sort of way. One is, as it were, perpetually inside his sphere of existence, as though within a hollow ball which seems to blur everything else to a strange haziness. It just isn't possible any longer to see and experience things as a mere lone individual—and this already weakens and dissipates one's surrender to the object. Even if you "can't help it", you can't quite escape that sadness, verging on a sense of guilt, at having something for yourself alone, not sharing it, not enjoying it together, and this bitterness is enough to make the object lose something of its special savour, i.e. it can no longer be fully discerned. Maybe this is somehow connected with that insatiable feminine urge to *share* everything, which a man probably doesn't know. Or the care, the anxiety always vaguely felt for the other person casts a veil across the inner mirror.

Looked at this way, it would seem that the demand for *apatheia* is the one sensible prayer for those desiring awareness of God: to clear one's consciousness of *everything* except the "one thing needful".

But here the snake already bites its own tail: Is this really permissible? The ivory tower on the highest level? May one isolate oneself like this, simply withdrawing oneself from everybody else—so as to experience God more intensely, i.e. to *enjoy* him more? Is this really honouring him? Is this what I'm here for, in this world? Surely it would be more obedient simply to submit in all humility to being "blocked"—by all human wretchedness?

For it isn't really true that one *loves* God more if one is more "aware" of him, rather one is more aware *that* one loves him and in what way. Just as you show more affection to someone you love when you're relaxed and at peace than when you're rushed and worn out. God isn't like a woman who needs to be told all the time that she's loved: we don't have to keep on saying it, showing it, assuring him—as though he didn't see all the mute, reticent, unobtrusive love of service and self-denial and having no time, and appreciate this just as much!

Aren't lots of our very twisted ideas about spiritual life rooted in just as distorted "ideals" for our human relations?— that notion of the Little Flower's, for instance, that "earthly fiancées" were always expecting gifts from their betrothed, etc.? All part of the same attitude: that we must be for ever "courting" God, that he wants us to spend all our time solely preoccupied with him. Surely typically feminine notions!

*

I've just finished a long essay about the activities of Protestant enthusiasts in the families and at the courts of minor German princes during the Baroque period (by F. Barthold, published in the *Historische Taschenbücher* 1852/53). Apart from anything else it is a grimly amusing comment and supplement to that book by Benz.* Very interesting, for instance, that the Awakened —including even some who could be called charismatics—far from being only "mystics" were often enough just as convinced— and crude—rationalists and apostles of the Enlightenment, even to the verge of atheism. Indeed their very enthusiasm seems in many cases to have been anything but religious—often downright pathological.

Seen thus, the role of the Enlightenment and the rationalism which flourished afterwards in both denominations takes on a new and surprising significance as a "necessity", even a providential remedy. What other course was left open to people who did not choose to sink and be swamped in such mental and emotional sloughs? That curious autobiography of Johann Christian Edelmann (1698–1767) illustrates the situation very clearly: it is as depressing as it's interesting. It is easy to see how even the ill-famed rationalism at its worst was sheer self-defence for such a man, the only way out of that revolting jungle of nauseating stupid superstition cloaked with "spiritual fervour", the only way any sane person could save himself from this flood of "religious" lunatics. Of course what emerged in the long run

* *Adam, der Mythos vom Urmenschen.* See above, p. 177.

was just as bad in another way—the Devil of Enthusiasm cast out by the Beelzebub of Reason and its idolatry. But what else could they do in the circumstances, hard pressed as they were?

*

I'VE been reading Fenimore Cooper again. Deeply troubled about the tragic "collective guilt" of the white race—not less, even greater than our German "collective sin" against the Jews and the East European people. It's the element of abuse— of waste—that is the real horror of it—for in all such super- crimes an incredible outlay in precious qualities and powers is invested: outstanding gifts, intelligence, energy, daring, organ- izing ability and drive, industry, efficiency, patience, generosity —gifts which, had they been put to proper use, could have been the source of incalculable blessings—gifts destined for some- thing great, entrusted with things which can never again be re- stored—gifts wasted, betrayed, ruined.

*

WE went to the cinema this afternoon: *Doctor in Stalingrad*. I thought the film had been made from Hans Dibold's book, but it turned out to be the most ghastly piece of *Kitsch*, probably adapted from some magazine serial. All the same one thing did shine out like a beacon: the doctor's special ethos. In this a doctor is a singularly pure image of God: he must offer the "salvation" of the body which is entrusted to him to every man alike, indiscriminately, to friend and foe: in this he must be "healer"—*Heiland*, like the Saviour, who was a physician, too, of a kind. So he must represent the Father, who sends sunshine and rain upon just and unjust alike, and the Holy Ghost, too, healing and restoring all things.

*

READING Karl Rahner's book *On the Theology of Death*,* it struck me that what he describes as the characteristics of this mystery are equally applicable to sex: the "veiledness", the openness, the ambiguity—consequence of sin—the humiliation,

* London and New York, 1961.

the mystery. I can't help it, there *must* be some profound correspondence between these two domains.

*

FOR most (white) people nowadays animals merely exist to furnish indispensable raw materials. I wonder whether that peculiar well-known taboo-attitude one finds among a certain type of Christian isn't really an outcome of fear—a barrier raised against all too intense "fraternizing" with animals, against a mental obliteration of their disparity and apartness from mankind? But I remember a quotation attributed to St Hildegard: *one* of the causes of the Flood was inordinate familiarity and equality with the beasts. Nowadays the only possibility of this kind would be intellectual—the kind of love for animals which is just transferred hatred of humans.

Yet what is really implied by all our teddies, Bambis, etc., perfectly harmless, yet significant? Wish-dreams for animal companions? Substitutes? And those animal pet-names in our love-language?

*

24 JUNE. In today's Office it suddenly struck me that John the Baptist is one of the greatest and most beautiful symbols of the Church—the prophetic Church, militant, preaching, proclaiming. Precursor of the Lord to come, preparing the way for his Second Coming—both mean the Church with her face turned to "publicity", to history, to politics: rebuking kings, teaching nations, directing all men towards the "One standing in the midst", unrecognized. John is the greatest of those born of woman: the Church the greatest of all the "religions" which, too, are all of them born *also* of natural parentage, *ex mulieribus natae*, growths of the soil and human institutions, and *as such* must take their place behind the lowest of those born of the Spirit. And the Church, too, is not the Lord, but just the Bridegroom's friend. She, too, must decrease that he may increase.

The iconographical attributes are curiously significant too: the lamb, the staff with the cross—with and without inscription— the camel hide, the beast's head sometimes beneath his feet, and in the icons the wings of the "Great Messenger". This is *man*, human being: beast-hide *and* angel!

*

THE pastoral on mixed marriage has caused quite a stir. Lots of people are exasperated. Yet I don't believe their annoyance is a refusal to accept the Church's principle in this issue, or a sneaking "apologetic" tendency in favour of mixed marriage— rather the feeling: there is something false in this too generalized assumption that "judgment is confused by passion" in such cases. I see it this way: The choice of a partner for life *is* an affair of primary and central importance; for most of our con- temporaries religion, let alone membership of the Church, is *not*: it's just a secondary matter, unimportant. In principle, however, it is right that people should sacrifice the peripheral for the central—the opposite would not only be madness, but morally irresponsible as well. "We needs must love the highest when we see it. . . . " The Bible tells us that "a man shall leave father and mother and cleave to his wife", i.e. to his new life, his future. If his Church means for him *only* childhood, origin, etc., then he's right to give it up. The solution is not, as the pastoral suggests in strengthening childhood ties, family feelings, clan- nishness, etc., "ghetto"—but rather in making the Church and membership of the Church a real and central experience, claim- ing and maintaining primacy among other conflicting claims and values—in its own right, not just through exterior defence measures. But how?

*

READING at random during this spa visit—the sort of books which one comes across here: novels, odd biographies, books on medicine, thrillers—but my Book Providence is working away as reliably as ever, patient, precise; like Hansel and Gretel in the wood, crumbs and pebbles are strewn before me, marking out the path through moonlight and shadows.

For example: Victor Heiser, *An American Doctor's Odyssey* = the world-wide campaign of the Rockefeller Institute of Hygiene against hook-worm, malaria, beriberi, etc. Most extraordinary how nowadays the craze for health can authorize super-demo- cratic—professionally democratic—people to resort to the kind of cold-blooded sanitary terror enforced in the Philippines, for instance, and other areas stricken by epidemics and pestilence. These shock-troops coolly did things which, done in a political cause, would be branded as the most flagrant infringement of human rights of every kind. Here they are apparently taken for granted, indeed even regarded as humane and commendable: houses broken into by force, families torn apart, removal of the sick, destruction of property, houses, furniture, etc. "The state of popular apprehension amounted to hysteria. Whenever possible, the sick were concealed by their families and the dead thrown into the sea or into the canals." "We could not avoid infringing the rights of domesticity, social intercourse and parliament." Indeed.

Rather distressing reports of how it was almost impossible to find nurses, since the Filipinas of the upper classes think every form of domestic work beneath their dignity—and they're strict Catholics! A schism occurred there thirty years ago—the Aglipayans—because no natives were admitted to ordination or the religious orders. I wonder if that's true? These things are the "barometer" for the change in the state of the missions.

The author's casual comment: "Our educational campaign against these deep-seated prejudices was like a conversion to a new religion" is much more telling than he knew: a new cult and a new scale of values was indeed introduced here.

*

Our Lady's called a throne, God's tent and canopy,
The sea, a star, the moon, an ark, house, keep, and tower.
A tree, a mirror, dawn, a hill, fount, garden, bower.
How can she all things be? Another world is she.
        Angelus Silesius* in *Der Cherubinische Wandersmann*

*

For the first time I've really read Arthur Schnitzler at length, the world in which my brothers grew up. The depths of Viennese rottenness and decay—*the* hot-bed of Freud's theories. But for me it was first and foremost a denunciation of its

---

* Pseudonym of Johannes Scheffler, Silesian doctor, convert and mystic poet (1624–77).

apparent contrast: our religious upbringing, which created an artificial hollow sphere, the most confined, smoothest, most impenetrable—open to God, yes, but hermetically sealed to our neighbour and his real and most burning needs. For whoever did not belong to the Inner Ring, whoever did not speak and understand our funny secret jargon—my own brothers, for instance—simply lived, for us, on another planet, as in Swedenborg's Other World. We had meals together at the same table and there was less communication than with the dead. The "world" was utterly unreal, the shadow of a shadow, nothing but a fantastic myth—and its inhabitants, for us, not "neighbours", but the remotest of beings, invisible, veiled from us by our own phantasmagoria, merely objects of our apostleship, lacking every right, any substance as individuals, nothing but material to be manipulated by prayer and a planned religious campaign.

And yet—how innocent we were, how well-meaning! How utterly unsuspecting! Was it really only irresolvable human limitation, narrowness increased by our "enclosed world" and faulty direction, or did it indicate the passing of a whole epoch, that "mystical" epoch in which devotion automatically implied turning from the world towards God, a turning to God only conceivable, only to be accomplished at all by turning away from the world and all its constituents, above all from worldly people? Deaf-dumb-blindness to all "worldliness"?

And on the other hand: if I think of some of these "worldlings" onc encountered in those days, or whose paths crossed our own—we were planets apart, not the remotest understanding between us, living cheek by jowl as we were: yet, theoretically speaking, each one of these people *could* have met a Christian, a truly convincing Christian, every day, just as others did, those notorious conversions we exulted in? Couldn't a sensible upbringing, providential books have done as much for A. and B.?

But: did God simply "permit" all this? Had he not fitted and joined and dovetailed everything into their lives, "arranging" it on purpose, just as in our own? It seems definitely *not* to be his will that things should happen as we imagine—"ideal" human developments—the way we would have arranged it. God loves roundabout ways—it's time we got used to this.

*

OH, and yet it *is* hard to have to live on reading—no longer to be able to take in "the world" either through nature or through people, but only through the thin drinking straw of books—the world, filtered through paper and printer's ink. No, this is quite different from the Brontës, with whom someone wanted to console me the other day. They still had incomparably more "world", for they lived in the heart of real, wild, elemental country, living really "in its heart".

*

CURIOUS how that talk on convents the other day increased my awareness how very much things are moving, changing, within the Church! How the mainland of a whole millennium is receding behind the departing ship—yet without changing in itself. That's the thing: it doesn't change. It simply remains behind: *en bloc*. Everything becomes much more difficult because this recession is an exclusively *mental* process—outwardly things are still there, unchanged—and we along with them. Only genuine contemporaries notice that in fact they are diminishing all the time, growing fainter, like a backcloth, two-dimensional— only those caught up in this current themselves. Other people, understandably, think them just obstinate and mulish, at best short- or dim-sighted, and offer their own spectacles. For, in their eyes, the settled world around them is, as ever, the only existing, complete, rich and tangible reality—a world not to be shaken.

*

OLD people ought to understand that children of emigrants and refugees are rarely acutely homesick for the "land of their fathers"—and even if they were, this would be rather by suggestion and sympathy. The same thing is happening everywhere, in space, in time.

*

THIS morning on waking, just on the threshold of a dream, I saw it quite clearly, standing before me, tangible, indisputable: the insight that freedom and necessity must be two aspects of the same thing and why. What a pity one can never "unfold" such things later on, it was so beautifully clear, crystallized on the point of a needle.

*

REVIEWING that big book on Spanish mysticism which is vexing me so, rather a good Trinitarian scheme occurred to me today: Mystics up to now sought either to experience the Father—the acosmic Abyss, the Inconceivable, beyond all worlds—or else the Son, in the historic figure on the Cross, in the Crib, in the Sacred Heart. The mysticism growing up today seeks and finds the Holy Ghost, experienced as love in Creation. But of course the great mystics always found the Trinity.

*

RADIO script *The Church in Transition*. Despite all the unsuccessful, abortive starts I've made, the theme is leading me on to ever deeper insights. As though—surrealistically—a corkscrew were turning into a winding staircase to climb into the heart of things. For instance, something vaguely sensed before and noted down already, I think: that the great historic impulse driving the Church forwards faded out, giving way to restrospective conservatism *ever since* her sense of eschatological expectancy ceased to be a living reality and was replaced by abstract doctrine. For in the Middle Ages the end of the world could have dawned with every new ruler, religious order, preacher: every new Emperor could have turned out to be the Prince of Peace, the Pope the Pastor Angelicus, the saint the last herald—or all of them Antichrist figures. All the time you were standing on the threshold, at least potentially, with the Kingdom of Heaven blazing through all the rifts and cracks into the old world. Every reign could have been the last but one. . . . Only when this living sense of expectancy ceased to exist did "progress" occupy the empty place.

*

IN the Napoleonic Museum in Arenenberg I was rather impressed just how richly clad in the costume of Antiquity the First Empire in fact was—dressed up even comically with its laurels and eagles and togas. Return to Rome wherever you look, though of course not to the *Holy* Roman Empire—to Caesar's Rome.

But the French Revolution itself had fallen back on more or less genuine or imaginary classical models: Brutus and the

Gracchi, consuls and Roman virtues—even these revolutionaries couldn't resolve to start from scratch with something really new. These dreams are outdreamed but not yet replaced.

*

THERE are "races in time", as well as in space; each of us localized also in his own particular time-area = era. Inhabitants of each different era speak a different language, and recognize each other this way.

*

READING Reinhold Schneider's *Winter in Vienna* I realize with a pang that I had no experience whatever of the real Vienna during those years I spent there. There, too, I was simply living within a hollow sphere—for though our Youth Movement was a native growth in those days, it was still claustral—Crusoe's desert island. With the difference that the others, my comrades, belonged willy-nilly, at least in their homes, to the real world; but I was a solitary "orphan", an "outlaw". Yet you must belong somewhere if you are to have any genuine experience of such an essentially sociable city: belong to Society, to the theatre, to the literary set, at least to the Bohemians, to some café or other. You must be asked to people's houses. Reinhold Schneider belonged to none of these circles, yet was a guest in many—also a genuine qualification, an entrée. For me in those days the Opera just didn't exist—or any other music either. Neither the (real) university, nor Art. I frequented neither drawing rooms nor coffee-houses, nor the typical Viennese chop-houses, nor the *Heuriger**—not one of the forms expressing the true essence of Vienna. The way I lived in Vienna I might just as well have been living in Berlin, and did indeed live later on in Dresden—in an unsubstantial, wraith-like world, without roots, in a no-man's land where others only penetrated as visitors or explorers to gratify an itch of curiosity. Institutions! Gehlen is perfectly right: "What is purely interior, subjective, scarcely exists: without a 'hold' in the outside world you cannot hold any content, it simply evaporates."

*

* Wine-drinking evenings in the vineyards on the outskirts of Vienna.

ONCE again: mysticism and mescalin—these words used as shorthand ciphers for all ecstatic states induced by natural means. Religious ascesis and such techniques as these can both serve as methods of enlarging our all too limited consciousness— "mysticism" towards God, "mescalin" towards the universe; even the mere process of "opening" could perhaps serve the same purpose, for a stretch at least—with man the subject. But the "object" revealed to faculties of perception thus intensified differs fundamentally—only the universe being an "object", God, on the other hand, always remaining a free "subject", disclosing or veiling himself of his own will. Perhaps the "nether heavens" are still natural objects which can be focused if the instruments of perception are rightly handled—but God is "discernible" only as far as he chooses to manifest himself within Creation—as far as he "borders" on us, so to speak. Anything beyond this is pure grace, not achievement.

*

PREPARING that lecture on marriage, etc. it strikes me how extremely difficult it is, for us, to think about this subject fairly and squarely, in plain sober recognition of the phenomenon. We're so prone to override our own very innermost insights— cancelling them out on the sly, deliberately—or at least hushing things up, scared by their possible consequences. We've been so conditioned to follow a particular line of conduct in this sphere —never to speak or to think about this subject except "to make a point", with a purpose, to warn, persuade, deter or encourage. And even those who fancy themselves as fearless critics and genuine rebels against conventions are actually more trammelled and lop-sided—driven by secret grievances and suppressed wishes—even their "theological" opinions are emotional.

*

HUGH WALPOLE's wonderful childhood story, _Jeremy_, again after many years. He has an amazing gift of conveying "the scent of things", that something which only our German word _Stimmung_ really expresses—cheap and rather sloppy though it is deemed today: the "mood of nature", as C. S. Lewis calls it, blended with the mood of the subject experiencing it—"atmosphere", but both ways, and here I'm stressing the *objective* quality emanating from external reality. Strange really how very few writers have the gift of creating this kind of atmosphere: you could count them on your fingers. Even in the greatest it is very often lacking. Adalbert Stifter, for instance, didn't have it, nor Thomas Mann; Bergengruen, yes, but just now and then, and Sigrid Undset only in patches. But it's there in much lesser writers, Elizabeth Goudge has it, though only in *Island Magic*—H. F. M. Prescott in *Man on a Donkey*: a clue—it seems to haunt reminiscences of the writer's own childhood and home. It means that the reader absorbs such descriptions neither intellectually nor by imagination, but directly, through his senses.

The scent of things, the goodness of things—for a long time now I've been toying with the notion of displaying this element as the "saving grace" of my childhood, making up, at least in some measure, for the coldness and bleakness of our upbringing, so soulless, so strangely devoid of love, "mind" and grace. "Atmosphere", meaning the very essence, the spirit of the house and its rooms, the woods and the changing seasons, revealing itself, a stream flowing out, strong, mute—touching the soul—the only "numinous" experiences of my childhood, to be replaced later on by far narrower deliberately practised exercises and their effects. Replaced? No, merely relegated to a less important place in my consciousness. But there they lingered for a very long time, an unconscious supplement, perhaps even corrective, to my "will-power religion".

*

LOTS of problems concerning the Spanish mystics. "Woe to the heirs!" said Goethe. I wonder whether the stamp of its period imprinted on classical mysticism may be explained along these lines: In the sixteenth and even the seventeenth century "good works" and devotional practices were of such paramount importance, so overwhelmingly in the foreground that they simply drained all religious energy—exhausting, in the double sense of the word. Religion was completely "externalized". A devout, even saintly demeanour with no "inwardness" behind it had become possible, indeed not only possible—by and large it was probably the only existing form of piety. A purely exterior form, neither reflecting nor expressing an inner state. These days we have a very striking parallel: the development of vast welfare schemes and social activities, devoid of charity. Surely an exact analogy. Which is why, in the past, they had to "invent", discover, explore a new kind of "inwardness"—and that was mysticism. Just as we today are seeking a new kind of charity.

Of course those good works were focused by their original intention on God, but they had grown so self-sufficient that they could be performed "independently", without really bothering about him. The mystics broke through all this, discovering a new approach to God Transcendent, to a certain extent without such works, and even beyond them. In our own day good works are focused on humanity without obliging anyone to bother about the real persons concerned—which is why modern mystics are proclaiming "Man as a Sacrament". Thus mysticism may be the divine, God-sent remedy, the response, the redeeming continuation of good human attempts, of starts made which have somehow got stuck on the way in blind alleys. One more reason, to my mind, why the classical way of mysticism can no longer be accounted the one and only pattern valid for us today.

*

BEING responsible means literally stepping out of the second dimension into the third. No longer hiding among the others, no longer ordered within the line and plane of generality, but standing out in relief, isolated, visible from all sides. Suddenly on a summit, blown by all winds. And what "depends" on my decision really does hang on this tension, a leaden weight, passive, motionless or resisting: woe if it should slacken.

*

JOSEF WITTIG's *Life of Jesus* again. For all its flaws—and these are very superficial—it's still a very remarkable book. He was a religious genius, an original thinker confined within the narrow ecclesiastical and clerical conventions of his day, really as in a prison—the clash was bound to come sooner or later—that

Index affair just happened to be the occasion. For his kind it's easier—I'm not saying better—if they're born outside the Church.

*

NOT even the most brilliant musician could invent every existing instrument by himself, any more than the most gifted painter could invent all the colours and proportions for himself. Yet where morals are concerned people still believe everyone can cheerfully undertake to be his own Robinson Crusoe.

*

WHY, I wonder, did Christianity have such a disastrous effect upon the attitude of the white race in general to the body? For me none of the countless answers provided really resolves this question. The tendency is always to trace it back to oriental, Platonic, neo-Platonic, Manichean influences. Yet none of the races and civilizations which hatched and propagated the quintessence of such anti-somatic, anti-material doctrines, purely dualistic religions and philosophies, have suffered the same consequences—Greeks, Hindus, Chinese (in so far as they were Buddhists), Japanese. They did not stunt the body-life of their adepts, they did not repress or maim their senses. With them thought and life were not set at cross purposes. Yes, and now a further step has been taken: today it's Christian Science—of all things—*the* doctrine most hostile to the body and all matter, far more drastic even than Hinduism: the total, systematic denial of matter and body, contesting their very existence, their reality: precisely this crazy system produces the greatest power of healing—i.e. the most powerful hold of the *soul* upon the body, shaping and saving it! These people really do possess powers which with us are pronounced a priori as miraculous. Can anyone understand such a thing? I can't.

*

I RECENTLY came across a curious collection of quaint Old Chinese texts (Lao-tse or the Tao schools generally): on the earthly immortality attainable by the chosen ones, without a break, "gliding" across. . . . Curious how the idea persists, everywhere, down the ages, from Old China to New America—for Christian Science denies death!—from fairy-tales and myth down to Prentice Mulford's speculations about "the absurdity of dying", in face of the most massive weight of evidence, universal experience, how the belief in the potential vanquishing of death endures: trees, apples, fountains of eternal youth, islands and mountains of immortals, etc.

*

I'M inclined to think that one root of the fascination of "the mystique of suffering" is the peculiar fashion in which it fuses charity, love of one's neighbour, with the desire for power. For the urge of charity, that fervent longing to help, to save, to ease pain, to work in the world—how desperately it suffers from the experience of its own weakness, impotence, helplessness! And then the whisper comes: "Through suffering you will find power, where you fail in practical action—power unlimited. The tiniest pain, the very slightest mortification, if only it is borne in love and integrated into the Passion of Christ, intervenes in an invisible, uncontrollable, yet supremely real way in the machinery of the world: helping, saving, atoning, redeeming." Sharing in Redemption! Surely something to grasp at? All the more so since the contribution demanded of us is at bottom only the very much easier role of passive endurance instead of active "achievement"?

*

PEOPLE who cannot fend for themselves in the house strike one these days as somehow crippled. As indeed they are, inasmuch as they are actually heads without hands or feet. For the great household of the old order was, in fact, a "body", not in the poetical metaphysical sense, but quite literally a body whose distinctive quality was not the equality but rather the inequality of its members. Messengers, for instance, were simply "feet"; other servants "hands", literally hands. All quite natural within an ordered domestic whole in which the father and mother really functioned as head and heart (or, if you like, as solar plexus, the second nerve centre). For probably there are lots of people who only exist "in part", as it were; and as members sharing in a larger body with wider scope, they are far from being maimed or mutilated, violated and humiliated—on the contrary: they are raised above themselves, elevated. This, for them, is the only possible way to achieve completeness.

The lord, the head, chieftain, chef, chief is, so to speak, the "larger man", possessing more eyes, ears, hands and feet than the average—which is why he is "powerful", demonstrating his power quite simply, massively, by the size of his household, the number of his servants and retainers—the very word "staff" expresses nothing else.

An invalid (it was my illness which taught me this) seems to be in a similar position, for he, too, stands in need of a "borrowed enlargement" by other hands and feet: but since these are only lent to him and not his own, this means dependence, i.e. weakness, not power.

Could this be one of the reasons for those ancient offerings for the dead? Man must enter the next world "complete"—so they gave him wife, servants and dogs to take along with him.

*

IT does seem strange that fairy-tales, stemming as they do from the archaic era of the most massive clan domination, should be concerned almost without exception with "love matches", triumphing over every difficulty, every obstacle, in the face of death and the Devil, power and magic spells. What is more, almost always "unsuitable" love matches: prince and Cinderella, king's daughter and charcoal burner, swineherd, etc. What does this mean, I wonder? Archetypes? Precognition? Hope? Or even: a forecast of the Incarnation?

*

MARRIAGE which is childless yet nonetheless valid and indissoluble is the first promise of "absolute" marriage, for it transcends fertility, both as motive and as object, denying neither, but finding fulfilment and completion beyond both.

*

LEVIRATE marriage clearly indicated the impersonal character of marriage within the old order. On the other hand, the fact of

270

adoption has always and everywhere proved (Japan!) that "blood" is more than just sap in the body, and that a sufficiently strong family tradition can completely assimilate and integrate strange, even unknown blood.

*

THE rejection of the visible began by creating a new and tremendous world of imagery in Christendom. For the Light Invisible, glowing ever brighter, was mirrored at first in all things visible —and in Its reflection they shone out as never before; transparencies, signs and symbols, glimpses. Formerly they had revealed the numinous immanent in Creation, now they mirrored the transcendent deity. At the same time the ever stricter demarcation between the sacred and the profane produced a new and separate world of imagery designed to embody the sacred in a wealth of figures distinct and aloof from the profane. But in time—beginning with the mystics—the Light of Lights began to consume his own bearers and mirrors, as the flame consumes the taper.

SELECTIONS FROM LETTERS

※ 1951—1959 ※

SELECTIONS FROM LETTERS

᎒᎒ 1951—1959 ᎒᎒

I GREW up with proud confidence in the "flawless edifice" of theology—not one stone missing in the great pile—in the conviction that for the Christian "there is an answer to every question in the Faith", the conception of that wonderfully perfect "cathedral" of the Fathers and the Summas, every detail finely chiselled, everything contained within it, the whole wisdom of the world, even if I myself were familiar with only the tiniest section of the gigantic structure. It seems to me that this notion fires the imagination of youth, aware for the first time of the boldness, the magnitude, the breadth, depth, clarity and courage of theological thought and scholarship—the intense and passionate struggle to achieve knowledge and truth at the Councils and the medieval universities; the power and volume of the rushing torrent of tradition. An intoxicating spectacle it is—and it is good to have felt it working, deep, strong, within me, to have been filled with awe and pride, feeling the weight of responsibility for this vast heritage. And I believe it does provide a sound foundation for the recognition which should follow: that all this, too, is but mirror and fragment, shadow and imagery. For it prevents what might otherwise be expected: that the shock of breaking through to the next step could produce scepticism and contempt for tradition. Naturally I feel at the same time that a great many of our theologians stop short here, at this rather youthful stage—nor do they really want to move on —perhaps in the lurking fear that by relinquishing this position they might lose their spiritual "fortune", or that this might dwindle instead of growing wider and deeper.

*

YEARS ago, before I came to know Newman better, these words of his took root in my soul: "To believe means to endure tension, questions unsolved."* I wrote these words on the flyleaf of every diary, still not knowing what they really meant, along with Leonardo's words about love being the daughter of knowledge. Then I read somewhere that Thomas called his work "chaff"—empty husks, remains. All of them "ferment words"! Or so many words in the liturgy. . . . And the growing recognition that on so many points theology is simply *silent*. And then in Newman, again and again, urgent, unveiled, the statement that revelation is not a "system", not a flawless whole by any means, and certainly not there for the purpose of "appeasing" our insatiable urge to *know* everything—blended as it is with so much sheer inquisitiveness and curiosity; rather it's "an economy" for our salvation, and so, necessarily, fragmentary. Single cones of light in an immeasurable, dark landscape, lighting only the way and the goal. Somewhere he uses the image (for doctrine as an existing body) of a huge building with a rugged open skyline—but you can gauge and guess many missing details from certain given points, filling the gaps and blanks of the outline almost to completion. This picture made a profound impression upon me and I see it in my mind's eye every time the theme is raised: the mighty broken silhouette of an unfinished tower, dark against the starry infinity of the night sky.

*

ALL the same we shouldn't be so hard on the "systematizers"— judged so harshly in some circles here. For they are important for laying the foundations, for maintaining the underpinning. Indeed we cannot do without them. And precisely their "Prince", Thomas himself, was very well aware of his limits and of the unachievable "background". But those who are not aware of this—since they aren't Thomases but merely systematizers— how can they help it? There is a grade or level beyond which no one can guide himself—he has to be pushed headlong through the vault of his own private world concept. But can anyone get through purely on the strength of his own thick skull? I doubt it. The wall must give way, revealing the new aspect. It feels like a sort of sacrilege at first to "accuse" this wonderful and hallowed

---

* According to a well-known German version. I have been unable to trace the original passage (*Trans.*).

fabric of being fragmentary, full of holes and contradictions. Not from arrogance, narrow-mindedness, pig-headedness—but rather from reverence, gratitude, love—and even a kind of true humility which could be expressed in the words: "Who am I to pass judgment here that the great, indeed the greatest have fallen short, indeed have even failed?"

How well I understand the first Jewish Christians from this standpoint: how hard it must have been for them to transcend the Torah for, and through, the Gospel—not for the Zealots, etc. but for those who really loved the Law, loved it for God's sake, as expressed in the endless meditations of Psalm 118.

*

TODAY I'm much clearer in my mind about the multiformity and complexity of the concept: the teaching office in the Church—which is as many-leaved as a cabbage rose. It is not only recently that I have stressed that the Church discriminates very nicely in what she commands us to believe: I've always tried to show people that there is a whole scale of actual *obligations*, meticulously graded, beginning with dogma, the essential "articles of faith", all the way down to the free, personal opinions of individual theologians. In fact, however, we were brought up to regard the sum total of religious teaching presented to us not as a slab of, let's say, slate, consisting of innumerable thin foliate layers, but rather as a solid lump of granite, to be accepted or rejected en bloc. And it took a lifetime of effort to train myself to discriminate. The more so because such discrimination must be practised in two different directions simultaneously—one positive, the other negative. This calls for an ever increasing and maturing independence of judgment—examine everything, retain the best—and *at the same time* an attitude of mind wary of regarding one's own private judgment as the supreme authority, the final "court of appeal". Anything but easy, as you know. Indeed it's so intricate a process, so subtle and delicate that it cannot be mapped out beforehand theoretically, psychologically. I couldn't tell you systematically why and when my "faith-conscience" decides to assess this bit of teaching as "genuine" doctrine of the Church and another as a theological surmise, an opinion without valid claim to demand our assent. Yet you'll find such estimates indispensable often enough—a haunting necessity —without ever having "learnt" to form them, and at the same time all this must take place in genuine, open, unconditional readiness to bow and submit to the authority of the Church.

Here, of course, I've learnt a great deal. For example, I understand today much better (what I've often explained to other people, converts, for instance), that "the Faith of the Church" is not identical with her theological system; this being just one of its elements, along with the liturgy, popular belief and devotions, *lex orandi*, etc. That this whole structure is by no means a tangible, definable system, rather a vast landscape, partly laid out like a park, with trees, and streams regulated in their courses—partly savage: forest, jungle and wild heath . . . and, basically, theology is the attempt to survey this immense landscape cartographically; yet still—thank God—with many white patches on the map. And with derelict mines once teeming with activity, river estuaries choked and buried in silt, with stretches of arable land, impoverished, exhausted, which no amount of cultivation can make fertile any more—and strips, long desert, now fruitful and green again, watered by subterranean springs.

*

I LOVE this feast (Pentecost) which always awakens a strange fluttering, trembling expectancy within me . . . Of all the feasts of the Church year it seems the most mysterious—for all that it commemorates the most "public" event of them all. It is made up of mysteries, perhaps the profoundest of these being the hidden reality of our own receiving of the Spirit . . . *Veni Creator Spiritus*—in the third verse we have "*Accende lumen sensibus*": some of our German translations garble it, turning it into a prayer for the light of grace, for the light of the mind, but it really does mean "Kindle our *senses* from above". How fervently the liturgy repeats the prayer from today on, right through the Octave: to renew the face of the earth—no, not the prayer, the assurance: "And thou *shalt* renew the face of the earth."

*

GOD appeared to me first of all in the Logos, later in Eros; and now, from both, I hope I am on the way to finding Sophia who contains both. And "Reason" within the Church is not to be understood first and foremost from its history in her, but from its origin, as reflection of the Logos, as longing for him—not simply hybrid human intellect, no matter how much this has always intervened, from the very beginning, even gaining the upper hand at times.

*

To my mind Joachim of Fiore's weak point lay in his understanding of Christ: for him the Lord is not the fullness, the zenith of history—not even the turning point of the ages: the arc spans from Isaias to Benedict almost above his head. Which is why he is not seen clearly in his working within his Church, and Joachim therefore can understand the sacraments only as purely institutional, pointing to something beyond, their effect only moral, life-reforming—and "the real thing" still lies ahead: for the mystical Christ, ever-present, active here and now, perpetuating his Incarnation, doesn't enter his ken at all.

On the other hand I'm coming to see more clearly all the time the real function of these "one-sided" figures in the Church —people "possessed" by a single thought, a vision. It would seem that human power is so weak, its energy just isn't enough —when it is "fairly" distributed—for the decisive step forward, or to rouse the lethargic masses, carrying them away, inspiring them—only these enthusiasts will do. As long as they do not cut themselves off from the body of the Church for the sake of their partial insights, as long as they do not despise and reject the whole for the sake of their personal recognitions—it's all right. That's what distinguishes the heretic from the saint, that and that only. And it wasn't Joachim's wish to break away from the Church—which surely obliges us not simply to leave his inheritance to the heretics to exploit at random, as though it were outlawed, but rather to integrate it ourselves, as far as this is possible.

*

[ON religion in schools.] The weight of the solely-institutional and wrongly-institutional (not the institutional in itself) is so

279

tremendous and the damage it inflicts so immense that the attempt to oppose it might well prove a crushing task. Yet I see more and more clearly that it's quite useless, and maybe even a trap set by the Devil, to involve oneself in a frontal attack. The best way is to ignore this dead world, as far as possible, and go on doing what one personally holds to be right. That conversation only further strengthened my conviction that the so-called religious education in our schools, though obviously indispensable, is an impossible affair from the start, and not even primarily because it's sandwiched in between gym and geography—even more because it occupies a completely isolated position in the children's lives, instead of being closely knit up with them. The same sort of thing as those American attempts at a separate sex education, with special courses and "rules of behaviour". This sort of thing is no use either. The whole network of life must support and sustain the "Gnosis" of sex.

*

I HARDLY think one could say that the Church has actually "forbidden" magic in general. What is termed "magic" under the First Commandment in the Catechism is, after all, quite clearly defined as the attempt to acquire and exercise power *"by the help of the Devil* and evil spirits". Something which has always gone on. Dom Daniel Feuling took the view that Hitler was a typical example of this, and that it accounted for his fabulous rise to power and his success at the outset.

A few years ago a Viennese priest told me an extraordinary story of a formal pact with the Devil which I can quite readily believe. Above all I'm convinced that this sort of thing "works", what's more—on the spot, and thoroughly. In contrast to the heavenly powers, evil spirits don't hang around waiting to be wooed and won: they snatch, in one fell swoop.

*

I WAS talking just now to our maid about ghosts and devils—she's so terribly "enlightened" and is astonished, horrified even, that "an educated person" like me can "still" believe in things which her whole village knows cannot exist! This always amuses me very much. Yet at the same time it's sad proof how rapidly religious life must be disappearing in the country: inevitable, I suppose, when the organ for one kind of perception atrophies, the other is bound to die too, at least to some extent, and other elements claimed to prop up the Faith nowadays, such as deliberate choice, intellectual maturity, etc. are naturally not to be found or fostered among the people, still more or less primitive. No, in this respect they really aren't "persons" at all, they must be embedded in the tissue of a larger body to share in the mysteries.

*

WHY is it that we Catholics can no longer create a real, living, *catching*, i.e. convincing utopia—whereas elsewhere in the Christian world the sects (above all the American ones) still seem to succeed in this—and, of course, in the non-Christian sphere we have the most glowing Messianic fervour in the political, social, economic and technical fields with all their aims and activities. Where is the Christian to place these phenomena —with the eschatological symptoms assuming ever crasser form, and Scripture, especially the Apocalypse, predicting the ever-increasing horror and dread of the end to come? On the other hand, every Christian-alive must surely also feel that "Christendom", as embodiment of the gospel of Christ, has scarcely passed the ABC stage, barely beyond the first pioneering experiments, often vague and along the wrong lines, and that the full range of possibilities to be realized still lies *before* us. "Forgetting what I have left behind, intent on what lies in view. . . ."

*

WHAT strikes me so forcibly in that small selection of Père Couturier's letters is how even such an original and in every respect free mind can still be so utterly convinced that the French are supreme among the human race, that where France is at stake the whole of the world is at stake, or at least the flower and the core of the world—and that France and France alone still represents the "light" and the "magisterium", liberty and justice in a sort of personal union.

*

DAME Julian: my mind is full of her all the time. She, too, had "ferment thoughts", the "shewing" that those whom God knows will be saved can never fall out of the fundamental oneness in love with him, even by mortal sin—which she recognizes and calls "deadly"!—even if they "be for a time dead". Isn't there an element of this in the doctrine of the ineradicable seal imprinted by certain sacraments? I believe I experienced something of this myself in my periods of opposition and sin. But I wouldn't have dared to say as much—though God knows such recognition in no way lessens the weight of one's guilt, making it "lighter" or "relative"—on the contrary: it's all the heavier weighed against such love and mercy.

*

I FIND our institution of the *Namenstag*★ so very fitting and a lovely custom—this emphasis upon "the family of God", not in the "idyllic" sense, but in the wider interpretation of lineage, spiritual generation, ancestors, the "name" perpetuated anew in each new bearer; "historical mission", looking back on the past and towards the future; living tradition binding the hearts of fathers and sons, the handing down of great models from generation to generation. All this seems to me embodied, simply, naturally, in the keeping of this feast day—the Christian standing in history and in the Church, on the road to the Kingdom of God and to eternity.

*

To consent to be a "pauper", i.e. "poor in spirit", without being a beggar—a beggar on the look out for alms, pushing forward, all eyes for what the others are getting; to consent to be a beggar, not extorting gifts by exhibiting his poverty, but really living like a Franciscan beggar from gifts, from surprises, from miracles—marvelling each time anew, full of joy and wonder at the grace of God falling, unexpected, from heaven—"at the appointed time": *that* should be one's aim. In the sphere of Eros too, in all its sorrow and its rapture, Francis is a mysterious "model". I always think his celebrated "Franciscan" joy is

★ The keeping of the feast of one's patron saint, a day often regarded as more important than one's birthday and celebrated accordingly in the family.

basically rooted in living solely from the surprises of God. Fundamentally his poverty was nothing else.

*

Two themes are preoccupying me incessantly—more sub-consciously than consciously: *"*Man the Creature*"* and "Revolt against the Mothers". And à propos my*"*central theme*"*: man and the world, "Devotion to Creation", I'm face to face with the problem of ascetic mysticism: I'm not concerned here with merely ethical ascesis, curbing and subduing every urge and impulse, nor with the dualistic Manichean variety, the false spiritualism which sets mind against matter—what I mean here is that truly mystical movement of "God alone"—the "*Solo Dios basta*" of the Spaniards, the "naughting" and "voiding" of all things created in the German mystics. I've been sparring with this problem all my life, ever since my first religious awakening, and not just theoretically either, as it might seem today. It draws me like a fascinating abyss—and all the same I know from year to year with increasing certainty that there must be another way, that there *is* another way.

*

ON the other hand, the element of piety, reverence, loyalty, constancy within me is very great, and all this shrinks back before the crushing, overwhelming weight of the consensus of (almost) all the masters of mysticism, inexorably unanimous in their interpretation of our Lord's words: "He that forsaketh not all that he hath cannot be my disciple"—at any rate as an inner rejection of all things created. Here they present a closed front: Francis, Bernard, Eckhart, Francis de Sales, a Kempis, orthodox and heretics alike, Ignatius, Tauler, de Caussade and the Spaniards. Who am I to venture here with even a hint of con-tradiction, or conjecture: "and yet *something* still escaped them, something *I*, of all people, see!" Sounds too crazy for words, grotesque, presumptuous—ridiculously impertinent. But what can I do? I cannot get away from it. This great and venerable tradition is but *one* aspect—the other has yet to be discovered, and there are lots of us digging away after it today like moles—still blind, still groping underground. All this talk about lay ascesis, secular orders, the hallowing of everyday life, Christians in the world, etc. is nothing but the fumbling search for this deep root not yet brought to light.

What I know myself on this matter is not derived from books, not even the most venerable, but truly knowledge "taught by God" in a thread of experience which forms the hidden marrow of my life. And it's the same for countless others, I'm sure. But it hasn't yet penetrated to the common awareness of the Church. It has still to be formulated—may God grant me strength to do my part in this.

*

WE call on St Joseph in our domestic troubles—the reason goes deeper than we realize! The liturgy on his feast links him with his Egyptian namesake which is surprising at first and is often attributed simply to the likeness in names. But our forefathers knew better: the Egyptian Joseph guarded the bread stored up, saved until the famine came, and then distributed it among the people. Joseph the foster-father was guardian of the Mystical Bread of heaven. That is why—and this is my own conclusion— he may help us towards our own daily bread: as a token of this. In this office moreover he is an image of God the Father—the Bible shows him as a good and faithful head of the household, providing the servants with food at the appointed time—that he may be the "hand" of the Father from whom we ask our daily bread.

*

WE modern Catholics are all of us Monophysites to a greater or lesser degree—in sentiment, that is, not intentionally, by reason. We are far more intensely aware of Christ's Godhead than of his human nature. The human mind is too small to be able to embrace both concepts at once in its poor consciousness.

*

THE last circular from Burg Rothenfels* brought a lecture on *Man and Creation* (everybody suddenly seems to be talking about this!). Some rather good things in it. But in a passage

* Since 1919 the centre of the German Catholic Youth Movement *Quickborn* (Living Fountain)—disbanded in 1939. Reopened after the war for religious courses, conferences and other Catholic activities for lay-people.

about "the attitude of man towards things created", based on the Bible, as the speaker says, he asserts: "Scriptural thought differs in yet another way from ancient pagan as well as certain modern points of view. The world is soberly and plainly regarded as finite—no intrinsic numinous glamour in things created, no religious 'virtue'. The 'divine' is not inherent in the world, *nor is it manifest* in its forms and powers. Rather this world is the clear-cut domain of created finality, and God is pure transcendence outside and beyond it. He moves in perfect freedom among his creatures, guiding and directing them according to his glorious will. This recognition results in a very sensible, cool and realistic attitude to the world. It is the combination of such lucid sobriety with a marvelling humility before the Creator which makes up the grandeur of biblical thought."

This goes very much against the grain with me. Since I've given up polemics I won't retort—and anyway the editors probably wouldn't print a reply. But I'm resolved to work out my own position for my next lecture in Hohenheim.

Of course X. is quite right in his view that the "novelty" of the God of Revelation, the great contrast to every form of paganism, lies in his absolute transcendence, distinct from all things, all forces, God as Creator, enthroned above and beyond the world. But I cannot agree with the consequences inferred from this, i.e. that, therefore, he is not manifest himself in the world, and that accordingly there is no numinous, religious power inherent in things. On the contrary, their very "createdness" *is in itself this powerfully manifest "holiness"*. Of course things are not "divine" and may not be called so: but—is there anything more awesome, more portentous than this knowledge: *that* they are created! Created, Creation—what more mysterious words exist? Thoughts, even fantasies of God, "in the beginning"—"out of nothing"—called forth solely by the deliberate choice of his love. Such things cannot be called "plain, sensible, sober statements". This assertion that Creation is just a matter of fact, "down to earth" affair strikes me as extremely modern. On this point I feel myself much more orthodox, for as far as I know St Thomas had lots to say about the "mystical" quality of "createdness". For him "the creature" is truly a mystery, a mystical reality. Sometimes this strikes me so forcibly that I shrink from crushing a gnat or plucking a blade of grass—how *dare* one do such a thing, except of necessity? Nothing sentimental about this—not even compassion at having to hurt things—simply awe before their Maker. I'd never dare to tear up someone else's sketch or manuscript without first asking the author's permission—unless, of course, he had asked me to do so.

I'd say that the very createdness of creatures makes them somehow "sacred". This is far too little realized. I suppose the monstrous destructive, perverting character of modern technical "civilization" has something to do with this.

*

TROCHU's *Vianney** book makes me shudder. Positively frightening—and the saint too. The first time I read it I was quite horrified. This book was one of the first to open my eyes to the falsity of that *fable convenue* of saints as sunny, amiable, "splendid" human beings, noble and charming. The Curé d'Ars was anything but this. Actually he is a second Simeon Stylites—he, too, stands on a ledge, barely a foot wide, between Heaven and Hell, a vertical figure, a pillar, perpendicular, height and depth, nothing wide and ample!—and how hard and stern he is—and not only against himself: he would excommunicate his parishioners if they even once went dancing or drinking—like the most rigorous Puritan.

I used to put this down to the flourishing Jansenism of his day—but now I have my doubts. Vianney was far too simple and uneducated to have been involved in "isms" of any kind. But he knew everything there was to know about sin, and saw that for his flock even very "harmless" things (by our standards!) led straight to really grave offences. And so for him there was no compromise, no consideration, no excuse. For him sin involved personal, direct single combat with Satan.

He is one of those saints who make one realize with terrifying clarity (or at least guess) the *gravity* of sin—not morally, but in the numinous sense. Yet all the saints were very hard—Francis no less than Catherine of Genoa, etc. Francis de Sales is really an exception—less, I think, because he was "well-bred", a nobleman, than because he set himself to express Agape in the

---

* Abbé Francis Trochu, *The Curé d'Ars*, London, 1949.

most perfect forms of Eros, and consciously became a master, indeed a past master, in the art of courtesy. Yet the iron hand was there too, in the velvet glove. But there's no glove to Vianney's peasant fist. He's really gruesome.

*

A PROPOS that theme of mine "Revolt against the Mothers", etc. I often wonder what really lies at the bottom of that curious dislike of Marian devotion I find in so many women—believers, too, even deeply religious women and girls—and which I felt myself for a long time. My conscience was always troubling me on this point, but there was nothing I could do about it. Yet one doesn't feel distaste for other saints or cults one doesn't share personally! One simply ignores them. But this was real protest and flight in one. Nor can it be attributed entirely to a personal mother complex, although this attitude is naturally very typical for people afflicted with one. On the other hand, precisely we could try to make up for the lack of an earthly mother by a doubly close attachment to our heavenly Mother. But there's more to it than that: it is the unconscious protest against woman-liness in itself, the feminine in its highest form, as appeal, obligation, vocation, in all its implications. As long as you do not *want* to be a woman, or rather are afraid of not being able to be one, you protest against the image of Mary. Only now do I know why and that our Lady is the archetype of all womanhood, and therefore our "model"—not in the narrow moral, educational sense, but an "example", an exemplar, in the deepest, most comprehensive meaning of the word. But this was exactly what one refused to accept.

*

IT's not my impression at all, by the way, that Couturier admires and commends everything "modern" *à tout prix*. He's far more concerned with the general break-through which had already begun at the turn of the century in "the world" and still hasn't "arrived" in the Catholic Church. And with the switch over from the bourgeois conventional point of view, with the recognition that art is more than artistic dexterity with educational or propagandistic possibilities, etc. For the rest he was dismally pessimistic: "I do not believe that modern religious art exists or is possible among nations which have grown virtually pagan—that is a chimera." Nor did he believe in a rebirth of Christian art in modern forms—merely that individual inspired examples could exist, here and there, in surprising ways, but by chance, more a miracle than anything else.

*

I ONCE argued with W. about the "right"—as contrary to the "leftist" attitude. I maintained that all "rightist" ideals were basically "numinous", descending somehow from the gods, which is why man can attach himself to them from different, deeper "strata" of his being and so really *serve* them—whereas the "leftist" ideals are merely related to man and his advantages, aims, well-being. A similar analogy to what Kierkegaard once said about Protestantism: its only point, its sole right of existence is as a corrective, an antithesis; it becomes impossible when one attempts to set it up in its own right. But of course he couldn't understand this. He probably thinks it's just my hereditary strain.

*

I'VE been mulling over those gospels for several Ember days, with their recurring theme of "power over evil spirits". To my mind the depth-psychologists and psychiatrists overlook this very important factor—it doesn't fit into their picture. Doctors and theologians can argue as to *how*, but it seems obvious to me that neuroses and psychoses and what is called insanity are far more closely linked with evil spirits than people like to think. Of course in the Middle Ages they tried exorcism to no avail on countless poor creatures who could be successfully treated nowadays with injections, shock therapy and surgery—today the boot's on the other foot. The Devil makes use of illness as a vehicle, as an "open door", slipping through the chink into the inner being; or else the mental and spiritual derangement reacts "sensibly" to the diabolical influence, expressing it through the symptoms of illness. If our Lord refers to the woman "bent down" (did she suffer from rheumatism?!) as having been "bound by Satan", how much more this must apply to mental diseases?

And the Church does possess the power and the strength to subject devils, not only in charismatic people, now and again, but in the office of the apostles to whom this power was delegated at first, originally, expressly. But we no longer believe in this power, which is why it is not activated.

*

How open we are, how kindly disposed, when we greet another person "in the name" of a friend! And how much more gladly ought we to do "in the name of Christ" what gives us such pleasure "in the name" of someone we love. . . .

*

I'M delighting in *The Sign of Jonas,** Thomas Merton's diaries of the first seven years in his Trappist monastery. In itself, of course, a grotesque, typically American paradox, but I don't find it "impossible" at all, on the contrary, deeply moving, a lovely book. "There are real monasteries after all, and real monks—somewhere this is still real life, not merely an institution; there the cost is truly worthwhile", I keep thinking at every page. . . . In spite of all the weaknesses, incrustations, etc., the "deep well" is there—genuine, passionate "life with God", surpassing all mediocrity. How glorious! For monasticism as a principle, a phenomenon, is a burning problem for me, a personal, vital issue. This book of Merton's really is a document of religious experience— not theory, but life—a very simple and powerful document. It rejoices one's heart.

*

DIONYSIUS the Areopagite is the perfect corrective to Joachim's weakest side: his total lack of a proper understanding of the priesthood. Not unlike certain trends of our own day, he viewed the clergy merely as social-pastoral "functionaries". In this it seems he couldn't break out of his own empirical subjective world. The idea of the "mystical hierarchy", indeed *any* conception of an archetype of the priest as exponent of the Liturgy, administering the sacraments, servant, voice of the Logos in

* London and New York, 1953.

theology—all this was utterly lacking. Which is why he expected specifically from the monk much that in Dionysius belongs essentially to the priest, and so could believe that the latter could well be dispensed with if only the former remained.

*

THAT abstruse reflection on the Trinity by C. G. Jung, with the Three and the missing Fourth—do you think me appallingly naïve when I say: The answer to me seems simple, even self-evident: the Fourth is the *World*—Creation. Utterly different, of course, from God, and in one way not to be named in the same breath with HIM—yet on the other hand still indissolubly bound up with him in one circle, with the Most Blessed Trinity. Not by nature, yet by his will. For we know them in no other way, we never encounter the Divine Persons in any other connection—we only know abstractly, i.e. as a mystery of faith, that they always "existed" without the world, since the world was their creation. . . . But the very word "existed" is wrong! It is true, on the other hand, that the world had a beginning and is not its own origin, yet we know, too, that even before its creation it was "in God", in what we call his decree, and in the sense that all things were in the Logos; and "now" it is in a state of pilgrimage, and in eternity it will be one with and in God in the state of transfiguration. This might well be the "Fourth"—what more do we want?

*

SOMETIMES one thinks, rather bitterly, that it would be better if the destinies and sayings of the saints were to remain arcane, so that not every Tom, Dick and Harry could identify himself with them, quoting and "applying" them in the wrong places and at the wrong times. But after all the destiny of our Lord and his words were only "inwardly" arcane and otherwise exposed to every misunderstanding, and there's surely nothing on earth more abused and misconstrued than the Gospel. This also is an aspect of the mystery "delivered into the hands of sinners"—the Word, too, delivered into their, i.e. our, thoughts and speech.

*

"HE among you who is concerned with nothing but love is a philanderer; he who is nothing but clever is an unbeliever; he who is nothing but devout is a thief," said Rabbi Bunam. The "occupational diseases" of the devout are curious indeed, and very revealing. It would be worth writing about them some time. Precisely the tension between the sinner and the "chosen" in the Christian strikes me as so important. Either of these extremes, isolated, without a corrective, can throw the soul out of balance. In the saints we see both these things in *fertile* tension —not slurred, uncompromising yet perfectly balanced.

*

YOUR allusion to "double think" in the Church rather grated on me. Of course there is this negative aspect as well, the sort of thing Fr Rahner describes as "subcutaneous heresy", real "double-dealing", i.e. official thought used merely as a mask to camouflage the true face which in this case is personal opinion in revolt. Nevertheless I hope that even where you do encounter this—and you will, more's the pity—it is still only the "shadow" of a positive phenomenon: that within the protective sheath of time-honoured thought something new and alive is growing. For then this tension in which we are living would be precious indeed, truly fruitful, really worth all the pain and confusion which we must keep on paying for it. I see it as an almost exact counter- part, on another level, to those lines of Hölderlin's I love so much: "The heart's fair wave would never surge up so nobly to the spirit's foaming crest did not the old mute rock of fate oppose it." You see, I don't believe the wave of the mind would surge up so splendidly either, touching truth and reflecting it, if the ancient rock of doctrine were not there to oppose it. Yet I can- not regard this solely as a check and a refutation—at the same time I see it rather like the prickly husk around the growing chestnut, the womb around the baby even, nourishing it, protect- ing it. If this shell weren't there we should fall an all too easy prey to the *Zeitgeist*—be swept into every blind alley by it. As it is, the fruit can only shed its husk in due time, when it is ripe. It would seem that this is how the Holy Ghost intends it to be: that the insight and perception he can rouse creatively in every mind must first pass through the maternal substance of the

Church's thought, to be coloured and stamped by it—the "issue" of both. Maybe it's different for people who've grown up outside the Church—but that is how it is with us. Possibly this way brings us more suffering—but I wouldn't want to miss this constant tension between the old and the new, between outside and inside—between the changeless and the ever-creative. The fact that we are living at this very moment, just when what is hidden and growing is beginning to appear in a recognizable shape—that's what reconciles me with this age of ours and all its otherwise hideous features.

*

ABRAHAM in my breviary. What touched me most this time was the threefold "I am here": to the call of God, to Isaac's call on the way, to the call of the angel on the mountain. If only one could answer like this to the call of God and one's fellow men!

*

I THINK I know now why Hieronymus Bosch's devils aren't really "sinister": it's because they still "belong". In spite of it all, they're still within Creation, even this Hell is still "inside the world".

*

I CAN'T help it, I can't stand Simone Weil. Of course she's magnificent in her way, and of a flawless integrity—but somehow I feel her to be awfully arrogant. That pride in being "different" from other people—at all costs and in every way, in everything she did or had or experienced—it's positively inhuman, like Rilke, whom I can't bear either, for precisely the same reason. The way she rejects every form of fellowship—for all her idealistic socialist solidarity, working in factories, Red Spain, etc., and her voluntary ration card starvation at the end. But all this was only exterior social solidarity and loyalty—in her heart of hearts she wanted to be alone, completely by herself, solitary, "unique", dependent on no other person—so much so that you must refuse even truth if offered by a friend!—I find this terribly inhuman. In fact it's refusing to be human, a being just as dependent on others as on God—not only noble, sublime, sovereign, but dependent on accepting *as well*, in poverty and gratitude. And that's precisely what she refuses to do. She's magnificent, yes, but to me she's simply unchristian. With all due respect for her truly terrible passion, I can't understand how people can set her up as a model—*admiranda, non imitanda*. Probably one oughtn't to say such a thing, but one has the faint suspicion that, had she met our Lord on earth, not even from him would she have accepted anything, taking it as a gift—or only on her own terms.

*

CHRIST never went about "transfigured" during his earthly life. Even as the Risen Lord he was always "disguised", as gardener, pilgrim, etc. Only the three apostles saw him transfigured, and then only for a single brief hour on Mount Tabor. Yet what they beheld was neither symbol, nor idea, nor promise, but reality irrupting from the world above, from the background of eternity into the earthly foreground. The transfiguration was never repeated and never again "confirmed", but it had given them a key to what was to come. And later on Paul knows that we should grow from light to light through the vision of his splendour, "and so we become transfigured into the same likeness, borrowing glory from that glory".

It seems to me that this applies to the Church as well. There may be stretches to come in her progress which will seem very close to this transfigured figure—and more dark periods as well.

*

A THEOLOGIAN, for me, is simply a man thinking for himself, independent thought grounded in a mastery of the fundamental, central principles and substance of theology—not merely passing on old formulae or applying the rather rusty stock of his young days here and there, in amateur fashion, wherever it suits his purpose, jumping elegantly over the things which don't. . . . And I see a great difference, too, between those who look upon systematization in theology as an attempt to trace the in itself indivisible Truth of faith from its sources, unfolding it for human comprehension—and those who are set upon pressing single shreds and fragments into the scheme of a given *Weltanschauung*, so as to make them "rhyme" on every point.

Which is why, so it seems to me, there must always be gaps in the theological system, and much must be left open—a building under construction, until our Lord's Second Coming. Yet just because the substance of faith, doctrinal faith, is one and indivisible, a whole in which every "point" singled out is yet knit together with everything else, I know also that I must be doubly chary about judging things with which I am not familiar from the single item with which I happen to be well acquainted. Certainly I often repeat just what is "merely traditional" in religious conversation. And what's wrong with that? I know perfectly well that what I have explicitly, deliberately "acquired" so intensely that I now have opinions and experience of my own about it are but fragments of the vast treasure of faith. But these fragments too, precisely these things which I've really got "by heart", I have received from the *Church*. And so other things which I have not yet penetrated and assimilated in the same way, things which, for me, are in a sense just marginal knowledge are no less important and valid for that; I hold them in obedience to the Faith, if not in understanding, confident in the hope that understanding will follow in due course, if once I can devote myself to them. In many points I have no other answer but the one I was taught, but this too is my own by faith. And by no means, as some impute to me, just out of love for things ancient and traditional—which, at the most, could colour my opinions but never produce vital decisions of faith—but simply in trusting submission, subjection to the divine sacrament of Christ in the Church. Of course I'm aware that within her own traditional heritage of doctrine, that vast conglomeration of the most diverse elements, the Church in her teachings draws many distinctions: what is revealed truth, what is its interpretation and deduction from it; what is dogma produced by an indissoluble fusion of both; what is opinion and conjecture, *communis opinio* or individual opinion, etc. But I'm no theologian and in lots of questions I cannot decide straightway to which of these many interlocking spheres this or that particular proposition belongs. Sometimes I know, sometimes I sense it—because I've got a rather good theological nose. But I'm extremely reticent about pronouncing that "something's wrong" simply because it doesn't fit my own personally acquired scraps of knowledge. If

I knew a bit more about the point in question, if the links between my shreds of insight were more fully developed, then the problem would very likely appear in quite a different light and fit into a place in the tapestry as yet invisible to me. But because I accept the whole, *en bloc,* implicitly, as "revealed by God and taught by the Catholic Church", as it says in the Catechism—it is far more *natural* to me to wait a while when I encounter something unfamiliar, not to my taste, biding my time rather than to turn it down right away—and certainly I won't reject it before I've examined the point in question as thoroughly as possible. And if—as is often the case—I don't really care enough to go to such trouble about it, then I feel I've not sufficient reasons either for refusing it, and simply leave it suspended, as far as my insight is concerned, not as to its objective validity. As long as, for me, it still forms part of the universal heritage of faith—good; when I see that it's merely a theological opinion, I might behave differently. As long as it *could* be even a splinter of the *depositum fidei,* I treat it whole-heartedly with loving reverence—until I'm certain that it does not belong, and not the other way round. Of course I realize that "what the Church really means" is—in innumerable instances—buried under a mound, no, a mountain of rubble of sheer historical, theological tradition. But I can hardly start boring at every point with a pneumatic drill! And so I swear by the treasure beneath the rubble.

*

I'M pondering a lot just now about the mysterious process of growing old—that stripping unto death. Yet I don't see it as something negative, not as descent into the dark valley, but rather as the climb to the last peak—before which one must rid oneself of all superfluous baggage, discarding all hampering equipment. The armour, the skins and wrappings the soul has laid upon itself for its own security would seem to be falling away, so that it must meet what is to come at last directly, naked.

*

I WAS reading Goethe's letters to Charlotte von Stein again last week—every time I feel the infinite pathos of this story. For me it's a pattern of love's mortality—a love so wonderfully deep, so genuine, grounded and moulded in the mind, the heart of genius—what else was lacking? Yet it's so cruelly, so humiliatingly bound up with the biological facts, with the inexorable consequence of the difference in their ages. Isn't it ghastly? The *necessity* of the development is what makes it so horrible, how even these two noble people "let themselves be lived", instead of determining their fate themselves—and in their friendship and passion there is nothing stronger than the gravitation of impersonal nature—no seed of eternal life. How *can* man bear to be "natural" and nothing more?

*

THE theme of Candlemas is never-ending: "letting go" in love, for love's sake. In marriage, too, we are two in one tissue of life—not one in two persons, and must respect and accept this "separateness" in our oneness. Funny that something so natural—a matter of course really—should be so hard. But anything else would only be "devouring", or "being devoured" if one's partner were stronger. And precisely the man can only exist, come to himself at all, if he can "realize" himself.

*

WE find the same thing in every heresy, in one form or another, a hidden attempt—subconscious in man very probably, but certainly all the more conscious in Satan—to dismember the Trinity. And, for the humans involved, presumably always with the best of intentions and motives. Yet all the extreme forms of Dualism seek to separate the world of the Father from that of the Son by attributing the world to an evil Creator; or the Old Testament is rejected, and only the New Testament accepted; or, in the more moderate, latent expressions of a Dualism more practical than dogmatic—even inside the Church—Creation, Nature—again "the ordinance of the Father"—is divorced and discredited, even damned in favour of the supernatural, of redemption, grace, the imitation of Christ, i.e. the ordinance of the Son. Or, in the various forms of spiritualism, the attempt persists, with almost devastating monotony, to split off the Pneuma, on the one hand from the world of the Father, i.e. Nature and its laws (sex, marriage, property, power, combat,

etc.) or—and even more intensely—from the world of the Son,
i.e. from the perpetuation of his Incarnation throughout history
and throughout the world = the Church. Every effort is made
to substitute for her embodiment in all its forms and features
the Spirit alone, a pure "inwardness", no longer requiring anything external, which means no longer in need of a body. In
other words, the Incarnation must be "overcome" in the name
of the Spirit. The Church is grazed by *all* heresies—from within
as well as without—she is infected and permeated by all of them,
she contracts every disease—and yet she has *always* embodied
the unity of the Trinity, maintaining this unity here on earth—
certainly not intentionally, i.e. by the deliberate intention of her
representatives, but, evidently, by the guidance of the Spirit
which unites Father and Son.

This trinitarian ground and key to all history is impressed
upon me ever more forcibly.

*

I'm afraid I do believe that all earthly love can die—since man is
mortal, why not also his most human feature?—and for me
pretensions such as "love that dies was never love", etc.
belong to schoolgirls' albums. To me it's part of the miraculous
power of the sacrament when in marriage love continually over-
comes its natural gravitation towards death, for its permanence
is not something to be taken for granted or even probable; and
I believe—and the belief hurts—that no seal, no fusion can
prevail, in itself, over the forces of destruction. But I believe,
too, that human love can stem so truly from God, and that
one of its roots can be kept so firmly sunk in him that from
this source—not from its own fire or yearning or tenacity—it
achieves a real share in immortality.

*

The marvellous thing is that God doesn't plan our vocations
without us, as ready-made ideal constructions to be climbed
into with difficulty—he makes them to measure, designed
individually to fit all our deformities and "humps", taking in,
from the start, all our faults and blunders and craziness, even as

component parts! Isn't it just like him—defying all the art of the human educator and psychologist.

*

THERE are prophets against the intellect, just as there are prophets against sex, lots of them: the analogy is exact. For inherent in both these comprehensive and yet central domains of human life is a very similar—perhaps identical?—combination of impulse, urge and fascination—in each the same translucency, reflection of God's image; in each the same lapse, corruption, seduction, pollution, falsification—each can lead to magic, intoxication, bondage—each calls for redemption. And you are perfectly right that as far as reason today is concerned (it was different in the nineteenth century—despite the Enlightenment, etc., sometimes even definitely opposing it) this aspect is far less recognized and admitted by us, if admitted at all, than in the case of "the flesh". Instead we've a movement doubly keen to "justify" sex, either by playing it down as harmless, or else exalting it to complete apotheosis; meaning at first relief after centuries of misinterpretation and one-sidedness, but it probably won't be long before it has grown out of all control.

*

I'VE suddenly realized—in my heart, not just intellectually—the full meaning of *Gnade*⋆ in the further sense of *gratia—grazia*—grace—graciousness: how, asking for it, we long for a smile from God—and how Mary is this smile turned towards us, heartening us to ask him.

*

I'M reading *Kristin Lavransdatter* again—as relaxation. Really it's one of the greatest poetic books, and the most powerful portrayal of medieval Christendom I know. And it's one of the greatest and most profound descriptions of love as a demonic force of destiny, with all its passion in both senses of the word—and yet, in contrast to the moderns, not a single brazen or crude word in it, for all its merciless realism. I must admit rather shamefacedly that it makes me cry every time—because

⋆ *Gnade* = grace.

it's so real, so true, reaching to the depths of human nature, touching one to the quick. An overwhelmingly convincing description how this elemental power seizes two beings, drawing them to one another, fusing them for their whole life; beyond reason and resolve, by no means for their happiness, yet in no wise as something base, animal; gripping and penetrating them both, as man, as woman, not impersonally, but in the sharpest relief of their individual characters, and yet it has nothing whatever to do with "understanding": they don't understand one another one bit, all along each still remains the great unknown for the other. They rend each other in the most cruel conflicts, yet still remain inseparably one, and their clashes result more from their all too great closeness than from their insuperable strangeness.

*

DIVERSITY of tongues. It hurts to feel how monoglot we've become in the Church and what an obstacle it is. It's my most ardent wish to break up the pack-ice somehow, to help to bring about understanding. Of course systematized doctrine is the river, the central stream flowing through the land; but it must be able to catch up the wild torrents and streams rushing or trickling down from all sides, carrying these along with it on its way to the sea: otherwise it will dry up itself, and these waters work havoc or drain away to no purpose. But the estuaries are silted up, blocked. Père Couturier, the Dominican artist, saw the Church as a tall tree, bearing leaves only at the top, while one great branch after another—Eastern, German, English spirituality—is torn away in the course of history. For me this picture is too tragic in its immobility. I prefer to stick to my own image of the river and the tributaries, hoping that the connecting channels of these other streams, alien but clamouring to flow into the great river, can once again be cleared.

*

A FALSE kind of Catholicism has spread here with us: the notion that every single Christian must realize in his personal religion everything the Church offers, i.e. we've either forgotten the figure of the Body and its members, or substituted the unreal idea of a toy church constructed out of children's bricks, all alike (as though even a building or a machine could ever be made up of exactly the same parts!). In the Church there *must* be "divers tongues".

*

IN private one can well be a cat that walks by itself, and without roots in any specific soil; but in the great battle for the Kingdom of God it seems to me one ought to belong to some brotherhood.

*

I LOVE today's Feast [Trinity Sunday] so very much, the Feast of God's sublime incomprehensibility. Koepgen is perfectly right: the Blessed Trinity is the very ground of our Christian existence. I've noticed that for all the saints it is, so to speak, the "last theme" of their lives.

*

BERGENGRUEN says somewhere: "What's the use of offering people choice wine? You can't make them drink it!" Is it the pitiable narrowness of human consciousness that it can scarcely ever grasp more than one thing at a time—either loyalty to the Faith or charity, for instance?

*

MAN is an enigma, a being full of contradictions, and one must learn to see him as such, accepting him and loving him. With lots of people one stops after a while, knowing that it's hopeless, or that it would be too much for one if the other person were to change from a figure largely constructed by oneself into a real human being. For in another person one sees, first of all, what one can *re*-cognize, what one knows, the kindred things, what is familiar, a corroboration of oneself—and *then* what is strange, contradictory, a barrier, what somehow puts me to the test, simply because it is so different. Unless, of course, one has penetrated to a deeper layer of love, a love no longer needing to cling to kindred, brotherly elements for support, but casting these aside in some curious way, reaching out of the freedom of one's own self across to the freedom of the other person in his dissimilarity. Here the arc is spanned far wider than between kindred spirits, based on finding rather than rediscovery. It stretches from one loneliness to another.

*

No, I can hardly believe there was ever a time in the history of living religion, whether Christian or non-Christian, antique or medieval, when *everyone* had the power to see angels and gods! More than in our own day, I'm sure, and certainly such things were potentially "natural". But surely—in every age—these visionaries were always in fact only a chosen few, marked with special grace, troubled by their gift, regarded askance by the broad masses as either holy or possessed. The universe as a whole has been "closed" ever since the Fall, and these powers, designed for mankind, have been locked and blocked for most people. Only a few did rediscover them in a lawful way, though many did so with the dubious key of magic. When one sees how inadequate man is in dealing with even the most commonplace situations in this world, how little he can discriminate between his fellow men—whatever would happen if he had to cope with all these other phenomena as well? What strength, what integrity, what grace would be needed! And don't you think, too, that some people must *choose* between these two domains?

*

Yes, I've lots of objections to Léon Bloy, despite his many impressive qualities. But what a hater he was!—wild and implacable, and what power of abuse! Strange, don't you think, that Ernst Jünger should comment at length in his war-diaries— along with some admiring observations—how irresistibly Bloy reminded him of Hitler in his paroxysms of rage and his foul and ribald tongue? All this goes against the grain with me, along with his—well, drunkenness—you can't call it anything else—with suffering, in which he knows no bounds. Yet he was undoubtedly a man with great gifts of vision and perception, and charity, too—even in the midst of his orgies of hatred. And much of what he writes about our Lady in his La Salette book is very fine and often goes straight to one's heart: for instance that Mary, weeping, suffering for her people, "is" the Heart of

Jesus—wounded, open. This is so clear, for me, that it seems like "something one ought always to have known". Scheeben already spoke of Mary as "the Heart of the Church"—and if the Church "is" the "form of a slave", the torn, wounded Body of our Lord, then this is perfectly obvious! Or, again, that because the children saw our Lady with a "living Crucifix" on her breast, she is the bride of the Song of Songs: "A bundle of myrrh is my beloved to me: he shall abide between my breasts" —things overpowering in their simplicity, yet, as far as I know, no one ever saw them before or at least thought of expressing them. You could also call the Mourning Lady: the Shekhinah.

But I can't help it, this La Salette book rouses quite a lot of objections as well. For instance that our Lady is reputed to have said in her message to the whole world: "There is no longer anyone"—"*personne*", unequivocal, unconditional!—"among the priesthood and those consecrated to God who can fittingly present the spotless sacrifice." "There are no *âmes généreuses* today who can pray for my people"—and that was 1846, when the saintly Curé d'Ars was still alive, and Don Bosco was already active and a whole crowd of other saints were working in the world (some of whom have already been canonized today, e.g. Pope Pius, Bernadette, Brother Conrad), not forgetting Newman who had just been ordained—Blumhardt the Elder, and certainly lots of others. It's hard to believe that our Lady could have said such things—but I suppose it's inevitable that certain subjective elements crept into the account of the visionary and can't be extricated any more. The actual message— apart from dubious details about Napoleon III, wars predicted (with neither Germany nor Russia mentioned, only France, Spain, England and Italy!)—is fundamentally the same as that of Fatima: penance and prayer—with special stress upon the hallowing of Sunday and of the Name of God, i.e. a damning warning against violation of the Sabbath and against blasphemy. (Just as in Fatima, as far as I know, the emphasis was placed primarily upon impurity and lack of charity.) All these things are very strange. Nor do I very much care for those lengthy reports by Mélanie in the appendix concerning her shabby treatment in Rome (she was indeed treated disgracefully, but at the hands of French prelates, not the Pope). These accounts strike me as so unbelievably eloquent, so rich in words—in both senses!—the journalistic style so very pat, so loquacious—it just doesn't fit into the picture of the taciturn mountain shepherdess who at fourteen knew no word of French, only *patois*, like Bernadette, and at seventeen still couldn't learn her catechism—and from there entered Carmel. And here she is, all of a sudden, writing like a Werfel novel. All very puzzling. For all his mother wit and the way he had of hitting the nail on the head, you couldn't imagine such a report from the pen of, say, the Curé d'Ars.

*

QUESTIONS which touch me particularly reading Julian of Norwich: her most impressive struggle to face and reconcile the frequent apparently glaring contradictions between what she had learnt and what she "saw"—between "what Holy Church teacheth me to believe" and "what our Lord shewed me at this time"—between personal mystical experience and the binding tradition of faith. Sometimes it just wasn't possible and she had "no other answer to the difficulty in this shewing of our Lord's except this: 'What is impossible to thee is not impossible to me'"; at times the contradiction is resolved as merely a question of perspective, things "seen from our earth" being so—but looking quite different "seen by God's eye", etc. But this tension can only be appreciated by someone who knows what the Church means in her concept of Truth, who understands her claim and the claim of her faithful to this Truth, and does not proceed a priori from the assumption that in religious matters everyone can think what he likes as a matter of course, whatever happens to occur to him or fits into his personal scheme.

*

REASON again—no, granted all its admitted dangers and the damage it can do, I still simply can't regard it as "the basic enemy of religion"—or at least only in one specific form, namely fallen *ratio*, reason in anarchy, unredeemed; but I love its Arch-Image so much, and even when clouded it is still the mirror of the Logos—and restored and redeemed it *can* mirror him most brightly. I feel rather like Socrates in Plato's *Phaedrus* fable who rebuked the lowest Eros and then faltered, "hiding his head, because he had reviled Eros and Eros is a god!"—Which is why I'm so keen about the purification and restoration of reason, as much concerned as others are about "the redemption of Eros".

Still it would hardly be fair to suppress the fact that Newman's views on reason were very similar to those of our extremists: that reason, not as it *could* be, but "as it acts in fact and concretely in fallen man . . . actually and historically", tends towards "a simple unbelief", in every religion and in every age. He regarded it as an "all-corroding, all-dissolving element" against which "no truth, however sacred, can stand, in the long run"; intellect, "that universal solvent" (quoted from the *Apologia Pro Vita Sua*). He saw in the Church specifically "the breakwater against the deluge", the only antagonist which has sufficient force and toughness to withstand "the wild living intellect of man". Of course in those days—only a century ago—the Church had not yet fallen a prey to "the sin of the intellect" to the same extent as today: this fact consoles me somewhat, for it shows that maybe it's just a disease of our age after all—widespread and severe though it is—and perhaps we'll get over it in time?

*

YES, I do fear evil spirits, "the powers of the air", as Paul calls them. The Church views spiritualism and occultism with such profound suspicion and aversion precisely because she is aware of these powers, really taking them seriously, making no bones about them, well knowing that they make use of various theories, systems, questions, etc., only as a pretext and "keyhole" for slipping inside a human being. "*What* is it that answers in I Ch'ing?" I once asked NN. "The world-fibre", he told me—but isn't this thoroughly ambiguous, filled with vague powers we cannot distinguish? Of course, as God's children, children of the Church, bearing the seals of baptism and confirmation, fed by the sacraments, we're protected and defended within this most powerful chain-mail. All the same—we ourselves, when we in some way uproot ourselves from the soil of God's love, present these powers with a chink in our "armour of salvation" through which they can penetrate. And who can be so certain that he is not in a state of sin, i.e. that he doesn't invite this situation?

*

WHEN one thinks what Mary Ward herself had in mind, her Institute of the Blessed Virgin Mary has really become rather a heterogeneous set-up. But I must put this delicately—I've no wish to hurt the dears. Mary Ward was a true visionary—a quality which, alas, isn't really shown in the book I wrote about her; for in those days I was too dense to understand this. And all her life long, on every rung of the ladder, she was guided and determined almost entirely by visions and voices. This fact is almost completely hidden by her remarkable fate and nowadays she merely has the reputation of an efficient pioneer of women's education and the lay apostolate. The seventeenth century is altogether a supremely mystical era, but this is lost in the outer layer of noisy political events in all their glaring colour: Thirty Years' War, Turks, *Roi Soleil*, revolution in England, etc. It is the Golden Age of mysticism in France, and of Puritan mysticism, too (foundation of the Quakers!). Mary belongs indubitably to this line. And her own true "heritage" is rooted in this soil—but it seems to have perished utterly in the Institute she founded, submerged in the bustle of merely scholastic activity, etc.

*

IN one of his sermons Newman said roughly the following: that one could credit Christ, i.e. Jesus, with almost all human merits and qualities—only one thing could not be said of him without a feeling of impropriety: that he was clever!! Nowadays practice of reason belongs wholly and exclusively to fallen man in the fallen world. In heaven intelligence will no longer exist. Made sense to me at once, to my joy, the more so since Newman himself was no obscurantist, shrinking from knowledge, but was one of the keenest, most intrepid, versatile minds—a typical intellectual of the highest calibre.

*

P.D. RECENTLY brought me another article by Karl Rahner in *Geist und Leben*—"The Eternal Significance of the Humanity of

Jesus for our Relationship to God". What he reveals here is an issue of the utmost importance: how essential it is for the Christian to recognize a "plural", numinous universe, made up of angels, saints, the dead and demons—which are not "the same" as God. He insists that modern man, i.e. the contemporary Christian, can no longer realize this plurality, regarding all these things merely as "names" for the one mystery of the uncreated God; and that if this "created numinous plurality" ceases to be understood as a reality, the very concept of God will be disfigured and distorted, until it finally devours its own Creation like a vampire. This, so he declares, is our temptation—the counter-temptation to polytheism—but to deny all such powers and figures is just as false, just as ominous as to succumb to them.

Karl Rahner has got a positively inspired "sixth sense", the way he puts his finger on theological "articular points". Reading him, one realizes how true that glorious quotation of Dionysius the Areopagite still is today (cited by Hugo Ball in his book about Byzantine Christianity): "Theology is the rallying point for all endeavours which make life worth living . . . the heart of the peoples and the very core of their enduring vigour. It is the last line of defence upon which all great destinies depend."

*

I SIMPLY can't understand how Christmas can have degenerated like this; for how it has come down in the world! Sometimes I wonder whether in the northern countries the old traditional Yuletide customs haven't gained the upper hand again? Maybe these have, in fact, always predominated in certain circles, merely covered by a thin Christian layer, and where this silver-plating has worn off the old boisterous feast of eating and revelling breaks through uproariously—and on top of that the commercial element! We ought to have the courage to dig in our heels and protest visibly, simply by going on strike. Let the unbelievers have their Yule racket if they want it, they're perfectly entitled to it, but we, as Christians, ought to demonstrate that what we are celebrating is something very different. The Christmas liturgy is so great, so austere—so utterly unsuited to a baby idyll and family revels.

*

I HAVE never considered before that the Son of God also took upon himself the complete humiliation—the indignity, if you like—of prebirth—by no means only "the likeness of man". During this foetal period he looked like some queer amphibian creature, tailed and furry, a tiny monkey—grotesque and eerie— *non horruisti Virginis uterum*. Well, and then it came to my mind: the Church is an embryo as well—fruit in her own womb—the Church, too, has ugly, repellent features, human and sub-human, even demonic. Her true face will only be revealed in its beauty and perfection when "her days shall be fulfilled", when she, the Great Woman, the Great Sign, can at last give birth to the Child threatened by the dragon. Seen thus, the Body of the Church in its slave's form which makes us all suffer so much is not only inevitable, but also profoundly significant. The "second Incarnation" in the womb of the Church seems to be following very much the same course as that in the womb of the Blessed Virgin.

*

"ZEAL for souls"—this, too, is a very ticklish business. I used to be very keen about "conquering" people for God, for their salvation—quite sincerely, yes, but via a personal attachment to myself. Tactics in which we were indeed schooled as a fundamental element of Jesuit strategy (Mary Ward surely offers the most obvious proof!). I practised such methods—for years— believing them to be good and right. Knowing me today, you'll find it hard to believe that once I ran after people who didn't mean anything to me, indeed whom I even disliked, "courting" them, lavishing favours and attentions on them—simply to "win" them.

At last I began to have serious doubts about the morality of this attitude—from the human angle—until I became aware that it was a sort of deception, no matter how "religious" the motives. Perhaps because in the meantime I'd learnt something about true Eros, true friendship, because I had learnt to take both these things seriously, reverently, and just couldn't go on making use of them as war-paint, merely as a means to an end. Perhaps because I had gradually come to see how offending, how deeply humiliating it is to be treated like this oneself, and then one day to see through the "apostle's" little game—that I suddenly no longer had the heart to go on duping people in this fashion, for their own good. Anyway I just couldn't continue in this way, and gave up. Of course I know very well that this attitude isn't good enough either, and that there must be a third approach here, as in all things, beside and beyond these opposite poles: after the naïve, well-meaning, purposeful pose of friendship and affection, after the resigned withdrawal from this "line"—true infused Agape, embodied in Eros, *lawfully* taking the shape of friendship and love, since it is more, not less, than these natural forms. I know quite a lot of people who can do this. But of course it is a charism, not to be obtained by one's own effort, and not to be pretended either—but probably one ought to pray for this gift day and night, even more than one prays for true and loyal faith. It is surely a sin simply to throw in the sponge.

*

TODAY I'm going on spinning my thread in our talk about friendship—in honour of St Mary Magdalene, the woman who —may I say so?—personified Eros in the life of our Lord, as St John represented it as his friend. Indeed in Umbria they call her "*Amica Domini*". In matters of love I rely very little on my "Catholic culture"—in this particular sphere it isn't sufficiently "initiated", and I prefer to stick to Plato—and to myself. The thesis that Eros plays a part in every sexual attachment, even the most base, seems probable—though with certain reservations! For me Eros is present wherever the attraction is *genuine*, no matter on what level—the phenomenon you describe rather well as "revolving around the sun of the 'Thou'"? And it is present—this magnetic attraction, this impulse, wheeling around its object, wooing—even in the lowest forms of Eros, at least in the biological order. It's that other view I'm questioning: that this attraction, this allurement, is already a "genuine" turning to the *other* person—I think its object is usually first and foremost self. Plato calls Eros a robber—and rightly so, since he is the son of poverty: but he is a son of wealth as well, and as such he wants to share, to give. But I suppose this only applies to the higher levels.

308

Agape has higher and lower levels, too, and the highest would be that which would succeed in embodying itself as Eros—yes, that's it exactly, it would "assume" Eros as its flesh, finding expression in Eros, in its force, in its forms. For if there's one thing I *don't* believe, it's that wide-spread "Christian" notion that "Agape is something quite different", i.e. that it needs must create an extra special form for its divine quality, a form non-existent here on earth. No, I refuse to believe this, but rather (and as far as I know this is even theologically correct!) that precisely here the maxim *"gratia supponit naturam"* applies, and divine powers become manifest *inside* natural powers, not distinct from these. Isn't it evident enough in saints with a special gift for Eros, such as Teresa, Bernard, Francis, Catherine, Suso, Newman, and probably a whole crowd of others? This was, in fact, the theme of that very first little book of mine about Elizabeth of Hungary: "The most human thing about Elizabeth was that she was a great lover, a veritable genius of the lavishing heart: and that is the exact formula for her holiness, too: a great lover, a genius of the heart, lavishing love."

In the saints, then, I'd say Agape dons Eros—and it is this which makes their charity so warm, delighted and delighting, so full of joy and tenderness. But—and *this* is the crux: who is capable of this? In most of us charity just hasn't got such a foundation, such material "to inform". In most cases it must be content with "social impulses" and moral attitudes for a vehicle and stuff to mould—which is why, even when genuinely inspired and potent, Agape so often takes the cold, gaunt, straitened (Berdyaev calls it "glazed") form we term "charity": Agape as "a duty", as "heroic achievement", turning to one's neighbour, yes, but not spontaneously, by effort. And yet, to my mind, not only is this way more usual but we couldn't do without it—for where would we be if we were forced to depend solely upon impulses welling straight from the heart to keep the world going? We'd just starve, most of us, on every level of existence. Which is why, to my mind, this respectable, tiresome, strenuous "will-power Agape"—(admirable, and a blessing as well, of course!)—is indispensable, since it hides the scarcity of Eros and makes up for what is wanting. It's as useless to try to hold our shattered world together with natural Eros as to drag tree-trunks along by silken ribbons or build houses with the stalks of flowers. A pity, I know, but that's what experience has taught me. Really turning towards the other person means turning to him *as himself*, as a whole, not just one part of him—his need, his problem—and not just with one part of my self either—my "interest", my readiness to help! Often enough we're capable of very little more, I know, but God will surely accept us here too in our wretchedness. All the same, I've long since ceased to believe the classic ascetics (including Francis de Sales) who maintain that love is more *precious* in God's eyes the more it springs from reason, faith and resolve, the less it is based merely on natural inclination. On the contrary, I feel that the less reasoned love is, the less deliberate, the more naïve and ingenuous, the more akin it is to the love of God, and therefore more pleasing to him. And if someone *is* taken in, made a fool of, not only by his simplicity, his innocence, but also by his loving-kindness—I think this finer than "keeping on the safe side" out of prudence and caution.

*

I'M only too well aware that people like ourselves must appear more as a muddle and a tangle than as clear-cut figures. How cruelly we must stretch the skin we were born and bred in to take in so many "novelties", wrenching our mental skeleton almost out of joint—anything but a harmonious picture! Every sleek synthesis would still be a falsification at this stage. The elements must blend together organically, must grow together into new structures, the shape as yet probably unknown to us— and such growth takes time! That is the fate of our generation. What the "keepers of the Faith" achieved in the past, externally, by pressure and compulsion as well, with ghetto walls, by authority verging on terror, with frontiers and barriers explicitly guarded to preserve the heritage of faith: all this we must now accomplish *from within*, yet at the same time remaining open, ravenously, passionately open to receive!—each of us alone with his solitary, agonizing decision. Moreover this only really begins after one has come to recognize for what they are (at least to a large extent) the "exterior" husks such as filial dependence, conservatism, the weight of inertia, aversion to novelty: painfully, as though peeling off one's skin, stripping it away, layer after layer. . . . And then, in this sore and vulnerable nakedness, one must build up one's own authentic resistance, in real counter-pressure against the *genuine* threats to the substance of faith, the disrupting, undermining, destructive elements present in these new impulses—beside so much that is precious and vital. Now that this counter-pressure, these strong defences are no longer "provided" from outside, one must provide them from one's personal resources, making hairspring decisions all the time where to open and surrender, where to shut up and hold on. For you must do both. But that's just it: the just proportion between "razing the bastions" and maintaining the frontiers, between stripping oneself and preserving things—this *proportion* is the supremely difficult feat for people like us, and certainly very few can really bring it off.

How good that beyond and apart from these inevitable struggles for innovations and renovations there are also people like Padre Pio—living unperturbed from the glowing Centre, shining out like beacons—personifying the heart and the blood of the Church, not like us poor "joints", almost always at breaking-point, yet still having to hold out. How good that we are fed from such sources.

*

I'm delighted to have your account of your visit to Padre Pio. For I must admit I was uncomfortable! The "visibility" of holiness is such a mystery—for me an impenetrable mystery. It seems to me that it is by no means part of holiness, a component to be taken for granted, but rather a supplementary grace, granted now and again for special divine purposes. Isn't the life of Jesus himself, hidden away so long in Nazareth, the very best proof of this? It would seem that he (and Mary! and Joseph!) was not a particularly "radiant" person, and no *"fama sanctitatis"* clung to him—no one even expected great things of him. On the contrary, when he returned as the famous prophet, people who had grown up with him, or had watched him growing up exclaimed: "What! He, of all people! Whoever would have dreamt of such a thing!" And, that time in the Temple in Jerusalem the Gentiles came to Philip asking: "We desire to

311

see Jesus"—which implies that they did not know him instantly, singling him out of the group—"That *can* only be him!" The kiss of Judas is further proof that they could well have mistaken his identity without a signal of some kind—though surely the Temple police must have seen him often enough among his band of followers—yet apparently they didn't know exactly. . . . How hard it is to realize this!

But the stories about St Francis in fact tell much the same sort of thing. Unless he deliberately *chose* to make himself conspicuous by some dramatic gesture, no one noticed him among his companions, begging his way through foreign lands. The women gave him less at their doors than Brother Masseo, for instance, because Francis was "small, ugly and unprepossessing". And when a saint was an impressive figure, he would probably have been imposing "naturally", without holiness, by his stature, nobility, intelligence, etc. In fact it seems to be the very rarest thing that the *heavenly* light does shine out, flooding its bearers. I don't think this has anything whatever to do with the "rank" of a saint, simply with his particular mission. Mary, for instance, was never "visible" her whole life long. And the posthumous visibility of the saints is a puzzling phenomenon indeed, and varies enormously. Little Thérèse emerged from complete obscurity to world-wide publicity; but Vincent Ferrer, for instance, one of the most prominent, most spectacular and dramatic saints in the whole history of the Church seems barely to have outlived his own lifetime. Today he's as good as forgotten. And in the Curé d'Ars the baffling thing is his personal insignificance and pneumatic fame—simultaneously. It would seem that it's really a matter of luck (what a trivial word!) whether one can recognize a saint as such—not merely as a "personality", if he happens to be this as well—whether one *may* recognize him.

*

I was thinking last night that almost all our modern hagiographical studies are retrospective, i.e. merely historical, reconstructing the bygone mortal appearance and behaviour of the saint as accurately as possible. So far so good. But something gets lost in the process, namely what the living Church has almost always seen *beyond* the figures of these perfect ones: that they (not all of them, but still quite a number) have *become something quite different* in heaven for the pilgrim still journeying on earth, a symbol, "a sign in the sky", pure transparencies, transmitting a message of which they themselves were not aware. In early times, certainly, but in those days this way of "beholding" things was natural, a living reality. What, for example, has Sebastian *become*, the officer of the Roman guard? What has grown out of that rather uninteresting figure Hubert (Eustace), and what of Agnes, or Cecily or George? The fate of St Agnes, for instance, wasn't, in fact, so very different from that of Maria Goretti—but how different an image did the imagination of the Church mould out of it! We ought to learn to see the more recent figures like this too, meditating them, "translating" them: what message has God to give us through these figures? What do they "portray"? What "word of God" do they personify? Historical facts, circumstances and events are important merely as letters in the alphabet: of course one has to know them, they must be investigated, meticulously examined, integrated, etc.—but after that we must really begin to "read". But most people stop at this point.

*

FROM the Aztec sun myth: "The Lord of the Sun flung himself into a fire that his heart might fly up into the heavens, a light to lighten the world. And so the sun was made. That is why it was thought that only human hearts were a fitting sacrifice to 'hold' him in the sky."

Another curious discovery: for these early Mexicans the supreme Deity, beyond their gods, was called "The Two", and took the form of a pair of identical figures placed opposite one another, like mirrors. Really not two at all, then, but "Three"?

*

I KNOW you (and lots of other people) think I'm too "Right-wing", "Papist", conformist, old-fashioned, too submissive to the clergy. In one of my last letters I told you that the Church has been both father and mother to me. I can put it even more precisely: I knew no other father but the priests, and my true brothers were "the theologians" (as we used to call our seminarists in the Youth Movement). How characteristic that I should have married from the Oratory in N.! I remember asking Father X.: "as I've no parents, no home", and so I spent the night before in their guest room, and our wedding breakfast after the ceremony was held there too. Only a symbol, I know, but very significant all the same. And so, for all my increasing remoteness, independence and criticism, I can never face priests, even very average priests, without a feeling of deep gratitude, devotion and reverence. For to them—after God himself—I owe the knowledge and experience of God gained in my life up till now. So much and so precious, really the marrow of my existence. Narrow as their "map" may seem to you, they taught me to walk in the Kingdom of God, to wander and to behold—and to long for things they could only intimate. And if here and there I now cross the frontier where their map ends, it's to them I owe the way up to this frontier.

Can you understand this? Which is why I'm so vitally engaged in discussions about our religious orders, actively, personally concerned when people talk about the blind alley in which so many religious get stuck, etc., etc.—this really matters to me. For I am flesh of their flesh, part of their destiny as well, sharing it all in painful, loving responsibility, even if they were no longer to "count" in what is to come. I'm as bound up with them as you are with the "pagan Christians"; or like Newman, whose heart was torn for years for his brothers of the Oxford Movement whom he could not take with him on his new way. Of course I know that precursors must always go ahead—and they must leave the others to God, they can't remain behind on their account. But it is real separation, a severing, and it hurts—very much.

Yet I know that this separation is not leading me away from the Church, nor from the Church of those left behind, but rather further in. Not least of all because I must fight so hard, so urgently, sincerely for almost every little bit which is changing before my eyes—nothing is surrendered lightly. Even if the substance is rarely at stake, merely certain aspects. But these, too, after all belong to my "mother tongue" and their roots go deep. Believe me, these pangs are more severe than the pain of the worst stage of my illness. Indeed there's no comparison. But

I gladly accept them in gratitude, knowing that something will be born of them. Moreover these are advent pangs, the pain not merely individual, but enacted within me as in a member of the Church—the Church of today, which is as much *my* concern as the Church of tomorrow is that of the reformers. In me the present Church is changing, if only in one tiny fragment, into the Church to come—that is the nucleus and meaning of my destiny.

*

JUST imagine, for the first time in my life I've read the whole of the Purgatory tract (Catherine of Genoa)—usually one is only served the middle section. And now I'm meditating upon it, all the time. It contains—expressed with most enviable, positively Latin brevity—an entire "doctrine of the soul", ranging from Paradise to Heaven. Catherine's Purgatory hangs, as it were, between the first and second Paradise. What I find most exciting of all is the *exact* parallel between her conception of the soul and that of Julian of Norwich—which, for me, throws a most revealing light upon Julian's vision of the Lord and the Servant. Since they were both "unlettered" women, yet at the same time under monastic spiritual direction, I conclude that this doctrine of the soul must have corresponded with general tradition, at least into the mid-sixteenth century: this conception of the soul as "queenly and divine" by nature, i.e. at its creation, dropping into the dark stream of original sin only by its union with the body. In baptism it is raised again out of this entanglement, pursuing then its earthly course towards a *second* perfection—with Purgatory as the final and most intense phase. Put another way this would amount to a repetition of the Fall in the creation of every human individual, though not, as in Adam's case, actively, by personal guilt, but purely passively. (Julian's vision of the servant who only falls into the ravine and "taketh full great hurt", getting himself dirty in the process, because he was running "in great haste, for love, to do his lord's will"!) Maybe I'm expressing this quite wrongly—I've scarcely begun thinking it out, it's just dawning, as yet barely outlined. Certainly it is nothing new, merely no longer clearly part of our present-day religious awareness. But I think I already see of which formulae and ciphers of the doctrine known to us this insight forms a part.

*

IN conversations with converts and genuine critics of the Church —not the unfair carpers, but those who are earnestly concerned —I invariably feel, to my sorrow and shame, how very much a part of it all one is—though one sees and acknowledges these defects as well and voices one's disapproval—how terribly one, i.e. I myself, am part of everything we censure and refute, all the things which go against the grain for us as well as for the others, things with which they hate being associated. But I'm part of all this, stamped with the same decay, bearing the mark of the same senility, limitations and rank growths in the Church. I'm steeped to the very bones in it, I grew up fed by this food, and was moulded at the most impressionable age in this form. I can only "withdraw" consciously, deliberately—yet still remaining part, and this can never be reversed. And I must readily accept this. For not only am I a child of the "Great Church" like the late-comers who have joined her of their own free will, unhampered by inheritance, I am a Catholic by birth, a cradle Catholic—child of this impoverished Church of the twentieth century, so disgracefully degenerate, in many ways so senile. One is a Catholic today *also* in the same sense that a Jew is a Jew—with the difference that a Jew can "step out" of the tragic hereditary guilt of Israel in history by baptism—but for us there's no stepping out any more. And in the most passionate, painful, burning zeal for reform we're in fact fighting and damning what we still are, or at least were—ourselves in certain aspects. Whereas the others need only fight from outside.

*

I'VE been thinking a lot lately that there's a certain historical similarity between parapsychology (and what is roughly termed occultism) and the development of anatomy (as a science): for this, too, was illegal in its beginnings, only possible by indulging in downright sacrilege: body-snatching, desecration of corpses, knavery of all kinds and petty crimes— bribery and corruption of officials on all levels, down to cemetery keepers and hearse drivers—and presumably none of it without the same sort of blackmail and denunciation among the accomplices themselves which I imagine must go on these days among smugglers and drug-traffickers. The "resurrection men" must have been sheer criminals, the doctors who made use of them reckless dare-devils, adventurers with an almost demonic curiosity and taste for things forbidden, caring nothing for respectability or reverence for the dead, for convention or tradition, law or commandment. And yet, in time, this very dubious business developed into a perfectly normal, respectable branch of academic study, the source of valuable and important information, knowledge rich in blessings. Parapsychology, etc. seems to me to follow a somewhat parallel course: the same bold venture to penetrate into a sphere, strictly taboo, rousing the spirits of the dead if they can, forcing them to speak and answer questions, etc., conjuring up ghosts, producing other phenomena of this kind by all sorts of arts. The same thing is happening in depth-psychology, in which the soul is forced open in its most secret and sealed recesses, dissected, X-rayed and photographed in mental states beyond the range of consciousness itself. The paradox lies in the fact that on the one hand secular and clerical authority had the right to forbid and were justified in forbidding such excesses, suppressing them from the start for a variety of very sensible and proper reasons—yet, on the other hand, God himself just goes on deliberately creating natures born to be smugglers and poachers, adventurers and pirates, who jump all barriers—even the most lawful ones—thus discovering things which would not have been revealed by "proper" means—yet still, so it would seem, were intended for man by God.

*

For his "Spiritual" Church Joachim of Fiore foresaw the continuance of the Papacy (much modified), but the bishops were to disappear. If I think at all of "the Church to come", then I hope and pray above all for a revival, indeed resurrection of the episcopal office. To my mind it is still a prisoner of its almost thousand-year long disastrous fusion with temporal power. Strange—only a few years ago I thought the Emperor Otto I just marvellous and was full of admiration for his genius in raising the bishops to *Reichsfürsten*—princes of the realm—thus securing an unshakeable foundation for his Empire. Politically it was a brilliant idea to counterbalance the incessant clan and hereditary feuds between his tribal dukes by a stable block of princes who would serve the Emperor without dynastic or political interests (without?—what about all the brothers, nephews and cousins?). Yet I can imagine no way in which a mortal enemy of the Church in all craft and cunning could have fastened a worse fate upon her. For then began her thousand-year Babylonian captivity, far worse than the brief imprisonment of the Popes in Avignon. And not all the many magnificent and doubtless also holy bishops of the Middle Ages and even the Baroque era can outweigh this. For how often was their charismatic office as *pastors* overshadowed, indeed frequently rendered impossible, by their *temporal* mission and worldly achievements, for all their importance to the *Abendland*, to Western Europe! And even today—all this "Your Excellency" nonsense, etc., i.e. the *false* distance of purely secular rank separating not only the bishop from the faithful, but also the bishop from his clergy—isn't this a last rather evil relic? In England and America, and in the Latin countries, things would seem to be better. Every single bishop, no matter how good he may be personally, must fight against the tremendous weight of a *false* tradition still part of the very atmosphere. For this really does exist, burying what is genuine tradition, washing it away, cropping up all the time in between. A miracle, to my mind, that the Holy Ghost manages to shimmer through at all, now and again. In Joachim's day this rank growth had apparently fused so inextricably with the episcopal office that he could only visualize the end of the one as the disappearance of the other. A transmutation into something like our present-day form was beyond his imagination. But even today how much needs still to fall away or rather grow anew before the true image can once again emerge. The bishop manifest once more as "the angel of his Church", as Möhler recognized him at a time of the crassest fossilization— the final suppression of the Church of the Holy Roman Empire.

*

I'VE just finished a (for me) very important book about the parents of the Little Flower: a detailed chronicle of her parents and sisters, lovingly pieced together into a mosaic by a French Franciscan. It confirms my thesis 100 per cent: that everything claimed by her super-heralds as her direct inspiration, her unique originality, in fact stemmed from inheritance, upbringing and repetition—down to the very last detail. I'd take on any bet: if I were to publish a collection of passages from letters of the Martin mother and the four sisters as "new discoveries" from Thérèse's pen—let's say in some periodical!—not one reader who did not already know this book would ever doubt their authenticity or suspect any mystification. Thérèse is indistinguishable—a homogeneous bit of family tradition. Most interesting for me is the recognition how alien and remote this "bourgeois" piety of the late nineteenth century has become, even for cultivated contemporary Catholic writers—a veritable *terra incognita*; otherwise this so wide-spread legend of Thérèse's uniqueness could never have grown up. It's as though one were today to ascribe the "invention" of Romanticism to one of its very last representatives. From the hagiographic point of view the whole phenomenon grows more and more baffling. And even psychologically I just cannot understand how the older sisters, having witnessed at home the more than heroic suffering and death of their mother (she had cancer of the breast), could not only have built up the relatively far shorter and less horrible illness of their sister into a martyrdom par excellence never before recorded—but furthermore drew no comparison whatever to the mother they loved so dearly—I cannot remember one single allusion to her suffering in the whole mass of documentary evidence. Always their implacable bitter resentment at the alleged "cruelty" of the prioress in permitting Thérèse's hard treatment of her own person for so long—austerity far less than that tolerated by their adored father in the case of his wife. What's more, these same sisters, now unable to forgive the prioress for not having put *"la petite"* to bed and made a fuss about her the very first time she coughed blood, thought nothing of dragging their half-dead mother—of her own wish—through the streets to a distant church, until she almost fainted. It really is a very odd story, and I must confess I can't contemplate the beginnings of this cult without a slight shudder. What an uncanny "family-mindedness" was involved in it all, barely Christian any more!—what strange shiftings and lapses of memory were not mobilized in the systematic propaganda employed for the one goal in view! As soon as one puts Thérèse back in her frame she disappears completely, like a little flower inside a thick wreath, one can no longer see what is her individual character and what is a family trait. But they've taken her out, removing her to a splendid isolation which has shifted the perspective, altered all the proportions, changing the whole picture. Surely this is one of the strangest triumphs of individualism and clannishness in the history of the Church?

*

IT seems a sort of law that with controllable regularity the Church should permit the very enemy she is fighting outside to penetrate simultaneously inside, by infection and infiltration, copying him, so that at times she appears almost as his faithful image. In their struggle against the ambitions of the medieval Emperors, the Popes became super-Emperors, aspiring to universal world domination. During the Renaissance the Curia grew into the largest and most typical Renaissance court; in the battle against the Reformation Catholic piety at once developed certain Calvinist features, as well as Lutheran traits (the "dark" image of man); in the late eighteenth century the leaders of the Church adopted Enlightenment and Rationalism, the nineteenth century witnessed a penetration of its materialistic, positivist cult of science and success which found its expression in a certain kind of "apologetics", together with "quantitative piety". No wonder that today we must resist the demons of collectivism, centralization, bureaucracy, totalitarian ideals, the managerial society, false socialization = levelling, within our walls.

As the vigilant and responsible Christians we would like to be, it's our primary task to be on our guard against these subliminal (Rahner calls them "subcutaneous") infections, and to find appropriate remedies and antidotes. There are plenty of other people engaged with "the enemy from without". Our task is all the harder since this "adultery with the *Zeitgeist*", as Anne Catherine Emmerich called it, will always have the majority on its side, for it has all the trumps in its hand—all the attraction and fascination of what is new and topical at its command. And if you speak up about this, or take a firm stand, you're branded at once as reactionary, hide-bound, a stick-in-the-mud, refusing to face up to life, etc., and, what's worse, you begin to feel yourself senile and sterile—a sore temptation I know only too well.

*

For me America is a symbol: symbol of the sort of "modernism" I cannot endorse or acknowledge, and can only accept with inner protest: not her theories and ideologies, for these are basically European, but their product, what would seem to be their fully developed fruit: a world devoid of tradition, born without roots out of a conglomeration of all the nations of the earth: counterpole to all ancient, organic worlds—*Abendland*, Antiquity, China, India, irrupting into them all, calling them all in question, critically. Indeed America, for me, is like a huge "retort baby"—yet still conceived upon the mysterious soil of a primitive race, virtually unknown to us, a race which had practically died out before it could be explored, before it even knew itself. Compared with this, Russia is actually a more kindred phenomenon, more comprehensible, sinister though she is.

*

I think I see exactly where the fascination, i.e. the spark of truth in Manicheism lay—that arrogant and grim abhorrence of matter and its limitations—the uncanny glimmer of truth in its doctrine that the Spirit has "fallen" into flesh. For me the answer to my own problem is expressed nowhere more succinctly, in its quintessence, than in the verse of the *Te Deum*: "*non* horruisti *virginis uterum*". If *that* wasn't falling—a sheer drop down below, into lowliness, into the ig-noble, let's admit it, messy—into the entrails of a woman, confined, dark and hidden. "*Non horruisti virginis uterum*." One must say these words to oneself out loud in temptation, when one is revolted and disgusted by the Church in her "form of a slave". And then, of course, one starts to remember the other connotations of "the virgin's womb": sealed garden, heart of the blossom and all that. Both aspects belong to the mystery of the earthly, not the

heavenly Church; we experience them by turns and must somehow cope with them both—and submit to both. But to me the
most wonderful thing of all is that the virgin's womb means first
and foremost an advent state, the way to birth. For not only as
individuals are we destined for rebirth: the Church too has her
carnal, mortal body "sown in corruption" for whom the promise
is equally valid that it will be transfigured to "the body of his
glory". But it's *this* poor, wretched body which shall be transfigured, this and no other more ideal form, unreal, abstract—
we cannot jump over it and can only be transformed ourselves as
its cells. No, I don't believe, as XX. so often hints, that it's my
temptation—the "home temptation", an infantile longing to be
"lovingly bedded in a warm nest". This may be true for others,
but for people like us the real temptation is just the opposite:
the desire to stand face to face with God in splendid isolation,
solus cum solo, far from the madding crowd. One must keep on
reminding oneself emphatically that God intended the *whole*, his
holy nation, the entire Vine. One loaf made up of countless
grains—each of us merely one grain, one drop, one single grape
in the cluster; and only as such do we participate in the Transubstantiation, the change—left to our own devices we would
simply end up as ashes, waste products. And so I can't believe
in any prophet who seeks to break away from this whole, content with a handful of disciples of his own—and in no "vocation" which could authorize this. Of course I believe at the same
time in solitude—but solitude *within* the community, sur-
rounded, upheld by the community—a painful but essential
counterpoise against collectivism, against uniformity; representing the "counter-principle" which must exist precisely within
the whole—so that it may remain "whole", sound.

*

I've a picture of Little Thérèse in front of me as I write—not
little at all. It's odd, but at the same time illuminating, to be
writing about her under the gaze of this strangely reserved,
proud face with its penetrating eyes and that faintly ironic smile
—a good yardstick, at once a spur and a curb.

*

READING Joachim of Fiore I'm beginning to realize something extremely difficult to express in words: that there are two kinds of time—horizontal and vertical. To the first belongs what we call progress, evolution, etc. A worm-like body, perpetually losing its hind "limbs", as it were, while it goes on growing "ahead". In other words the earlier phases of its development are ignored, simply dropped, lost en route; the only thing which is "real" is what in fact exists at the moment, what is "there", and this, too, is continually moving on towards further growth. But in "vertical time" things develop organically like a plant—never for a moment can the stalk be parted from the root, the blossom from the stalk, that would mean death: never can the past be excluded, discarded as unnecessary. Yet all the time new things are turning up—genuine in themselves, wholly distinct from what has gone before. This, to my mind, is how Joachim foresaw the growth of God's Kingdom in its three phases. Of course such growth takes place within time, all growth as such being a temporal process—yet such time is not chronological, it cannot be fixed by dates. That Joachim in fact tried to do this, falling a victim to the hobby of his day for juggling with numbers, etc. strikes me as his weakest side. Yet this was surely his own personal limitation, subjective, never really part of the structure of his vision as such. 1260 is a concept of horizontal time, "now" and "once" and "later" are valid within vertical time as well.

These stretches of time are diverse yet simultaneous, for within the Church there are always certain individuals and groups already embodying what is to come, or still personifying the past: what is important is the proportion between the representatives of these eras. What's more, each individual Christian passes through the three "Kingdoms" in his personal development: yet this is by no means a private, subjective and therefore unimportant process, rather it is THE CHURCH which is progressing within him. It is her development which both bears and impels the growth of each individual, urging it forward—and the other way round too. And "from God's view" maybe this wave-pattern mirrors in some mysterious way the workings of the Blessed Trinity in man—which, I suppose, is what Joachim in fact had in mind. This is no toning down of "*Stirb und*

*Werde",** of the essential withering and disappearance of so much—as sheer necessity: the husks, the skins in all three phases which are continually being embodied. And all the time the body this process creates is growing old, withered, rigid— to be rejuvenated once more. No different from the human body in its various phases. That's how it grows.

*

FOR me, as for so many people today, moral theology has become more and more an indispensable but somewhat questionable structure patched together out of widely diverse materials, like a carpet made up of silk, wool, straw, gold and hair: biblical and philosophical components, Greek, Jewish, Roman, German, purely abstract stuff, as well as logical consequences and the richest human experience; many honest attempts somehow or other to reconcile what is valid in the morality of many and various peoples, ages and cultures with its own first principles, incorporating it as far as possible. And all this must be achieved in the fulfilment of the Church's difficult vocation to summon the faithful to perfection and holiness in a corrupt and disordered world *and yet* to be "the advocate of our frailty"—still concerned with saving the minimum, while keeping the summit of perfection in view—an impossible undertaking really, and therefore a truly heroic venture!

The questionable aspects are as clear to me as to anyone. On the other hand, ever since the campaign against moral theology started in certain quarters, with the battle-cry of "situation morals" to relegate the whole structure in one contemptuous sweep to the scrap-heap of Jewish legalism and pagan ethics, ever since then something has flared up in my heart, and I *know* that for all its short-comings it is an irreplaceable treasure, granted by God, even if built up from frail and often ambivalent human materials. And it's our task to dig down, fervently, lovingly, humbly, to retrieve the store of gold hidden under all the packing and deformations, separating it from the rest, showing the difference. Not in the wish to make things easier, but to reach a closer understanding of the "Way", which is Christ. In this sense I *love* the Law because for me it is the

* "*Stirb und Werde*" = "Die and relive", a household word with Goethe.

earthly form of God's will, just as dogma is the earthly form of God's truth—slave's forms, both of them, yet manifest. Legalism, as such, the law as a fetish, obedience to the law *not* for God's sake—all this is so alien to me, so impracticable, that it's a real effort not to think of such things as mere polemical constructions.

*

CONVERTS find it hard to understand how intensely Catholic readers are schooled, even from nursery days, to ask instantly when confronted by any kind of religious statement: "Do I *have* to believe that?" The notion of religious ideas and opinions as not obligatory, as submitted to individual judgment, as wholly or partially "right"—or perhaps not—seems barely to exist among us any more. A very dangerous state of affairs. Which is why so few people are even dimly aware, for instance, that various lines and streams of tradition in fact exist alongside one another. We grow up believing that on every point there is only one rigidly binding tenet (for what do we ever hear about the history of dogma?), and in contrast to this a heap of entirely irrelevant private opinions which one needn't, indeed shouldn't listen to. That's what makes us so arrogant, intolerant—and lazy.

*

WHAT does the Church actually mean for me? What is my answer, my *"sentire cum Ecclesia"*? Not stability in law and order, not the world's spiritual treasury, the Ark of culture, the Mother of the True West, the last bulwark of tradition and all the other things to which NN. is so fond of attributing my attachment to the Church—no, all that could drop away and nothing would be changed. How simple, how uncomplicated, how direct this bond in fact is—a relationship of love, nothing else. I'm really not a bit "mystically-minded"—and when people come telling me—like G.S. only yesterday—about "the prayer of quiet", long hours of nightly meditation, etc., it just staggers me, I look at it rather sadly from afar, with respect, as not for the likes of me. And although I've done my best for more than thirty years, I still have only a shamefully meagre, poor and colourless "picture of Christ", as far as the historic figure of Jesus is concerned—and perhaps this will never change. There's simply nothing I can do about it. But it has pleased God to reveal himself and his Son, truly his countenance, to me in the Church—in the shape of the meanest slave. Here I really see and touch him, here I meet him, experience him, live with him. And submission, compliance, obedience to the Church in my case has nothing to do with "objective" delight in order and solidarity—but solely with love. Must love not strive to accept the beloved in his actual epiphany, as ordained by God, taking this as it is, the Church with all her blemishes and wrinkles, with all the incomprehensible malformations, mutilations and scars? with a sharply critical eye and in sore pain at it all, yet always on one's knees and in complete *acceptance*?

This is a pure gift, pure grace: I haven't struggled for it, it is something which has been put into me and which I must guard. By nature I've even got a fundamental, deep-seated resentment against the very names and notions of order, duty and the like: I've never quite got over this complex: I "trembled too long before their diabolical distortions", as Baader puts it, at home and in the petty narrowness of our boarding schools. (A palmist once told me my hand bore "the mark of the prisoner" like a scar!)

It was reason which taught me, late enough, to acknowledge and honour authority and the like as components without which man's world could not be constructed. Emotionally I still twitch irritably, rebelliously at the very sound of these words.

*

I'm just reading Sholem Asch's book about Christ, *The Nazarene*. It touches my innermost being, reaching the very root of my faith. Rabbi Jeshuah ben Joseph—yes, I can address him this way, too. How the Gospel comes alive, how full of colour it is! You feel you are there yourself, in the midst of it all. In reality we modern Catholics are all of us—to a greater or lesser extent—Monophysites in sentiment. That naïve question of one of the girls in my Bible-reading group, for instance, when we were discussing the Ascension story: "So now, of course, he's just God and nothing else?"—the Docetic interpretation in fact: the Lord merely as "God veiled", barely concealed in a phantasmal human body, all-knowing, omnipotent, suppressing, as it were, this knowledge and power every moment by a deliberate effort.

But, after all, it's asking a great deal of anyone to envisage the figure of Christ in its immense multiplicity: the Second Person, the Logos, the Wisdom of the Father, the Transfigured Lord, the Head of the Universe—and the Son of Man, Jeshuah ben Miriam! Each single aspect so profound, so rich that one could spend a whole lifetime caught up—held up—in its contemplation, to the exclusion of all the others.

*

I've spent the whole day—with a kind of disgusted fascination—going through the official documents concerning Anne Catherine Emmerich *before* her meeting with Brentano: reports by the various doctors, records of commissions of inquiry, statements by priests set to watch her, interrogations of clergy, relations, former fellow-nuns, girlhood friends; the diary kept, at the instructions of the Vicar-General, by her ex-confessor. My general impression: depression. How narrow, petty, how fusty, musty and measly—how very nasty, all of it! It brings me back once again to that same old problem of mine: what were the saints really like? (But—*was* she a saint?). I'm still a long way from realizing in my heart all the things I explained so neatly, so wisely with my mind in the book I called *The Church Incarnate*.* In reality I'm still haunted by the longing, as unreasonable, as it is unsatisfied, to find perfect man in the saints, perfect in his *nature*, not only morally, aesthetically as well—I want to see *gods*! And it seems there's no getting over this yearning—at least for me. The image of man as he could be, as he should be, is branded so deeply within me that the sight of his reality shatters and grieves me each time anew. I'm resigned to the fact that I can never be such myself, but when others in whom I expect to find it turn out to be failures too, then I'm floored, disappointed—I feel it to be a bit of confounded bad luck! People really living in God, truly dedicated to him surely

* Ida Friederike Görres, *Die leibhaftige Kirche*, 1950.

must—so I think—be transparent, radiant, from top to toe, whole = holy. And this is just how I feel now about Anne Catherine Emmerich: it's there all right, the purity of intention, the shining quality—and beside it all the typical low-class features of the born-servant type, sly and fawning on the gentry, easily hurt, enjoying complaining and being pitied, wheedling all round, which can't be done without a good deal of dissembling. Everyone who listened to her believed he was her chosen confidant, the one and only to whom she was disclosing "everything", whereas in fact she was playing off one against the other all the time, often only from weakness, under pressure—how typically feminine! And yet one has to admit in the end: there's nothing actually *evil* about any of it—as little "wicked" as bad breath.

*

I read in a rather shrewd English book the other day that *the* characteristic of the Jews is their perpetual preoccupation with what is to come. They're for ever looking ahead, whereas Europeans, even in Homer's day, have always looked back in their search for a Golden Age, an age of heroes, an "ancient law", a once upon a time. . . . The craze for Progress only appeared in the late eighteenth century (simultaneously, by the way, with the emancipation of the Jews—could there be any connection here, I wonder?). Even the various "renovation" movements can be interpreted each time as recourse to an historical ideal—Antiquity, the early Church, or the Middle Ages, the Holy Roman Empire, etc., as *Re*-naissance, *Re*-formation. How true this is of NN.

*

"First-fruits of his creation. . . ." I asked that nice lay sister in charge of the Wurzach convent gardens (she was just planting out the first seedlings from the frames) what, from the gardener's point of view, characterized these "early" plants: are they any better than what comes on later, do they stand up better to bad weather, do they flower better or bear more fruit? "Not a bit of it", she replied, almost crossly. "They make more work, that's all, give more trouble, grow less well and are far less hardy. One loves them simply because they're the 'firstlings', that's the only pleasure one gets out of them!" I had to laugh, and made a note of this, as a lesson from the Holy Ghost. Perhaps we Christians will be such "firstlings" until he comes again.

*

OH how ghastly, how boring, how unreal so many of our Catholic lectures, articles, etc. are nowadays: not although but just *because* they're so "right"—polished so smoothly. Yet only what is jagged, sharply pointed, can really make an impression. But we've cultivated a specifically Catholic style, all our own, in which everything which can be said at all must be said simultaneously, in one go, and that's what people call "Catholic". I'm beginning to see what nonsense this is, and that the corpus of Catholic opinion mustn't be like a sack full of balls and glass marbles, all smoothly rounded—for these just roll away in all directions and get lost—it must rather consist of sharp-edged bits, which can be fitted together to form a mosaic. I realized this for the first time reading a criticism of my beloved *Heloise und Abelard* by Helen Waddell. The reviewer condemned the book as "not really Christian", since it is only concerned with sorrow, with no mention of "the meaning of Easter"—as though a novel, a literary work of art, must always be a compendium of every truth in the catechism! All the difference between false completeness and true wholeness.

*

I JUST revelled in that High Mass at Beuron Abbey on All Saints' Day. Once again "the liturgy as drama", nothing purposeful about it, praise and thanksgiving to God as *art pour l'art*, as natural as the liturgy of the angels before the heavenly throne, devoid of all pastoral instructional "consideration" for the congregation which, for that very reason, was carried away by it all, borne on its wings. X's inevitable disapproving comment: "The monks merely play-acting, with the congregation just spectators. . . ." But this wasn't what I felt about it. Of course it's a "spectacle", but that's just what makes sense, the very same sense as monasticism in general: to be a foreshadowing, no, a fore-sight of the liturgy of heaven, ritual as the

reflection of glory. How marvellously impersonal it is—the strict
anonymity of the monks, even more impressive when they raise
their hoods. They are just figures and voices. What an achievement to divest oneself of everything private, individual, to
enact this holy drama day after day, indifferent to one's personal mood, representing all of us simply as "mouth of the
Church". Far from being exhausted after the long service, I
felt stronger and fresher than I had felt for ages. Pure beauty,
pure senses, heavenly bread and wine.

*

THE Church is the princess in misery of fairy-tales—even
Allerleirauh in her coarse patch-work dress, pieced together out
of rags, of all the mistakes and false attitudes, past and present,
with ridiculous scraps of "fashion novelties" stuck on all the
time as new patches . . . and we, we contemporary Catholics,
we ourselves are this garment, this camouflage which scares off
the others!

*

MARGARETE SUSMANN's interpretation of biblical figures—
Moses, Ezechiel, Saul and David—throws a highly significant
light upon Jewish piety. I see so clearly now, for instance, that
NN's vehement abhorrence of rational theology is simply a form
of the primitive Jewish protest against "God made visible":
"The most deeply rooted impulse of the Jew . . . , his primitive
vigour in abolishing every image of God for the sake of his
truth . . . the power of utter abandon which, desiring God and
God alone, rejects every hint of a divine face and figure, even
as the vaguest of yearnings. To renounce every figure of God,
surrendering oneself utterly to him, is to be a complete human
being." (Behind this, of course, is M. Susmann's own denial
of the Incarnation!) The "gentiles" are quite unbiased towards
the world of imagery, which is probably why iconoclasts are
necessary, from time to time, and perhaps this is why Jewish
converts are so valuable. Moreover all this is somehow linked
with the Jewish struggle for change, con-version—the struggle
of living reality against rigid tradition—and here M. Susmann
cites Henri Bergson as an outstanding example. She interprets

the love of David and Jonathan very beautifully as "the love of the Jewish world knowing no magic, no enchantment (is this really true, I wonder?), no intoxication, or delusion: pure human love from soul to soul". This book has also shown me very clearly the strange way in which Catholics and Protestants have divided the specifically Jewish inheritance between them: Barth, for instance, strikes me as being as "Jewish" as Calvin —and maybe Bultmann also belongs to this line of the radical abolition of every picture of God; ritual, the priesthood, the liturgy, on the other hand, are *our* Jewish, not pagan, heritage.

*

You see, the mystic realizes his return from ecstasy (perhaps even his entire existence?) as an exile—of which all outward emigrations and banishments are but pale symbols. This is the real origin of that "revulsion from the world", which people who hate ascetics as well as those exclusively ascetically-minded will insist on interpreting simply as a moral (or Manichean) attitude. In fact it arises from the contrast of the two realities—from the harshness of a return that is not a home-coming, into the prison of this empiric world, this broken, dim, transitory remnant of reality in which we are living.

And the *doctrinal* inference drawn from this fact seems to me manifestly wrong: that such statements of mystics are to be taken at their face value, quite plainly and squarely, as precise pronouncements about "the world" in general, valuations of its quality to be handed down as such. Whereas in fact they express *nothing* but an experience of contradiction, a negative proportion, a highly personal, concrete shock of dissonance. But the ardent pupil, who hasn't an inkling of the real connection, goes all out to apply these hard sayings directly, flatly, to the world he is living in—*and* to justify them to boot. What ensues is a nightmarish tangle of crooked pretensions and stilted and insecure attitudes. How well I know that kind of thing from my own way!

*

OPTIMISM and pessimism in judging human character. I'm inclined to think that such attitudes are less the result of experience or training than of temperament and instinct. Take my own case: from nursery days we were taught to believe the worst of people—quite apart from the fact that we never experienced warmth, kindness or trust, in the family, from governesses or from servants. We were drilled, in principle and emphatically, never to believe anyone, never to trust anyone, all people are liars, people are always hypocrites, especially if they are nice to you, "everyone can be bought . . .", etc. Scandal was the sole topic of conversation in Stockau: "Just to show you what the world is really like." And for our brothers it was the greatest fun to "enlighten" us—in every way. Oddly enough, this was what I wanted myself, in the helpless feeling of growing up in such isolation, ignorant of the world, utterly "at sea", I was fiercely determined to have no illusions, to confront even the ugliest reality face to face. I would smuggle *The History of Prostitution* and such-like books out of the library, disclosures of financial scandals I couldn't understand, books on the crimes of colonial government, and H. provided me with appropriate fiction—Strindberg and horrible society novels popular at the time. And what was the result? I believed every word people told me, they could lie and swindle and make up whatever they liked. I was a perfect fool, duped all the time. Nor did my later training as a social worker and all the professional wallowing in criminal neglect and depravity help at all in this respect. Only much later—and what a price I paid for my experience!—did I acquire a certain scepticism, but, in fact, only through physiognomy. Today I think I can detect falsehood in a voice. I'd still be taken in by the actual words, only my instinct warns me—occasionally. Could it be that my insatiable and often so incautious hunger for people who are good, pure, beautiful and holy is in fact the direct result of that early training to despise people?

*

I'M always coming up against the Curé d'Ars—that unrelenting supranaturalist, upsetting all our fond ideas of "the Christian in the world". And yet I must love them, very much—these fierce jets of flame darting straight to heaven. Compared with them all the others seem just like domestic animals. There must be both sorts—the paradoxical and the congenial, understandable saints, the irritating and the useful saints. The trouble only starts when one kind is played off against the other.

*

TODAY's feast (New Year) ought to be especially significant and dear to the hearts of Jewish Christian converts. God became Man at Christmas, but Jesus became a Jew by his Circumcision, entering into the Covenant of Abraham, irrevocably, as the promised "secd" of salvation, embedded in the history and mission of his people.

Throughout the last week of Advent the antiphon is repeated again and again: "Virgin Israel, turn back to thy cities—how long wilt thou turn away in sadness? *Thou* shalt bear the Lord Thy Saviour. . . . " And then: "Lo, all is fulfilled that the Angel foretold of the Virgin *Mary.*"

I see so clearly here that Mary "is" Israel as well, the faithful Israel of the Covenant, just as she "is" the Church.

*

WHO really knows what a bishop is any more?

We've allowed his significance to fade, our notion of his office infiltrated by the Protestant as well as the old "princely" understanding of it. For most people he is just the highest clerical authority, the "top man", the peak of the administrative pyramid built up from below. We've quite lost sight of him as the high priest, of all bishops as "emanations" of the One High Priest. Anointed—and how he is anointed at his consecration, both head and hands! But Anointed means Messiah = Christ: David and Samuel come alive again at his consecration, king and prophet. And Moses and Aaron, again and again, the entire Old Testament is there: the mitre is the "helmet of salvation", Pauline, yes, but its form is linked expressly with the "horns of light" radiating from the face of Moses and "the golden plate, sacred and set apart" placed upon Aaron's brow; the gloves too are linked with the skins which covered the hands of Jacob when he brought his father "the roast dish such as he loved well". And the whole New Testament is there as well: throughout the long ceremony of consecration the candidate bears the Gospel resting on the nape of his neck, until it is finally taken from him and placed in his hands with the words: "Receive the Gospel, go forth and preach to thy people what has been entrusted to thee: God hath power to increase his grace in thee!"

The high priest is the summit, from whom all power and grace flow, streaming down, showering down from above: the other priests are in fact "his" priests, his own "hands", yet in turn representing him, his reflections, almost emanations; branches of one tree without which their own office would be inconceivable—by no means individuals raised democratically from the community. All this is obscured and forgotten today: we no longer see the "tree of consecration" with its many branches, the hierarchical body with its rays. Incidentally the bishop's pectoral cross is still blessed with the same words used in blessing the crosses once laid upon the Crusaders.

*

IF there's one thing I can't stand it's that kind of piety solely preoccupied with sin and its punishment and avoidance—nosing it out and tracking it down, discussing it—yet this was the atmosphere in which we grew up. And then Fr B., O.P. comes telling me that there isn't a single chapter in the whole *Summa* directly concerned with sin; St Thomas never dealt with it as his principal subject, always just in the margin, in relation to other questions. They "cultivated" our consciences along basically Pelagian lines at our convent schools, i.e. the doctrine was never stated explicitly, but always taken for granted, that man is capable of avoiding *every* sin by will-power; his normal state being essentially virtuous, sinless, sin in itself always being just an accident, a technical hitch which need never have happened with a little more good will and dexterity. Which accounted for the weight—and the shame—attached to even the tiniest fault. But also for that curiously deep-rooted notion that other people, i.e. the "good" people were really as blameless as they were made out to be, and only oneself was the dismal failure.

*

I'M reading a very quaint American book, *The Power of Positive Thinking*, written, so I'd suppose, by a sectarian minister, presumably of Methodist dye.* He's full of stories of prayers heard, faith healing, etc.—and extols the power of prayer. In one way it's staggering and makes me feel ashamed for us—but on the other hand—good heavens, what innocence!! An unwavering trust in God, a seriousness bar every doubt, leading dead straight to the assurance: "My well-being, including my health, success in business and in money-making, is so obviously the right thing, a matter of course, so important and essential, that God just must give it to me as soon as I ask him for it. Before leaving for an important business conference I brace myself with texts like 'If God be for us, who can be against us?' or 'I can do all things through Christ which strengtheneth me!' Then I stalk into the conference room, sure of my victory, and carry off the most marvellous deal: all my rivals just shrivel up on the spot, for Christ is my ally. . . ." This, in essence, is the burden of the whole book, That's what people call Christian optimism. But it's wasted on us—we've been spoilt for this sort of thing. Certainly such "positive thinking" is a tremendous power, and maybe it can move mountains. But isn't it rather self-suggestion than authentic religious impulse? It doesn't seem to have dawned on him that suffering, disappointment, defeat or loss might also have some point too, or that God's designs could sometimes be hidden. . . . The good man is so utterly convinced that his salvation and his material well-being must be identical, that God's support must pay immediate dividends, that if things go wrong, it certainly wasn't Providence at work but just his own lack of faith which unfortunately shut the door—out of the question, all of it. I read him with the funniest mixture of envy, admiration and exasperation: "Lord, I thank thee that we are not like them. . . !"

*

A WONDERFUL lecture by Heinrich Schlier about the First Epistle to the Corinthians. He in fact described the prototype of all heresies, for all ages, without even touching on the Reformation. He reduced the beginnings of schism among the Corinthians to their glorying in self-appointed spiritual fathers and their personal experiences and charisms, set up against the "scanty,

* Dr Norman Vincent Peale. *The Power of Positive Thinking* was published in 1953 (*Trans.*).

hard and dry kerygma" of the apostles and their disciples, *who are not themselves prophets*, but only ministers—not themselves creative, but merely handing on, administering, distributing. But the enthusiasts had no patience with the provisional character of this kerygma, couldn't put up with the modest offer and the poverty of "the given word"—heresy is, basically, refusal of acceptance—"refusing to accept the 'folly' of dogma in ready, open obedience". The heretic places his faith instead in his own charism, deliberately nourished on exclusively private, if as yet still Christian experience; *he exalts "experience" as the ground, norm and light of his faith.* And, as Schlier says, "there is nothing more intolerant than the small group confusing their charism with dogma". And there is no way of healing the breach (was it a hint at personal experience, I wonder?) except surrender of one's "superiority"—a *genuine* superiority of knowledge, intensity of experience, richness of the mind—for the rough-hewn kerygma opposing you in the testimony of mere "office". Surely this sums up, in a nutshell, the problems and conflicts of all our modern reform movements within the Church? Most important of all, to my mind, was the bold statement that heretics quite often really *are* superior to the "average believer" and often enough to clerics, too—though we usually only discuss fictitious superiority. But this gives the decision, the struggle, the conversion its real weight.

*

I OFTEN feel that the nineteenth century was simply "too short", rather like a room too small for all the bulky furniture crammed into it.

This accounts for the general impression of hopeless tangle and topsyturviness. I mean, they did glimpse such an overwhelming mass of new things for the very first time, things so novel, strange and puzzling that their first attempts to express and realize them were bound to fail, or at least to fall short. And often enough it was just those crude and sketchy experiments which congealed and froze hard into patterns—and now we must try to get rid of them, even with pick-axe and dynamite. Yet I'm convinced that quite a lot of their bright ideas were basically sound, but their efforts to express and embody them went wrong.

For instance things like socialism, emancipation of women, early Bible research, eugenics, unhampered science, etc.—perhaps Romanticism as well, and within the Church lots of minor religious foundations. What stood behind these ventures, in the minds and hearts of the pioneers, may, time and again, have been something entirely different from things dubbed with the same label current with us today. I'm immensely drawn to contemplating this strangely fruitful, multicoloured chaos. And with what envy I regard its "flowers", those magnificent specimens, men and women, exquisitely moulded, rich and mature, fulfilled in their scope and their achievements! What wraiths we seem by comparison—mere hints and sketches of what we *could* be!

*

THE long recluse existence of illness somehow turns one into a kind of embryo again, growing into one's room, like a mussel in its shell, so that it becomes a sort of skin without which one would be afraid to venture out into the world, among people. *How* I can understand the deadly *nakedness* of the refugees— more than mere poverty. For precisely for people with least substance of their own, individuality consisted far more in their "belongings" than in their person, and their "persona" was much more a matter of things than of the soul. Lots of them have "died", in the strictest sense, as a result of this "separation of body and soul" and are still wandering around like ghosts, wraiths of their former existence, really "Poor Souls".* Indeed it's astonishing that so many have succeeded in building up a new "body" for themselves. But how many others in the camps, etc. are still living this ghost-life, and die in this state.

*

GOD is almost more hidden in his Church than in Creation or in history. Of course he has concealed himself in these, too, so much so that many people never find him all their lives long. But in the Church, so it seems to me, this hiddenness does not only mean our guilt, our cowardice and tepidity, our own defence measures against the immediacy of God—there is also something in it of the deliberate hiddenness of Christ, of his mystery,

* The German term for "Holy Souls".

of Nazareth, of his humility which spurned everything conspicuous, sensational, "showy", even in religion—of his "annihilation": which accounts for the fierce and poignant tenderness one feels for everything which could be even a thread on the hem of his garment, be it ever so poor, so ridiculous—and, at the same time, for the wide-awake criticism, sensitive as a raw nerve, the smarting indignation and impatience, the soreness at the way his 'Body'—*everything* about it!—is hiding him, muffling him, letting him down.

Fools of God. I well know the evil, dark, destructive kind of folly—so-called society abounded with such fools, ruthlessly wrecking every order. But ever since my religious awakening I have known, loved and honoured the other kind: the folly of the children of God which shows they are strangers in this world: fools dazzled by the nearness of God—"*quia te contemplans totum deficit*".

*

LYING in bed I can still just see the arm of the great crucifix beside the window in the looking-glass of the wardrobe, and every time "Shekhinah!" comes to my mind—the *dextera Domini*, the "right hand of majesty", manifest in the mirror of our world as the crucified left hand, nailed down in its weakness.

*

BACK again to Julian of Norwich, and beside her a short collection of lesser known mystics of the Eckhart school. People claim that the dignity and rights of man were invented by humanism, or even the French Revolution! The image of man, man's understanding of himself, the Christian's claim upon himself never soared higher than on such wings of thought about "the godlike soul". Of course I'm aware of the inevitable danger here: you simply can't avoid it: that brand of spiritualism *bound* to arise from flights to such heights, the shrinking, dwindling, extinction of the rest of Creation under the eye of the mind soaring above it all. Now we need an entirely new eye to perceive Creation from this same lofty perspective, yet not in defiance or rebellion!—restored once again to its greatness and significance. But this seems only possible consecutively, not simultaneously.

*

I've been reading a long novel by Pearl Buck about a Chinese emigrant family in New York: father, mother and four children, each of them reacting entirely differently to their émigré destiny: some of them adjust themselves inwardly, others assimilate externally into the New World, some return to China, but can't stand life there any more. All the time I was reading I kept transposing the Church for Old China, and I realized how very closely you could compare the existence of the Church today with an exile's fate. By and large the older generation *chez nous* is still living in the past, looking back proudly and wistfully upon the bygone classical culture, purposely disregarding the revolution, dreaming of restoration, loud in their praises of past glories for the benefit of outsiders. But all this splendour of the past leaves the younger people quite cold, they couldn't care less, concerned only with what is to come. I saw the whole drama of our decline (or at least transition) mirrored as though in a looking-glass as I read, the irrevocable disintegration of all one cherished in pride—and our groping for what is yet unborn but already shimmering through everywhere. Of course such "mirroring" only applies to *forms* within the Church. Never for one moment do I forget that the Holy Ghost is hovering above our fading and reflowering, dying and rebirth, working in it all in his thousandfold power. Still, this world of old forms was very real, and to watch its passing is intensely pathetic.

*

I wonder what really lies behind the fact that so many funny saints are canonized nowadays, such utterly insignificant, uninteresting people? On the one hand it disturbs me as a sign of decadence (for there *is* something amiss with it), yet, beyond this, as a "second intention" of the Holy Ghost, it could mean that today the holiness of the Church is showing in "the dark side of the moon", i.e. no longer in "solar" figures, radiant, fascinating, but in little people, mute, anonymous, simply serving and suffering—*and* in martyrs and prisoners who are even more sacrificed, hidden, trampled into the earth. Both reveal the depths of the Church, not her peaks: the ground, not the crown—the silent, enduring element upon whom everything else rests, the force bearing and forbearing: in this sense the maternal—the Marian element in an unknown form. The very things discredited in the rest of the world today.

*

I wonder sometimes whether the almost complete disappearance of animals in our modern cities isn't a symptom of more far-reaching significance than we think. Newman once said—not as a "point" in itself, just casually, as something taken for granted: it oughtn't to be difficult to believe in the existence of a world of angels since we're constantly living together with animals, i.e. with a whole world of living creatures with whom we share only half our natures; why shouldn't there be another world of beings corresponding to the other half and embodying this in pure essence? It seems man lives, by nature, between "elder and younger" brothers. If he loses contact completely with the one, must he not lose it with the others as well? And with his own kin too, since he no longer has any authentic standard for comparison? I loved G.V.'s letter the other day (they have a Newfoundland puppy since the New Year): "Play and work, fight, sadness and the yearning for the New Creation—this links us to them, and, adding love—knowledge—worship, to our fellow-humans as well. But if the things we share with the animals are lacking or seep out of our relations with men, then the essentially human fellowship is imperilled." Fits in perfectly with what I've just said.

*

Why do I object to make-up, or rather to lipstick?—for all the rest is just a matter of taste and of fashion. The mouth is a supremely central organ, spiritual, like the eyes, the brow—expressive in the highest degree, in some people even more expressive than their eyes. Medium of speech and of smiles—weeping belongs to it, too, and singing, and kissing—organ of love, then—as Eros, not as sex, even if not unrelated to it; at the same time organ of eating, the lowly, most primitive necessity

340

of life. And so, in a unique way, the mouth is at once spiritual and physical, human, serving and expressing the spiritual and the sensual, the soul and the purely vegetative. That's why it requires special guarding and a kind of chastity. And it contradicts this, to my mind, to go painting it conspicuously with glaring colour, crude and unnatural, turning it into an eye-catching device for all and sundry, even for the total stranger. What's more: things displayed in shop-windows are offered to the public, for sale. . . . Lots of people sense all this instinctively—that is, if they've got any instinct left!—without being able to express it: for instance: the mouth shows whether a person is "open" or "closed"—children's are prone to gape, and people who are naturally reserved usually have rather tightly pressed lips. How can one turn one's mouth into an advertisement for the public?

＊

FIFTY years ago Péguy wrote: "Our conception of matter is even more confused and less serviceable than our conception of the mind."

This seems to be in everybody's mind just now. Only recently NN. wrote in a letter: "The secret lies in the body, not in the mind." But surely such statements are characteristic of the intellectual, not of the naïve type, and certainly not of the average person. It's we who take the mind for granted, the inward, invisible world. It is forms and shapes we are ever marvelling at—matter, materiality, bodies—that's what we feel to be "different", strange. Sensuality as the universal organ for perceiving "bodiliness" is in fact truly developed only in intellectual man, since in his detachment his sensibility is "redoubled" (as Kierkegaard would say) by his very remoteness. For a "sensible", i.e. "sense-*minded*" person the outline of a flower, the tint of a stone, a scent, the faintest caressing touch can be "an event", thrilling his very depth, where the senses of a carnal man remain dull and irresponsive to much cruder impact. To a genuinely "physical" kind of person taking matter literally as "a matter of course", our awe and wonder in the face of bodiliness must remain wholly incomprehensible; whereas to him things of the mind, "ghostly" (as the English mystics would

341

say) seem an adventure, mysterious, baffling or simply improbable. That's why he either flatly denies them altogether or else falls a victim himself to books, intellectual talk, etc. with a respect and uncritical awe which can amount to narcotic effects.

I think medieval people still lived with fairly equal intensity and zest in both spheres—of the body and of the soul. The purely "intellectual" domain was, on the contrary, so new to them, so exciting, that I can well understand the supreme and exquisite delight with which they threw themselves into things of the mind, pure thought, differentiating, assessing, formulating, with a vigour and passion very different from the dry and bloodless rationalism of later ages. That's why I'm always defending the scholastics so maligned today—I believe I know exactly how they must have felt!—Just think of Thomas and Albert, for example, friars wandering on foot through foreign lands—the countless nights they must have spent out under the stars, bedded with all the fibres of their being in landscape and heaven, weather and the changing seasons—how *understandable* that they should have constructed the crystal towers of their abstract thought above it all in the sheer delight of play! We can experience something of the same sort—in pale reflection—in adolescence, that quiver of rocking light-headedness, that sudden upsoaring exuberance, thrilling with the first flashes of genuine intellectual perception—when walls recede and undreamt of horizons are revealed.

*

SOME French novels give the impression that sex—for you couldn't possibly call this sort of thing love—is nothing but a bloody, merciless war between two vanities. The role of the senses is relatively unimportant! They merely serve as "ammunition". The real sport consists in conquering, humiliating, wounding, keeping the other person on tenterhooks, tormenting, insulting, making it up—and starting all over again. Nothing but a refined game played with the urge for ambition, possession, domination, and all the attendant aggressions. The coldest, most "affected"—literally—form of passion, calculating, self-idolizing, in which the partner, he or she, is just another peacock's feather to be stuck in one's cap—prey, victim, trophy, decoration—even scalp. In every way the dead opposite of love, even of the "natural" kind, disguised and made-up as love with a perpetual frothing cascade of artificially whipped-up, lying emotion.

*

It seems to be NN's disquieting function in my life to come tapping with his little hammer at stones well built into the fabric of my house, remarking: "That sounds hollow." Sometimes I hear it then, too, and sometimes I don't. The exciting feature is that if you take a stone out of the wall in the right place, you may well gain a window or a door—but if you take it out of the wrong place, all kinds of bits may start slipping and toppling and the most awful damage can result. You'd need to know a lot more about building and the architect's plan (system? dogma?) in order to tell at once what's the matter: whether, for the sake of the whole, one ought to leave a gap bunged up with inferior material, rather than risk undermining an important staying point, etc. Obviously it would be preferable to have the right material handy so as to stop the hole properly. Sometimes, of course, one just goes on strike, simply too tired to start rebuilding, and makes do with mere patching up. Newman seems to have said somewhere that we must make up our minds to living under branches or in huts—as a makeshift—while a whole wing of the mansion is being demolished for renovation. But if you've lived in this old building for so long, if you're rooted in it with the very fibres of your being, embedded in it in so many fond memories—then this is rather hard. It's so much easier for converts. They don't have to tear away bits of themselves to make room for the new building—though of course the same sort of thing does apply to their own general past. . . .

*

I don't know, that is, I cannot really judge, how far I'm involved in a far-reaching melting process. I'd say what one could call ecclesiastical "local patriotism" is being smelted out of my innermost image of the Church. Not the solid frame itself, not the clear firm mould, rather something within myself, in my own attitude to this. What, in fact, found its outlet in the savage review I wrote long ago of Walter Nigg's book about heretics. But this element is rooted deeply within me—it isn't just a matter of temperament, my notorious "hedgehog's spines"— rather it's part of the very bones of my spiritual substance. This is a slow, continuous process, this dissolving in the centre of my soul, an extremely painful, consuming crisis, an incision into real living tissue, touching the most sensitive nerve points. It is not "dangerous", because I know I am under the scalpel of the Divine Surgeon—and because I know that, slowly and surely, like my outward recovery now—this interior supporting substance will also grow again, purified, more resilient, stronger than what is now being destroyed. But—it hasn't got that far yet, or at least I don't feel it has. I'm simply living on hope. This, too, is a sort of conversion—from my old conception of the Church, rather smug, self-satisfied and somewhat pig-headed —to an ever-deeper perception and recognition of "the Church herself". A pity one can't talk to anyone about it. It is a bit of real dying, part of the crumbling of the exterior house which is to be clothed upon with our house which is from heaven.

*

I was asked today what I'm doing at the moment. I ought to have answered: "I'm translating", for that—apart from being married—is, in fact, my main occupation. I'm not really a "creative" person at all, rather I'm a "translator"—and I do this in various languages. This means puzzling out complex and often half-buried trails, a net-work linking all kinds of spiritual and intellectual positions, aspects or whatever you like to call them, to their corresponding points within traditional Catholic thought and life where they're so often only embedded as ciphers—or fossils. It's anything but easy and most important. Not for me personally, not even for certain friends, but for some contemporaries in the Church, the "natives" boxed up in their own little capsule for whom so many channels have been blocked up—as well as for those outside for whom important links, bridging links, into the core of the Church are missing. So I'm trying to explore the hidden traces connecting the most diverse yet secretly related insights, knit with one another into one great star pattern, trying to sketch the design, at least bits of it.

*

NN. WRITES that he's been wrestling for weeks with his understanding of the Church. I'm not doing anything else either. The picture is expanding and concentrating, growing transparent, at the same time taking on a positively frightening hardness—an undreamt of degree of reality which makes me tremble for I feel utterly unequal to the consequences. I feel like the people in the Bible must have felt when they saw an angel— yes, that's just how I feel at the glimpse of these flashes of the reality hidden behind "the Church", that worn word, anything but transparent. But he who is revealing himself to us—isn't it up to him to see that we can bear him?

*

EVERY alert Christian is seized now and then by a fit of despair at the state of Christendom—and why wouldn't he be! Then he may choose between four ways of escape: if he doesn't elect to spring overboard altogether. First he can capitulate and resign, either negatively: "What's the use anyway!"—or, positively: "Things must remain the way they are, everything must be kept and defended, nothing changed at all." Secondly, flight into the Church Invisible; thirdly, flight into the past—reconstruction of the Early Church, or some other ideal form, hand in hand with the invention of a scapegoat: everything since Constantine or Gregory VII or Scholasticism or Trent or the S.J., etc. is degeneration, falling off, decline: let's get rid of it all, abolish everything and start afresh "before the parting of the ways": here Reformation and Restoration and many sectarians are of one mind. And finally the fourth way out into the future: salvation lies not in beginnings but in what is to come. Here, too, there are two variations: first to clear the decks of the past, setting up something entirely new in its place—as the more recent (e.g. the American) sects are trying to do—the other the "Joachite" way: the new growing out of the "genuine" old, out of tradition buried or vitiated.

*

THE Assumption of Our Lady. No, I'm sure the blessing of herbs* doesn't mean the supplying of "amulets", withered bunches to be stuck behind the looking-glass or behind the crucifix in the bedroom. The traditional fifteen flowers are nothing but the principal medicinal herbs: arnica, pimpernel, camomile, valerian, etc., and I'm sure they were originally blessed for their function as remedies. Around midsummer every household had in any case collected its store of herbs and these were simply intended for practical use, naturally and supernaturally; just as St John's wine† is meant to be drunk and not used to sprinkle things, and Easter bread to be eaten and not saved up as a pious relic. Just another thing which has fallen into that false spirituality which can so easily slip into superstition. In fact one could just as well bring one's herbal teas and tinctures to be blessed in church.

*

ALL the time in his writings on the Assumption Rahner keeps handling the problem: "What do we in fact mean by 'Resurrection'—what do we really believe?" Classical theology, the sharp, polished instrument wielded with utmost skill, almost artistically—but not a bit like a game of patience which must "come out". Quite the reverse: as though with the finest blade he carefully lays bare one layer of thought after another, thereby showing how little in fact "comes right", how little is fixed, how open the most vital questions still are, not even really asked indeed, often only intimated and then hastily slurred over and circumvented: how much has *not* yet been defined in doctrine and how, at the same time, tiny quick flames of truth are flickering everywhere in the bronze cups of dogma, as though in the moulded polished cups of a candlestick—a breath-taking, fascinating spectacle. Of course the style is rather difficult—after all the whole thing is a cautious egg-dance in front of an audience of critical theologians always ready to pounce on him, and his book must pass the test—you wipe your brow, as it

* The custom—largely confined nowadays to country churches—of bringing herbs to be blessed at Mass on the Feast of the Assumption.

† Wine is blessed in German churches on the Feast of St John and taken home to be drunk in accordance with the priest's words: "Drink this wine in the love of St John!"

were, as you read. But it's incredible the way he manages to get on across this dangerous territory with all its hidden mines and barbed wire entanglements, making his own imperturbable way.

*

Esoterics! No, for me the golden table leg* remains the golden table leg. It will be more than enough for me, if I come to know "the splendour of reality" *after* I've crossed the threshold of death. Here in the realm of the pilgrim Church I'm content with the contact with God as permitted to the "poor"—in the mysteries and demands of unseeing faith, and in the so infinitely modest sacraments and symbols of his Church. For, after all, this too is a question of poor and rich—and probably in this sphere the ecstatics, visionaries, etc. count among the "rich" and the privileged—whose number will never exceed a very limited few. But precisely this strikes me as an essential difference between Christianity and other religions: that God does *not* have to depend upon "religious talent"—and certainly not psychic and parapsychic gifts—to touch people, to fill them with grace and love. They don't need to know the faintest thing about such out of the ordinary possibilities—see Little Thérèse, etc. or the Curé d'Ars. Yes, they were poor all right, little people, child-like, to whom the universe remained closed: they found God "only" in their own narrow world. But they *did* find him, and it's to them that I belong and not to the magicians, seers and those who wander along the frontier. . . . I don't think this is sour grapes—if I could choose between reliving my own poor, meagre experience of God, his actual gift to me, or the way of cosmic mysticism—I'd say: oh please, the same way again, just as it was, and the Golden Table intact—when I get across!

*

Not only the Pietists, not a few among us also pretend that doubt and sin are absolutely necessary pre-requisites for a true

---

* Allusion to a story of Bergengruen's based on a Jewish legend: In a time of Roman persecution three rabbis are brought into dire peril. In their despair they resort to magic. A fourth rabbi almost succumbs to their persuasion to join them, but his wife has a dream: she sees the blessed in Paradise feasting at golden tables —but the table of one who has evaded suffering is lacking a leg. The rabbi stands firm, and as he is beheaded has a vision of the Golden Table awaiting him, intact.

conversion—there can be no rebirth without the experience of the Prodigal Son.

That isn't true at all. The son *is* already a son when he runs away, and before it—he isn't "promoted" only when he comes home. His guilt and tragedy lie precisely in the fact that he runs away as the son of this Father! And the objectionable brother who stays at home is his son too and remains his son, and it's to *him*, of all people, the Father speaks with such tenderness: "My son, thou art always at my side, and everything that I have is already thine." By the way, I think that elder brother shows precisely that there are tests and trials other than those of flight and exile. Even in his Anglican days Newman was always fighting against those groups (Methodists? Evangelicals?) who mistook the psychological experience of "awakening", the struggle of penance and penetration for regeneration. For such confusion in fact nullifies the sacramental effect of baptism as rebirth. The turmoils of growing maturity, of growing awareness are something entirely different from the "silent" process of birth—which does not take place primarily in the consciousness of the newly-born.

*

A MOST interesting discussion with W.B. about Newman. Pity I can't think of resuming my book about him. But I could never catch up with all the newly-discovered, or rather newly-published material which would certainly alter the current picture profoundly. W.B. himself has already unearthed 250 hitherto unknown manuscripts of sermons dating from his Anglican days. And then all those letters, correspondence with his woman friends, as yet unpublished since they don't fit into the established notion of the Cardinal—and "the great solitary". Yet, in reality, he had a genius for friendship—and not only for men—and the few women in his life, not only R.G., were passionately devoted to him. Biographers to date seem not to have noticed this, going, I suppose, by the strictly or largely spiritual theme of the letters —or did they ignore facts on purpose? But we moderns have sharper ears—and we're less discreet—so that a slightly awkward situation arises. By the way, it's part of the same legend that

Newman dismissed everyone from his deathbed with the words: "I can die alone." In fact his last words were: "William, William!", the name of his last young friend in the Oratory. I think this far more pathetic, far more lovable than the fiction.

As a saint I see Newman as the counter-pole to figures like the Curé d'Ars or Padre Pio, "poor in spirit" with a superabundance of charisms. But isn't this just one further proof of how inessential such gifts are for holiness? Was there ever any talk of such phenomena in the case of Augustine or Albert the Great? But perhaps such a mind, such great intellect is already a charism *in itself* and ought to be recognized as such?

*

NN. COMPLAINS that the "cure of souls" in the Church has completely swallowed up the "cure of the spirit", or rather it hasn't given this kind of pastoral work any chance at all. I think we ought to discriminate. The soul which is the object of Catholic pastoral care is not at all the same thing as the "psyche" treated by psychotherapists, any more than it is the "mind" which grapples with problems. What the Church calls the immortal soul, the soul to be saved, is a third idea—I'd call it the root from which both stem, from which both radiate: what is often called "the Self" these days, or "the core of the person" —the entity of our interior, invisible being, the object of redemption—unfortunately only too often divorced from the body, combined with which this soul becomes the object of salvation = man. Not much thought seems to be given to the structure of the soul here, or so it seems to me; nor, alas, is it often considered that this soul can, in fact, only be grasped, addressed and reached through the psyche and the mind. Generally speaking the psyche is only very vaguely hinted at as "emotion" or "lower nature" (or rather left to itself as something uncontrollable and somehow uncanny), whereas the mind is seen merely as reason, in the narrow sense of intellect. It was rather typical at one of our first meetings of a group of doctors, psychologists and pastors—arranged for interchange of experiences, therapy, etc.—when one of the priests remarked serenely: "We're only concerned with the *person* of the penitent in confession—*the soul doesn't interest us at all!*" "Why, *whatever else?*"

exclaimed the horrified psychologists, and I had to step in and do a little interpreting to unravel the terminological tangle. Basically the same thing applies to the pastoral attitude towards Eros—whereas in the first instance they reckon only with either reason or "emotion" in the dull, torpid sense, here it's usually either physical "impulse" and "urge", or, straight off, Charity = Agape—the point of amalgamation seems to escape attention.

*

ROY CAMPBELL*: how God must have loved such a life!—even if the smug and respectably pious think it an utterly useless existence: praise incarnate. How God must delight when a man so exults in the work of His hands, finding it all so glorious! Surely such insatiable joy in Creation is a thousand times more incense in his sight than the timid "abstinence" of countless *dévotes*, afraid of biting into the apple in case they might "endanger" themselves or get themselves dirty—fearful of touching God's splendour, even with their finger tips? But this book was written, as the introduction says, "so as to repay my debt both to Almighty God and to my parents for letting me loose in such a world to plunder its miraculous literatures and languages and wines: to savour its sights, forms, colours, perfumes and sounds, etc., etc." The man who wrote these words —he has died in the meantime—was a war invalid, a cripple, a man who knew poverty in the most various forms for long stretches of his life, as well as hunger and need and hard physical work—he was no spoilt child of fortune. A gay adventurer, his childhood spent in South Africa, a hunter and horseman, later a painter and poet in England, the wildest of Bohemians, in between spells as a sailor or fisherman, cattle-drover, bullfighter, acrobatic super in films, tramp. Even if half of it is a hunter's yarn, it's still, unwittingly, a book for meditation.

Of course to "know" the world like this it takes a body equal to the mind and spirit in strength and capacity—a body which can swim and ride, dance and climb, spin and spring, fight and work like a giant.

*

* On reading *Light on a Dark Horse*, Autobiography, 1901–35, London, 1951.

WHAT Leopold Ziegler, Guénon, etc. call "tradition" and what this means for us—and the relation between the two—could perhaps be described by the image of a half-open oyster-shell—outside it's black, shaggy, cracked, so overgrown and incrusted with strange drifting weeds and foreign matter that it has almost lost its original shape: that's how the ignorant see it, and they take it at face value, thinking it's the real thing: they call this rough shell superstition, darkest heathendom, etc.—and look down their noses at it. The inside is vaulted, rainbow-coloured, shimmering: this is the "tradition" of the mythologists and symbolists—literally the mother-of-pearl: and in its heart lies the pearl itself: the faith of the Church which for *us* is Tradition. Of course the pearl is born of the mother-of-pearl; it would be inconceivable without it—to a certain extent the pearl is indeed less "original" than the "mother". For this existed first, the shimmering, iridescent cave, closed, mysterious. The pearl resulted from a deep wounding, by the penetration of an extraneous element, but it did result, and now it is far more precious than the maternal element. Nor is it merely part of this "mother", or permanently joined to it. On the contrary, it can—once formed—exist apart from it, since the substances which have formed it are part of itself. Indeed its beauty only then becomes fully apparent. Of course its "essence" must be protected and given proper care, otherwise the pearl will lose its lustre and go black. The pearl, the pearl of great price of the Gospel, outweighing all the treasures of the world—no matter how hideous and trashy its setting may be. But for some people the mother-of-pearl is more important than the pearl itself, indeed they only seem to value it at all as the product of the former.

*

IT's awful how imprisoned people are, confined in their solitary "language cells", often only able to communicate with the outside world by the prisoner's code of knocking. I can well understand how theologians took refuge in Latin for centuries—for when they tried to discuss spiritual and intellectual matters in the various barbaric tongues they found themselves in exactly the same position as a musician who discovers that half the keys are missing on his piano. In those days Latin gave them room to move, but today it has become a cell itself, a tower even, a code in which only certain things can be expressed. In Burg Rothenfels,* just as in other Catholic—and, I'm sure, Protestant —religious centres an exclusive style of talk has grown up— and it's the same in other spheres, I suppose.

*

No, spiritualism is *not* the supreme state in the religious life. It's merely an inevitable phase in a certain curve of development, equivalent to infatuation in the curve of love. It embodies the nostalgia of youth, not the fulfilment of maturity. And at this point the dangers lurk. For instance one can well linger on this level, concentrating—as lovers do—solely on what is related directly and exclusively to the beloved and mutual affection, in this case on the "purely religious", i.e. things stamped by us as "devotional", or "raised" to this status. Everything connected with divine service, Mass, the liturgy, "the spiritual life", etc. —down to clerical activities. Much less attention is paid to things whose relation to God stems "only" from him, from his fingerprint on what he made. That is why it's so typical of this phase to demand unconditional precedence of religious and ecclesiastical matters over everything else, theocracy through the Church, for instance, clerical control of education, etc. And this already involves the first dangerous step towards mistrust and contempt of the profane.

*

THE Assumption of Our Lady. Apart from whatever else it is, this is also the feast of the anticipated wedding of the Shekhinah with the King. The Church "recognizes" this too, for all the breviary texts are nuptial in character—Mother and Son are completely submerged in images of bride and bridegroom, the marriage of the King, the King's couch—"His left hand under my head, and his right hand shall embrace me"—plain enough that here, in Mary, the whole of Creation is gathered up by her Lord in his embrace.

*

* See above, p. 284n.

PEOPLE talk about the Catholic ghetto as a thing of the past, a period phenomenon, long since overcome. Yet in reality—at least over wide stretches—it only *seems* to have opened, and only towards a hectic form of modernity, only horizontally at that, no depth, no growth "upwards". And even this new "broadness" isn't real breadth, spacious. Even educated, cultivated Catholics are still living, to an astonishing degree, on an island all by themselves, as though in a Red Indian reservation—and they don't know it. It may be different in France—possibly in England (though only among the *converts*, I think, for the "native" Catholics there the ghetto hardly seems to have been broken yet)—but here this is surely the rule.

On the other hand I don't deny for one moment that "in exchange" the Catholic mind often has a peculiar quality of compactness and concentration which is very valuable—people coming from other "thought climates" where the air is thinner, more diffuse or less clear sometimes find it surprising and even attractive. Catholics live in a world of their own—that's at once our strength and our weakness—especially if in this enclosure the windows and doors are hermetically sealed.

*

NN. THINKS, as he told me in his last letter, that the history of the medieval Church could teach us better to realize something about the Papacy today—how vulnerable it is, liable to changes, anything but impregnable. He's right, of course, but at the moment I'm far more interested in the eighteenth century and the turn into the nineteenth. One hardly ever considers what a crisis took place within the Church in those days—truly a matter of life and death—and more dangerous still since her most determined opponents were inside not outside! How impotent she was, externally and internally, robbed of all power in the State Church of France and Austria!—by Josephism just as much as by the French Revolution, then by secularization in Germany and by the absolutist rule of Freemasonry in the so-called "Catholic" states. In fact her situation was little different from today in the totalitarian countries. When one considers, for instance, the war waged against the Jesuits prior to their abolition—the fact that in "Catholic" Portugal 800 Jesuits were held prisoner for twenty years in underground dungeons—who knows anything about this today? Or the two imprisoned Popes, indeed the whole treatment of the Popes by Napoleon (and by Joseph II, too, only with velvet gloves!), then the incredible break with tradition and culture in the demolition of the old Church of the Holy Roman Empire, the destruction of the most powerful and ancient centres of spiritual life by secularization—it's a marvel to me that the Church recovered *at all* over the past hundred years—and recovered so well. And it's no wonder that she is still suffering from the after-effects, from the deep internal damage and loss of substance which every lost war involves; for that's what they were, a series of lost wars, besides those waged against the enemies outside.

*

In one way Mary Ward has grown rather strange to me, remote. For her external story represents a model belonging to the very earliest phase of my spiritual life, a model now outdated; the typical zealous figure—almost zealot—of the Counter-Reformation, through and through. And yet, underneath I glimpse a second face, the face of the English mystic, painted in water colours, strangely vague, almost without contours, misty, dreamy. My book described her destiny from the outside, her heroic legend—as I quite rightly first called it. Shall I succeed now in showing the other side? An attempt to grasp the inner figure, revealing this not as an X-ray photograph (which is what I rather tried to do with Little Thérèse), but rather in the way one might work on a palimpsest, exposing the script scarcely visible under the second layer.

There's a third element in her life as well, so alien to us today that one can hardly realize it, indeed even imagine it at all. At any rate I myself find it very hard to "think myself into" this attitude, caught up as I am in the very opposite current of our age. It's that inexorable, unhesitating, strictly aristocratic, hierarchical attitude which divides up society—spiritual in *exactly* the same way as temporal—into ranks, as unyielding as in the Hindu caste system! Class here is rigid, really "station", fixed, either from above or below, and upper-class "is" better and worth more, quite apart from its individual representatives—

and there's no modification. The aristocrat "is" better than the burgher or peasant, since he personifies a higher form of life. And the same thing applies to priest and layman, as well as to simple and solemn vows. For us today this last point is purely a legal nuance, but for Mary Ward it was the turning point of her destiny. She fought for this privilege with all the passion of her being: to be recognized as a community with solemn vows. This, not her "emancipated" work, was the real bone of contention. She did not only claim the right to perform certain tasks within the Church not hitherto behoving to a nun—she wanted à tout prix to do these as a nun. It wasn't enough just to work in the kitchen, she had to do it as lady-in-waiting. They would have been glad enough to accept her services if only she would have deigned to renounce her rank of lady-in-waiting—but she stiffened: either both or nothing at all. It wasn't even a question of humility.

*

FOR what is nowadays usually termed "projection" in love Baader uses the words "divinatory phantasmagoria"—which is so much more appropriate, profound and true. For this means the very opposite of beholding the beloved through a haze of one's own making, investing him—or her—with qualities and features which he doesn't possess. This means recognizing the true potential Self of the other person à travers his own incomplete ego. What I've always thought myself, by the way. And then it occurred to me that there could be a negative "divinatory phantasmagoria" too—but not the evil kind (which I know only too well, when the Devil tries to poison a budding relationship)—(Baader rightly says the Devil is the enemy of marriage and love because he is the enemy of rebirth)—but "divining" in the sense that the lover also recognizes the hidden perils within the other, not desiring to guard himself against them, rather to protect the person he loves—as "custos animae". Who invented this wonderful name for friend?

*

PORTRAYING a saint, either in a picture or in words, one ought to discern between the face of holiness and the face of the saint himself. And the one must be recognizable in the other. A difficult task. In the liturgy the type is predominant. Nowadays people ask for the individual face, but this must be transparent for "the face of holiness", otherwise all you get is just a private human face, at best a hero's biography. And you must also show what has been "added" with time, the "second image", the clothing with a new garment, that fashioning "like unto his glorious body". Isn't this rather like painting a portrait, but on a higher level, as it were? Seeking the true face, the valid one among the many chance faces of one's "sitter" and depicting this, not as a construction, not abstracted from his own material: race, age, sex, etc.—but expressed in this very stuff, this and no other?

For instance: let's take it that Newman were in fact to be canonized and someone were commissioned to paint him as an altar-piece. Sounds awful, I know, but was it any different in the case of Little Thérèse? That's why those trashy pictures they turned out in Lisieux were so ghastly! For any mere "portrait", no matter how piously stylized and garnished with "attributes" of rays or clouds, is a monstrosity in a place of worship, over an altar—downright scandalous, almost blasphemous. But what would be the difference between a true "holy picture" of Newman and an "ordinary" portrait? What is the clue to the genuine, valid "translation" of a significant, interesting human face into the countenance of holiness? What—whom—would the artist try to picture? The holy philosopher? The saintly old man? The Doctor of the Church? The sage and priest? The misjudged, lonely, the sorely tried man, purged by suffering?—and all this "in English", Victorian to boot, summarized in the unique character head of John Henry Newman, 1801–90.

*

I'm reading a biography of St John Baptist de la Salle—woefully badly written, but highly interesting. Extraordinary what educational insights and experiments have existed already—and what has been forgotten! That reformatory, for instance, which he founded on the most amazing principles somewhere around 1680. The young delinquents were detained in solitary confinement to begin with, being promoted later, on improvement, to community life with the more "advanced" inmates. But in their single cells they were given flowers and plants to cultivate and singing birds to breed! The prisoners took their meals together with the Brothers, and each of the boys in solitary confinement was entrusted to one particular Brother. They were trained to the utmost courtesy in their relations with one another and were treated likewise. De la Salle also introduced "Courtesy" as a subject to be taught in his elementary schools, recognizing that many crimes were committed by young people simply grown wild in the habitual coarseness of the lower classes. Equally astonishing is the chapter on the rules for his schools, regulating the punishments to be employed by the teachers, down to the very last detail: "If the punishment is to do the pupil any good it must fulfil the following ten requirements: be pure and impartial—moderate—dispassionate—careful—respectful—silent"—and, what impresses me most: "voluntary", i.e. it must be accepted freely by the pupil, not forced upon the unwilling culprit! Despite all these limitations—in an age of the most savage corporal punishments!—flogging was only permitted in exceptional cases. There are detailed instructions about considering the individuality of each child. Teachers are warned emphatically to avoid sermonizing in religious instruction, etc. On the other hand everything is immensely practical. Not only "texts and maxims" should be set as copy-book tasks, but the boys were to write "bills, invoices, receipts, working contracts, notaries' agreements, warrants of attorney, rent and tenancy agreements, deeds of mortgage, etc." Drawing and singing—the "artistic training" so fully recognized today—were already introduced by de la Salle as subjects in his elementary schools, as much an innovation as the crafts and gardening taught in his curious boarding schools for "degenerate boys of good family" (we could do with similar establishments these days!)—the most modern "work therapy".

The Jansenists were bitter opponents of the Brothers, for in all his schools de la Salle laid great stress on frequent Communion, and also wrote something on this. They did their best to oppose him personally and to hinder his work. The Revolution wrecked his Institute, some of the Brothers were executed, others emigrated.

*

THESE books I've been reading about stigmatics, including Fr Herbert Thurston's *Physical Phenomena of Mysticism*, all serve to strengthen my conviction how sharply and uncompromisingly one must discriminate between such parapsychological and paraphysiological phenomena and genuine religious processes. It's extraordinary how people will go mixing up the two—people who ought to know better at that! I'm repelled and disgusted by this sort of thing, not merely astonished or baffled. Or don't you think it's revolting, such pious inquisition, nosing about with bleeding, sweating or "odorous" corpses, the way they go poking and prying, cutting and pricking, bending and kneading to examine their elasticity and "freshness"—not to mention the appropriate descriptions of coral lips and rose-petal cheeks? . . . Their accounts supplement one another, Höchst the uncritical enthusiast, and the sceptical and very sensible Fr Thurston. And that nasty interest people have in the excrement of the fasting mystics—thank God it would seem they hadn't yet acquired that taste in the days of Brother Klaus. But the things they get up to in the name of science plus piety! And not only doctors either—which does make sense, after all—clergy and devout laymen as well—measuring the "abdominal crosses" above the navel of Anne Catherine Emmerich with rules, and so on—whatever is supposed to be edifying or spiritual about such things? What has it got to do with religion? Why should such signs be "a triumph of grace", a badge of the divine? It makes my hackles rise. All I can see in any of it is that among the *dévotes* and perhaps truly saintly people you can find a certain percentage of "psychic" constitutions—much as you find a certain number of aristocrats, artists or organizers among them. So what? Such types seem to express their spiritual fervour in the language of their mould, just as others do by writing verse or books or music. To my mind such peculiarities are no more "supernatural" than the ability to build or to paint— after all it's not everyone can do this either.

*

ONLY the other day I came across two bits of "evidence" showing that even for the Chinese—for all their cult of the family and love of children—the act of giving birth is considered as something low, ignoble, involving countless taboos, not only for the mother, but also for the whole household.

*

No, reading the Zohar and other Gnostic books isn't undermining my faith—on the contrary, it is a strangely refreshing tonic to my orthodoxy. One's ears grow sharp, sensitive for certain qualities and tempers of doctrine which one would never perceive without the contrast. The *Ungrund** of these immense systems—no, this is *not* the God of the Bible, the God and Father of Jesus, the God one may address, to whom the psalms call out, to whom one may say: "My Lord and my God!" This is just a gigantic shadow-image of God spread out across the endless cloud-heaven of imagination. When I say the Creed afterwards, I keep saying: "I believe in the *real* God, in the real Father Almighty, the real Maker of heaven and earth—and in his real Son. . . ." And the Gospels, or their reflection in the Rosary, are like the cool freshness of early morning after a display of strange, gigantic fireworks in a dazzling and terrifying night. It's then that I sense the simplicity of Christian thought about God as against the Oriental or Asiatic, its own particular simplicity, humility and chastity—a taste of "Nazareth", a unique, all-embracing quality, the incomparable character of God's condescension to the creature, his "lowering" into the small, the simple, the unpretentious; what's expressed in its quintessence in "*non horruisti Virginis uterum*", in the swaddling bands of Bethlehem, in the house in Nazareth: profound, unutterable mystery of silence, of hiddenness, unfathomable—a *different* mystery, not iridescent and spectacular and complicated like the pagan and esoteric mysteries. As inconspicuous as the secret of pure water, of early spring, of buds. Yes, it's a kind of poverty, this incredible simplicity of contour, something which belongs to Jesus—a poverty which is not need or want, but transparence, openness, silence. It is the same quality which stamps the sacraments: *accessibility*, devoid of pathos, decoration, sensation. For me this inexpressible quality—this humility of God is what

---

* Literally the "Non-ground", a term of Jakob Boehme's for the ultimate divine mystery as beyond even the "ground", i.e. the uttermost foundations of Creation.

calls for adoration—to be talked about only on one's knees or prostrate.

I think I had the first glimpse of this as a boarder at the convent in St Pölten—I sometimes used to slip away to old Sister Anselma in the sacristy and help her to bake hosts. There was no electric drum in those days, only an open fireplace in the wall, a heavy black waffle-iron and a bowl of batter, and out of this we made the most fragile and poorest dress for the living Godhead. How far from here to the dazzling, dreadful mysteries, towering peak above peak, of the Gnostic heavens, powers, essences—and yet it is good to remember that both are somehow connected by strange threads. That the Enthroned Lord of the Apocalypse is the same as the Son of Man on the roads of Galilee, and the wafer in the monstrance.

*

St John Nepomuk also belongs to the "symbol saints". Not in real history. As far as I know he was merely a forgotten local figure in some medieval Prague chronicle—the Court confessor thrown into the Moldau by wicked King Wenceslaus because he had refused to reveal his queen's confession to her jealous husband—a tragic and edifying story, nothing more. Apparently it was the Jesuits who first unearthed him in the Counter-Reformation, setting him up, they say, as a counterpart to John Hus—he too a Czech, a priest and a martyr, but not against the rule of the Church—a martyr for the Church. Anyway this propaganda won the day—for there's not a village in Bohemia—and far into Austria!—where he is not standing guard over a bridge, a ford or a pond, his finger raised to his lips, the crucifix in his hand, and around his head the twelve stars supposed to have shown his corpse floating down the Moldau. To me this image means far more than simply the historic figure: the holy man of silence, standing above the water, watching over the bridge, indeed he "is" a bridge as a priest = *pontifex*. Of course speech is a bridge from man to man—but so is silence. Many ties can exist only because and as long as silence is kept. "Would not the whole order of the universe be destroyed if secrets were revealed?" says Bergengruen in one of his novels, curiously enough in direct reference to John Nepomuk. And his silence stands above the *water*: the depths, the surge, the abyss—well, in the end this very element engulfed him, he was sacrificed to it.

And what about those twelve stars? Aren't they the attribute of Mary, victorious over the dragon? And is not Mary herself holy silence, the greatest symbol of protecting, inviolable silence, the obedient "keep" of the Word, belonging to God alone? And surely precisely in this silence she is the bridge between God and his world, triumphant over deluge and dragon, abyss and darkness? And in this a radiant reflection of Christ—the Word, no doubt, but I've heard about an icon somewhere depicting him as Divine Silence. Nowadays in the age of indiscretion all this seems especially significant.

In the figure of John Nepomuk the priest's office is revealed as much in its "militant"—martyr!—as in its "motherly" function. For the protective, healing silence of forgiveness is just as much part of confession as its quality of judgment stressed so much more. For in confession sin is not so much subjected to the "light" of the word, of judicial sentence, as received into the darkness of merciful, secret acceptance, sunk into divine oblivion.

*

IN my concern for the Church to come I must never forget the Church of today—or of yesterday either. Could I ever love only the youthful figure of someone dear to me, or the hope of his future face? Must I not see both *in* him, here and now, beholding both, no matter how buried, or barely hinted at, not as yet realized? I cannot simply withdraw, "distancing" myself from his present state as irrelevant, of no interest to me (as so many of our enthusiastic reformers do with the Church), even if I should feel that he was more lovable or more attractive at some earlier phase of his life, more "himself"—or that he has yet to achieve full stature.

I don't mean this just in an inert or conformist way—I know well enough that everything is moving, flowing—and in the present-day Church more than ever. But in this whirlpool of conflicting currents and counter-currents of development for us living here and now it is our most serious duty and responsibility to strengthen (and, if one could, to guide) those who are pointing in the right direction.

*

CURIOUS—and rather humbling—that it should be NN., a non-Catholic, outside the Church, indeed I don't even know whether she'd call herself a Christian—that it was she who opened my eyes to the fact that the signal from Rome recalling the worker-priests sprang not *only* from inertia, conservative fears and "curial demonism", but also from the wisdom of experience. For even if many of these priests are saints—and who could deny this?—in the movement as a whole, and even more in its echo, particularly its literary echo, there is also the modern tendency to glorify the proletarian as *the* human being, absolute man, setting valid standards for all; idolization of manual labour; deliberate levelling; the trend to take man seriously as a "mind" only if he's a labourer as well; the maxim: "Only brothers, no father!"—in short, the very leftist principles which are morbid symptoms of our *Zeitgeist*—and for deep and most decisive reasons unacceptable to the Church—even if represented by saints. Of course I hope—and fervently believe—that there'll always be individuals with a charismatic vocation to follow this path—but it must not be in the assumption that they're the only ones, that they and they alone are "real" priests, compared with whom all the others are failures or degenerates.

*

I'M realizing more and more strongly the consoling truth of St Paul's words (Ephesians 4) that the Church is growing towards "perfect manhood", "the completed growth of Christ", *in the diversity of her members*, and that we may confidently accept and acknowledge this variety—chequered and multi-coloured as it all is—together with its inconsistency and incongruity. "Glory be to God for dappled things"—after all it is this fullness that builds up her body, and not that uniformity which a notorious German and Roman bias is for ever striving after. The whole is complete just *because* one has what another has not. If each one is intent on spreading the message which is nearest and dearest to his heart, "the faith of the

362

Church" will be proclaimed—whereas a uniform and invariable proclamation will *not* be universal, but, on the contrary, so onesided, with so many bits dropped beneath the table, that heresies are bound to spring up from them.

＊

BOUYER's book on Newman* has made me see with a startling clarity how very much Newman "went into the desert" after his conversion—not in the least entering into the alleged Catholic abundance. Nowadays, after a hundred-year interlude of relative "peace" in the history of the Church (over and done with now, I'm afraid), we've no longer any idea of the impoverished state of the Church in that revolutionary era after Napoleon, how badly things, in fact, stood with her—the period unthinking people these days regard as her gay Biedermeier days, her seven fat years, as it were! Yet spiritual and intellectual culture were in a kind of D.P. state—rather like a crowd of survivors after an air-raid, sitting around higgledy-piggledy on a heap of odd bits of furniture and junk, among broken glass and rubble out of which they must now start building a new house. When Newman, the learned Anglican scholar and divine, came to Rome (1845–46) to prepare for his ordination as a Catholic priest—in those days *persona gratissima*, cordially welcomed, with recommendations to the very best colleges and professors —he discovered with a shock that in fact no theology existed at all. Rome itself was as ignorant of Thomas as of the Fathers with whom he was so thoroughly at home. When he enquired about Thomas they told him: "Certainly a great saint, but we hardly know anything of his doctrine any longer—*nor do we want to!*" Teaching was exclusively positivist, there was no groundwork, no sense of continuity. At first Newman had dreams of founding an English school of theology and a college for theologians, but he gave up the idea as he came to see that there was simply nothing to link up with. All the same I get a certain confidence out of his tragedy—hoping that what annoys us so in present-day systematic theology may well be merely an emergency structure, like those buildings they knocked up in our bombed cities by no

* Louis Bouyer, *Newman, his Life and Spirituality*, London and New York, 1958.

means "built for eternity", easily demolished and rebuilt by better builders, should any turn up.

*

I'VE been ruminating on Mother Frances Xavier Cabrini, surely a classical example of that special, perfectly genuine and lawful brand of Christian piety which can be completely unintelligent. On the face of it, that is, for obviously all these saints are, in fact, filled with the Holy Ghost; but with them the Spirit makes no use of their "mind" as intelligence, only of their practical sense—not of *ratio* in the grand, ancient meaning, the whole realm of speculative, i.e. reflective thinking, where questions are raised, depths plumbed, answers sought, where ideas are stimulated and truths are discovered—in short, the sphere of "gnosis". They are wise in practical choice, in their decisions, their whole way of life. But their wisdom is so unconscious that it doesn't even crystallize in remarkable sayings—as it did so abundantly with the Hasidim, for all their simplicity and everyday way of life. In 67 years of holiness truly lived—most of which were spent in working among people, and even in the professional guidance of souls!!—there is no record of a single "unforgettable sentence". I've been keeping a sharp look out for significant anecdotes, but haven't found one in the whole book. Mute, all of it. Completely devoid of self-reflection. One feels almost inclined to say : if animals could be holy, they would be holy this way.

What can this mean ? That charity—i.e. wisdom *lived*—can exist without the mind. But intelligence, for the Christian, can *not* exist without charity. A salutary snub for some of us.

At the same time I realize from all this how very much intellect (in our sense!) is not only a "talent", but also a charismatic gift : a privilege and special mission, in truth awe-fully respons-ible. How godlike, and yet at the same time how questionable : sphere of the lowest fall and the worst corruption. Which is the more deeply fallen, the mind or the body? Which, in fact, is more deeply perverted ?—not only in the sense of moral abuse, but also in the sense of decadence, depravity, degradation, de-generation to the point of self-abolition. Which needs redemption more—the power of knowledge or the power of love ?

We hear much too little about it, and about the mind's special way of purification, ascesis as related to brains—yet such knowledge would be at least as important as the corresponding problems concerning Eros. I'm sure one could find a lot in Newman —I'm thinking particularly of his Oxford University Sermons.

*

I'M still spinning my Huxley (mescalin) threads. Nowadays anti-rationalists, tired of purely abstract thought, only too easily forget that for countless people reasoning was *the* "gateway to reality", leading to a higher level of life—just as people expect to find this approach today by means of intuition, inspiration, a sort of medium-like "discernment". Besides the "higher" sensuality, which reveals the transparence of things, there's the other "lower" sort, far more common, alas—in both senses of the word—the "vulgar" kind which shuts people up in a nothing-but-empirical cage. For the person who started—who starts—from that point of departure the discovery of the intellectual realm means a break-through—exactly like the picture of the universe in that old woodcut attributed to Cusanus,* even on this side of the Nether Heavens.

I'll never forget how it was long ago—this unbelievable, stunning experience, turning life topsy-turvy—truly *vita nuova* and the discovery of a new dimension. Nothing less than, somewhat later, the discovery of love and of religion. That's why I can so readily understand that for lots of people this remains "the real thing", the goal beyond which they have no wish to progress.

I think I know exactly how the medieval monks must have felt when they first discovered abstract thought—for "barbarians" they were, *goyim*, nobles or peasants, closely confined within their own immediate, animal, physical, clannish bounds. How intoxicating it must have been, the new game with concepts and definitions, syllogisms and formulas—the first venture of flight into a strange unknown space and element. And behind this fantastic sparkle of an ice-clear crystal world was always

* A fifteenth-century engraving showing a pilgrim on his knees, his head and hand thrusting through the vault of sidereal heaven, with new suns, clouds and celestial wheels revolving round him.

the sound counter-weight of "normal" life, the ponderous, inescapable reality of kin, family and home.

Maybe it's easier to understand this experience today as a woman, we're still so much closer to it, having ourselves only just been admitted to this domain, whereas men are already sophisticated (and Jews most of all—as in King Solomon's day silver was rated "as clay" in Jerusalem!). For us having brains, or being allowed to use them, is still a novel experience, still glistening rainbow-like. I've often felt how typically "academic" women are bound fast in this self-fascination, narcissically spellbound, incapable of growing beyond it.

*

MEETING converts—from unbelief rather than from disunited Christendom—we must ever and again see and understand the spiritual vagrant, homeless, unsheltered, lest we grow too rusty and set in our own ways within the Faith. But we must be very gentle towards the other kind too—so tightly snuggled up in their fondness for their own little nook that they're scared of every step—even peep—across the border. There are cosmopolitans as well as provincials within the Church, and both have a right to exist. (Even if the smug and pig-headed sort are the hardest to put up with.)

*

IT's the special and very uncanny gift of hysterical people that they can force one to take part in their emotional play-acting— in the role in which they have cast one; for instance to go on miming a friendship which has, in fact, died. And yet you mustn't do it, for it's deception, even from the noblest motives, a deceit worse still since it involves the very heart of trust. (But don't they know this really, deep down, but just don't want to admit it?) And isn't this "pity", which draws one into being an actor in love or in friendship really mostly cowardice—dread of a row, a scene?

One must accept the fact that relationships are mortal—something I absolutely refused to admit when I was young. The adolescent's notion of "eternal" love and friendship! Human relations can die because they are living, like plants, they have seasons, they spring up, budding and flowering, they ripen, bear fruit, wither and die. The process of withering, once begun, can't be stopped. Resolutions, intentions or pleas are of no avail; what drifts apart, drifts apart, and it can't be helped. Good will and a bit of play-acting can veil the true situation for a while but cannot stop the process. Every single experience of what I used to call my faithlessness was every time sheer terror, a taste of death. Perhaps that's how I realized that the world is transient. For years I felt this as guilt—irremediable. Now I tell myself (is this wise old age or resignation?) : People who have a higher "curve of life" than others *must* inevitably grow out of contacts and encounters, growing beyond them. How can I help it if the other stays put! I can't drag him along—not even out of "loyalty", nor can I stop growing myself, for his sake. I'm *convinced* that it's part of the sacrament of matrimony that love's natural mortality is here transcended by powers of resurrection, in a way not to be defined, but experienced. Yet even here—often enough!—grace must vanquish the inertia of mortality, renewing what is passing from a deeper fount of life.

Perhaps something similar exists for friendship—not promised, of course, not guaranteed—but one may still hope that God will permit such an affection to take root within the rhythm and measure of the true growth of soul and spirit.

In Goethe's life this phenomenon has always fascinated me, and I've often defended him when people accused him of fickleness. Once, when I was still very young and utterly inexperienced in matters of love, our beloved German mistress told us: "Goethe was just a frivolous butterfly flitting from one blossom to another, leaving each flower as soon as he tired of it." It made me furious. I felt this couldn't be true—that a tragic destiny, a compulsion was behind it.

*

I'M revelling in the new *Fountain of Juda.* This strange mingling of Bible and Arabian Nights. So often it's like a subtle middle tone blended between the parables of Jesus and the tales of Harun al Rashid; the stories of Israel's royal judges, for instance, of Solomon's judgment of the two harlots, of Daniel and Susanna, and similar fables of the wise vizirs of the Arabian Nights. I keep wondering: did Jesus listen to such tales as a

367

child, as a boy, sitting there, all ears, as the story-tellers told of
kings sailing across the sea, leaving faithful stewards or
treacherous knaves behind, of poor widows and unjust judges? I
love to imagine this: as though one were glimpsing a *natural*
thread shimmering through here and there in the tapestry of his
life and work.

*

I'M so often struck by the fact that almost all the "representative" saints between Christ and the middle of this century
broke the bonds of the family, demonstratively, dramatically,
brutally: Alexis, running away on his wedding night; Francis,
flinging his clothes at his father's feet, renouncing even his
name; Elizabeth, sending her children away; Perpetua, leaving
her baby and her old father, despite all his pleading; Bernard,
drawing his married brothers into the monastery; Bridget and
her husband who agreed to part, each entering the convent—
and she even separated her daughter Karin from her husband,
refusing to let her go home; Brother Klaus, who gave up what
was surely the most Christian of families; Jane Frances de
Chantal, stepping over the body of her youngest son to leave her
house—and certainly scores of others, known and unknown.
Even the tragedy of Cornelia Connelly belongs to the series (and
my cousin Fanny C., too). But what confessor or bishop would
approve of this sort of thing nowadays? To my mind this all
belongs to the bygone struggle of Christianity for freedom
against the domination of kinship. Today the front takes a very
different line. Today the Church is defending the last ruin of the
institution with all her might, for this has suddenly become her
last bulwark against the new leviathan, the State.

*

IT's terribly exciting to read in that Mecca book the text
from the Koran, Mohammed's prophecy of the figure of dread to
appear at Doomsday—in fact an apocalyptic image: "The being
called Daddchal: he is blind in one eye, but possesses mysterious
powers bestowed by God. With his ears he can hear what is
spoken at the farthermost ends of the earth, and with his one eye
he sees what is taking place in the infinite distance. He flies in a

few days around the whole earth; treasures of gold and silver suddenly appear out of the mines of the earth; rain falls at his bidding, and plants sprout up; he kills and restores to life—so that all those weak in faith fancy him to be God himself, falling down before him in adoration. But those who are strong in faith can clearly read what is written across his brow in letters of flame: DENIER OF GOD—and so know that it is but a phantom, sent to test the faith of men. . . ."

Is this Antichrist, or simply our civilization?

Appendix

THE GERMAN YOUTH MOVEMENT

THE German Youth Movement was an extremely elusive, short-lived and strictly circumscribed phenomenon set apart from the vast array of contemporary youth associations organized and run by schools, welfare authorities, Churches, canvassing political parties or adults promoting interests and activities of all kinds. The units of the Movement, or rather Movements, called themselves, most emphatically, *Bünde*—plural of *Bund* = league, confederation, to draw the line between themselves and the rest of the groups mentioned above—a designation smacking strongly of Covenant, in the old religious sense. Though non-denominational in its origins, indeed even hostile to organized religion, it bore a much closer resemblance to the sectarian movements of history—the early Quakers, for instance —than to any modern educational enterprise.

The German Youth Movement was, in fact, very definitely the shared personal experience of a comparatively small number of young men and women during the years between 1897 and 1933—some people insist only up to the First World War, regarding the later development as mere backwash: it was and remains a unique phenomenon which could neither be prolonged indefinitely and deliberately nor imitated and reconstructed, all of which has been attempted, though without success.

The Youth Movement began neither as a creed nor as a doctrine, not even with a programme or a slogan. The *Wandervogel* ("Birds of Passage", as the first and main group was called) started quite inconspicuously: a band of secondary schoolboys in Berlin, bored to death by their homes and schools and grown-ups in general, sought to elude this adult world by spending their Sundays and holidays roaming the countryside— what we would call hiking, an unheard of pursuit in those days. They began by camping out, sleeping under haystacks or in the woods—tents and hostels came in much later—mixing with peasants, gypsies, travelling journeymen, tramps, breaking

370

down class barriers and shedding city habits. This practice proved infectious among adolescents (girls, incidentally, were admitted later and reluctantly, increasingly only after the First War). Being Germans, they—and even more the adults who joined them on strictly equal terms—could not refrain from distilling a *Weltanschauung* from their pursuits. Hiking—combined with fierce repudiation of all other social activities or amusements—and hiking kit, flaunted defiantly on every inappropriate occasion in open rejection of fashion—became symbolic, standing for "Back to Nature" against modern civilization; hardihood and outdoor life against urban effeminacy; the free lance spirit as against gregariousness, yet, paradoxically, the urge for comradeship against atomizing individualism; rustic simplicity against sophistication and artificiality; health against morbidity; independence opposed to authority in all its forms. In short, revolt against their whole middle-class background. (Neither the upper classes nor the proletariat were involved in the Movement, with the exception of stray individuals prompted by curiosity.) In this respect the Youth Movement coincided with the general restless protest fermenting in many countries around the turn of the century in the birth throes of a new era.

It followed that its members should adopt or champion almost all the contemporary trends concerned with reform: social, artistic, valetudinarian—pacificism, teetotalism, vegetarianism, the Simple Life, arts and crafts, folk-lore, folk-song and dance, "physical culture" and athletics, Socialism of a kind—but politics, commerce and technology were shunned. Yet they never identified themselves with any of these aims, merely making use of them as bricks in their own scheme for a Brave New World.

The idea was to create a "Realm of Youth" (*Jugendreich*) between childhood and what they considered corrupt and warped adult life, a kind of Red Indian reservation of adolescence; to build the model of a new and better world on a fresh set of values, combining Greek and archaic patterns with some Christian ideals, the Noble Savage with chivalry and brotherhood, with Nietzsche and Romantic pantheism included. In 1913 at the first and only general meeting of congenial groups (never centrally organized) the "Free German Youth" proclaimed their Magna Charta of independence (alas, only spiritual!), autonomy

371

and self-determination, based upon *"innere Wahrhaftigkeit"*, i.e. radical sincerity of self-expression. This claim probably led the few and scattered professing Christians in the Movement to muster in separate denominational groups, Protestant and Catholic. Slightly later several existing Catholic youth associations of the traditional kind, infected by the *Wandervogel* spirit, "converted" wholesale to the Movement. The main Catholic branch, *Quickborn* made Burg Rothenfels on the Main its centre (1919), with Romano Guardini as our leading mind. We went in enthusiastically for the Liturgical Revival, Biblical studies and every other spiritual and theological trend, nascent and renascent.

In 1933 the Nazis swallowed up the groups on the nationalistic fringe and shattered the bulk of the *Bünde* as bulwarks of the individualistic and independent spirit. Many of the resistance martyrs came from their ranks, Fr Delp, S.J., for instance, and the undergraduate brother and sister, Scholl, who were beheaded in Munich in 1943. Nevertheless the Nazis kept up a good deal of the apparel of the *Jugendreich* for some time as bait and policy for their Hitler Youth organization, but this pattern gradually became submerged by military forms and finally supplanted altogether.

But the Movement had really petered out much earlier due to the sheer irrefutable fact and process of people growing up. Many of its members entered the teaching profession or turned to educational and welfare work or the arts; others took up community farming, slum work in teams, engaged in youth hostel activities, the planning of new school types or training in physical culture; the Christian groups produced a significant number of religious vocations—the German Oratory of St Philip Neri has its origins in a group of students of the 'twenties. There were some, admittedly, who refused to grow up, presenting a rather ludicrous picture of middle-aged men sporting corduroy shorts, lutes strung round their necks, and women in long-waisted dresses, their hair coiled archly in braids around their ears. Others concentrated on fads such as teetotalism and uncooked foods. A great many drifted back to normal bourgeois conformity. Today, I suppose, for many of its former members the Youth Movement represents no more than a store of youthful memories. But a small but by no means negligible minority did receive a basic shaping and moulding which held good for the rest of their lives, the essence of that fleeting spirit of the Movement: a shared vision of the true nature of man and his place in the universe, integrating seemingly disparate values, historic and modern, into a sound, reliable whole; a special kind of awareness to Nature; an extremely keen sense of intellectual and spiritual responsibility and a peculiar sanity and sobriety of judgment. This is quite a lot to be thankful for.

I. F. G.

INDEX OF SUBJECTS

INDEX OF NAMES